ENGLISH-AS-A-SECOND-LANGUAGE (ESL) TEACHING AND LEARNING

ENGLISH-AS-A-SECOND-LANGUAGE (ESL) TEACHING AND LEARNING

Pre-K–12 Classroom Applications for Students' Academic Achievement and Development

VIRGINIA GONZALEZ ▪ **THOMAS YAWKEY**

University of Cincinnati   *Pennsylvania State University*

LILIANA MINAYA-ROWE

Professor Emerita, University of Connecticut

Foreword by Josefina Villamil Tinajero

Boston ▪ New York ▪ San Francisco ▪ Mexico City ▪ Montreal
Toronto ▪ London ▪ Madrid ▪ Munich ▪ Paris
Hong Kong ▪ Singapore ▪ Tokyo ▪ Cape Town ▪ Sydney

Senior Series Editor: *Aurora Martínez Ramos*
Editorial Assistant: *Kevin Shannon*
Marketing Manager: *Krista Groshong*
Composition and Prepress Buyer: *Linda Cox*
Manufacturing Buyer: *Andrew Turso*
Editorial-Production Coordinator: *Mary Beth Finch*
Editorial-Production Service: *Stratford Publishing Services*
Electronic Composition: *Stratford Publishing Services*

For related titles and support materials, visit our online catalog at www.ablongman.com

Between the time Web site information is gathered and then published, it is not unusual for some sites to have closed. Also, the transcription of URLs can result in unintended typographical errors. The publisher would appreciate notification where these errors occur so that they may be corrected in subsequent editions.

Library of Congress Cataloging-in-Publication Data

Gonzalez, Virginia.
    English-as-a-second-language (ESL) teaching and learning: pre-K–12 classroom applications for students' academic achievement and development / Virginia Gonzalez, Thomas Yawkey, Liliana Minaya-Rowe.
        p.   cm.
    ISBN 0-205-39251-2
    1. English language—Study and teaching—Foreign speakers. I. Yawkey, Thomas D. II. Minaya-Rowe, Liliana. III. Title.

PE1128.A2G653 2005
428'.0071—dc22

2005042133

Printed in the United States of America

10 9 8 7 6 5 4 3 2 1   10   09   08   07   06   05

To my son, Christian Emmanuel Fernandez, now an eight-year-old, growing up proud of his bilingual English–Spanish abilities. And to his large group of 11 cousins in Lima, Peru, and San Jose, Costa Rica, who make him proud of having a bilingual and bicultural family. For the joy that the new generation of nieces and nephews has brought to my family.

V. G.

To my wife, Dr. Margaret Louise Yawkey (now retired), for her strong, steadfast support of educational endeavors, and who despite many setbacks continues onward, never letting despair penetrate her positive life's outlook and these endeavors. And to our son, Brian Michael, for his developing dedication to academic interests and directed focus on life's pursuits.

T. D. Y.

To my father, Carolino Minaya, for his support and encouragement over the years.

L. M. R.

To ESL and all educators, in honor of their important service as role models, mentors, and advocates for ESL students and their families. This book celebrates the dedication of ESL and all educators and encourages them to continue their professional development.

V. G., T. D. Y., & L. M. R.

CONTENTS

CHAPTER TWO

Understanding the Demographics and Policies of Language Diversity in the United States   77

CHAPTER THREE

From Theory to Practice with ESL and *All* Students   109

CHAPTER SIX

Increasing Academic Achievement and Language Acquisition for English Language Learners across Grade Levels 227

CHAPTER NINE

Conclusions: A Dialogue about Myths Held by Educators and Recommendations for Better Educational Practices for ESL Students 329

LIST OF TABLES AND FIGURES

FOREWORD

Josefina Villamil Tinajero

ESL teaching and learning is destined to fail unless a new attitude gives it new vigor and direction. Recent reports identify dramatic demographic changes in the United States with particular emphasis on shifts in the ethnic composition of school-age children. The increase in the number of students who speak a language other than English has been dramatic and is expected to continue growing. At this writing, nearly one of every five American students entering school is a native speaker of a language other than English. By the 2030s language-minority students are predicted to account for over 40 percent of the school-age population. Currently, ESL students are present in over 42 percent of all school districts nationwide. Moreover, 20 percent of all public school teachers have at least one ESL student in their classroom, who is not fluent enough in English to complete most of the assigned work. The picture presented here underlies some of the most critical educational challenges that educators must address, quickly, responsibly, and creatively. The knowledge and skills required of teachers to work well with ESL students include reflective and responsive understanding of diversity, culture, and language. A very timely response is given by Gonzalez, Yawkey, and Minaya-Rowe's book in which they assert that the fundamental characteristic of a highly qualified teacher is a new attitude, based on culturally appropriate sensibilities and commitment to social equity and respect for their individual rights and responsibilities.

How can ESL students survive and perhaps even thrive? In *ESL Teaching and Learning*, Gonzalez, Yawkey, and Minaya-Rowe explore the conditions necessary for ESL students to thrive in our schools. Their goal is to provide all teachers, particularly those in ESL settings, with theoretical and practical knowledge or know-how on ESL instruction and its contexts to enhance classroom performance. The work they present will increase the possibility of students' academic, social, linguistic, cultural, and global success. A significant and unique element of this book is the infusion of a social, affective, and moral dimension in the preparation of teachers. The end result is the development of a sense of advocacy, commitment, and empathy by teachers as they get to know and work with their ESL students.

This book makes two distinctive thematic contributions to the field. The two underlying themes are: (1) developing in teachers a personal connection to the socio-historical presence of ESL immigrant students in our schools, and (2) becoming a committed advocate to better serve ESL students. The authors successfully communicate their theses in an extraordinary way. They help readers understand the importance of the multiple roles that ESL immigrant students and their families have played in the social history of the United States and help them develop a connection to their own personal family history and professional experience. In doing so, they help the reader make a conceptual connection between the sociohistorical, political, economic, cultural, and linguistic issues associated with the quality and characteristics of the educational programs offered to ESL students in our schools today.

The authors also work to dispel the prevailing myths that have done a grave disservice to ESL students. Central among these myths is the belief that yesterday's immigrants prospered without special programs and that the public schools successfully weaned students from their native languages by immersing them in English. Educational attainment data, however, show neither of these misconceptions to be true. Indeed, bilingualism was an accepted fact of life among the early immigrants to the United States. New arrivals strived to preserve their heritage by preserving their native languages and cultures. European immigrants established schools in the New World that provided instruction in native languages. Italian, Polish, Czech, French, Dutch, and German immigrant groups, introduced their languages into elementary and secondary schools either as separate subjects or as the languages of instruction (Crawford, 1989). According to Crawford, German-speaking Americans operated schools in their own tongue as early as 1694 in Philadelphia, a practice that prevailed until the early twentieth century. For much of the nineteenth century, the structure of U.S. public education allowed immigrant groups to incorporate linguistic and cultural traditions in the schools, which supported the transition to second language programs. Nevertheless, immigrant children were more likely to sink in English-only classrooms, where they experienced considerable difficulty with no special program to help them acquire either the English language or academic content. Historically, and contrary to popular beliefs, English-only instruction devoid of special program support has consistently been ineffective in achieving purported goals yet very effective in isolating and intimidating immigrant children, making sure they are stripped of their first language, and uninterested in formal schooling.

There is no empty theorizing here. Based on sound history and theory, the authors suggest practical, relevant ideas for teachers and administrators. The historical and theoretical base provides a meaningful framework from which the authors recommend research-based instructional practices. The research cited provides the reader with substantive evidence for best and promising practices and sets the stage for the application sections presented throughout several chapters. The application sections describe state-of-the-art policy, practice, and related issues associated with effective teaching, learning, and assessment within an ESL context. Their goal here is to enhance the confidence of teachers relative to the selection and use of best or most promising research-based practices in ESL instructional contexts. These practices are based on a cognitive/humanistic/constructivist model of learning theory and teacher education, in which teachers articulate fundamental principles that allow them to fashion their own models of effective teaching for ESL students.

Advocacy for a positive difference is a part of the new attitude essential to a reinvigorated approach to ESL teaching. The concluding chapter (Chapter 9) is particularly powerful. Here Gonzalez, Yawkey, and Minaya-Rowe bring closure to the book in the form of a dialogue that focuses on the two central themes and myths discussed in this outstanding publication: developing in teachers a personal connection to the sociohistorical presence of ESL immigrant students, and becoming a committed advocate to better serve them. Based on this discussion, they provide recommendations for effective educational practices with ESL students, such as the implementation of two-way bilingual education programs, which can make a positive difference in the academic achievement of ESL students.

Any teacher who seeks to be challenged in ways that will make a difference for our ESL students will welcome this book. *English-as-a-Second-Language (ESL) Teaching and Learning* provides teachers and administrators with the information to make insightful choices for themselves and for their ESL students. It challenges them to use this information to advocate for, and make personal connections with, ESL students. At the same time, *all* teachers can create learning environments where learning is facilitated and stimulated by caring adults. The authors' purpose is met in showing how best practices for ESL students can be distributed across significantly more classrooms in the United States. Their hope is that the critical reading of this text will influence all teachers to view ESL students' backgrounds and experiences as the assets that they are. I'm confident that Gonzalez, Yawkey, and Minaya-Rowe have achieved this goal.

The content of this book is empowering. It will encourage you to reach and teach each and every one of your ESL students.

Dr. Josefina (Josie) Villamil Tinajero
Professor of Bilingual Education &
Dean of the College of Education
The University of Texas at El Paso
Past President, The National Association for Bilingual Education (NABE),
and current NABE board member

REFERENCES

Crawford, J. (1989). *Bilingual education: History, politics, theory and practice.* Trenton, NJ: Crane.

> *Not like the brazen giant of Greek fame,*
> *With conquering limbs astride from land to land;*
> *Here at our sea-washed, sunset gates shall stand*
> *A mighty woman with a torch, whose flame*
> *Is the imprisoned lightning, and her name*
> *Mother of Exiles. From her beacon-hand*
> *Glows worldwide welcome; her mild eyes command*
> *The air bridged harbor that twice cities frame.*
> *'Keep, ancient lands, your storied pomp!' cries she*
> *With silent lips. 'Give me your tired, your poor,*
> *Your huddled masses yearning to breathe free,*
> *The wretched refuse of your teeming shore,*
> *Send these, the homeless, tempest-tossed to me:*
> *I lift my lamp beside the golden door!'*

Emma Lazarus, *"The New Colossus,"* carved at the base of the Statue of Liberty

STATEMENT OF PURPOSE AND PHILOSOPHY OF THIS BOOK: CENTRAL THEMES IN RELATION TO MYTHS

Emma Lazarus's poem reminds us of the sociohistorical reality of the United States as a nation of immigrants, who came seeking better social, economic, and educational conditions. A large proportion of these immigrants, who entered through New York harbor and the Ellis Island facility, came with diverse language, ethnic, cultural, and socioeconomic backgrounds.

As Emma Lazarus's poem depicts, our purpose for writing this book is to make English-as-a-Second-Language (ESL) teachers and *all* educators aware of the historical continuity of the educational challenges when serving ESL immigrant students within the U.S. public school system. Our philosophy endorses a developmental and humanistic view of learning and academic achievement in ESL students and *all* students, supporting a socioconstructivistic theoretical perspective, a pluralistic pedagogical approach, and an ethnic educator advocacy position (see Gonzalez, Brusca-Vega, & Yawkey, 1997, for an extended discussion of this proposed advocacy position).

Throughout the book we have chosen to use the term *English-as-a-Second-Language* (ESL) student over the former terminology of *limited English proficient* (LEP) student, or the more recently coined term *English language learner* (ELL), because the former term has achieved continuity and stability in the research and applied fields serving this population. The term *ESL student* has become a classic that has endured pendulum shifts in theoretical and political educational arenas. More specifically, the term *ESL student* conveys that the student is in the process of learning English without connoting that the student is in some way deficient until full English proficiency is attained. Finally, the term *ESL student* complements the philosophy that we endorse in this book: a developmental and humanistic view of learning and development, a socioconstructivistic theoretical perspective, and an ethnic educator advocacy position.

From a developmental and humanistic perspective, teaching as a social and affective experience is emphasized throughout chapters, stimulating ESL teachers and all educators to develop advocacy, commitment, empathy, and rapport for assuming social and moral responsibility when serving ESL at-risk students. From a socioconstructivistic position, the importance of educating the "whole" child is highlighted (i.e., academic, social, emotional developmental areas), as well as developing in teachers a holistic vision of education that aims to develop cognitive, socioemotional, and moral abilities in ESL students. We acknowledge the interaction of internal and external factors in development and learning in ESL students and all students, with the need to stimulate verbal and nonverbal conceptual development as mental tools for thinking and learning. We endorse pedagogical theory, principles, and strategies that ESL teachers and all teachers can use to develop high-level critical-thinking skills and problem-solving strategies that can actualize students' potential for learning into academic excellence. Within a pluralistic framework, we celebrate cultural and linguistic diversity as an asset that can enrich the developmental and learning potential of ESL students into brighter bilingual, bicultural, and bicognitive minds and spirits. We endorse *transculturation*, and not assimilation, in order to use education as an enrichment tool that nurtures ESL students' culturally and linguistically diverse identities. Transculturation allows ESL students to move freely between their minority and mainstream personalities, enjoying the freedom provided by a truly democratic classroom and schooling process. In this way, the American Dream pursued by ESL immigrant families will become a reality for their children.

Following an ethnic educator philosophical position, throughout our two main themes for the book we exhort ESL teachers and all educators to: (1) develop a *personal connection* to the sociohistorical presence of ESL immigrant students in the U.S. public schools, and (2) become *committed advocates* for better serving ESL students. The first central theme invites ESL teachers and all educators to understand: (1) the role of ESL immigrant students in the sociohistorical context of U.S. education since the Ellis Island years (late 1800s to the 1950s) until today, and (2) the connection to their own personal family history and professional experiences. By inviting educators to engage in reflection we hope to raise their awareness of the historical nature of ESL immigrant students in U.S. education. Moreover, this invitation to engage in reflection also urges all educators to examine their family history and engage in a search for ESL immigrant ancestors, since about one-third of U.S. citizens today have at least one ancestor who entered through Ellis Island. By finding a personal connection through family history, we can stimulate ESL teachers and all educators to become committed advocates for better serving the needs of ESL students and their families, and to endorse an ethnic educator advocacy position.

Furthermore, the first central theme of the book urges ESL teachers and all educators to dispel myths, such as the misconception that ESL immigrant students entering the United States during the late 1800s throughout the early 1900s learned English, became literate in English, graduated from high school, and entered mainstream American society without experiencing academic achievement, economic, and social problems. Indeed, ESL immigrant students historically *have* experienced numerous educational, social, and economic problems, and it *did take* several generations for Ellis Island immigrants to achieve the American Dream and enter mainstream American society. It is our main purpose to dispel these myths and make ESL teachers and all educators aware of the many parallels between Ellis Island ESL immigrants and contemporary Hispanic and Asian immigrant ESL students and their families.

The first central theme of the book discusses the historical presence of ESL immigrant students and their impact on U.S. education in the past, present, and future; with particular attention to sociohistorical, socioeconomic, and demographic issues (this topic was introduced by Gonzalez's article published in 2001). Educational challenges are examined throughout the book centered on the theme of the continuous presence of ESL immigrants in the U.S. public educational system, and the educational myths about their development, learning, and academic achievement.

In relation to the second central theme of the book, the audience for this book, U.S. preservice and in-service educators, will be exhorted to make a personal connection between their own family history and the role of ESL immigrants in the sociohistorical context of U.S. education. Out of the 270 million Americans today, about 100 million are descended from at least one ancestor who had an ESL background and immigrated within the last 120 years (see Gonzalez, 2001). This factual statement describes the sociocultural reality of the United States as a nation of immigrants and will be used for motivating educators to develop a personal connection or rapport with the ESL pedagogical content presented throughout the chapters of this book. Building rapport with ESL students is key for educators to eliminate affective filters that prevent them from implementing high-quality pedagogy that fosters ESL Pre-K through Grade 12 students' learning and academic achievement at excellence levels. Building rapport connotes in this book infusing among educators *cultural awareness* of the effect of teachers' attitudes and motivation on their own and their ESL students' instructional and learning processes and products.

Thus, the central themes of the book are related to myths commonly held by pre-service and in-service ESL teachers and all educators about the effect that having a culturally and linguistically diverse background can have on Pre-K–Grade 12 students' learning, development, and academic achievement. Research evidence and educational implications presented through examples of how high-quality teaching can make a difference for dispelling these myths about ESL learners is presented throughout the book and also in the companion Web site (www.ablongman.com/gonzalez1e), a major multimedia instructional and learning resource for the book.

In relation to these two themes, the coauthors discuss myths throughout chapters, and more explicitly in Chapter 9 as a dialogue among the authors for reaching conclusions in which our three voices become one. These myths are related to controversial issues and dilemmas, commonly held by pre-service and in-service educators when serving ESL students and their families. The main idea underlying these myths is how *internal* (i.e., developmental and psychological characteristics) and *external factors* (i.e., school and family environments) interact for making ESL students resilient or at-risk of underachievement.

The four most important myths, and related issues, discussed throughout the book and more explicitly in Chapter 9 include:

1. Understanding and differentiating between external and internal factors affecting development, and learning in ESL students. The need for educators to fully understand that low socioeconomic (SES) factors and cultural and linguistic differences (all external factors) can have on intelligence, development, and learning (internal or psychological factors, including first- and second-language—L1 and L2—learning); and that may result in low SES children needing extra developmental time and individualized, high-quality, ESL and/or bilingual instruction

2. Understanding similarities and differences between monolingual students' learning and developmental needs, and ESL students' idiosyncratic educational needs. For instance, developmental time needed for L1 and L2 learning among ESL students (i.e., readiness for reading and writing, difference between social and academic English language proficiency, the role of L1 in learning) resulting in most effective ESL and bilingual pedagogical strategies (i.e., need for establishing rapport between students and educators, individual differences and learning styles, and accommodations for cultural and linguistic diversity)

3. Understanding the need for linking assessment to instruction, through performance-based or classroom-based assessments, for separating cultural and linguistic diversity from genuine learning difficulties and fulfilling the instructional purpose for assessment. A battery of alternative and standardized assessments across contexts and evaluators, and across developmental and content areas needs to be used by an interdisciplinary team of professionals to fulfill two purposes: (a) measuring validly and reliably academic achievement and development in ESL students, and (b) fulfilling the accountability purpose of assessment mandated by federal and state and local educational agencies in relation to high-stakes standards. This assessment battery needs to evaluate both the individual child (i.e., readiness for learning) and the social learning and developmental contexts within the school (school readiness) and family settings. Assessment as an inseparable element for high-quality teaching requires the use of instruments that have demonstrated lines of validity evidence for a particular use and population, as well as highly trained educators who can test, evaluate, assess, and diagnose accurately ESL students' learning and development

4. Understanding the need for all educators, not only the ESL teachers, to reach out to minority parents to become collaborative partners, mentors, cultural mediators, and committed advocates in the successful schooling process of ESL students

OVERVIEW OF THE BOOK

English-as-a-Second-Language (ESL) Teaching and Learning: Pre-K–12 Classroom Applications for Students' Academic Achievement and Development, as the title conveys, establishes foundational knowledge in teaching and learning for ESL students. The three authors build on research-based knowledge and transform it into best educational applications for Pre-K through Grade 12 ESL students to develop and achieve at high-stakes standards established by federal mandates and recommendations made by professional organizations (American Educational Research Association [AERA], American Psychological Association [APA], and National Council on Measurement and Statistics [NCME], 1999; Teachers of English to Speakers of Other Languages [TESOL], 1997).

The book is divided into two complementary parts that present foundational knowledge and its transformation into best assessment and instructional practices for teachers of ESL and all students. The first part of the book is comprised of Chapters 1 through 3, and is entitled "Foundations of ESL Teaching and Learning: Thematic and Theoretical Perspectives, and Demographic and Policy Realities of ESL Students." The second part of the book is represented by Chapters 4 thorough 8, and is entitled "Best Assessment and Instructional Practices for ESL and *All* Students: How Can Teachers Stimulate Development and Academic Achievement in ESL Students and All Students in Their Classrooms?" Finally, Chapter 9 brings closure to the book in the form of conclusions in relation to the two central themes and myths discussed across chapters.

The first part encompasses Chapters 1 through 3 and introduces (1) the two overarching themes of the book as a motivational tool for readers to develop a personal connection to the ESL area; (2) a sociohistorical context for the presence of ESL learners in U.S. education's past, present, and future; (3) the theoretical perspectives and approaches endorsed in the book; (4) the demographic reality of ESL learners and their teachers in the United States; and (5) federal policy and national and professional standards regulating educational services for ESL learners. Then, Part I provides foundational knowledge for ESL teachers and all educators aimed at raising their awareness about the sociohistorical context of the continuous presence of ESL immigrant students in the U.S. public schools, since the Ellis Island years (i.e., late 1800s until 1950s) until today, with contemporary Hispanic and Asian students and their families. The context for Part I is built around two central themes for the book: for ESL teachers and all educators (1) to develop a personal connection to the sociohistorical presence of ESL immigrant students in the U.S. public schools, and (2) to become committed advocates for better serving ESL students.

Thus, together, these three chapters build a foundation that establish a state-of-the-art thematic, sociohistorical, theoretical, demographic, and policy context for ESL teachers and all educators to understand language, cognitive, and socioemotional development and academic achievement in ESL students. That is, this foundational first part of the book brings state-of-the-art research into practice for ESL teachers and all educators to broaden their knowledge base on: (1) *What* is the demographic and policy reality of immigrant ESL students in the U.S. public schools; (2) *How* ESL students learn and develop; and (3) *Why* some instructional approaches are better educational practices for stimulating ESL students' L1 and L2 learning, development, and academic achievement.

The second part of the book, Chapters 4 through 8, has the purpose of transforming foundational research-based knowledge into recommendations for best instructional and assessment approaches and practices for stimulating learning, development, and academic achievement in ESL Pre-K through Grade 12 students and their families. Part II also presents educational applications of recommended ESL instructional and assessment approaches and practices for the education of ESL students that are connected with: (1) federal policies and standards, (2) standards for best practices from professional associations (AERA, APA, and NCME, 1999; TESOL, 1997), (2) educational implications of data-driven research studies, (3) successful ESL models—including two-way bilingual education—at different grade levels (across preschool, elementary, middle school, and high school levels), and (4) research-based assessment models and approaches to validly and reliably measure L1 and L2 learning, development, and academic achievement in ESL students.

Thus, Part II has the goal of illustrating best assessment and instructional practices for ESL students, and responds to the following questions often asked by ESL teachers and all educators: (**1**) *What* assessment and instructional approaches work for ESL students?, (**2**) *How* can we implement these best assessment and instructional approaches for ESL students?, and (**3**) *Why* do these assessment and instructional approaches work? The companion Web site, www.ablongman.com/gonzalez1e, provides a supportive multimedia instructional environment that offers readers electronic links to documents available on the Internet, multimedia vignettes that model best instructional and assessment practices with ESL learners, digital recordings of interviews with ESL teachers and ESL students and parents, and other valuable information.

AN OVERVIEW ACROSS CHAPTERS

As explained above, **Part I** is comprised of Chapters 1 through 3, and it builds a foundational context for the book representing thematic, demographic, policy, and theoretical frameworks. The first part of the book is entitled "Foundational Context of ESL Teaching and Learning: Thematic and Theoretical Perspectives, and Demographic and Policy Reality of ESL Students."

Chapter 1 is entitled "The Role of Immigrant ESL Students in the History of U.S. Education: Making a Personal Connection." Chapter 1 develops the first and second central themes of the book: for ESL teachers and all educators to develop a personal connection to and cultural awareness of the role of immigrant ESL students in the sociohistorical context of US education since the late 1800s until the present. The first and second themes are summarized as building rapport, that is, infusing cultural awareness among educators about the powerful effect of their attitudes on Pre-K–Grade 12 ESL students' learning, development, and academic achievement.

Thus, Chapter 1 develops the first and second themes for the book by inviting the audience to make a personal connection with the role of immigration and ESL in their own family history, and to develop advocacy and commitment for assuming social and moral responsibility when serving ESL at-risk students, who are part of a language diverse society. In addition, readers are invited to compare the needs of immigrant ESL students within a sociohistorical perspective and recognize similarities and differences between Ellis Island's waves of immigrants and today's Hispanic and Asian immigrant groups. This motivational tool can help mainstream and ESL educators to develop rapport or empathy through a personal connection between their cultural and linguistic backgrounds and their ESL students' social, economic, and educational realities. Most educators come from European backgrounds but not necessarily English mainstream backgrounds: Out of the 270 million Americans today, about 100 million are descended from an ancestor who had an ESL Southern or Eastern European background and immigrated within the last 120 years (see Gonzalez, 2001). We use this sociohistorical fact as a motivational tool for readers to develop an ethnic educator perspective when serving ESL students and their families.

Chapter 2 is entitled "Understanding the Demographics and Policies of Language Diversity in the United States." Chapter 2 provides an overall view of demographics for ESL students in the United States based on recent census figures with emphasis on sociocultural, historical, linguistic, and economic factors—documented as important contributors in educational outcomes by demographic data, as well as by previous research and practice. The latest U.S. Census demographics are discussed, which include a majority of "minorities" within the next decade in the most populated states. Demographic information is desegregated in relation to ESL students' educational, social, economic, cultural, and linguistic realities. In understanding the effect of educational structure factors, we emphasize the role of external factors on ESL students' learning, development, and academic achievement.

Chapter 2 stimulates teachers of ESL students and all students to embrace the challenge of valuing and celebrating diversity, endorsed by an ethnic educator perspective. This challenge for teachers of ESL students is presented as part of the current federal and state policies and educational standards for all learners. These are important policies, mandates, and recommendations that teachers need to be aware of for better serving ESL students (e.g., high-stakes assessments for documenting progress in academic achievement in ESL students—related to the movement of accountability and standards). Having knowledge of policies and standards, ESL teachers and all educators can use this information to become advocates for assuring that equal educational opportunities are provided for ESL students (given their cultural, linguistic, and SES differences in comparison to "the norm" established in the school culture by middle-class, mainstream students). Educators need to rethink and rediscover the learning potential of ESL students and all students, and forcefully endorse that teaching can make a difference. Thus, Chapter 2 is squarely connected with the second theme of the book: to infuse cultural awareness to motivate teachers to develop moral responsibility and to become committed advocates for ESL students and all students.

Chapter 3 is entitled "From Theory to Practice with ESL and *All* Students," and it provides a socioconstructivistic theoretical framework for understanding conceptually the process of L1 and L2 learning and the derived educational principles for ESL students and all students taking into consideration a research-based knowledge perspective. Chapter 3 discusses cognitive aspects of learning and teaching, bringing research-based knowledge from cognitive and developmental psychology, and its educational psychology applications for the classroom. More specifically, Chapter 3 discusses educational principles derived from research-based knowledge in learning and teaching, with an emphasis on pedagogical approaches and strategies that are proven to work with ESL students and all students.

Chapter 3 is connected with the book's second theme because it aims to increase ESL teachers' and all educators' understanding of: (1) the internal and external factors affecting the ESL learning process (low socioeconomic [SES] factors and cultural and linguistic differences—all external factors, can create the need for extra developmental time), and (2) best educational strategies to better serve ESL learners and their families. Teaching as a social and affective experience is emphasized in Chapter 3, with the endorsement of the education of the "whole" learner (i.e., academic, social, emotional developmental areas), as well as developing in teachers also a holistic vision of education that aims to develop cognitive and ethical and moral abilities in ESL students. With teachers' gaining understanding, we also aim to infuse cultural awareness and therefore make their attitudes toward ESL students more positive. In turn, by aiming to make teachers' attitudes more sensitive to value and celebrate diversity, we also aim to increase their motivation, commitment, and advocacy levels for better serving ESL students. Chapter 3 emphasizes the idea that schooling of ESL students may take generations, and that the value of schooling lies in ESL teachers and all educators serving as a "mediational" social agent or cultural broker to facilitate ESL students' adaptation process to access and integrate into middle-class America. Endorsement of an ethnic educator approach for teaching is presented in Chapter 3 leading to integration (leading to multiple languages and cultural identities), and not assimilation (leading to enforcing mainstream culture and language only), as a cultural adaptation process for ESL students and their families.

Chapter 3 presents foundational theoretical knowledge about learning, development, and academic achievement in ESL students. Chapter 3 also examines myths commonly held by ESL teachers and all educators that are connected to the second theme of the book such as: (1) the developmental time needed for L1 and L2 learning at the social and academic levels; (2) the effect that having an ESL background can have on intelligence and development; and (3) the effect that high-quality teaching can have on ESL students' learning processes.

Thus, together, these three chapters build a foundation for the first part of the book by establishing a context for readers to understand the multidimensional factors affecting teaching and learning in Pre-K through Grade 12 ESL students and all students. These multidimensional factors stem from sociohistorical, theoretical, demographic, and, policy frameworks; and by gaining knowledge in these areas, ESL teachers and all educators can apply high-quality teaching for improving academic achievement in diverse students. This foundational knowledge is presented by the first part of the book in relation to the two central themes of the book. Chapters 1 through 3 aim to motivate ESL teachers and all educators to build a personal connection and raise their cultural awareness and commitment about how to better meet the educational needs of ESL students and their families.

Part II is entitled "Best Assessment and Instructional Practices for ESL and *All* Students: How Can Teachers Stimulate Development and Academic Achievement in ESL and All Students in Their Classrooms?" The second part of the book encompasses Chapters 4 through 8 and increases readers' understanding of recommended teaching practices for stimulating ESL students' learning, development, and academic achievement. In Part II we provide a connection between: (1) *Why* sound theoretically grounded and data-driven approaches do work for ESL students and all students, (2) *What* best practices for ESL students and all students are derived from these methodologically sound theories, and (3) *How* these best theories and methods can be implemented into procedural knowledge for teaching ESL students and all students.

Chapter 4 is entitled "An Historical and Contemporary View of Best Instructional Approaches for ESL and All Students." The accumulation of knowledge about the best instructional approaches to teach second language (L2) and foreign language (FL) learners, English-as-a-second-language (ESL) students, and all students during the past five decades has paved the way for a promising new millennium in terms of the applications of this knowledge to help build a global society. By the middle of the last century, language educators witnessed the emergence of one field of L2 teaching with instructional approaches based on sound applied linguistics research about the nature of language learning and the successful acquisition of L2 and FL in the classrooms.

Chapter 4 presents a spectrum of educational approaches and strategies from traditional grammar-based perspectives of the 1960s until contemporary meaning-based approaches. These contemporary educational strategies use dual-language or two-way immersion and transitional bilingual educational models, which help ESL students to learn social and academic English in a contextually and culturally appropriate manner. Chapter 4 translates the instructional theories, concepts, and principles discussed in Chapter 3 to further descriptions, discussions, and best educational programs and instructional strategies to improve ESL students' oral, reading, and writing skills in English at the social and academic levels, and their overall academic achievement. Thus, Chapter 4 is connected to the second theme of the book because the recommended instructional approaches for developing L1 and L2 academic skills in ESL students can be successful if used by committed teachers.

Chapter 5 is entitled "A Bilingual Developmental Model and Curriculum for Increasing ESL and Mainstream Young Children's Academic Achievement." Chapter 5 presents a bilingual developmental model with its derived philosophical, theoretical, and pedagogical principles. Two bodies of research are interconnected as a theoretical framework for the bilingual developmental model proposed in this chapter, including: (1) mainstream studies in cognitive and developmental psychology and cognitive science, following a traditional paradigm, resulting in educationally applied recommendations made by the National Research Council (1999a, 1999b); and (2) studies in the area of bilingual and ESL education, following an ethnic educator philosophical paradigm, resulting in educationally applied recommendations that are interfaced with ESL *Standards* (TESOL, 1997). This model is translated into a two-way bilingual curriculum that represents the best educational practices derived from contemporary socioconstructivistic and developmental research. The bilingual developmental model and curriculum can effectively stimulate cognitive, linguistic, and socioemotional development and academic achievement in young, at-risk, low socioeconomic (SES), ESL and all students. Chapter 5 illustrates the first theme of the book: to infuse an ethnic educator philosophy among ESL teachers and all educators for developing cultural awareness of the powerful effect of their attitudes and educational practices on ESL learners and all low SES, young learners' development and academic achievement.

Chapter 6 is entitled "Increasing Academic Achievement and Language Acquisition for English Language Learners across Grade Levels." The purpose of Chapter 6 is to expose all teachers, whether they are in bilingual, ESL or mainstream classrooms, to a number of important concepts and effective research-based applications in: (1) language and content teaching methodology and strategies, and (2) instructional models and lesson plans that have been successful in the classrooms across the United States. Chapter 6 has the goal of making ESL and mainstream teachers aware that ESL students may be able to participate in content courses at grade-level objectives as the teachers deliver modified instruction to make information comprehensible to them. Chapter 6 uses the information presented in Chapters 3, 4, and 5 on methods and describes specific state-of-the-art, research-based strategies translated into teaching modules and lessons. By implementing national standards for academic achievement, ESL teachers and all teachers can use Chapter 6 as a resource from which to apply, revise, and implement best educational models and lesson plans for ESL students. Through the presentation of the book's second theme, Chapter 6 encourages ESL teachers and all educators to gain awareness of philosophical and educational models, and best applications of classroom teaching strategies across content areas for better serving ESL students. By addressing the second book theme, Chapter 6 also encourages educators to dispel myths about L2 learning, and to realize that there is no quick fix to teach ESL students because language and academic development take time.

Chapter 7 is entitled "Assessing Learning and Academic Achievement in ESL Students for Instructional and Accountability Purposes." Chapter 7 provides ESL teachers and all educators access to research-based and educationally applied knowledge, principles, and national standards to conduct classroom-based assessments of learning, development, and academic achievement in ESL students, and to do so in a systematic, valid, and reliable manner that fulfills both instructional (i.e., links assessment to instruction) and accountability purposes (i.e., program evaluation) of the *Standards* movement. This objective is achieved by integrating research-based knowledge with best educational practices for ESL students in two areas: (1) a contemporary view of the psychometric paradigm, centered on issues of validity and reliability, and (2) an alternative assessment model proposed, which is based on an ethnic educator philosophy and an ecological perspective, with its derived applications on developmental stages of L1 and L2 learning and principles of alternative assessment. For both areas, national and professional *Standards* (AERA, APA, & NCME, 1999) and research-based knowledge are used as guidelines of best practices for educational and psychological testing.

Chapter 7 connects to the first theme of the book: to infuse an ethnic educator philosophy in order for ESL teachers and all educators to develop cultural awareness of the powerful effect of their attitudes and assessment and instructional practices on all low SES students' development and academic achievement, including ESL students. Together, all chapters of this book bring the same ethnic educator philosophical and theoretical approach for ESL teachers to establish a smooth connection between instruction and assessment when serving ESL students in their classrooms.

Chapter 8 is entitled "Integrating Technology for Assessing and Instructing ESL Students." Chapter 8 addresses the issue of integration and implementation of educational technology with quality assessment and instructional services to ESL students. It includes practical applications of educational technology in the daily classroom setting and of action research for teachers of ESL students to use these tools in the classroom to support their teaching. It also includes ways for teachers to become familiar with and involved in the use of technology as an instructional tool and to stay abreast of developments through communities of teachers, learning and working together toward this goal. Thus, Chapter 8 relates to the second theme of this book as it provides information for teachers to better understand how instructional technology can help them individualize assessment and provide instructional service delivery for ESL students. By integrating educational technology with best practices in ESL education, teachers can use instructional technologies as a tool for enhancing the learning potential and learning outcome in ESL students.

Chapter 9 is entitled "A Dialogue about Myths Held by Educators and Recommendations for Better Educational Practices for ESL Students." More specifically, Chapter 9 provides closure for the book in the form of a dialogue among the coauthors, centered on myths commonly held by educators, and some recommendations for better educational practices with ESL students in relation to the first and second themes of the book, referring to educators: (1) developing a personal connection to the sociohistorical presence of ESL immigrants in the U.S. public schools, and (2) becoming committed advocates for better serving ESL students. In relation to these two themes, the main idea underlying myths is how internal (i.e., developmental and psychological characteristics) and external factors (i.e., school and family environments) interact to make ESL students resilient or place them at-risk of underachievement. The book, throughout its chapters, presents evidence and examples of how high-quality teaching can make a difference for dispelling myths about ESL learners. The companion Web site, www.ablongman.com/gonzalez1e, also presents abundant information centered on the first and second themes of the book, and can be used by readers as a major instructional and learning resource for the book. The need to dispel myths commonly held by educators has also been mentioned by the *ESL Standards for Pre-K–12 Students* (TESOL, 1997). According to TESOL *Standards*, it is necessary to dispel the myth that

> In earlier times immigrant children learned English rapidly and assimilated into American life . . . [in fact] . . . Many immigrant students during the early part of this century did not learn English quickly or well. Many dropped out of school to work in jobs that did not require the kinds of academic achievement and communication skills that substantive employment opportunities require today. (1997, p. 3)

OUR AUDIENCE: ESL TEACHERS AND ALL EDUCATORS MAKING A PERSONAL CONNECTION AND DEVELOPING CULTURAL AWARENESS FOR BETTER EDUCATING ESL STUDENTS

The intended audience for our book is the wide cadre of ESL teachers and all professional educators and upper undergraduate and graduate students interested in serving ESL students and their families in the U.S. public school system. This target audience of pre-service and in-service ESL teachers and all teachers from Pre-K through Grade 12 are in need of mandated continuous professional development. Then, we intend to reach out to all education majors, pre-service and in-service ESL and mainstream teachers educating the increasing number of ESL students in their regular Pre-K through Grade

12 classrooms. Therefore, this book can be used in foundational ESL and related major area courses (i.e., bilingual and multicultural education, diversity of learners; and all early childhood, elementary, middle, and high school teacher education majors) at the upper undergraduate level (i.e., junior and senior), as well as at the beginning and more advanced graduate levels (i.e., endorsement and masters and doctoral levels), depending on whether courses are geared toward ESL or mainstream educators.

The book goes from research to practice, and consequently it is appealing for university faculty and students who can use the book within an academic context, as well as in-service ESL and mainstream teachers using the book for professional development. That is, this book can also be used for staff development training workshops required by state and local education agencies for ESL teachers and all educators serving ESL students. Therefore, this book responds to the academic and professional development needs of both audiences trying to meet the wide range of diverse characteristics of today's ESL students in the U.S. public school system. Then, besides the *target audience* of ESL teachers and all educators serving Pre-K through Grade 12, there is a long list of stakeholders in the education of ESL students that we are writing this book for: bilingual and special education students and professionals; cognitive, developmental, educational, and school psychology students and professionals; educational diagnosticians; school counselors; speech pathologists; social workers and all school personnel involved in the assessment of ESL students; school administrators and support personnel; and all university professors and administrators in higher education providing training for ESL and all educators.

It is important to highlight that, according to the *ESL Standards* from TESOL (1997), all education personnel need to share responsibility and engage in collaborative teaching for the education of ESL students. All educators need professional development to

> expand their knowledge base . . . [toward] . . . the understanding of similarities and differences in first- and second-language (L2) acquisition, the role of native language in L2 and content learning, instructional methods and strategies that facilitate both English language and content learning, instructional practices that accommodate individual differences and learning styles, the interrelation between culture, cognition, and academic achievement; alternative approaches to assessment, and the importance of community-school linkages in education. (p. 4)

ESL Standards also promote that "native-English-speaking students, teachers, administrators, and school staff should learn about the world and its languages from ESL students, their families, and their communities" (TESOL, 1997, p. 5).

This book responds to this current issue, the professional development of *all* Pre-K through Grade 12 pre-service and in-service teachers, with a fresh approach: infusing research-based knowledge on best instructional and assessment approaches for ESL students through making a personal connection and developing cultural awareness. Presently, ESL teachers and all educators are required in many states with large numbers of ESL students (e.g., Florida, Colorado, Texas) and at the national level by federal legislation (i.e., the No Child Left Behind Act—NCLB, December, 2001) to show teachers' effectiveness in ESL students' progress in academic achievement across content areas according to high-stakes standards. Then, our goal in creating this ESL book is to bring a fresh approach to presenting this topic through two overarching themes that will grab the attention of readers. Our goal is to build rapport in readers, and to stimulate them to develop positive attitudes and cultural awareness by making a personal connection through the sociohistorical context of immigration in U.S. history. By using these two pedagogical tools, we are making the ESL topic real, alive, and relevant for readers.

ACKNOWLEDGMENTS

There are many individuals who have supported and made possible the production of this book, which has certainly become a team collaborative effort. Our sincere thanks go to our colleague, Dr. Josefina (Josie) Villamil Tinajero, who wrote the compelling Foreword for the book. We admire her inspirational role as a national scholar, leader, advocate, and mentor for bilingual and ESL educators, students, and their families.

The authors express their appreciation to Dr. Rita Brusca-Vega for her valuable help during the planning stage of this book, as she provided feedback for improving the content and format of multiple chapters. We would like to acknowledge the assistance of colleagues Dr. Abie L. Quinoñes-Benítez, University of Connecticut and New Haven public schools, and Dr. Evelyn Robles-Rivas, Waterbury, Connecticut public schools, for their advice during our many brainstorming sessions and discussions on the chapters. We also want to recognize and express our appreciation to Ms. Carla Amaro, a doctoral student at the Teaching English as a Second Language (TESL) Program at the University of Cincinnati. She designed the companion Web site for the book, a very valuable interactive and multimedia instructional environment. We are also grateful to the teachers, students, and parents who volunteered to participate in the vignettes included in the book and companion Web site.

Foremost, we want to acknowledge the support of numerous people at Allyn and Bacon who made possible the production of this book. Our appreciation goes to the key person who made this book project possible, our editor, Aurora Martinez, for her vision and commitment to publishing high-quality professional books to support ESL educators and their students. She provided us with outstanding editorial support, together with her team of editorial assistants, and production and marketing support professionals. Finally, the authors extend their appreciation to the reviewers who provided wise and useful feedback to improve the content and format of the book and companion Web site:

Edmundo F. Litton   *Loyola Marymount University*

Judith B. O'Loughlin   *New Jersey City University*

Beth Anderson Smith   *California Lutheran University*

Lawrence Krute   *Manhattanville College*

Happy readings!

V.G., T.D.Y, & L.M.R.

REFERENCES

American Educational Research Association (AERA), American Psychological Association (APA), & National Council on Measurement in Education (NCME). (1999). *Standards for educational and psychological testing*. Washington, DC: AERA.

Gonzalez, V. (2001). Immigration: Education's story, past, present, and future. *College Board Review, 193*, 24–31.

Gonzalez, V., Brusca-Vega, R., & Yawkey, T. (1997). *Assessment and instruction of culturally and linguistically diverse students with or at-risk of learning problems: From research to practice*. Needham Heights, MA: Allyn and Bacon.

TESOL. (1997). *ESL standards for pre-K–12 students*. Washington, DC: TESOL.

ABOUT THE AUTHORS

Virginia Gonzalez is an associate professor of English as a second language (ESL) education at the University of Cincinnati. She has an interdisciplinary professional and academic background, with a M.A. in Bilingual Special Education and a Ph.D. in Educational Psychology, both degrees from the University of Texas at Austin. She received a bachelor's degree in Clinical Psychology with a minor in Educational Psychology from the Pontifical University of Lima, Peru. She was formerly a faculty member at Texas A&M University and at the University of Arizona. She is an expert in ESL/bilingual instruction and assessment. One of Dr. Gonzalez's major areas of expertise is the generation of research models explaining cognitive and linguistic development in ESL Hispanic students, and their implications for assessment, learning processes, and instruction and teacher education programs. She has taught pre- and in-service teacher education courses in child and human development, diversity in learners, assessment of mainstream and ESL students, second-language development and learning, instructional methods in ESL/bilingual education, research methods in ESL, and development and achievement in ESL/bilingual students in the three universities where she has worked. She has mentored a large cadre of masters and doctoral students in the three universities where she has worked. These American and international graduate students, representing several Asian, European, and Latin American countries, have collaborated in research projects and published extensively with her. Dr. Gonzalez has published numerous books and journal articles, which have been applied for the assessment and instruction of diverse students, and for the training of ESL/bilingual educators in higher education. She has served on national boards for major professional organizations and other research and advisory committees on ESL and bilingual education. Since 2002 she serves as editor for the National Association for Bilingual Education's *NABE Review of Research and Practice*. Dr. Gonzalez is multilingual, with Spanish as her native language and Italian and English as second languages. She was born and raised in Lima, Peru, and came to the United States in 1986 as an international graduate student, with Austin, Texas, as her U.S. hometown. She and her husband, Emmanuel, have a bilingual English/Spanish child, Christian, who is first-generation Hispanic American and was born in Tucson, Arizona.

Thomas D. Yawkey is professor of education at the Pennsylvania State University. He formerly conducted research and taught at the University of Maryland, College Park, the University of Illinois, Champaign-Urbana, and the University of Wisconsin, Madison. Dr. Yawkey received his Ph.D. from the University of Illinois, Champaign-Urbana and master's degree from Duquesne University (Pittsburgh, Pennsylvania). He has extensive experience working with culturally and linguistically diverse families and children. He is of Greek ethnicity. While in the Midwest, he worked with Native Americans and Mexicans. At Pennsylvania State University, Dr. Yawkey worked with Puerto Rican,

Mexican, Russian, Chinese, and Vietnamese families in community, agency, school, and migrant programs. In addition, he has taught in day care programs in Illinois, infant and kindergarten programs in the District of Columbia and Baltimore, Maryland, and intermediate through high school classes in Pennsylvania. Currently, he advises international graduate students from Taiwan, China, Kuwait, South Korea, Saudi Arabia, Ghana, and Turkey. He served as director of the Title III project ADELANTE Pennsylvania State Univerity ESL Graduate Courses for In-service Graduate Level ESL Training and Staff Development, and as director of the Title VII project P.I.A.G.E.T. Bilingual Academic Excellence Programs. He has in-serviced ESL, bilingual, and migrant teachers in school districts and social service agencies in Pennsylvania, Puerto Rico, Wisconsin, Maryland, Alabama, and other states and countries. Author and co-author of numerous books and articles on ESL, bilingual parenting, and young children, Dr. Yawkey has worked with distance-education course development for Penn State's World Campus–based Family Literacy Certificate Program. His international work includes sabbatical and research leaves in countries such as Taiwan/ROC and South Korea, and he has served as keynoter of national and international conferences in these countries. Dr. Yawkey's wife, Dr. Margaret Yawkey, is a lifelong educator and teacher. She specialized in literacy programs for pre-Kindergarten through grade 12 for the Wisconsin State Department of Education, for agencies and intermediate units in Pennsylvania and Wisconsin, and for colleges, and is now retired. They have two sons, Shaun Nicholas and Brian Michael, who both reside in Pennsylvania.

Liliana Minaya-Rowe holds a Ph.D. in education from the University of Texas at Austin with an emphasis in bilingual/bicultural education, linguistics, and anthropology. Dr. Minaya-Rowe is professor emerita of the Neag School of Education at the University of Connecticut, where she developed a graduate training program in bilingual education. She directed quasi-experimental and experimental doctoral dissertation research studies in the areas of teacher education, professional development models for effective teaching, Spanish-English reading development and teaching, two-way program development, first and second language acquisition and teaching methodology, social aspects of education, parent and community involvement in schooling, and linguistic processes in K–12 students. She is currently a researcher at the Johns Hopkins University's Center for Data-Driven Reform in Education, where she is co-principal investigator with Margarita Calderón, principal investigator, on the Carnegie Foundation of New York's *Project ExCELL: Expediting Comprehension for English-language Learners* (ELLs) to design, implement, and refine a staff development program for middle and high school teachers of literature, science, and social studies who have ELLs in their classrooms. Additionally, Dr. Minaya-Rowe has served as consultant to school districts and conducted numerous workshops, seminars, and institutes for teachers of ELLs on all facets of second-language instruction, classroom assessments, and literacy. Her more than 80 publications include journal articles, books, chapters, teacher manuals, and guidebooks on professional development, plans and practices for two-way, bilingual, and ESL programs, and parent/family involvement strategies. Dr. Minaya-Rowe is a native of Peru, where she codirected staff development programs for Quechua-Spanish bilingual teachers in the Andes. She has also taught in public schools in Peru and the United States.

ENGLISH-AS-A-SECOND-LANGUAGE (ESL) TEACHING AND LEARNING

CHAPTER 1

THE ROLE OF IMMIGRANT ESL STUDENTS IN THE HISTORY OF U.S. EDUCATION
Making a Personal Connection

LEARNING OBJECTIVES

1. Develop knowledge of the four immigration waves present in U.S. history, and the continuous presence of ESL immigrant students in U.S. public schools since the middle of the 1800s until the present

2. Understand sociohistorical factors affecting the academic achievement and cultural adaptation to the school culture of ESL immigrant students

3. Become aware of the philosophical and political movements present in U.S. education history

PREVIEW QUESTIONS

1. Has there been a history of ESL immigration waves in the U.S. public schools since the middle of the 1800s until the present?

2. What are some of the similarities and differences of sociohistorical factors affecting the Ellis Island and today's ESL students?

3. What political and philosophical education movements, and their derived policy, have affected the educational process and outcome of ESL immigrants since the middle of the 1800s until the present?

PARALLELS BETWEEN IMMIGRATION WAVES THROUGH ELLIS ISLAND AND TODAY'S IMMIGRANTS

Chapter 1 presents the theme of our book: stimulating educators to gain awareness of immigrant English-as-a-second-language (ESL) students' continuous presence throughout the history of U.S. education, from the steady influx of eastern and southern European immigrant students with non-English-speaking backgrounds during the Ellis Island years (1850s to 1950s) to today's Hispanic and Asian immigrant ESL students.

Through the presentation of the book's theme, Chapter 1 also encourages educators to recognize that more than one-third of today's U.S. citizens are descendants of at least one ancestor who came through Ellis Island as an ESL immigrant, within the period of the 1850s until the 1950s. By gaining this awareness of their own or their students' family history, educators can make a personal connection with the sociohistorical reality of the presence of ESL students in U.S. public education. By making a personal connection, educators can build rapport and become empathetic and committed **advocates** to better serve the culturally and linguistically diverse needs of ESL students and their families. In Chapter 1, readers are presented with the idea that schooling of ESL students may take generations, and that the value of schooling lies in serving as a social agent to facilitate their **cultural adaptation,** the process of interacting with and integrating into middle-class America. Emphasis on the conceptual difference between integration (leading to multiple languages and cultural identities; see transculturation) and **assimilation** (leading to enforcing mainstream culture and language only) as a cultural adaptation process is made. Box 1.1 presents an example of cultural adaptations through integration by using an excerpt from an interview with an international graduate student from Taiwan.

In order to present and discuss the book theme, Chapter 1 provides for readers a discussion of historical content that compares the needs of ESL immigrants during the **Ellis Island years** (late 1800s to middle 1900s, Waves 1 and 2) to contemporary immigration trends of Hispanics and Asians (1960s to the present, Waves 3 and 4) in terms of significant parallels—and also some differences—across sociohistorical, socioeconomic, and demographic issues.

■ ■ ■ ■ ■

BOX 1.1
INTERVIEW WITH KIM, AN INTERNATIONAL GRADUATE STUDENT FROM TAIWAN

Interviewer: What is your definition of your culture?

Kim: My culture is very dependent. Other people depend on other people. That's why I can't understand it why my classmates won't let me use (their) notes. Only they will just say "Okay, I will let you know" and then they just break their promise. In Taiwan, we don't do that. We are very dependent on family and friends. This is one cultural difference. Also, Asians are very obedient. We won't offend our professors or our elders. But I just think somehow American students should have some respect for their professors and their elders. Americans are very individualistic. Professors are very knowledgeable in their field. I did not say that you should not challenge their knowledge. No, but just have some respect because I always see, especially undergraduates, they just leave the class early and that disturb the professors, I mean their motivation in lecturing, or also it disturbs other students in the class. I know that students can assess professors. I think they should not do that. In Taiwan, we respect all professors very much. I think this is a good virtue.

BOX 1.1   CONTINUED

But in some way Asian students are too obedient. They don't speak up in the classes. They don't express their ideas like American students do. American students always speak up their ideas in class and they always ask questions if they don't understand. But Asian students, they just keep quiet and they take whatever the professor said; they won't even ask questions in the class. This is another big difference.

Interviewer: How similar do you think your culture is in comparison to the American academic culture? Explain using examples.

Kim: I don't think that Asian culture is very similar to American culture because we are just so different, but now, maybe they are a little bit more similar. I mean in my time, when I went to school, I don't think it was very similar, but now maybe it's becoming more similar because now the professors in the university or in the college are all graduates from a university in America. They got their Ph.D.s in America so somehow it changed our academic culture in Taiwan because of the professors. When I move back to Taiwan I expect that the culture will be more like the American academic culture now.

Interviewer: What difficulties have you faced in adapting to the American academic culture?

Kim: It was very difficult because (the) American academic culture is very different from (the) academic culture in Taiwan. In Taiwan, we are always memorizing stuff. We are not used to have our own ideas and to think critically.

Interviewer: Has your lifestyle changed since you came to the U.S., and are those changes positive or negative? Please explain.

Kim: My lifestyle changed since I came to the U.S., definitely, and I believe these changes are positive because I learned to be more independent, to have my own ideas and have my own opinion. I don't follow other people's opinion always like before anymore. I think you need to screen the American culture and decide to what you want to adapt to because I believe Chinese and American cultures have their own strengths and weaknesses. I would like to adapt to the strengths of the American culture instead of its weaknesses, so I don't really adapt to everything in a culture and I can kind of screen what I want.

Interviewer: Are there things that you used to do before you came that you don't do now or the other way around?

Kim: For example, before I came here I was very obedient to my parents. When they said something, I just did whatever they said, but now when I don't agree with my father or my mother, I won't argue with them, but I will tell them my opinion later with a soft voice because I'm still Chinese. I won't offend my parents. And now I learned to express my opinion and I try to be objective, that to let my father know that this is my thinking and maybe you can consider it.

In relation to the theme for this book, four immigration waves will be discussed:

Wave 1   *Middle 1800s and up to early 1900s*, Ellis Island years in relation to: (i) causes and effects of immigration of eastern and northern Europeans to the United States; (ii) immigration quotas, policy, and anti-immigration views of U.S. public; (iii) cultural adaptation in relation to the melting pot or assimilation philosophy; (iv) assimilation movement in the U.S. school culture; (v) schooling conditions of immigrants; (vi) the role of public schools as a social institution for the transmission of cultural heritage; (vii) post-World War I years (1918–1929); (viii) intelligence tests; (ix) marriage and social status of women; (x) housing conditions of immigrants; and (xi) working conditions of immigrants

Wave 2   From *1901 to 1930*, Ellis Island years in relation to: (i) cultural adaptation through name changes; (ii) cultural adaptation through adoption of American dress code; (iii) factors affecting the degree and pace of cultural adaptation and assimilation, (iv) gender roles; (v) returning immigrants to Europe; (vi) housing conditions of immigrants; (vii) working conditions of immigrants: effect on their economic status; and (viii) the internal migration of African Americans: schooling conditions

Waves 3 and 4 From the 1960s to the present, in relation to: (i) interwar period; (ii) the **civil rights movement era** (including segregation in public schools; equal educational opportunity for the poor; legislation—Head Start and Elementary and Secondary Education Act, Bilingual Education); and (iii) the new immigrants of the 1980s, 1990s, and the early 2000s

COLONIAL AND REVOLUTIONARY ERAS (LATE 1500s TO LATE 1700s)

Even though our discussion of immigration waves begins in the mid-to-late 1800s, an overview of immigration waves during the colonial, revolutionary, and early republican periods in America (the late 1500s through the late 1700s) will be presented in the next section and in abbreviated form in Table 1.1. We consider it important to present for our readers historical immigration trends and how they influenced the origins and development of the United States, and to serve as a reminder that the United States is a nation founded by immigrants. In fact, in trying to make a personal connection to our own immigrant family history, we educators need to realize that over a third of U.S. citizens today descend from at least one ESL immigrant. Some questions that educators can pose for themselves include: What is the U.S.-born generation that we and our students represent? What was the ethnic, cultural, and linguistic backgrounds of our ESL immigrant ancestors? What were the major reasons or motivators to immigrate to the United States? What were the **socio-historical conditions** that our ancestors endured at the time of immigration? What was the U.S. public education reality that our ESL immigrant ancestors experienced? In the sections below, we will examine these questions in relation to Immigration Wave 1.

The First Settlers: America from the Late 1500s through the Late 1700s

French, Spanish, Dutch, and British immigrants colonized most regions of North America. Colonists were motivated to come to North America for several reasons; among the most important ones were religious and political freedom, and economic opportunities. The first permanent settlement established by European colonists in North America was St. Augustine in the late 1500s, in what is now the State of Florida, then under the control of Spain. In addition to some territories in North America, the Spaniards explored and settled South and Central America using the Spanish language and the Catholic religion as tools for acculturation of native Indians.

The first permanent English colony in America was Jamestown in Virginia, established in 1607. These earliest colonists were motivated by economic reasons; they arrived with the idea of making money by trading with Europe, and of finding gold and silver as the Spaniards had found these precious metals in South and central America. They were not motivated to become farmers, but to find gold and become rich. One of the colonists, John Smith, became a leader, making everyone work building cottages, planting food crops, and cutting firewood so that they could survive. However, due to the hardships of cold winters and sickness, less than half of the Jamestown colonists survived the first few years. The colony was able to survive only because of new settlers and supplies from England that continued to arrive, and the discovery of tobacco as a trading crop.

The second permanent settlement founded by Englishmen was Plymouth, Massachusetts, in 1620. These settlers were called the Pilgrims and came to North America because they were looking for religious freedom. The Pilgrims arrived on board the *Mayflower*, on which they developed the *Mayflower Compact*, a government agreement stating two important principles: that the people would (1) vote about their community's government and laws, and (b) accept whatever the majority chose. These two principles later became very important ideas shaping the U.S. Constitution. Again, as had happened to the Jamestown English settlers, the Pilgrims also suffered during the cold winters, with only half surviving the first year. The settlers had to learn how to adapt their farming and fishing techniques to survive in the North American continent. The Pilgrims are best remembered for the Thanskgiving tradition they helped to establish with their first harvest meal in the fall of 1621.

The third group of English settlers, the Puritans, also came to America in search of religious freedom. The Puritans established their settlement in the Massachusetts Bay area in 1630. Learning from the experience of the Pilgrims, the Puritans had come better prepared for adapting to the new land by bringing with them the necessary supplies and skills. Later on, some colonists left Massachusetts for other parts of New England because of lack of religious freedom in the Puritan colony, founding New Hampshire in 1632 and Connecticut in 1636. Also in 1636, Roger Williams founded Rhode Island because of political and religious persecution. The new colony was the

TABLE 1.1 Immigration Waves and Major Historic Milestones from the Late 1500s through the Late 1700s

YEAR OF SETTLEMENT	PLACE OF SETTLEMENT	GROUP	MAJOR MOTIVATION FOR IMMIGRATION	MILESTONES
Late 1500s	Florida St. Augustine	Spaniards	• Religious and political freedom, and economic reasons	• Spanish language and Catholic religion were used as major tools for acculturation • Spaniards colonized most regions of South and Central America, and some territories in North America (current states of former Spanish territories: California, Florida, Texas, Colorado, New Mexico, Arizona)
1607	Virginia, Jamestown	English	• Economic reasons (colonists came to find riches such as gold and silver)	• Survival became a major problem, with high rates of mortality due to inclement winter weather, starvation, and sickness
1620	Massachusetts, Plymouth	English, the Pilgrims	• Religious freedom	• Development of the *Mayflower Compact*, a government agreement (introduced important ideas that later helped to shape the U.S. Constitution • Colonists learned how to survive by adapting farming and fishing techniques • Establishment of the Thanksgiving tradition—first harvest meal in 1621
1630	Massachusetts Bay Area	English, the Puritans	• Religious freedom	• Learned from Pilgrims about adapting fishing and farming techniques; and brought supplies and skills needed to survive
1632	New Hampshire	English, the Puritans	• Religious freedom from 1630 colony	• Difficulty of dealing with religious and cultural diversity among colonist groups
1636	Connecticut, Rhode Island	English, the Puritans	• Religious persecution from 1630 colony	• First colony to separate church and state (later became basic principle of U.S. Constitution
1663	North and South Carolina	English settlers from Virginia		
1664	New Netherlands; renamed New York	English Navy took away Dutch territory	• Economic reasons	• Dutch settlers kept their rights, and their land, language, and religion
1664	New Jersey	Dutch, Swedish, and Quaker groups	• Religious freedom	

Date	Location	Event	Significance
1681	Pennsylvania	• Religious freedom and separation between church and state	• Separation between church and state
1682	Delaware	• Independent from Pennsylvania	
1732	Georgia	• English • Refuge for people in debt with England	• Southern pioneer territory
1689–1763	America	• Original 13 colonies were established	• Colonies enjoyed some freedom and self-government because England was at war with France in Europe
1754–1763	America	• French and Indian War with Americans and British	• War ended with Treaty of Paris. During war British took control, with France losing most of its colonies in American territory
1774	Pennsylvania	• American Revolutionary War	• First Continental Congress of the original colonies as a reaction to enforced new laws by Britain (i.e., enforcing taxes, and restrictions of trading) • New American identity and self-confidence, separate from the British, prompted willingness to fight for their principles under leaders (Thomas Paine and George Washington). • Principles and values represented by Paine's pamphlet *Common Sense* that appealed for moral obligation to the world to become a democratic republic • Americans decided to fight for independence
1776, July 4	Pennsylvania	• Second Continental Congress • Thomas Jefferson wrote Declaration of Independence • Thomas Jefferson, 13 original colonies	• July 4, 1776, date of Declaration of Independence from England • Establishment of basic American principles of freedom and self-government (i.e., the belief that all men are created equal, all people have certain unalienable rights including life, liberty, and pursuit of happiness, and a government exists only by consent of the governed) central to U.S. Constitution

(continued)

TABLE 1.1 Continued

YEAR OF SETTLEMENT	PLACE OF SETTLEMENT	GROUP	MAJOR MOTIVATION FOR IMMIGRATION	MILESTONES
1781	Yorktown, Virginia		• End of Revolutionary War	• Final decisive victory for the Americans, marking milestone of control of war against England
1783		American representatives, Benjamin Franklin, John Jay, and John Adams	• Treaty of Paris was signed	
1787		13 states	• Constitutional Convention • Great Compromise for a Bicameral Legislature	• Revision of Articles of Confederation, resulted in the U.S. Constitution document • Debate between sovereignty and independent power of states resulted in agreement about two issues: (i) federal government becoming stronger and more centralized, and (ii) a new strong federal government cannot take away liberty or freedom from people • House of Representatives elected on the basis of number of people in each state, and a Senate represented by two elected people from each state regardless of size
1619	Virginia		• First Africans brought to American	
1789	Northern states versus southern states		• Debate of slavery and guarantee of civil rights • Three-Fifths Compromise	• Southern states supported slavery because of need for labor force to sustain a farm-based economy • Northern states opposed slavery as city's economy was based on business or trade • Political issues for counting state population for paying taxes and determining number of House representatives (5 slaves = 3 people)

Date	Event	Details
1789, April 30	• First U.S. President	• Principle of government was that autonomy needed to be part of institutions. No one person, not even the president, would keep all the power • Foreign policy of political neutrality led to isolation for over 100 years
1791	• Two government periods • Bill of Rights was added to U.S. Constitution	• Bill of Rights was added to U.S. Constitution in the form of 10 Amendments that are central in establishing the civil rights and liberties of all Americans • The First Amendment guarantees the right of freedom of speech, press, religion, peaceable assembly, and requesting changes of the government. It also states that church (any religion) and state (any part of the government) should be separate
George Washington		
1798	• Second U.S. President • Naturalization Act of 1798 • Aliens Act expanded	• Kept peace with French and British • First legislation to limit immigration to United States was the Naturalization Act of 1798 (raised number of years an immigrant must live in United States—from 5 to 14—to become a citizen) • Gave the president the power to imprison immigrants whom he considered dangerous to the United States or to force them to leave the country • Both acts were aimed at keeping poor or revolutionary immigrants from coming to the United States
John Adams, Federalist (now Republican party), and Vice President Jefferson (Democratic Party)		
1800	• Both Acts were never enforced strictly	• Democratic Party represented large number of immigrants • America reconfirmed its commitment to an open-door and free immigration policy
Jefferson became President (Democratic Party)		

first to separate church and state, a basic principle of the U.S. Constitution. Other territories became proprietary colonies, such as North and South Carolina, colonized by settlers from Virginia and newly arrived Europeans during 1663.

All together, the pioneer colonies established in North America between 1607 and 1732 came to a total of 13. Other colonies were founded as settlements by various European groups. The British Navy took New Netherlands away from the Dutch in 1664 and renamed it New York; however, the Dutch settlers kept their rights, their land, their language, and their religion. In the same manner, New Jersey was also formed during 1664, when additional settlers joined the Dutch and Swedish pioneers and Quaker groups who were looking for religious freedom. Quaker groups were also the founding settlers in Pennsylvania, which they established as a colony during 1681. Quakers advocated for religious freedom and the separation between church and state. Delaware later became independent from Pennsylvania in 1682. Georgia was the last of the 13 original colonies: It was founded in 1732 as a refuge for people who were in debt in England, as they could receive a piece of farming land in this southern pioneer territory.

The Colonies

During this early colonial period, the colonies were regulated by the king of England, who appointed governors and members of the two assemblies (i.e., the upper House and the governor's council). Even though the colonies had much freedom and self-government, the process was not completely democratic because members of the government needed to meet some qualifications: (1) only men who owned property could vote; and (2) in some colonies, individuals also had to meet religious qualifications. During the period between 1689 and 1763, the colonies were mostly left to their own devices because England was at war with France in Europe. These political problems eventually manifested themselves in North America as a war between French settlers in Canada and British colonies in North American territory. The French and Indian War lasted from 1754 to 1763, with the French helped by some Indian tribes and the Americans helped by the British. French troops won battles at the beginning of the war, both in Europe and in North America, but eventually British troops took control, with France losing most of its colonies when the war ended with the Treaty of Paris.

With Americans gaining self-confidence in fighting and winning battles, and with a less threatening situation with the French, the colonists became more independent from England and saw the need to unite and solve common problems. After the war with France ended, the British government was enforcing new laws for the colonies, asking them to pay new taxes, establishing new policy for settling land, and restricting trading of goods to only England and enforcing high taxes for trade with other countries. In order to discuss common problems and unify, the colonists held the first meeting of the Continental Congress during 1774 in Philadelphia. Twelve of the thirteen colonies sent representatives, including such famous leaders as George Washington and Patrick Henry. The newly formed Congress wrote a Declaration of Rights, which petitioned the king of England to correct problems, and voted on a boycott of British goods. Patrick Henry's stirring words to close the Congress, "Give me liberty or give me death," stated clearly that the colonists identified themselves as

Americans. A new, separate identity from the British one was emerging among Americans and they were willing to fight for their principles.

From the Revolution to Independence

Because the British legislature and the king rejected the Declaration of Rights, the disagreement started the American Revolutionary War. During the first year of the war, the colonists were unsure of whether they were fighting for their rights as British citizens; however, some factors helped Americans decide to fight for independence. For example, colonists were angered that the British hired German soldiers to help them fight the war. Some Americans were also influenced by the principles and values expressed by Thomas Paine in his famous pamphlet entitled *Common Sense*. Paine appealed to Americans' moral obligation to the world to become a democratic republic and support the revolution. Political and military leaders, such as Commander-in-Chief George Washington, were also key players for Americans to develop a new identity and self-confidence.

The Second Continental Congress met during 1776, and on July 4 decided to declare independence from England. The Congress asked Thomas Jefferson, a lawyer and farmer from Virginia, to write the Declaration of Independence, which established the basic principles of the American government. Among the most important founding principles is the belief that "all men are created equal," which is central for a democratic government. Jefferson's claim to independence was based on two basic principles: (1) all people have "certain unalienable rights," including "life, liberty, and the pursuit of happiness," and (2) "a government exists only by consent of the governed." To show that England had ignored their rights, the Americans also wrote a list of complaints or grievances the colonies had against the king.

Even though the Declaration of Independence claimed freedom and self-government as a democratic unified group of independent states, still the war against England had to be won. The final, decisive victory for the Americans was at Yorktown, Virginia, in 1781, where they took control of most battles against the British forces. The Revolutionary War ended formally in 1783, when the Treaty of Paris was signed; Three negotiators represented America and helped to write the peace treaty: Benjamin Franklin, John Jay, and John Adams.

After the Revolutionary War, problems arose for establishing consensus among the newly formed United States of America about its basic form, with some people defending a centralized federal government, and others favoring giving most power to each individual state as declared in the Articles of Confederation. The Constitutional Convention was called in 1787 in order to solve the big issue of whether there would be 13 sovereign states, each acting as an independent country; or 13 mutually dependent states, acting as one united country. The Constitutional Convention was charged with revising the Articles of Confederation, resulting in the document, the U.S. Constitution. The debate between sovereignty and independent power of states resulted in agreement about two issues only: (1) the federal government needed to be made stronger and more centralized than it was; and (2) a new, strong federal government must not take away any of the liberties, or freedoms, of the people. The controversial issue of state representation was difficult to solve, and resulted in a Great Compromise for a bicameral legislature. Thus, the House of Representatives would be elected on the basis of the number of people in each state, whereas the Senate would include two people elected from each state, regardless of the size of the state.

There were two issues that were also debated: slavery and the guarantee of civil rights. The first issue had a deeply rooted historical background; slavery had existed in the colonies since 1619, when the first Africans were forced into slavery and brought to Virginia. The southern states supported slavery because they perceived it to be necessary to supply the intense manual labor needed to sustain with their farm-based economy. In contrast, most northern states based their economy in business or trade that occurred in city areas, and historically had not supported slavery and were planning to make it against the law. The controversy over slavery between southern and northern states was not based on moral issues, but on political issues such as counting state population for paying taxes and determining numbers of House representatives. The states settled for the Three-Fifths Compromise, in which five slaves would be counted as three people for both representation and taxation.

Regarding the second debatable issue, many state delegates supported the idea that the Constitution should guarantee the rights of the people, and that the federal government should be given more power than it had under the Articles of Confederation. In addition, some states guaranteed such rights as freedom of speech and religion in their own constitutions, and some state representatives also supported the need for the U.S. Constitution to guarantee those rights. All states ratified the U.S. Constitution soon after George Washington took office as the first president of the United States of America on April 30, 1789. The young republic had the central idea that the authority was in its institutions and that no one person, not even the president, would keep all the power. The young country also followed a foreign policy of political neutrality in its relations with other countries, following a policy of isolation for over 100 years. The central idea or philosophy of the Constitution is federalism, in which the powers of the government are divided between the central (federal or national) government and the state governments. The Bill of Rights was added by the delegates to the Constitution in 1791, in the form of ten Amendments that are central in establishing the civil rights and liberties of all Americans. The First Amendment guarantees the rights of freedom of speech, press, religion, peaceable assembly, and requesting changes of the government. It also states that church (any religion) and state (any part of the government) should be separate.

FIRST IMMIGRATION WAVE: MID-1800s TO EARLY 1900s

Causes and Effects of Immigration of Eastern and Northern Europeans to the United States

A European potato blight in the 1840s began the immigration era, after Ireland and other areas, such as some provinces of Germany, were devastated by famine, resulting in about 1.4 million people immigrating to America (Weatherford, 1995). For example, the population in Ireland was estimated to be 8.5 million in 1845; by 1851, its population was reduced to 6.5 million. The loss of 1 million Irish people is attributed to starvation and resulting disease, and another million emigrated to America. An immigration of such magnitude had never been experienced before. Even during its founding years, only 850,000 immigrants entered between the American Revolution and the 1840s (Weatherford, 1995). A synopsis of major historical and social similarity patterns is outlined in Table 1.2, showing such comparisons as ethnic, cultural, linguistic, and educational backgrounds, access to educational services, job conditions, and so on.

Another major cause for the drastic loss of lives among immigrants to the United States during the mid-1800s was the very poor sanitation conditions endured on the ships, which often led to epidemics and death on board. The normal mortality was 10 percent for steerage passengers of early ships, with 17,000 Irish immigrants dying during 1847, the peak of the famine period, and another 20,000 dying soon after arriving in the United States (Daniels, 1990; Handlin, 1951).

During this immigration era, around 2.6 million Europeans arrived in the 1850s, with some reduction of numbers during the Americans Civil War, and continuation of the large number of immigrants during the 1860s, which brought over 2 million newcomers, with numbers doubling during the 1880s to over 4.7 million arrivals. The 1880s marked a milestone in the history of U.S. immigration: "For the first time, more than a million immigrants . . . were from central—as opposed to northern—Europe" (Weatherford, 1995, p. xiv), with large numbers of Jews, Italians, and various Slavic groups. In most instances, men came first, and millions of women followed some time later, bringing their children with them or sending the earning-age children before the rest of the family came. Grandparents were most often left behind, primarily due to two reasons: older adults had more difficulty coping with the strenuous traveling conditions, and age was viewed as a handicapping condition by immigration officers. In most instances men, who were often illiterate, could not provide sufficiently detailed information to prepare their families for the difficulties of the voyage. Women did not know exactly what to pack and what items to sell or leave behind, or what to expect during debarkation at Ellis Island. Most European peasants were fatalistic, as explained by Weatherford (1995): "[The immigration journey] was a confused process, and more dependent on luck, than [it] should have been [Most immigrant women had a] . . . self-protective belief that what would be, would be" (p. 297).

The 1890s brought some economic depression, reducing the number of immigrants to 3.6 million, with the following decade (1901 to 1910) experiencing an immigration peak of 8 million, in partly because of the introduction of faster ships, (marking a milestone; see Table 1.2.), reducing the voyage time from months to weeks and days. The steamers also could maintain regular schedules independent of the inclemency of the weather, such as unfavorable winds. Steamers also provided dining facilities, and medical inspections and vaccinations were required at the port of embarkation in Europe. Even though steerage sanitation was still in need of improvement, the mortality rate decreased tremendously and almost disappeared. In response to the change in the ethnicity of immigrants to the United States experienced since the 1840s, legislation restricted the number of southern and eastern Europeans by

TABLE 1.2   Similarity Patterns between Ellis Island and 1980s through 2000s Immigrants

PATTERNS	ELLIS ISLAND (AND PRECEDENT) IMMIGRANTS (1840S–1950S)	1980S–2000S IMMIGRANTS
Ethnic Backgrounds	Mostly eastern and southern European from rural backgrounds (in order of size of foreign-born groups: German, Italian, Russian, Polish, Irish, Swedish, Austrian, Hungarian, Norwegian, Danish, Greek, French, Finnish, Dutch, Swiss, Romanian).	Mostly Latin Americans and Asians have immigrated to the United States since the 1980s until the present. Mexicans and Chinese are the largest groups, with other secondary groups such as other Central and South Americans, Cubans, and Asian refugee groups (e.g., Vietnamese, Hmong, Cambodian).
Cultural and Linguistic Backgrounds	Foreign-born groups had different behavioral codes, such as dress code, nutritional and eating habits, hygiene habits, gender roles (related to women's role and birth rate), religions, values and beliefs, principles guiding behaviors, and social conventions related to family life (e.g., communication patterns between spouses and parents and children). Multiple L1 spoken by diverse eastern and southern European immigrants, with children gaining some proficiency in English if schooled and adults rarely learning any English. Different religions (e.g., Catholicism and Judaism) and cultures were represented, unfamiliar to the Anglo-Saxon mainstream population in the United States during 1800s and early 1900s	Most Hispanics are from a rural background, with a mix of educational levels for Asians. Multiple languages spoken by Asians (Mandarin is most commonly used) and uniformity of Spanish as an L1 among Hispanics, but with dialect and ethnic cultural variations (e.g., vocabulary, pragmatics). Multiple religions brought by Asians, and uniformity of Catholic backgrounds among Hispanics.
English Proficiency Level	Most did not speak English, which prevented them from getting better paid jobs and higher occupational status	Most do not speak English, which prevents them from getting better paid jobs and higher occupational status
Educational Level	Most likely illiterate in first language (L1), with no schooling in country of origin	May be illiterate in L1, or with primary or elementary level of schooling

TABLE 1.2   Continued

PATTERNS	ELLIS ISLAND (AND PRECEDENT) IMMIGRANTS (1840S–1950S)	1980S–2000S IMMIGRANTS
Educational Opportunities in the United States for Children of Immigrant Families	Access to city schools' regular, English-only programs at the elementary levels (during 1800s and early 1900s), and later to secondary schools	Access to low-income neighborhood schools, or mixed-income suburban schools with other non-English-as-a-second-language (ESL) minority and economically disadvantaged groups (e.g., African American and White). Some availability of ESL and bilingual education programs, but limited resources and trained personnel to comply with policies. Schools (especially inner-city ones) suffer from high attrition rate due to at-risk social conditions connected to low socio-economic status (SES) such as high dropout rates, teenage pregnancy, violence, overrepresentation in special education, low academic achievement, and so on.
Fertility Rate and Size of Family	No birth control education available for foreign-born women, who had a much higher rate of birth and infant mortality than American-born women	Immigrant families are much larger than the 1.5 children average rate of U.S. families. Age of mother, number of children, years of separation between pregnancies are factors connected with SES of mothers (e.g., level of education, occupational status, etc.).
Housing Conditions	Live in immigrant ghetto sides of urban areas, isolated from mainstream areas	Live in low-income ethnic area neighborhoods ("barrios") in inner city or suburbia, isolated from mainstream areas
Job Conditions and Occupational Status	Unskilled laborers working in factories (Industrial Era) in menial jobs, with low wages, nonunionized Immigrants from eastern and southern Europe who came to the United States prior to the 1900s formed the large mass of laborers in farms and factories that help found and build the Industrial Revolution, and later U.S. economic and political power	Mostly unskilled laborers (or with invalid degrees or certifications in the United States) working in manufacturing, service industry, farming in menial jobs, with low wages

imposing quotas in the 1920s. However, it was the poor masses of early immigration, prior to the 1900s, that formed the largest group of laborers in farms and factories, and that helped create the Industrial Revolution. Furthermore, the immigrants helped establish the political and economic power of the United States as a leading world country.

Because of the large number of immigrants who entered the United States through the New York City Harbor during the peak immigration period, the Ellis Island facility was built and inaugurated during the late 1800s. The first immigrant who sailed to the United States and entered through Ellis Island was Annie Moore, an Irish teenager who arrived on New Year's Day, 1892. She represented over 17 million immigrants who entered through Ellis Island since its inauguration until the mid-1950s, with 70 percent of all immigrants arriving through New York City Harbor (Weatherford, 1995). Annie Moore also represented a large group of Irish women, who comprised 52 percent of those leaving Ireland between 1899 and 1910.

Prior to the 1900s, before Ellis Island opened as a port of entry, immigrants came through several cities in the East Coast, such as Boston and Philadelphia, and mostly settled in northeastern cities. The 1900 census showed that New Jersey had 1,883,669 residents, with 431,884 born overseas (23 percent), and that Connecticut had 908,420 residents, of which 238,210 were foreign born (26 percent). For instance, Boston received "no fewer than twenty thousand immigrants annually, most of them Irish" (Weatherford, 1995, p. xi). Cities such as Boston attracted immigrants because of the availability of factory jobs, such as the textile mills industry that employed large numbers of Irish, Italians, Jews, Portuguese, Greeks, Syrians, and Armenians toward the late 1800s.

Other immigrants arrived into these northeast ports of entry but then moved into midwest industrial centers such as Detroit, Cleveland, and Chicago, in urban industrialized areas such as cities "from Cincinnati and St. Louis to Milwaukee and Minneapolis" (Weatherford, 1995, p. xii), and in farming towns in the upper midwest "from the plains of Kansas to the woods of northern Michigan" (ibid). Most of the immigrants settling in the midwest region were from German, Scandinavian, Polish, Italian, Russian, and other Eastern and Southern European backgrounds.

Immigrant communities were present across the United States. Other immigrants entered through southern parts such as New Orleans. These immigrants settled in some southern regions that became exceptions to the trend of settling in the east coast and midwest cities and farm towns, and attracted immigrants to work in coal and copper mines (e.g., Arizona and Colorado) and some smaller "niche" or enclave communities (e.g., German centers in Texas). For instance, as early as 1844, Austin County received 400 Germans, and in 1845, 21 ships arrived at Galveston with 3,084 German immigrants.

Industrialization Creates the Need for Immigrant Laborers.   The northern part of the United States became industrialized sooner than the more rural southern region, which was dedicated mostly to farming lands. The United States had many of the natural resources needed for industrialization including energy sources, such as coal and rivers to provide electrical power. The government also passed some policies to support the growing industries by erecting tariff barriers to keep out low-priced foreign goods. The steady arrival of immigrants and growing U.S. born population provided industry with a large source of laborers and consumers for goods in growing metropolitan areas. In addition, many of the inventions of the Industrial Revolution were the work of Americans, such as the cotton gin that separated the cotton fiber from the seeds and the sewing machine that allowed the mass production of cotton clothing.

Though the birth rate was high in the United States during the mid-1800s and early 1900s, the demand for workers was even higher. Thus, immigration was the major source of steady availability of farm workers and industrial manufacturing laborers. After 1830 more immigrants worked in the factories than on the land, and government policy reflected the openness to immigrants. Immigration was perceived by early-eighteenth century Americans as a way of making the United States even greater than it already was. Immigrants contributed the people needed to help the country grow, and many immigrants became inventors and businessmen who led the economic development. The companion Web site, www.ablongman.com/Gonzalez1e, highlights some Ellis Island immigrants who later became famous Americans, including Bob Hope, Samuel Goldwyn, Rudolph Valentino, Elia Kazan, Isaac Asimov, Xavier Cugat, Father Edward Flanagan, Baron and Baroness von Trapp, and Bela Lugosi.

Immigration Quotas.   Immigration policies started to be enforced long before the peak immigration years of Ellis Island; they date back to the late 1700s. A summarized list of immigration policies is presented in Table 1.3. The first policies intended to regulate immigration were enforced during John Adams's administration, where he became the second president of the United States, after George Washington's second term as president. Adams continued Washington's foreign policy of isolation and neutrality and was able to keep peace with both the French and British. Adams supported the first legislation to limit immigration to the United States, the *Naturalization Act of 1798*. This policy increased the number of years an immigrant must live in America (from 5 to 14) before becoming a citizen. In addition, the Alien Acts gave the president the power to imprison immigrants whom he considered dangerous to the United States or to force them to leave the country. Both acts were aimed at keeping poor or revolutionary immigrants from coming to the United States. Adams represented the Federalist Party and his support for these acts was opposed by his vice president, Thomas Jefferson, who represented the Democratic-Republican party, which had a large number of recent immigrants. The Alien Acts were never enforced strictly and were allowed to expire in 1800 when Jefferson became president, with the United States reconfirming its commitment to an open-door and free immigration policy.

After World War I, Americans began to worry about the increasing numbers of immigrants, as the cities were becoming crowded and unsettled land was becoming scarce. In addition, after the 1840s most immigrants were from eastern and southern Europe, and brought with them cultures and languages that were different than the northern and western Europeans who came earlier. The fear of different immigration trends led to legislation limiting immigration, which added to some of the already existing restrictions on Chinese immigrants (e.g., the Chinese Exclusion Act of 1882). In 1917, Congress passed the first law to apply to all immigrants, called the Literacy

TABLE 1.3   Immigration Waves and Major Historic Milestones and Policy, Late 1700s–Late 1960s

YEAR OF SETTLEMENT	GROUP	MAJOR MOTIVATION FOR IMMIGRATION	MILESTONES
1774 to 1840s, American Revolutionary War 1840s (peak 1847), Famine Period	Estimated 850,000 immigrants came to America 1.4 million eastern and southern European immigrants	English, and majority of northern and western Europeans immigrants • *Immigration Era* began, motivated by a European potato blight in Ireland; some provinces of Germany were devastated by famine	• Most immigrants were from eastern and southern European cultures and languages, different than previous majority of northern and western Europeans immigrants
1850s	2.6 million immigrants	• Civil War Period	
1860s	Over 2 million immigrants		
1880s	Over 1 million immigrants	• Looking for economic and job opportunities to make a living	• Prior to 1900s the poor masses of immigrants formed the most numerous groups of laborers in farms and factories
1882	Chinese	• Chinese Exclusion Act	
1892, January 1	Irish immigrants: Annie Moore was the first immigrant to enter through Ellis Island 17 million immigrants entered through Ellis Island from 1892 until the 1950s, when it closed	• Ellis Island opens	• 70% of immigrants arrived through the port of New York • Prior to Ellis Island years immigrants came through several ports of entry on the east coast (such as Boston and Philadelphia) and the South (such as New Orleans) • Immigrants moved into industrial centers in the east coast and midwest regions (e.g., Pittsburgh, Detroit, Cleveland, Chicago), farm towns (from Kansas to Michigan), and even the southwest region (e.g., Arizona, and Colorado) and the southern region (e.g., Texas, received German immigrants since the 1840s) to work in mines and farming
1900s	3.6 million immigrants All immigrants		• Major milestone in the history of U.S. immigration: Steam ships created easier travel situations by decreasing trip from months to weeks and days, and decreasing the mortality rate

1917 through 1920s	• Immigration legislation	• Restricted the number of southern and eastern Europeans by imposing immigration quotas • Notions of Darwinism with the philosophy of the "survival of the fittest," with 10% of immigrants entering through Ellis Island marked with some sign of physical or mental problems • Psychological testing of the time had serious problems of cultural and linguistic discrimination; testing them in English using culturally unfamiliar stimuli
1917	Congress	• Literacy Test Act	• Only immigrants who could read in their first language (L1) or English were allowed admission into the United States
1921	Congress and President Warren Harding Congress	• Emergency Quota Act	• 3% of the people of nationality living in the U.S. in 1910
1924		• National Origins Act: Favor northern Europeans and restricted immigration	• To deny entry to criminals, the "feeble-minded," those likely to become "public charge," and those who had violated the Contract Labor Law (i.e., prohibiting immigrants to accept employment before coming and been admitted to America) who were subject to deportation • Pushed base-year back to 1890, before massive immigration wave of eastern and southern Europeans
1952	Asian and all nationalities	• McCarran–Walter Act	• Increased immigration quota by nationality slightly above the former 2%, and gave quotas to Asian countries excluded before
1965		• New Immigration Act	• Settled quotas for areas of the world, including 120,000 for the Western Hemisphere, and 170,000 for countries outside the Western Hemisphere • Certain categories gave preferences for relatives of U.S. citizens, individuals who had needed job skills, or were refugees from Communist governments or natural disasters

Test Act. Only immigrants who could read in their native language or in English were allowed admission into the country. From 1921 through 1924, immigration was limited to a certain number of people per country, based on 2 percent of the people of that nationality living in the United States at that point in time. In 1952 a new immigration law was passed, the McCarran-Walter Act, that increased the quota slightly to 150,000 and gave quotas to Asian countries that had been excluded before. In response to some criticism about certain groups of immigrants, a new Immigration Act was passed in 1965, that established quotas for areas of the world, including 120,000 for the western hemisphere and 170,000 for countries outside the western hemisphere. Certain categories gave preferences to relatives of U.S. citizens, or individuals who had job skills needed in the United States, or who were refugees from Communist governments or natural disasters.

In 1921, Congress and President Warren G. Harding approved an Emergency Quota Act that restricted immigration to the United States to "no more than three percent of the number of foreign-born of that nationality living in the US in 1910" (Carlson, 1970, p. 458). Restrictionists supported these quotas and successfully fought for into more stringent policies during the 1920s. President Calvin Coolidge in 1923 commented in his State of the Union message that "America must be kept American" (ibid). In May 1924, Congress passed the National Origins Act, pushing the base year back to 1890, before the massive entrance of southern and eastern Europeans to Ellis Island. Immigration Quota Acts of 1921 and 1924 became increasingly complex, requiring large amounts of paper work and red tape that were difficult to follow for immigrants, who most likely did not speak English and were illiterate in their native language. Quotas favored the immigration of northern Europeans, and "discriminated against those from the southern and eastern parts of the Continent" (Weatherford, 1995, p. 320). Quotas also favored literate immigrants as American Nativists supported regulatory legislation with more rigorous standards to deny entry to criminals, "the immoral" (i.e., bigamists, prostitutes), paupers, criminals, the sick, the insane or "feeble-minded," those "likely to become a public charge" (Weatherford, 1995, p. 301), the illiterate or unlearned, and those who had violated the Contract Labor Law (prohibiting immigrants to accept employment before coming to and being admitted into the United States, with penalty of deportation). Regarding provision of the law for avoidance of "the immoral," immigrant women who came by themselves were required to show evidence of their intended residence, which was rigorously inspected for sanitary and "moral" conditions. For instance, a teenage girl was deported because the immigration inspector in Chicago determined that her intended address was "too crowded and unsanitary" (Abbott, 1924, p. 212).

Social Darwinism, with its philosophy of the "survival of the fittest" prevailed during the early 1900s, with 10 percent of immigrants entering through Ellis Island marked with some sign of physical or mental problem (such as lameness, trachoma, pregnancy, etc.). As noted by Thomas and Znaniecki (1958) even a high-ranking official acknowledged that the era's psychological methods were not capable of overcoming the variables of language and individual exigencies to deal fairly with these serious decisions. In relation to psychological testing, the problem was that intelligence testing was in its early stages of development during the 1920s, and contained very serious and ingrained problems of cultural and linguistic discrimination against immigrants due to testing them in English using culturally unfamiliar stimuli, such as asking immigrants to tell time in English (Weatherford, 1995).

These quotas separated families for years, as most men immigrated first and even when enough money was earned for passage, their wives and children needed to wait years for a visa. As explained by Bird (1924, cited in Weatherford, 1995), even though separation between immediate family members resulted in some incidence of desertion, the immigranto nevertheles held family life as a high priority.

> The average separation in this wartime-restriction era was 'ten to twelve years'—an entire childhood. The result was a situation in which 'we find desertion, non-support, divorce . . . and general deterioration as a result of long separation of the man from the wife and minor children. (p. 321)

However, as noted by Weatherford (1995), "they [husband and wife and parents and children] did miss each other, and most clung steadfastly to their belief that marriage was forever and that the family was the most important aspect of life" (p. 324). Thus, immigration quotas posed some obstacles for immigrant individuals and families trying to enter and become adapted to the American cultural lifestyle.

Cultural Adaptation: Assimilation, or "Melting Pot," Philosophy.   Americans were proud of their special culture: a blend of all different cultures from their ancestors and recent immigration trends, but yet uniquely "American." The cultural traditions in the United States had been strongly influenced by immigrants, such as the different religions and language traditions (e.g., idioms, phrases), food, music, and leading cultural institutions, such as mainstream organizations that were interested in helping immigrants to gain cultural adaptation faster. For instance, the Red Cross and the YMCA provided much needed help to immigrants during the early 1900s. During 1911, the YMCA set certain goals to assist in the cultural adaptation of immigrants: was to help them learn English; to provide technical classes to increase their job skills and employment opportunities; to help them understand accurately American standards and ideals; and to encourage aims and mold character (Baldwin, 1911, cited in Weatherford, 1995, p. 307). However, as in the case of today's Asian and Hispanic immigrants, back then it was also difficult for parents to adapt to the new American culture and language and lifestyle as fast as their children, resulting in generational gaps and cognitive dissonance for the children who lived "between two cultural worlds." Cognitive dissonance results from cultural identity confusion after exposure to two different or even clashing value systems between the American mainstream cultural environment and the home and family setting, or even the ethnic community.

Challenges present for the first-generation Americans were many, because they were in between their parents' European cultural values and beliefs and the prevalent American standards of their mainstream peers, resulting in cultural clashes and cognitive dissonance. An example of a contrasting value was that in Europe, male and older figures had higher status in the family, with grandfathers, fathers, and sons receiving more respect and higher ranking than female figures such as mothers and daughters.

For instance, a Hungarian or Italian family would provide more freedom to sons and would expect them to receive an education, whereas daughters would be expected to work both inside and outside the home to help sustain the household. In contrast to the superior status of the European male, "Americans have traditionally revered motherhood" (Weatherford, 1995, p. 332). Among immigrant families, the older daughters would typically help their overburdened mothers with their many siblings, assuming the role of "little mothers" (a virtually institutionalized role of becoming a mediator between her parents and siblings for the negotiation of old and new cultural values and behaviors). As will be discussed in the next section, another major challenge for first-generation American children was to bridge between their school experiences with the mainstream American culture and their home and family lives still tuned to their parents' ethnic immigrant identities, resulting in cognitive dissonance for the children (see Boxes 1.2 and 1.3).

The Assimilation Movement in the U.S. School Culture

During the early 1900s, urban areas and major U.S. cities grew at a fast pace due to large numbers of southern and eastern European immigrants settling in ghetto ethnic areas.

BOX 1.2
EXCERPTS FROM CASE STUDIES OF INTERNATIONAL GRADUATE STUDENTS: ILLUSTRATING COGNITIVE DISSONANCE

Victor (pseudonym): A Mexican, middle-aged, graduate international student, majoring in engineering in a large, Southwest state university.

When asked about the source of his support for cultural adaptation, he considered that he had received social support to adapt to the American college culture from his family (case study excerpted from Gonzalez, 2004). He stated, "It is essentially a family support. I do not socialize very much with people other than my family. I have two or three friends, and they are also Mexican people, but I do not see then very often. I spend most of my free time with my family. Because when my wife and children got to the U.S., they didn't speak English. So, they needed a lot of help from me. I did have some experience with English before coming here to the U.S. I'm trying to be successful in this program because of them, I want to give them an example, I want to be a good role model because I want to be in a better condition to provide for them, they are my motivation." Victor came to the realization that "My children are a bridge between me and the American culture."

Alejandra (pseudonym): A female, young adult, Spaniard, graduate international student, majoring in psycholinguistics at a large, Southwest state university.

When asked about the differences between the American culture and her culture of origin, she considered that Americans move a lot. She stated (case study excerpted from Gonzalez, 2004), "In my country, people don't move as much. You grow up in a city, and you are already part of the idea that people grow up in the same city and go to the university in that city. And then, you stay in the department that you chose for studying after graduation,

■ ■ ■ ■ ■

BOX 1.2   CONTINUED

so your working environment ends up being the same. So, there is never renewal of ideas, nobody new enters, nobody with new ideas. So, in Spain they are a little bit fossilized. I like the fact that here people move. So, always some new people are constantly bringing new ideas. On the other hand, you have the disadvantage that you are losing your friends or your family. They are left behind, and you are entering a new situation. You don't know anybody, so moving has its advantages and disadvantages."

When asked about similarities between the American and Spaniard academic culture, Alejandra replied: "Well I guess the similarities are mostly in the curriculum. But, I don't know because in America there's more money and more freedom, more exchange of ideas. In America, it seems that everybody has the right to say what he or she thinks about other people's ideas. Sometimes a little bit too much, because sometimes they are a little bit too rude. But, in any case I think it is good that these discussions are allowed even with students. Certainly, there is also much more money here that allows for investigation and better resources. So, I don't know about the similarities. I can think of the differences."

Job (pseudonym), a male graduate student from Kenya, majoring in agricultural engineering at a large state university in the Southwest, when asked about value changes, explained (quotes excerpted from a case study, Gonzalez, 2004)," I don't know if my values have changed from what they were, but I think I've learned different things, and my experience is richer. I know things that I never used to know. I know different ways of believing, so maybe I have richer values now that what I had earlier." When asked about the process, sequence, or transition that he went through, Job replied, "I just become richer. I still value the way of living I came from, I still value the village life that I lived. I still value the different ways my community life is different from here. I think the sequence was from realizing that there are different things out there, there is always something new and different out there."

Job reported that he prefers to spend his free time with his family now, and he explained, "Before I came to the U.S., I wasn't very involved in raising up my children, because of the way we live. Before, the grandmother took care of them, but now we are forced to be with them all the time, the two of us [himself and his wife]. So, to speak the truth, I don't have a lot of extra time here. I had a lot more extra time back home. I had time to just call on a friend, and walk off with him and go see places, but I must go home now." When asked with whom he preferred to socialize and why, Job responded, "It depends on what kind of socializing. Family socialization is what I prefer now. I also enjoy socializing with colleagues at the university."

Leonardo (pseudonym), an Italian graduate student, a young adult, majoring in humanities at a large, Southwest state university. When asked about cultural differences and similarities between the American and his home culture, he said (quotes excerpted from Gonzalez, 2004), " The hardest part of this transitional process is to find a balance between your own values and the behaviors and attitudes that you need to show here." For Leonardo it was hard to draw a line between being "too Italian" and being "too Americanized," and finding a balance or making a choice when the value system clashed (such as the dissonance of having to prioritize both valuing family and career goals, and the hard experience of making a choice). He said that the hardest part for him was "making a choice."

BOX 1.3

SUMMARY OF A CASE STUDY OF A HISPANIC HIGH SCHOOL ESL STUDENT: ILLUSTRATING COGNITIVE DISSONANCE

The actual interview was conducted in Spanish by the first author of the book. The digital recorded interview is available on the companion Web site, www.ablongman.com/gonzalez1e,. In order to better organize the information provided by the interviewee, four areas were created: (1) background, (2) schooling experience in the United States, (3) English-as-a-second-language (ESL) history, and (4) extracurricular activities influencing English social language and socialization abilities.

BACKGROUND

Melissa (pseudonym) is a 16-year-old, female sophomore student, who has been born and raised in a middle-size city of Peru. She had been living with her father for 1 year and 7 months in the United States at the time of the interview. Her parents separated and she and her father came to the United States because of job opportunities for her father, and settled in a mixed neighborhood in the suburbs of a middle-size metropolitan area in the Midwest.

She considers that her father does not speak English, and can get by with speaking Spanish only because he works in construction. Melissa spoke only minimal English when she first arrived in the United States, having had only two-and-a-half years of English instruction as a content area during high school in Peru. She completed in Peru up to the equivalent of eighth grade, and quit to move to the United States during the middle of ninth grade.

SCHOOLING EXPERIENCE IN THE UNITED STATES

Melissa stated that her schooling experience in the United States has been "horrible, terrible because of my problems to communicate in English." During her first year of schooling in the United States, she could not understand anything that the teachers said in the classroom and used to fall asleep out of boredom. She started schooling in the United States in an ESL magnet school, located in a mixed suburb, and was placed in ninth grade. Melissa explained that during this first year, she had a very bad experience because "the content was too low for me, too repetitive, the teachers spoke only in English, and they wanted that I first master English before promoting me to a higher grade. So I moved to another school at the end of the first year because if not I could have been in ninth grade forever, until I finally learned how to speak English!" At the end of her first year in the United States she changed schools and was placed in a mainstream high school sophomore classroom, where she also received the help of a pullout support ESL Program, the placement that she was in during the time of our interview. Even though she considered her U.S. experience to be difficult because of her lack of English command, Melissa stated that "there are more opportunities in the U.S. because in Peru you have to pay lots of money for private education in college in order to get a job, and here there is access to public education."

The most difficult subject area for Melissa was considered to be U.S. and world history due to her lack of familiarity with its content, as she had not studied that subject in Spanish. On the other hand, math was easy for her because she has studied the content before during her high school years in Peru and felt that she could transfer her knowledge.

ENGLISH-AS-A-SECOND-LANGUAGE (ESL) LEARNING HISTORY

Because Melissa had come with very little English, as she explained "I knew only few words in English because I had studied it only as a subject for two and a half years at

■ ■ ■ ■ ■

BOX 1.3   CONTINUED

school in Peru." She started to improve her English with the help of bilingual classmates who would translate teachers' explanations into Spanish. Even though she felt that she had improved her English skills, she still considered that her vocabulary and pronunciation skills were poor by the end of her second year of U.S. schooling, and therefore still experienced difficulty in speaking English. However, she felt that her writing had improved some because she could use a dictionary and also received the help of ESL teachers in completing homework and projects.

When asked about learning opportunities that could help her to improve her English skills, she believed that tutoring could help her in learning how to pronounce and understand the meaning of new words, which in turn can help her better understand new content that she is learning in her classroom. She also considered that she needs further help in the use of new tenses and social language. She felt that the ESL pullout program was helping her to have more time to do exams and to complete writing projects and homework with the help of the ESL and a Spanish-speaking teacher's aide. However, she also felt puzzled by the fact that teachers gave her answers to homework questions, and all that she was required to do was copy ready-made responses, which she felt was not helping her to really learn and understand content and be able to become an independent learner. She believed that ESL teachers gave ready-made homework answers to ESL students because there was no time for explaining answers because the teacher-student ratio was very high. She would prefer to have more one-to-one tutoring help, in a lower teacher–student ratio, and have ESL teachers explain to her grammar rules and the meaning and pronunciation of new words, and help to improve her writing skills.

EXTRACURRICULAR ACTIVITIES INFLUENCING ENGLISH SOCIAL LANGUAGE AND SOCIALIZATION ABILITIES

Melissa felt that participating in extracurricular school activities was also helping her with improving her ability to speak in English because she could learn words about themes and content areas and could also learn from bilingual classmates.

In terms of her social language abilities, she felt that she could talk with American classmates at a superficial level, but sometimes she could not understand them because of her poor vocabulary and lack of familiarity with their Midwest accent and jargon (e.g., idioms, phrasal verbs). She also felt that her American classmates were "immature" and she became bored when talking to them; she preferred to interact with her bilingual classmates, with whom she could establish a more interesting conversation.

In terms of her socialization abilities and her perception of cultural values, Melissa felt that her American classmates did not respect teachers, and that they did not respect authority as much as students in Peru, who valued more responsibility and discipline. She felt puzzled by how American teachers could not make students respect them and did not have authority to discipline students.

Her perception of American classmates being "immature" was also colored by the fact that she was very aware that they were a year younger. In terms of her age, Melissa also felt discouraged because in the United States she would finish high school when she was 19 years old, versus in Peru where, due to a shorter educational system, she would have graduated at the age of 17. She felt inadequate and homesick when remembering that her former high school classmates in Peru were graduating at the end of her sophomore year.

For instance, the yearly numbers of eastern and southern Europeans immigrants to the United States between 1905 and 1914 was always higher than three-quarters of a million. Table 1.4 presents a synthesis of major historical milestones achieved in the early 1900s as part of the assimilation movement of immigrants into the U.S. school culture.

At the same time, the Progressive movement was gaining popularity at a rapid pace among middle-class Americans, the descendents of earlier northern European immigrants who had created the Protestant, Anglo-Saxon mainstream values and culture and its social institutions of government and law. The Progressive Era was influenced by general economic prosperity, nationalism, and race pride supported by social Darwinism, a "scientific" movement that supported an ideology that classified northern Europeans as a "superior" race. As explained by Carlson (1970), "It [the social Darwinism] described the blond, long-headed Teutons of the north, the so-called Old Stock immigration to the United States, as inherently superior to the round-headed or dark-skinned central and southern Europeans" (p. 441); the latter group included the German, Irish, Italian, and Jewish immigrants of the mid-1800s. Because of the support of social Darwinism by the Progressive movement's followers, the cultural and genetic superiority of American mainstream culture and values needed to be instilled among new, and very diverse, groups of non-Anglo-Saxon immigrants. The newcomers had to be assimilated, or Americanized, into the mainstream American culture, using social institutions, such as the public school system, as major vehicles.

The Social Justice or Liberal Progressive side of the Progressive movement wanted to help immigrants' living conditions in overcrowded and unhealthy ghetto areas by providing some training in homemaking and industrial arts, and English classes in order to improve their skills for getting better paid jobs and gaining cultural adaptation, and ultimately gaining higher stages of Americanization or assimilation in a faster manner. The Social Justice side of the Progressive movement also understood the importance of building respect for the ethnic background of the first-generation American children's background, but at the same time supported instilling within immigrant children a community spirit and support for mainstream social institutions and organizations.

However, this humanitarian initiative to maintain the immigrants' cultures was overridden by the Americanization or assimilation efforts, resulting in an ambivalent attitude toward large numbers of immigrants during the early 1900s. On one side were the politically dominant Industrialists who wanted to maintain the flow of cheap labor that newcomers provided. On the other side were the American, middle-class citizens who disliked the conditions in which immigrants,—who looked, dressed, and behaved in a "foreign" manner—lived in the ghetto areas. During the Progressive Era (late 1800s to early 1900s), educational reform was initiated with the organization of the modern school system. Social reform also focused on improving the living conditions of the new immigrants from southern and eastern Europe and other urban poor populations, whose problems were perceived as a major social crisis. To help new immigrants adapt to their new social and cultural environments, social settlement houses were developed in cities' neighborhoods with large numbers of newcomers, such as Chicago. The philosophy of social settlements was to maintain native cultural backgrounds in new immigrants while helping them to adapt to their new life in America.

TABLE 1.4 Historical Milestones Achieved in the Early 1900s in the Assimilation Movement of Immigrants into the U.S. School Culture

YEAR	GROUP	EVENT	MILESTONES
Early 1900s	Progressive Movement (traditional side)	• General economic prosperity, nationalism, and race pride supported by Social Darwinism, a "scientific" movement advocating northern Europeans as a "superior" race	• Assimilation or Americanization of southern and eastern Europeans into the Protestant, Anglo-Saxon mainstream values and culture, and its social institutions of government, law, and education; established by descendents of earlier Northern European immigrants
Early 1900s	Social Justice side of Progressive Movement	• Wanted to improve overcrowded conditions of immigrant ghettos in large urban areas • Humanitarian initiative	• Increase cultural adaptation by: (i) citizenship, (ii) training in homemaking, (iii) providing English classes, and (iv) improving skills for getting better paid jobs • Building respect for immigrants' cultural and linguistic backgrounds, and develop a community spirit and organizations • Resulted in bipolar attitude of Social Justice and Americanization • Solution was to continue accepting immigrants, but to Americanize them
1910	Progressive Movement (Traditional side)	• Four major arguments for imposing restrictions on immigration	(i) Industrial argument: Newcomers would depress wages of Americans (ii) Social argument: The "foreignness" of behaviors and thoughts of immigrants as a major obstacle for assimilation (iii) Political argument: Incapacity to appreciate freedom and cultural values represented by democracy (iv) Racial/biological argument: Eugenics or Darwinism advocated superiority of northern European race over southern and eastern European races

(continued)

TABLE 1.4 Continued

YEAR	GROUP	EVENT	MILESTONES
1912	YMCA	• Advocated creation of "Melting Pot" resulting in Christian American nation	• To help immigrants adapt culturally to the United States by providing classes for learning the English language and citizenship • To maintain a single-minded nation by instilling among immigrants the dominant cultural values and language • Fear that immigrants would "foreignize" U.S. society • Conformity of immigrants to middle-class standards and the maintenance of the status quo in American society
1914	Committee for Immigrants in America created by Miss Frances Kellor		• Apply business efficiency to schooling, factories, and businesses (social mainstream institutions) to Americanize immigrants • Implementation of the industrial "factory model" to schooling, with the use of English only to gain efficiency for communication and encouraging like-mindedness in thought and behavior (to eat the right kinds of food, to wear the right kinds of clothes, to understand what constitutes fair wages and decent working conditions, to understand the mission of unions and human civil rights, and to spend in the United States the money earned
1920	John Dewey	• Cultural Pluralism	• Opposed Americanization and Assimilation movements by advocating exposure of immigrants to the benefit of American democracy (i.e., better educational and economic opportunities, and greater individual freedom) for instilling cultural values of nationalism and identification with the United States

As discussed in the previous section, the philosophy defended by the Liberal Progressives in the Social Reform movement supported cultural sensitivity and diversity and sought social justice for the poor, urban population, including new immigrants from eastern and southern Europe.

A solution for this polarity was to continue accepting immigrants, but to Americanize them. In general, every Progressive movement advocate held in common the belief in "the traditional American faith in education as the means of solving 'The Problem' . . . to Americanize those immigrants" (p. 443). Miss Frances Kellor led the Committee for Immigrants in America, which unified efforts of public and private agencies in Americanizing immigrants (Cubberley, 1919). In 1914, this committee attempted to apply business efficiency to schooling, in an effort to Americanize the children of immigrants in the least costly way for society (i.e., "Americanization as the science of nation-building," Carlson, 1970, p. 449).

Like a factory, the elementary and secondary schools were recommended to "gain efficiency by requiring a single language for communication and by encouraging like-mindedness in thought" (Carlson, 1970).

> The immigrant would have to learn to spend his wages more wisely, to eat the right kinds of food, to wear the right kinds of clothes, to understand what constitutes fair wages and decent working conditions, and to spend in America the money he earned here. (Kellor, 1914, quoted in Carlson, 1970, pp. 912–13.)

The industrial model of the time was applied to Americanize immigrants efficiently through social institutions (such as school, factories, and businesses) via educating them in citizenship and the English language. The *American Federationist* magazine, published in 1916, discussed the importance of Americanization for industry workers who needed to understand the mission of unions: "The trade union movement has been teaching them that human lives and human rights are of greater importance than exploitation for private profit" (p. 690).

Ellwood (1910) discussed the four major arguments presented by defenders of the traditional side of the Progressive movement in relation to restrictions for diverse immigrants: (1) the Industrial argument (newcomers would depress wages of American workers), (2) the Social argument (the "foreignness" of behaviors and thoughts of newcomers was a major obstacle impossible to overcome through assimilation), (3) the Political argument (incapacity of immigrants to understand and appreciate the freedom and cultural values represented by democratic institutions), and (4) the Racial or Biological argument (based on eugenics and Darwinism's claims of superiority of the northern European race over southern and eastern European immigrants).

Commons (1907, cited in Carlson, 1970, p. 447) defined assimilation as a "union of minds and wills by educating the immigrants to enable common life and action." Commons also recognized the importance of learning English for integrating the newcomers to the mainstream culture. He argued that "the instrument of a common language is at hand for conscious improvement through education and social environment" (p. 447). The YMCA organization in 1912 emphasized the importance of creating a "melting pot" that resulted in a Christian American nation, but was afraid that the diversity of the newcomers would destroy the melting pot. The YMCA had the mission of helping the immigrants to adapt to American culture by providing classes for learning the English language and citizenship. Hodge (1912) complained that "masses of suspicious, clannish people from southern and southeastern Europe had 'foreignized' the centers of congested American cities. Unless we Americanize them they will 'foreignize' us" (p. 175). The interest of mainstream social organizations, such as the YMCA, was to maintain a single-minded nation by instilling in newcomers the dominant cultural values through control of social institutions. According to Carlson (1970, p. 459), Americanization meant to establish conformity to middle-class standards and the maintenance of the status quo in American society.

In the 1920s, John Dewey exhorted Americans to endorse Cultural Pluralism, instead of Americanization or assimilation, which allowed them to enjoy the liberty of keeping their cultural and language background as they settled in their adopted country. The idea was to permit immigrants to enjoy U.S. democracy through its institutions, and not to impose on them cultural values and the English language. Dewey thought that by exposing immigrants to the benefit of enjoying a better life in the United States than in their native countries, such as new educational and economic opportunities and greater individual freedom, immigrants would gain values of nationalism and identification with their new nation.

In fact, part of the pursuit of the American dream of immigrants of the past and present has been to advance in their social and economic status, an opportunity that only true democracies can give to citizens. In most European societies of the middle 1800s and early 1900s, a person born into a servant status would never be given opportunities to change his or her social and economic status, and so they came to America looking for those opportunities, changing from the European fatalism and destiny to the American optimism and freedom. As described by Weatherford (1995),

> where one was born was where one stayed . . . many peasants found a certain mental comfort, a sense of safety and security, in "knowing their place." These Europeans who questioned the wisdom of this attitude took their first risk with emigration. In America, they would . . . take more risks, and so evolve from fatalism into the New World creeds of progress and faith in the future. (p. 257)

Most Hispanic and Asian immigrants of recent decades also come to the United States motivated by a desire to leave traditionalist societies that enforce social and economic status quos. Within these traditional Asian and Latin American societies, educational and life opportunities are mandated by individuals' socioeconomic status at birth with no opportunity for social mobility. As discussed in the next section, the role of education as a vehicle for social mobility is a new experience for most ESL adult and children immigrants of the past and present. The challenge for educators becomes to offer genuine educational opportunities to meet the needs of culturally and linguistically diverse students in the U.S. public educational system of the past, present, and future.

Schooling Conditions of Immigrants

Immigrant children during the late 1800s and early 1900s also had to endure stereotypes and discrimination from their peers. A Swiss immigrant girl experienced teasing from her schoolmates because her ethnicity was confused with the Dutch or Irish; it was a common misconception during the late 1800s that all foreigners conformed to these two most common nationalities. Presently, the same pattern repeats itself, with all Hispanics being attributed the same, stereotyped Mexican nationality, or all Asians attributed the stereotyped Chinese nationality. Not that long ago, the first author of this book (a naturalized American citizen, Peruvian born and raised) had a revealing conversation with one of her neighbors in southern Ohio, who had limited exposure to Hispanic newcomers. During the conversation, the author's then 5-year-old son commented that his mom cooks delicious food. The neighbor replied, "She must cook wonderful tortillas!" To the neighbor's astonishment, the author's son remarked, "But my mom never cooks tortillas!" Probably this Ohio resident had limited experience with Hispanic food, such as eating occasionally at Mexican restaurants, and thought that all Hispanics eat tortillas. Stereotypes are the result of lack of exposure to and lack of knowledge of diversity within cultural groups, such as Hispanics, due to ethnicity and national origin—in this case, the idiosyncratic differences between Mexicans and Peruvians, who do not eat tortillas—a basic item in the diets of Mexicans and Central Americans, inherited from the ancestral diets of the Mayan and Aztec civilizations—but instead have potatoes and rice as basic items in their diets, as do most countries in the Andes region of South America (potatoes were part of the ancestral diet of the Inca civilization, and rice was introduced by Asian immigrants). Knowing some world history and geography can encourage educators to become more familiar with the idiosyncratic cultural backgrounds of diverse ethnic subgroups of their ESL students and help to dispel stereotypes.

In spite of stereotypical images that past and present immigrants still have to endure, a major advantage they enjoy in the United States is that their children can benefit from free public schooling, available for all school-age children regardless of their social class or national origin. A summary of an interview with a group of Swedes during the 1850s clearly shows that early northern European immigrants were aware of the advantages of immigrating to the United States for the education of their children (Bremer, 1924, cited in Weatherford, 1995,). This notion is also portrayed by Melissa, a Hispanic, high school–aged, immigrant ESL student, whose interview is summarized in Box 1.3, and whose digitally recorded interview can be heard at the companion Web site, www.ablongman.com/gonzalez1e.

However, free access to public education for *all*, regardless of national origin, emerged as a new social concept of democracy during the late 1700s and early 1800s. A precedent for the more modern notion of equality of educational opportunities for all individuals, including the diverse immigrant population, is found in the Liberal side of the Progressive movement, long after the American Revolution and the early U.S. Constitution years.

In contrast, and as discussed in the previous section in relation to the assimilation movement, the Conservative Progressive movement of social reform supported

Americanization through using social institutions for acculturation. Following this Conservative Progressive movement, many cities used the public school system as a social agent for acculturation, assimilation, or Americanization of the new immigrant children and their families. The philosophy of the Conservative Progressive era was to assimilate new immigrants to the American way of life through their school experience. Based on an anthropological definition provided by Urban and Wagoner, "Americanization was an acculturation program . . . that was assumed to be superior to that of the 'old country' " (p. 188). Conservative Progressives endorsed social reform as the establishment of social order through the rational management, order, and control established by trained experts. Conservative Progressives were much more influential than liberal Progressives.

The more traditional faction of the Conservative Progressive movement took control and organized the school system, and its supporters became more influential in directing the modernization of the school system. Schools were reorganized under new scientific principles stemming from educational psychology: development of more child-centered pedagogical innovations; extension of educational opportunity from an eight-four elementary–high school organization to a six-three-three elementary–junior high–high school system, still prevailing as of today; addition of extracurricular activities; use of educational and psychological testing for grouping students in classrooms; improved education of teachers; and changes in school administration. School innovations were a response to multiple social changes occurring by the end of the 1800s and the beginning of the 1900s, which in turn affected the nation's social, political, and economic life and thus increased dramatically the number of children enrolled in public schools.

The huge increase of students in public schools in cities throughout the nation created a climate of public concern and the need for introducing changes in the school system. As stated by Urban and Wagoner (1996), "For example, enrollments in the city of Cleveland, Ohio between 1900 and 1930 went from 45,000 to 145,000, while in Detroit they climbed from 30,000 to more than 250,000" (p. 191). Some of the social changes during this Progressive Era include the passage of compulsory school attendance laws, the massive numbers of immigrants coming from Eastern and Southern Europe, and internal immigration from rural to urban areas.

Beginning in the mid-1800s, the increased number of immigrants from very different backgrounds than those of earlier settlers in the United States brought a new social situation to public schools. Teachers and school administrators were suddenly asked to serve immigrant students whose diverse and "exotic" cultural and linguistic backgrounds they were not familiar with and who often had a Catholic background, all of which evoked fear and was interpreted as a threat by the (predominantly protestant) administrative Progressive movement. According to Urban and Wagoner (1996), "Most southern and eastern European immigrants were Roman Catholics and were largely responsible for the increased enrollment in Catholic parochial schools through much of the twentieth century" (p. 205). Furthermore, "the cultural diversity of the immigrants meant that the public schools were now facing students whose backgrounds they did not know, whose language they did not speak, and whose habits they often found strange and threatening" (p. 202).

Typical negative attitudes toward new immigrants expressed by administrators endorsing the Conservative Progressive movement are illustrated by Urban and Wagoner (1996) in the case of Ellwood Cubberley. Cubberley was a school superintendent and Dean of the School of Education at Stanford University, and author of several textbooks used for the education of teachers and administrators. In one of his textbooks, *Public Education in the United States*, published in 1919 by Houghton Mifflin, the positive characteristics of nineteenth-century immigrants from northern and western Europe are presented against the social problems introduced by new eastern and southern immigrants. These southern and eastern Europeans were very different from the northern and western Europeans who preceded them, and were described in negative terms by Cubberley in his 1919 book, as culturally and racially inferior to Anglo-Saxon Americans due to different cultural value systems and the lack of literacy skills in English. Cubberley concluded that these immigrant groups could not be easily or successfully assimilated into American culture (cited in Urban & Wagoner, 1996).

On the other hand, the more Liberal side of the Progressive movement in education had as a goal to use school reform to achieve social justice. John Dewey was a practical philosopher who supported the pedagogical Progressive movement, and who conducted some studies applying scientific methods to test educational principles supporting democratic social reform. Dewey considered schools and social institutions as learning laboratories for improving democratic society. To achieve this goal, Dewey proposed that teachers and students design cooperative learning and the curriculum to respond to real-life occupational and democratic experiences present in society. This curriculum would be child oriented; instructional methods would use inquiry and would concentrate on meetings the needs of children and society. Educators had to be prepared in gaining knowledge about how children learn and on becoming more knowledgeable in subject matter. This pedagogical philosophy generated the foundations of modern educational systems, still in place today.

After the Progressive Era,

> [Eastern and southern European] immigrants made their way out of poverty, and they were replaced by newer migrants and immigrants to the inner cities: blacks, Hispanics, and Asians. These groups also would find themselves underserved by school systems focused on the needs of mainstream American culture. (Urban & Wagoner, 1996, p. 203)

The present Asian and Hispanic immigrants share with the Ellis Island immigrants a low socioeconomic status (SES) background (see Gonzalez, 2001a), and their poverty was (and still is) conpounded by educators stymied by difficulties posed by their culturally and linguistically diverse educational needs, as discussed further in the next section.

Impact of Poverty on Academic Achievement of ESL Immigrants.   According to a report written by a Commission on Immigration established in 1911, some groups of immigrants could integrate and achieve at school in the early twentieth century, such as Jewish and northern European immigrants, but non-Jewish and southern and eastern European children performed significantly lower than mainstream and Jewish immigrants. Eastern European Jewish children excelled in school during the early 1800s, but immigrant Italian and Slavic children did poorly in school. Immigrant children of northern European background (e.g., English, Scottish, Welsh, German, and Scandinavian) had academic achievements comparable to their mainstream American counterparts.

However, besides cultural background's effect on the school achievement of immigrant children, other socioeconomic factors were clearly affecting their performance. Factors associated with poverty such as social class, occupational status of parents, literacy and educational level of parents, and economic resources available at home negatively affected the school performance of eastern and southern European immigrants. The same poverty conditions affecting new immigrants during the beginning of the nineteenth century affect immigrants today—now from a Latin American and Asian background (for further discussion of this topic see Gonzalez, 2001b; see link in companion Web site, www.ablongman.com/gonzalez1e). It is in fact poverty, and not ethnic or cultural background, that is the most pervasive factor negatively and significantly affecting achievement and exacerbating learning difficulties among immigrant children in the U.S. public school history. As stated by Urban and Wagoner (1996),

> Regardless of cultural background, students from families mired in poverty generally brought with them negative attitudes toward the school and consequently, whether they were immigrant or non-immigrant, did poorly in school. The fact that more immigrant youngsters fared poorly in school, then, was in large part due to the fact that more of them were from the lower classes. (p. 204)

Another factor negatively impacting achievement among immigrants historically has been ESL parents who may also be illiterate in their native language, typical of poor populations coming from rural backgrounds. Urban and Wagoner (1996) identified the interaction of socioeconomic factors with poor achievement in school.

> [F]actors such as urban or rural origins and wealth or poverty in their native countries influenced immigrants' school success or failure. These factors surfaced in areas such as students' facility with words and abstractions, behavioral dispositions toward schooling, and responsiveness to school reward. . . . These factors are culturally based and operate somewhat independently from socioeconomic characteristics. (p. 204)

In fact, there is an interaction between poverty and cultural values and attitudes toward schooling. Some immigrant children from poor backgrounds have been able to succeed in the U.S. public school system throughout history. First it was the eastern European Jewish children during the early nineteenth century; more recently, Asian children have achieved at high levels, and in many instances outperformed the mainstream American population. In some situations, these children and their families have a low socioeconomic condition at the time of immigration, but their parents may be literate and put high value on attaining success in education, such as eastern European Jews immigrating at the beginning of the 1900s, and some Asian groups that entered the United States during the 1980s, 1990s, and 2000s decades. Furthermore, as discussed by Perlmann (1988), when the socioeconomic conditions of the underachieving immigrant groups improved, their school performance also rose. The achievement of Irish students increased in the early twentieth century as they started to move up in SES and attained positions of political, economic, and social power and entered the school system as administrators and teachers. Thus, as teachers' and administrators' attitudes and actions became more favorable to children of Irish descent, and the SES of their families in society improved, their school performance also increased and was comparable to American children's achievement levels (who were descendents of earlier, northern and western European white immigrants).

Cultural and Economic Factors Affecting School Performance of Immigrant Children (1850s–1930s).   Historically, the difficulty of adapting to the mainstream American school culture for the earlier groups of eastern and southern Europeans who immigrated to America, has been forgotten by the general public. A myth has taken root that assimilation was easy for the earlier groups of ESL students in the U.S. public school system. Scholars, however, have acknowledged the difficulty of the immigrant experience, although very few scholars have differentiated the degree of difficulty in relation to immigrant groups' nationality in comparison to native-born, white Americans' school achievement. Information for two periods will be analyzed in relation to ethnic and nationality groups, first for the period of the middle 1800s in the city for Chicago, and secondly for the periods between 1900 and 1930 for the larger immigrant cities in the United States.

Chicago: The Mid-1800s.   During the middle 1800s, Chicago grew primarily because of the steady incoming population of immigrants. According to the 1860 Census (as cited by Galenson, 1995), Chicago's population grew from 30,000 in 1850 to 110,000 in 1860, with 70 percent of adults foreign-born (with German, Irish, and English as most numerous immigrant groups).

In terms of the schooling process for the most common immigrant groups in Chicago,

> Boys began to enter school in large numbers at age 5, when just over a third attended, and two-thirds were in school at age 6 . . . 80 percent at age 7 . . . 80 and 90 percent through age 12 . . . more than half of the boys were still in school at 16, and one-fifth at 18. (Galenson, 1995, p. 373).

However, when groups are analyzed independently, differences in schooling patterns emerged by nationality and place of birth. German and Irish boys born in the United States had higher attendance rates than their foreign-born counterparts, and equal to the mainstream group up to 15 years of age, and only lower than the mainstream group at the high school level.

According to Galenson's (1995) multivariate analysis of the 1860 U.S. census data, two major variables (i.e., occupation of mother—whether she worked outside home—and single status of mother; both indicators of economic need or wealth) negatively, and significantly, affected whether a teenage boy would continue high school education. The presence of older siblings increased the probability that boys could attend high school, just because there were more potential (and older) breadwinners who could help the household economics and who allowed young siblings to attend high school. Galenson also reported that statistical analysis showed a significant tendency for U.S.-born children of immigrant families to have a higher rate of school attendance at the high school level than their foreign-born counterparts. This latter tendency has been interpreted in the literature (e.g., Ferrie, 1994; Pope, 1989) to indicate that immigrant families with U.S.-born children, would normally have spent longer periods in U.S. residence than a family with a foreign-born son, of the same age, would have. Longer U.S. residence could also mean higher levels of cultural adaptation and economic and social status. Thus, variables associated with income and family demographics were more significant, and predictive of school attendance, than ethnicity.

Another statistically significant pattern observed at all ages, as reported by Galvenson (1995), was the effect of family location within a community (in turn associated with income level and occupation status—unskilled versus skilled laborer, and white-collar versus blue-collar status) on the children's school attendance. More specifically,

> the first ward, located along lake shore south of the Chicago River, had both the largest proportion of American residents and by far the highest mean household wealth among the city's wards, the Tenth Ward, on the city's far southwest side, had the highest proportions both of immigrants and of unskilled workers and the lowest mean wealth of any ward. (p. 387)

In addition, Chicago became a city of immigrants from various national groups during the middle 1800s, and responded by creating a system of parochial schools that served primarily two of the largest increasing immigrant groups: the Catholic Irish and German-speaking children. Parochial schools emphasized proper religious training and offered instruction in the children's first language. Therefore, public schools in Chicago were competing with parochial schools to attract immigrants as clients, with both systems closer in size and influence in Chicago than in other eastern cities. Moreover, the social reality of immigrants in urban areas in the Midwest region of the United States during the middle 1800s was that they enjoyed a more prosperous situation than that of immigrants on the East Coast. Then, within cities, even by ward, the schooling reality of immigrant families and their children may have differed; with bigger gaps across cities and regions of the United States.

U.S. Cities: 1900–1930.   Olneck and Lazerson (1974) made a comparative analysis of the differential patterns of adaptation to U.S. institutions, and the role that schools played in assimilating immigrants to mainstream culture and in offering social mobility through education. Even though Olneck and Lazerson had only limited data available for analyzing the period between 1900 and 1930, the data on school attendance, school continuance, school completion, retardation rates, and gender rates can suggest relevant patterns of immigrant adaptation. Their analysis was focused primarily on two nationality groups—southern Italians and Russian Jews—because their school achievement was dramatically different in relation to some cultural factors (e.g., parental length of residence in the United States, home language, age at school entrance, standardized test scores, and occupation and income levels), resulting in a negative school experience for the former group and a very positive experience for the latter group.

As reported by Olneck and Lazerson (1974), elementary-level immigrant children had similar patterns of school attendance as that of mainstream American children, but differences arise for older students in high school grades. Older immigrant students did not complete school, had slower rates of progress through school, and dropped their attendance when legally permitted in higher proportions than American mainstream students. Larger numbers of immigrant children were in a grade that did not correspond to their age (called school "retardation" at the beginning of the 1900s), and as stated by Olneck and Lazerson, "some portion of the apparent gap between the two groups [immigrant and mainstream] was due to disproportionate late entrance among immigrants" (p. 456). Percentages of seventh-graders dropping out of school before entrance to high school were about 40 percent for native white students; 50 percent for native black and English, Swedish, and Hebrew-German and Hebrew-Russian immigrants; 70 percent for Germans, Irish, and southern Italian immigrants; and about 80 percent for Polish immigrants (according to information available in 1908 for large U.S. cities with high ratios of immigrant students, such as Chicago, Boston, and New York City; U.S. Immigration Commission Report, Washington, D.C., 1911, as cited by Olneck & Lazerson, 1974, p. 457).

Between 1908 and 1916, some nationality groups showed raised school attendance rates, such as Germans and Hebrew-Germans and Hebrew-Russians, but other groups remained stagnated, such as Italians and Poles. However, once the immigrant student reached high school, then the chances of completing his studies was similar to the mainstream group. The differences in school achievement between immigrant and mainstream students were marked by two major patterns: age of completion of elementary school and high school entry. The school difficulty patterns of earlier immigrants are very similar to more recent patterns of school performance in the U.S. public schools for Hispanic and Asian immigrant groups, as is the mismatch between their native cultural value systems and the mainstream school cultural expectations and value systems.

It is important not only to realize the difficulty of cultural adaptation to the mainstream school culture of some of these earlier groups of ESL learners, but also their similar characteristics with the Hispanic immigrants of today who also are becoming underachievers in U.S. public schools. The major difference is that employment opportunities for young boys and men without high school diplomas were greater in the past than today, but still were bound to be in industrial, untrained jobs in the past and low-wage service industry jobs in the present. Completion of high school was also the route to college preparation, and remains so today. The difference is that, in the past, only a small number of children from any group would follow the college track, including mainstream, native-born Americans. There was an exception, though: in the past, Russian Jewish immigrants prioritized the education of their male children, and supported their completion of high school in order to pursue a college career. As quoted by

Olneck and Lazerson (1974), "In Bridgeport in 1922, for example, 90 percent of the Russian Jew boys were in the College or Scientific tracks of the high school compared to 75 percent of the males with native-born fathers" (p. 464).

Thus, cultural factors had a strong influence on school completion, such as cultural gender roles and cultural values for offering academic education to children. Even though Russian Jews shared a number of other characteristics with southern Italians, the cultural values of the former group helped them succeed in public school, in contrast to the poor performance of the latter group. Both Russian Jews and southern Italians arrived during the same time period (the 1880s until the 1930s), were very poor, spoke almost no English, and had the tendency to settle in East Coast cities in ghetto urban areas. Both groups entered school at the same age, did not use English at home, and their fathers had been U.S. residents for about the same period of time. However, Russian Jews performed at higher levels in school, showing higher retention rates and lower retardation, and higher scores on standardized tests.

In spite of the similarities in social characteristics at the time of immigration, there were also differences between Russian Jews and southern Italians. Russian Jews came to the United States with a different occupational history that allowed them to earn higher wages in the clothing industry, resulting in some differences in economic and occupational status. As reported by Joseph (1914, cited in Olneck & Lazerson, 1974), between 1899 and 1910, about two-thirds of Jews immigrants were prepared to enter skilled labor jobs in the United States, in comparison to only one-fourth of southern Italian immigrants. Based on the U.S. Industrial Commission Report (1911), the occupation of foreign-born Russian Jews and southern Italians in seven major U.S. cities (i.e., New York, Chicago, Philadelphia, Boston, Cleveland, Buffalo, and Milwaukee) showed 55 percent of Russian Jews working in manufacturing and mechanical industries versus 29 percent of southern Italians, and 34 percent of Russian Jews working in trade versus only 13 percent of southern Italians. This document also showed that most Southern Italians were working in general labor jobs. This same document showed that the average annual income of Hebrew Russian immigrant families was higher ($647 in Chicago and $501 in Cleveland) than their southern Italian counterparts (only $504 in Chicago and $412 in Cleveland).

Another major difference between Russian Jews and southern Italian immigrants was that they had a different group history and traditions in the Old World that translated into different responses and group adaptation patterns to the American institutions, such as the school culture. Traditional cultural group behavioral patterns (i.e., "reinforced habits of mind that stressed mental agility, close attention to the meaning of words, and lively criticism," [Olneck & Lazerson, 1974, p. 473]) and high value in studying, learning, and engaging in scholarship activities resulted in success for Russian-Jewish children in the U.S. schools. Russian-Jewish parents trusted that U.S. schools, and American society, provided opportunities better for their children to become anything they wanted if they studied hard. Jewish families believed in American opportunity and were willing to make economic sacrifices for their children to complete their education. As explained by Olneck and Lazerson (1974), "Parental attitudes, like beliefs about opportunity, are tied up with attitudes about the future. The view that the conditions of the present can be improved in the future is a central tenet in Judaism" (p. 473). The positive parental attitudes about education translated also into higher expectations and childrearing practices aimed at pressuring children to succeed in school, such as to show early individual mastery by requiring them to study harder and for longer periods of time. Psychological studies conducted in the 1950s and 1960s (e.g., Kohn, 1969; Psathas, 1957; Rosen, 1956) showed that Jewish children developed earlier positive school attitudes and behaviors such as motivation to succeed, belief in an orderly world, belief in rational mastery and planning, self-direction, and preference for individual credit for work. Moreover, according to Gans (1962) and Whyte (1943), the traditional dichotomy of Jews versus Gentiles lost its boundaries for most non-Orthodox Jewish families, allowing their participation in secular and civic society.

In contrast, the cultural background of southern Italian immigrants in the United States represented a rigid social structure and chronic poverty of a rural class of *contadini* (farmers who worked land for landlords). Therefore, southern Italians held negative attitudes toward social institutions like the schools, resulting from negative experiences in the Old Country with authority and officialdom, which translated into negative responses toward American public schools that represented in their past experiences "alien institutions maintained by the upper classes" (Olneck & Lazerson, 1974, p. 476). The American value of using the school system as a tool for social mobility for immigrant families did not coincide with the cultural background of southern Italian parents in which "education as an agency of upward mobility had little meaning" (p. 476). Based on the cultural experience of southern Italians, the extended family was the social institution of trust and loyalty to kin and peer groups, which encouraged dependence and collectivism. Olneck and Lazerson described the conflicting attitude toward social mobility experienced by southern Italian children of immigrant families, who experienced at home cultural values of filial obligation, a childrearing philosophy of obedience and control, and parental expectations that the achievement of their children would not exceed their own.

Consequently, as discussed by Olneck and Lazerson (1974),

> This [cultural] background ill-disposed southern Italian immigrants to respond favorably to American schools. Schooling was seen as a direct challenge to family values and parental control . . . [parents were fearful that] . . . school would indoctrinate their children with ideas antagonistic to the traditional codes of family life. (p. 476)

In addition, economic needs of lower-income southern Italian families, in comparison to other national groups of immigrants, interact with their traditional cultural values toward and experiences of social institutions and the family, resulted in lower retention rates for school children beyond the early elementary grades. In fact, most southern Italian peasants went to school only until third grade, in school buildings in poor condition staffed by teachers not able to encourage children to stay in school. The traditional value of religious and secular knowledge was based only on folklore, oral traditions, and exposure to the Catholic church and mass—a mystic and supernatural and emotional identification to be accepted, and not texts to be analyzed and debated. The value of knowledge as scholarship, of religious or secular texts that needed to be studied and learned, present among the Jewish families, was not common among the southern Italian *contadini* (peasant, rural) culture.

Thus, an interface between cultural and economic factors may have affected the school performance of Russian Jewish and southern Italian children, such as levels of literacy of their parents in their native language; group cultural values for supporting their children through academic work; and higher family incomes and occupational status. These cultural and economic factors were much more powerful influences on school achievement than the other social characteristics shared between immigrants. The same argument regarding significant and powerful effects of cultural value system and beliefs can also explain the higher income levels of Asian immigrant groups today and their higher achievement levels in comparison to mainstream and other underachieving immigrant groups (e.g., Hispanics and other underachieving minorities, such as African Americans). Immigrant Asian and first-generation Asian students perform higher than subsequent generations of Asian Americans, a phenomenon explained in the literature by the strong effect of cultural values that prioritize academic achievement and pursuing college education and professional careers. In contrast, the traditional religious and cultural values of southern Italian immigrants resulted in dichotomies and polarities that translated into underachievement in their children.

U.S. public schools of the early 1900s did not respond to the cultural diversity present among immigrant groups, but rather were insensitive to cultural and individual differences. Only some ethnic cultural groups, whose cultural background and values matched the mainstream American culture, could succeed academically and showed higher degrees of cultural adaptation and social mobility. Other groups lagged behind for decades, taking significantly longer to integrate with mainstream society. After about one century, this story repeats itself in contemporary society; only the specific ethnic groups have changed identity, and so instead of underachieving southern and eastern Europeans, such as southern Italians and Poles, we have now underachieving Hispanics from rural Mexico and Central and South America, a poor rural culture similar to the Mediterranean Europeans.

Institutionalization of Public Schools as Sociocultural Agents

According to Drake (1961), the public school system in the United States became institutionalized in the early 1900s when federal and state regulations started to control the training and certification of teachers. With education becoming institutionalized in the early twentieth century, "the public school [became] the major agency for the transmission of the cultural heritage and for maintaining social order" (Drake, 1961, p. 42). The philosophical framework of the public education movement in the United States was provided by the Jeffersonian emphasis on the rights of the common citizens and the Hamiltonian emphasis on American nationalism.

The nineteenth century's history of education is divided into two periods: (1) the Construction period, encompassing 1750 and 1860, in which the American patterns for education were built; and (2) the Expansion period, from 1860 to 1930, in which there was growth toward universality in the U.S. educational system. During the

Construction period, the Civil War marked a milestone in which the foundations for all aspects of American education were laid, including: (1) the graded and ladder-type system embodying the eight-four-four plan, (2) teaching based on knowledge of child nature, including developmental teaching, (3) teacher–pupil empathy (introducing women as teachers, especially for younger children), and (4) introduction of formal teacher training.

Some of the philosophical underpinnings for the knowledge base of teaching come from Locke's seventeenth-century ideas following the tabula rasa concepts of Aristotle and Comenius. Locke's ideas were based on the assumption that human nature is neutral-passive, that is, ideas are not innate but originate in the experiences with the senses and begin early to form a child's attitudes, habits, and character. Locke helped to secularize education with his emphasis on educating the moral, and not religious, character and using education to form useful habits. Locke recommended that children develop experiences first, and then language, and that education develop in children the ability to use impressions as a sensorial bases to assign words. Therefore, play could be used for an educational purpose, when controlled and organized.

During the eighteenth century, elementary education became more secular, but still retained a quasi-religious character and used recitation and memorization as major pedagogical techniques. The science-based teaching, rooted in pedagogical applications based on knowledge of how children develop and learn, tended to follow the assumptions of Rousseau's theory, and the Progressive education movement, which considered human nature good and active, and education and development as child centered.

The major milestones achieved during the 1800s that allowed for the establishment of the U.S. public school system during the 1900s were: (1) the mass training of teachers with the establishment of the American state university system, (2) the increased federal and compulsory taxation system funding educational activities, and (3) the establishment of the public high school. However, by the beginning of the 1900s, public education still had not attained central unity because of opposition to the secondary public education system. As described by Drake (1961), "Illiteracy was still a major problem . . . teachers had little if any professional consciousness; [and] only the wealthy attended high school and the university" (p. 42). The increase of federal funds toward building a state system of secondary and higher education helped tremendously to close the gap between the public school and the university during the 1900s, with the resulting unification of public education. Within this continuous educational system, "the public school system has become a fixed institution in the life of our people, reaching from the kindergarten through the graduate school of the university" (p. 44).

As an institution, this continuous public education system has become part of the general society and the American culture, and, in turn, it also contributes to producing a specific subculture, the so-called "American school and college culture." Education as an institution tends to follow the purposes, and endorse the democratic ideal and cultural value systems of the particular sociocultural reality that it is part of mainstream American cultural institutions. The educational system qualifies as a cultural institution because it is an organization that exerts a significant influence on the lives of social members. The schools and universities are a social institution comparable to state, church, and family. Culture is a term that includes the activities of a given society in the social, economic, religious, and political realm; both as processes (e.g., patterns of behaviors, habits, traditions, folklore, etc.) and products (e.g., music, food, clothing, and any other artifacts created by humans such as technology).

Post–World War I Years (1915–1929)

During the period between 1915 and 1929, the completion of the modern school system took place within the context of World War I (WWI). As explained by Urban and Wagoner (1996), during this time

> Anglo-Saxon dismay [at social and cultural changes] was also directed at the new wave of immigrants that had flowed into America at the turn of the century. It produced immigration restriction laws in 1921 and again in 1924. The earlier legislation limited the number of immigrants from each country to a small percentage of its current American population. The latter tied the number of immigrants from each country to a percentage of their number in 1890, before most southern and eastern Europeans had arrived in this country. (p. 219).

The previous section about immigration policy expands on this topic (information summarized also in Table 1.3).

Up until WWI, German language was taught together with English in many private and public schools in cities with a large number of German immigrants, such as Cincinnati. During the WWI years, and the postwar years, pro-German curriculums and even teachers and administrators were penalized.

Intelligence Tests.   Intelligence tests used during WWI, the Army "Alpha" and "Beta" tests, were applied to the public school system during the postwar years as an integral part of the modernization process of the U.S. public school system. The measurement movement in educational research was also a reflection of the successful use of psychological tests by the U.S. Army for recruitment and selection of personnel. As documented by Urban and Wagoner (1996), "School systems soon began developing elaborate bureaus of educational research whose major function was to purchase and administer the standardized tests that were believed to measure educational potential and achievement of students" (p. 220). Intelligence tests were promoted by a first generation of school reformers in order "to sort and to adjust the differences within and between different age, sex, and class cohorts [that is, for] overcoming social differences" (Heffron, 1991, p. 82).

Heffron also highlighted that the intelligence testing movement has an innate argument that is very conservative, that "removes people from the social compact and obviates the need for external controls" (1991, p. 82). Initially, intelligence tests were supposed to be more objective and modern methods replacing older and subjective methods that selected and placed students in the school system. According to Heffron, "intelligence testing was a revolution from above, the work of an elite vanguard of professional psychologists, educators, and administrators who, allied with the publishing industry, sought to impose new classificatory schemes on an unwitting public" (p. 85).

However, what seemed to be a panacea became part of the contemporary problem of discriminatory issues in assessment because, as Heffron (1991) put it, "there are no psychometric solutions to questions of fairness to individuals or groups and that only a consensus of value judgments can solve these problems" (p. 84). Some representatives of the Liberal Progressive movement, such as "Dewey, warned of the threat to democracy made by the indiscriminate labeling of people on the basis of intelligence test scores" (Urban & Wagoner, 1996, p. 221). As demonstrated repeatedly by contemporary research, intelligence and educational standardized tests measure the effect of external factors on learning and development (i.e., amount of cultural and social information and knowledge learned). These tests can discriminate against immigrant and poor schoolchildren who are members of minority and/or language-minority groups such as African Americans, Hispanics, Asians, and Native Americans. For instance, intelligence tests were used during the pre-and postwar years in the South to track African American students into low level, nonacademic, industrial education programs. Validity and reliability flaws are still present today for standardized testing with ESL students in the U.S. school system. We have come to realize the more complex theoretical and methodological underpinnings and limitations of standardized tests; nevertheless, political and economic needs reinforce the application of more traditional, not alternative, assessment methods. Chapters 7 and 8 discuss the topic of assessment of ESL students in a more extensive manner.

Family Life of Immigrants

Social Status of Immigrant Women.   It was more likely for women of most immigrant groups to follow their husbands and to come during the post-WWI xenophobia. Some exceptions were Irish, Bohemian, and English Canadian women who emigrated by themselves in higher numbers, and, in smaller numbers, Italian women married to men doing compulsory military service. Irish and English Canadian women had no language problem; they were English speakers, and found better jobs and wages in U.S. factories than in their agricultural home countries. Bohemian women started coming in the 1870s, working skilled jobs in the cigar-making factories of the time. Irish women were more likely to remain single until later in life and to be devoted to parents and siblings rather than to husbands and children. With these exceptions, most immigrant groups of the late 1800s and early 1900s had many more men than women. Thanks to the relative scarcity of women in immigrant America, they attained a higher status than in Europe, and were granted civil rights during the 1920s, including the right to vote and to enter workers' unions.

Because older generations were left behind in Europe, and also because of more egalitarian status and legal rights of women and children in America, immigrant wives gained a higher social status than in Europe. Even farm wives had a final say in matters of general interest for the family, such as buying and selling land. In many instances, it was women who managed the financial matters in the household, such as paying bills and buying necessities, and who also took the lead in Americanizing the family (e.g., learning how to cook American dishes and buying American-style clothes for family members).

Marriage Traditions among Immigrants.   Most immigrant men sought wives from their own ethnic group; because there were fewer of them women had a better opportunity to select husbands than in Europe. Women also preferred to marry men of their own ethnic group, and "even as late as 1920, some 700 to 800 of every 1,000 new mothers listed the fathers of their children as having been born in the same country as themselves" (Carpenter, 1920, cited in Weatherford, 1995, p. 328). In general, according to Carpenter, during the early 1900s most men and women immigrants, including Austrians, Hungarians, Russians, Italians, Poles, and even Irish (who had no language barriers and a longer history of immigration), preferred to marry within their nationality group (approximately around 70 percent), or first-generation, U.S.-born individuals of their same ethnic group (approximately 20 percent) or a close one (approximately 10 percent, such as Irish marrying Scots, Welsh, or English; with Hungarians choosing Austrians; and with Russian marrying Poles). Endogamous marriages (i.e., within the same nationality groups) tended to prevail longer in cities than in rural areas.

Eventually, during the middle 1900s, the most important factor for choosing a spouse became the merits of the individual, a change to the individualistic cultural values of U.S.-born citizens, and the subsequent loss of the family's power and preference toward religious and ethnicity factors. Americans formed nuclear families rather than the traditionally extended European Mediterranean families. Immigration policy also supported marriage ties and bringing in wives and children, rather than extended families, so that married immigrants would have more children in the United States and establish "new American-born families" (Weatherford, 1995, p. 341).

Typically, almost all immigrants courted and married within their ethnic groups, and even their children would prefer to marry a spouse of their own nationality to please their parents. According to the European heritage, individuals would not follow the romantic notion of love as Americans would; instead, property exchange and parental approval were the two most important factors to consider in marriage decisions. This idea of deciding marriages on the basis of property typically meant men were much older than women when they married, because men needed to accumulate property to bid for a wife (and in many eastern European countries, complete military service). Because women were considered economically dependent on their husbands, they were expected to bring money or property to a marriage, with a bridal dowry remaining important for a decade or two after emigration. Immigrant women viewed marriage as necessary, as a step to secure their future economic security. Immigrant men viewed marriage as a natural state, and ethnic communities, such as Italians, perceived single men with prejudice. Eastern Europeans were used to celebrating weddings for two or three days, as women's only goal and identity came from her marriage. Immigrants' ambivalence about American-style dating continued for one or two generations, and was eventually overcome by women entering the workforce and becoming acquainted with men through the workplace.

From Extended to Nuclear Family Structures.   During the period between the 1840s to the early 1900s, immigrant families were frequently larger than the average American families, with immigrant women giving birth to two or three times the number of children borne by American women, especially those of higher SES status. Repeated pregnancies with little time between babies left immigrant women weak, malnourished and in poor physical health, and with a large number of children to care for. Even though immigrant women had more children than American women, they also lost more babies (child mortality was 30 percent in native mothers versus 60 percent among foreign-born mothers in 1910 in the State of New York, Weatherford, 1995).

Infant mortality rates were also related to ethnicity among immigrants. For instance, the rate of Italian infant mortality in New York in 1905–06 was five times higher than native white Americans and twice as high as other groups of immigrants. This difference in infant mortality rates was related to the quality of infants' nutrition, which varied considerably between groups (Senate Documents, 1912), and to when solid foods were started (e.g., Italian, Polish, and French Canadian mothers started babies on solid foods earlier than Jewish and Irish mothers). Moreover, immigrant women suffered from a disruption of their eating habits, and familiar foods that had offered some nutritional balance, such as milk and cheese, were expensive and difficult to store properly in cities. One reason why many immigrant families preferred to stay in ethnic neighborhoods in cities was because they could find familiar foods in stores, as their shopping and language needs were met by store-owners in Little Italy, for instance. Immigrants also were exposed to new food items, originally from the North American continent, such as pumpkins, sweet potatoes, and watermelons, and within one or two generations their diet became more varied and unique to their new American home.

Several factors led immigrant women to have more babies, such as getting married at young ages, religion (e.g., Catholic priests considered contraception a sin and supported having babies as a gift of God when consulted by immigrant women), and cultural beliefs (e.g., poor status of women and the dominance of males who believed that children were proof of virility or that they represented economic well-being because they were potential earners). The cultural belief in using children as workers proved useful in U.S. farmlands, where immigrant families could use young boys and girls to take care of crops and animals. Therefore, daughters of immigrants who remained on farms continued to have large families. However, in the cities, immigrants soon learned that large families were a liability, and that poor young children were not productive in the urban industrial society. This fact resulted in immigrants learning how to limit their pregnancies (as noted by city social workers, Weatherford, 1995). In general, as immigrant families changed their religion and cultural beliefs, their values in relation to family size also changed, resulting in fewer children.

The stress of cultural adaptation took its toll on marriages among immigrant families, such as unemployment among males, and the need for women to work outside the home. Given the great disparity in age, most marriages did not offer mental or spiritual companionship or shared experiences, but a formal and conservative relationship. Ambivalence and fatalism were common attitudes toward marriage among immigrant women and were also related to American society's views of the time: women, who never married or who were divorced were not accepted. Instead, women's place in society was to be married and dependent on their husbands. Certain European immigrant groups had a tradition of desertion, especially during pregnancies, which continued in the United States, leaving women with the burden of supporting the household in the absence of the male figure. The solidity of marriages in Europe could end in the United States, given cultural changes and ambivalent attitudes toward marriage. Because immigrants did not understand the U.S. legal system, divorce was not seen as an option even if marriages were broken. Most often, immigrants' religious prohibitions and conservatism prevented ending marriages through divorce.

Even though elderly grandparents typically did not immigrate to the United States, within a decade or two, families had their own elderly members due to the strenuous work conditions for immigrant parents. Adults in their forties suffered from early "old age" due to overworking in hard conditions in the industrial engine, and as a result had a hard time finding jobs. The Americanized attitude toward the elderly and aging adults was to view them as a liability, in contrast to the traditional European perception of authority and respect for the wisdom of elders. Sometimes, the immigrants' cultural backgrounds emphasized the extended family ties and collectivism, such as closeness between siblings, which contradicted the American emphasis on the nuclear family and individualism. Immigrants were encouraged to establish new, U.S.-born families separated from the Old World family ties, with more equality between gender roles and less emphasis on respect and authority to the elders, allowing the young to assert themselves.

In contrast to their mothers who had married very young (in 1920, 14 percent of foreign-born women over age 15 were married), first-generation American young women married later and consequently had fewer children. As explained by Weatherford (1995), "Certainly to some extent it was because young women saw the difficult lives of their mothers and saw that America offered alternatives" (p. 343). First-generation American women worked in jobs with a higher status and earned better wages than their mothers, moving upward from domestic jobs (employing approximately 70 percent of their immigrant mothers) to work in trade and manufacturing, and even office clerical jobs, such as typists. As explained by Weatherford, "being treated 'like a lady' indeed became the goal of almost every immigrant girl" (p. 347). The sons of immigrant families also experienced upward mobility, achieving a higher educational level than their parents and increasing their leisure time. Both U.S.-born girls and boys found greater freedom and fewer employment barriers, as they now spoke English and could aspire to an education, resulting in more flexible gender roles.

On the other hand, rural U.S.-born boys and girls needed to marry in order to build a farm, to raise children who could work on the farm, and to overcome loneliness in the vast expansions of the prairies. In fact, farm life was considered healthier and more in tune with the former agricultural labor of rural immigrants. Children of immigrants growing up on farms were more likely to speak the native language of their parents and to respect their cultural backgrounds more. Family members developed closer relationships in farm settings than in urban areas because the large farms placed neighbors far apart from each other, and they were also far away from villages and towns. The typical perception of immigrants about farming in the United States was one of commitment and gratitude because they appreciated the privilege of becoming landowners, free and independent of landlords and inborn social and economic power (Weatherford, 1995).

Housing Conditions.   Since the mid-1800s, millions of immigrants settled in the upper Midwest region, and most of these new settlers were from a German and Scandinavian background, with some eastern and southern Europeans. However, most Irish, Italian, and Jewish immigrants preferred to settle in urban areas on the East coast. During the period of the late 1880s and early 1900s, most immigrants lived in tenement apartments in large urban areas such as New York City, with unventilated and dark rooms, and a kitchen stove as the only source of heat. Conditions became worse as immigrant numbers increased, leading to overcrowded immigrant households that included friends, relatives, or strangers who rented a space and slept on cots or tables, in closets, and under stairs. Sanitation conditions were very poor: sewage lines backed up, sometimes for weeks, while indoor toilets off of hallways were a rare commodity shared by many tenants.

Because of the poor housing conditions in the late 1880s and early 1900s, epidemics were common. A cholera epidemic struck a New York City suburb called Gotham Court in the 1880s, killing 195 out of each 1,000 residents. In addition, the physical and mental health of immigrant families suffered from overcrowded rooms in buildings so close together that city blocks could have a population as great as an entire town. Another threat in these conditions was fire, which could trap hundreds of people because of the proximity of the houses. For instance, the great Chicago fire of 1871 killed primarily German and Scandinavian immigrants who could not outrun the fire once it reached their poor wooden shacks. During the tenement era, fire escapes were nonexistent.

The conditions outside the cities were also crowded for immigrant families, who roomed in small houses packed together in mill towns. The boarding business, mostly run out of tiny homes in urban areas, also offered extra income for immigrant families. Unmarried or married men or women who had emigrated without their families used boardinghouses as a social support system to stay close to their ethnic groups and maintain familiar life styles. Boarding immigrant families used the extra income to save money toward buying their own home (i.e., achieving their American dream), but in the meantime had to endure overcrowded, unsanitary and dangerous conditions not in compliance with the mainstream American family standards (Weatherford, 1995).

Other occupations of immigrants were related to farming, with some groups following crops in the Midwest and in areas near northeastern cities, such as Long Island. Russian, Bohemian, Southern Slavs, and Polish immigrants were the groups most likely to do itinerant farm work, with men, women, and children being hired as extra help during harvest. In farm towns, sanitation conditions were also very poor because people built their outhouses and wells close to their homes, for convenience but so close together that diseases developed quickly, especially during hot weather. Insects such as flies and mosquitoes spread disease to immigrant families who had not yet built immunity defenses comparable to native-born Americans. Often, farmhouses were as crowded as city tenements, because newcomers would ask for refuge until they could build their own homes.

Farmers assimilated faster than their urban counterparts because they invested their hard work in building a farm, and contributing to the growth of new settlements in the wild. Consequently, as landowners, they did not have any intention of returning to Europe, whereas immigrants settling in the cities could have some hope of returning to their Old Country homes. As Weatherford (1995) described it, the immigrants settling in the prairies had the mission of building "churches and schools where the tall grass had grown free, to make farms and fences where the buffalo had grazed . . . The purpose of civilization was to subdue the natural" (p. 269). Immigrants settling as farmers in the midwest region had to work hard to fight against the freezing cold winters and summer prairie fires, and therefore "showed a greater commitment to their land than most American settlers. . . . for without the belief that they were entitled to the land that they tilled, their decision to emigrate and all of their plans for the future would fall apart" (pp. 261, 268). Therefore, place of settlement, and urban or rural origin, were factors that made a difference in the identification of immigrants with their new land, the quality of their living conditions, and their economic well-being and found opportunities in the United States.

Working Conditions

Working conditions for immigrants were difficult in the new, emerging industrial era of the mid-1800s in large urban areas such as those found in New York, New Jersey, and Pennsylvania. As stated by Ernst (1965, cited in Weatherford, 1995), during 1855, "two-thirds of the New York City dressmakers, seamstresses, milliners, shirt and collar makers, embroiderers . . . and artificial flower makers were foreign-born" (p. 204), with the majority of manufacturing workers coming from a Jewish background, and skilled European women running the silk-mill centers. As explained by Weatherford (1995),

> As soon as the Irish arrived in the 1840s, they began to replace Yankee farm girls as laborers in the textile mills of New England. Experienced workers from Britain joined them, as did Germans and French Canadians. By the end of the century [1900s], these mills employed Poles, Italians, various Balkan peoples, Greeks, Syrians, and Armenians—in some [mills] more than forty languages were spoken. (p. 206)

Most immigrants worked in factories, and avoided jobs in stores because of the language barrier, but even if they were English-speaking, they preferred the higher wages offered by factories. Regardless of earning higher wages, immigrants still suffered from job discrimination in factories, with the newcomers being given "almost invariably the dirtiest, least rewarding tasks" (p. 230), but the attitude of foreigners was almost always positive toward work, and "most immigrants saw all work as honorable, and the job that paid best was the one to choose" (p. 229). As explained by Weatherford (1995), the opposite attitude was held by U.S.-born workers, who perceived working in a factory as losing their social status, and instead preferred to work in stores regardless of the lower wages offered. "Department stores were infamous for low wages, long hours, and arbitrary rules" (Weatherford, 1995, p. 228), and yet were perceived by Americans as more socially acceptable jobs for working-class women.

Even though some immigrants worked in factories, others had to stay for their entire working career in ghetto sweatshops that belonged to people of their own nationality. Among the reasons why newly arrived immigrants worked in the sweatshops of their ethnic ghetto were an unfamiliarity with the subway or tram system in urban areas, inability to speak English and read signs for using public transportation and operating machinery in factories, and ignorance of how to look for a job in factories (i.e., where to look for advertisements of positions and when, such as city newspapers on Monday mornings). These small sweatshops actually offered worse working conditions than the larger factories: they were not only more overcrowded, unsafe, and underventilated, but also paid lower wages. For instance, in Chicago in 1912, most small men's garment shops employed German, Bohemian, and Polish immigrants. A more detailed account of working conditions for women, policies, and working conditions in specific types of jobs (i.e., mills, farms, households, etc.) is provided in the next section.

Labor Protection Policies.   During the middle and late 1800s few labor protection policies existed; especially problematic were poorly-enforced safety regulations protecting women's and children's working conditions. Factories operated without safety standards, providing inadequate buildings equipped with unsafe machinery, and following unsanitary practices that allowed oil, rags, and lint to accumulate, turning wooden structures into firetraps. Another problem for workers was seasonal unemployment, such as builders during winter, or higher seasonal demand, such as overproduction during Christmas season—no policies were in place to make employers pay either unemployment compensation or mandatory overtime. In the absence of such policies, many industrial managers acted as authorities not to be questioned, and perceived workers as in need of discipline. Many new immigrants from rural areas, such as Italians, did not question these authoritative practices in nonunion jobs, and "it was common for immigrants to take jobs without knowing what one was to be paid" (Weatherford, 1995, p. 226).

Most immigrants understood the need for create unions for workers. If immigrants found working conditions in the United States that did not conform to their expectations, especially if they were coming from unionized working experiences, then they would try to establish workers' unions. For instance, a dress manufacturing company in New York City, Triangle, denied the right of workers to organize in unions during the early 1900s, and always employed newly arrived Italian and Jewish immigrants willing to work in a nonunion shop. As discussed by Weatherford (1995), "The Swedish women [working in the Chicago garment industry during 1897] insisted on the inclusion of the ill-paid Italians in their union, and they 'lived well, maintained good homes and aspired to general education and culture'" (p. 238, cited in Senate Document, 1912).

Women's Situation in the Labor Force.   Many times it was easier for young single women to find jobs than it was for married women. Many women who got married could no longer get the same jobs they had earlier when they were single, especially after they had children. Employers paid lower wages to single women who did not have the responsibility of supporting a household, especially when teenagers still lived with their families of origin and just contributed their wages to their parents' and other siblings' earnings. As stated by Weatherford (1995), "Discrimination against married women was so severe that a number said they had to resort to concealing their marriage to get work . . . most of whom were Irish and German" (p. 230). Some sociological reports of the late 1800s and early 1900s, documented that most immigrant married women worked because they needed extra income to provide necessities for their families.

However, married immigrant women also perceived that working outside their homes also helped them to improve their mental health, and "viewed their work as an escape mechanism that allowed them to ignore fundamental depression" (Weatherford, 1995, p. 243). While most middle-class American families during the middle 1800s to early 1900s debated whether married "respectable ladies" should work outside their homes, immigrant families took it as a given that wives should earn an income, helping to ensure the family's economic well-being. Actually, the early Puritan settlers supported the idea that women and children should work, in order to avoid idleness and encourage good work ethics.

According to Weatherford (1995), immigrant values

> were closer to those of the Puritans, and productive work was seen as good no matter who did it. At the same time Americans began to look down on work—especially work done by women—as something suitable only for blacks, foreigners, and occasional poor whites. The immigrants kept for a while a different value system. (p. 244)

As soon as economic stability was achieved by the breadwinning men of the family, then women were required to adjust their roles to the expectation of becoming housewives in Victorian American society. However, there was always a dichotomy or ambivalence between the Victorian values of the late 1800s and early 1900s and the American values of freedom and individuality that encouraged women to become assertive and independent earners actively contributing to the income of their families. It was not until World War II that women discovered their power as breadwinners for their families.

Mill Work.   Working conditions in industrial America of the mid-and late 1800s were difficult for all immigrants, who were assigned and expected to accomplish a much higher amount of manufacturing than in Europe. Weatherford (1995) enumerated the difficulty of working in factories: long hours, low wages, high competition between workers (e.g., publicly posting worker's production charts), and unhealthy facilities (no ventilation and inadequate light). For instance, mill workers had a higher tendency to die of respiratory diseases, such as pneumonia and tuberculosis, due to lint and dust and machines fumes, than farmers. A study in

Lawrence, Massachusetts, in 1912 revealed that "one-third of the spinners in the mills died before they had worked ten years" (Cole, 1963, cited in Weatherford, 1995, p.25). Even after the 1860s, German, Scandinavian, and Irish immigrants completed many tasks in the garment industry on home contract. "The cut clothes were brought home, and all members of the family worked at sewing and 'finishing'—hemming, stitching buttonholes, and attaching buttons. The 'sweatshop' had begun" (Weatherford, 1995, p. 208). In the 1880s, electricity revolutionized the garment industry; with the availability of electric machines, seamstresses and tailors now became machine operators, completing repetitive work at a hurried pace. The garment industry required cheap work so that ready-made clothing could be offered to working-class Americans.

Work in Other Industries.   Besides the garment and mills industry, other typical manufacturing jobs for immigrants were candy, candle, artificial flowers, and cigar making. Candy and chocolate making employed immigrant women from many ethnic groups; payment generally was low for tedious, repetitive tasks such as wrapping or packing candy, with some exceptions for more elaborate candy-making tasks. However, working conditions were demanding because workers stood for long hours and were exposed to cold temperatures to prevent candy from melting; during summers, there was no employment because the heat would melt the candy.

Cigar making required more skill and paid better, employing a large proportion of foreign-born women, primarily from Bohemia, since the late 1860s until the early 1900s. Most women working in the cigar industry did not speak English (in larger percentages than in other industries, as reported by a New York study with Italians, [Odencrantz, 1919]), were older and married, and considered themselves "unassimilable" (Weatherford, 1995). Cigar making attracted larger percentages of men due to higher wages, and also older and married women with children because this industry offered flexible hours; most likely not available in other industries. However, the cigar industry also had the risk of illness for workers, such as nicotine poisoning and eye strain for rollers and packers. Cigar making also attracted some Cubans of Spanish descent and Sicilian immigrants to the southern states, such as Tampa, Florida.

In contrast to cigar making, artificial-flower making was one of the worst-paid immigrant industries, and became a feminine task completed on home contracts, offering work for married women and their young children. During the early 1900s, it was Italian immigrants who entered this trade, with men working as dyers in shops, and women and their young children (as young as 3 or 4 years of age) making the artificial flowers, mostly on home contracts. Demand for artificial flowers was high during the Victorian Era because they were used as decorations on hats and in homes. During the 1920s the fashion changed and this industry ended.

Mines, oil refineries, construction jobs building railroads and infrastructure such as bridges and homes, and the metal industry also provided work for immigrant men. Educated immigrants also worked in the publishing industry, editing immigrant publications or as typesetters and book binders. Educated women immigrants became nurses, midwives, or teachers in parochial schools serving immigrant children and their families.

Working in Laundries.   Another typical employment for immigrant women in urban areas was laundries, with most starting to work as teenagers and employing northern as well as southern Europeans such as Irish, Swedish, German, Italian, and Polish women. Older married women also worked in laundries, if they became widowed or needed extra income to supplement their husband's wages to be able to sustain a large family. Most women did not stay long in these jobs, because of the exhausting and dangerous working conditions. Newcomers knew that laundry work was hard and paid badly, and it was accepted only as entry-level work for short periods of time. Other married women accepted other people's clothing to wash or iron them at home, providing extra income for their family with homebound work.

Working in Households.   Another traditional employment for immigrant women was to become a household worker, which also helped the Irish, German, and Scandinavian immigrant groups to gain faster acculturation to the American lifestyle. Learning English and cultural habits, such as food preparation and childrearing, was easier and faster when immigrants were living with American families. Besides earning much higher wages for their domestic work and gaining knowledge of American domestic arts, immigrant women also received democratic and considerate treatment from U.S. household owners, all benefits resulting in increasing their self-esteem and assertiveness. Foreign-born domestics were better paid than U.S.-born women, and household work was not as hard and fast-paced as the routine of unskilled machine operators in factories.

Young foreign women with no family in the United States preferred domestic rather than factory or store jobs because they were provided with room and board in addition to a salary, so that they could save money. The ability to send money back to their families in Europe to help support them or pay for their passages to immigrate to the United States was an important factor for choosing household work. Because marriage was the ultimate goal expected by society of the mid- to late 1800s and early 1900s, domestic work was a better option for immigrant women to prepare to become mothers and housewives. As explained by an American social worker of that era, "Some families [in which] the woman was a servant before her marriage . . . [demonstrate] the superiority of domestic service over factory training for developing intelligent homemakers . . . [who took better care] of their children's diets and health" (Weatherford, 1995, p. 251, cited in More, 1907). In contrast, Italian and Jewish women avoided domestic work because of cultural traditions that did not allowed females to live separated from their families. It was more difficult for Italian and Jewish women to acculturate to the United States without the experience of living in a mainstream family.

However, domestic work also had its downside: long hours due to live-in conditions, isolation, and lower social status than factory or store jobs. Aspiring young women wanted to work their way out of the serving class and find opportunities for advancement in other jobs, and look for work among equal coworkers in industrial settings. Eventually, with the opening of new jobs during the 1910s and especially after World War I, foreign-born women left domestic jobs permanently to pursue new opportunities for unskilled workers in the general labor market, the result of social changes and the emancipation of women.

SECOND IMMIGRATION WAVE: ASSIMILATION

What's in a Name? Cultural Adaptation through Name Changes

Many times it was through their children that immigrants started to "Americanize," such as changing their names. For instance, an immigrant woman named Rahel would change her name to Ruth or Rose, which was easier to pronounce for their teachers, employers, and new American friends. Actually, while the first author was writing this book, she went through the naturalization process herself. During the naturalization ceremony the judge announced that about one-fourth of the applicants had changed their names, with the author herself going from two last names to one and switching around her original first and middle names. On her alien resident card her name read "Maria Virginia Gonzalez de Fernandez," with the "de" used within the Hispanic culture to mark her married status. In her certificate of citizenship she chose to change her name to "Virginia Maria Gonzalez," shortening her name to the typical American pattern of one first name, one middle name, and keeping her maiden name as the only surname. It was a formalization of what she already had adopted many years before as a resident of the United States. Her husband underwent naturalization at the same time, and in his "rebirth as an American citizen" he also changed his name from three first names and two last names to one first name and one last name.

In a way, this subtle, but nonetheless, important variation in names at the time of adopting U.S. citizenship also marked the process of identity change to biculturalism and transculturalism that they had started many years ago. The concept of transculturalism applies in this case because cultural identity changes were taking place for the adoption of a new citizenship, and the resulting name adaptation to symbolized the new cultural identity. However, the "original or old cultural identity of Latin American citizenship" is latent and still alive in many facets of identity processes, such as the selective use of the Spanish language according to cultural context and other traces of personality traits (e.g., spiritual value systems, such as religion, emotionality and affectionate use of language, speaking English with a nonnative accent, etc.).

What's in a Clothing Style? Adoption of American Styles of Dress

The assimilation level of immigrants was judged by their clothing, which needed to show adoption of American styles of dress. For immigrants to get jobs, they needed to "look like Americans" and show their cultural assimilation to lifestyles and values through their manner of dressing. For women it meant wearing hats, a central dress piece prior to WWI, and abandoning the shawls and "old country" dress patterns that marked them as "greenhorns" (Weatherford, 1995, p. 30). Hats also symbolized for immigrant women the changing social standards, that is, the passage from a peasant or serving-class status to achieving the social status of a "lady," because in Europe only upper-class women wore hats. Society approved of unmarried women dressing fashionably; however, as soon as a woman married, her dressing style became frugal and her major concern became how to dress her children and husband warmly (Weatherford, 1995).

Many immigrants adjusted their dressing style even before they left their countries of origin, following the advice of relatives in the United States who asked them to abandon and sell their garments in Europe. The most important expense for immigrants after arrival was to buy American-style clothing, so that they could find a job. Adoption of American-style dressing could prevent some prejudice against immigrants, and was also a symbol of social advancement and a practical investment in achieving a better social status in the future. During the early 1900s, thanks to the Industrial Revolution, mass-produced clothing was readily available in the United States. Immigrants considered this mass-produced clothing costly, but also a symbol of American sophistication and style, as their countries of origin were still in the preindustrial era. Because clothing was rather expensive but not very durable, many immigrants could afford to buy only a few pieces of clothing and had to launder them often.

Factors Affecting the Degree and Pace of Cultural Adaptation and Assimilation

Age at the time of immigration was a major factor affecting the ability to change habits and cultural behaviors (e.g., eating and dressing) from the Old World ways to the new American ways. Besides age, the degree of contact with native speakers of English and mainstream U.S. society also influenced the opportunity to learn the new culture and language. Young children who grew up within immigrant communities and who received no schooling showed low levels of acculturation to mainstream American lifestyles. This situation is well illustrated by a quote: "A child . . . put into the shop remained in the old traditions, held back by illiteracy. Often it was years before he could stir away from it, and even sometimes it would take a lifetime" (Cohen, 1918; cited in Weatherford, 1995, p. 358).

Another common situation that typically slowed the pace of assimilation was faced by housebound wives who, lacking contact with the "external world," would develop homesickness and loneliness, and did not adapt to the new culture and language. In contrast, their children and husbands had a higher degree of contact with mainstream society through schooling and work, and therefore showed higher degrees of cultural and linguistic adaptation. This phenomenon is still common today among Hispanic immigrants, with housewives typically remaining monolingual Spanish and men and children developing English-language skills at a faster pace, due to their higher degree of contact with mainstream U.S. society. This phenomenon results in a generation gap between children and their mothers, as immigrant women cannot speak or read to their children in their preferred, and dominant and more proficient, language: English.

A case that illustrates this phenomenon of slower-paced assimilation experienced by housebound immigrant wives is an incident that occurred at the Bilingual Preschool Developmental Center (BPDC), featured in Chapter 5. In one of the bilingual preschool classrooms, a Hispanic 3-year-old girl had developed a preference for speaking English over Spanish, and was asking her monolingual, Spanish-speaking mother to talk and read to her in English at home. By the middle of the school year, we implemented an introductory-level English and cultural adaptation course for parents, and this Hispanic mother learned how to use basic phrases for communicating socially in English. One night, this mother said to her child: "Go to bed!" The astonished little girl hugged her mother and happily declared: "Now you can speak English, mom!" Suddenly, the gap between the bilingual preschool classroom experience, and the monolingual Spanish-speaking home experience had closed for this little girl. Even though both languages, Spanish and English, were equally emphasized in the dual-language bilingual preschool program, this little girl had developed a marked preference for communicating in English at school. Perhaps an explanation would be the fact that the Spanish-speaking teacher was also a native-speaker of English, and that the rapport that the child had established with her called for a bilingual model for adults, which was not repeated at home with a monolingual Spanish-speaking mother, and a Spanish-speaking father who also had a limited degree of English competence. It was a happy and revealing experience for this little Hispanic girl to hear her mother using both languages at home. Suddenly, the gap, and cognitive dissonance, between a monolingual Spanish home and a bilingual Spanish/English classroom had dissolved: She finally had some degree of bilingualism at home, too.

Another factor affecting degree of assimilation to the mainstream American culture was the historical point at which the national group had immigrated. Most immigrant groups carried with them established European prejudices against other national groups or ethnicities. For instance, Weatherford (1995) mentioned the case of immigrant Polish women in Cleveland at the beginning of the 1900s who held biases against Greeks, Syrians, and Italians, and even against some ethnic groups such as Galicians; but admired English nationals as "all cultured, refined, and educated" (p. 362). The process of accepting "newcomers as alike American-born" took time, because new groups of immigrants replaced the older groups as targets for prejudice and discriminatory biases. Eventually, older immigrants became part of the settled American groups who would discriminate against newer groups of immigrants.

Cultural adaptation was not an easy process for immigrants, especially if they had initially thought to go back to their country of origin, but ended up staying for various economic and family reasons. Many immigrants lost economic and social position when coming to the United States, and only regained those social commodities after hard work over a long period of time, of even over a generation or two. It was actually the children, or even grandchildren, of immigrants who could become fully fledged Americans and enjoy all their civil rights. It was the well-being of the family, and of their children, that kept many immigrants in the United States. The difficulties of changing cultural identities the long and dynamic process of "re birth" symbolized by name changes, lifestyle changes such as dressing styles, and adoption of a new language and cultural values and ways of thinking were rewarded by the thought that American-born children would one day prosper. Many immigrants adapted culturally to their new country, but did not necessarily renounce their old cultural and linguistic identity.

Thus, many immigrants become bicultural or even transcultural, by learning how to bridge their use of their native language and adopted English language across cultural contexts. In this balance between Old World and new American cultural and linguistic identities, a new identity is created, a bicultural or transcultural one that is very different from their original identity and yet dissimilar to the mainstream American identity. For instance, as exemplified by Weatherford (1995), European immigrants, when visiting their countries of origin, felt uncomfortable with the docility, fatalism, lack of social mobility, and authoritarian governments; and felt relieved when coming back to a "free" United States. The first author of the book is an immigrant herself, and she can empathize with this feeling of impatience and lack of adaptation when visiting her country of origin, and Latin America in general. When visiting Latin American countries, it takes her about three days to readapt to "old" familiar places and people, and to switch her "cultural being" and "verbal mind" to the other side of her identity—the Latin American side of her Hispanic American identity. This is the reality of biculturalism and transculturalism: to be able to maintain some features of the "old self," enact the "new self" when necessary (with both, the "old" and the "new" self, forming the bicultural self), or to transform to the hybrid self (the latter is the genuine transcultural self).

Cultural identity changes and the ability to adapt to a new cultural and linguistic reality depend on many factors, some individual and others specific to national groups. To be able to adapt to a new culture, immigrants needed to take risks and to be willing to change psychologically and behaviorally. This mind-set was captured in the phrase of a German woman who immigrated to Missouri during the late 1800s; she wrote to her relatives back in the Old Country that she liked her immigrant experience because she was "a pioneer by nature" (Bruns, 1988, cited by Weatherford, 1995, p. 379).

Cultural identity changes also make most immigrants aware of advantages and disadvantages in their experience in their adopted country. As documented by Weatherford (1995), most Ellis Island immigrants identified educational opportunities, freedom, and social mobility as some of the advantages of coming to the United States; distance from relatives back in their home country was one of the most common disadvantages. Recently, during the ceremony of naturalization oath, held at a public elementary school in Cincinnati, the first author of this book was interviewed by a fourth-grade schoolgirl about her reasons for immigrating to the United States and what she liked the most and the least in this country. Her most immediate responses to these questions were attaining higher education and enjoying liberty and democratic rights as a motive to come to the United States and what she saw as positive factors; and poverty among minority and majority children as the most negative social reality.

Gender Roles

Some immigrant groups perceived women working outside the home as more acceptable because it corresponded with their former experience in Europe. For instance, Bohemian women were used to working outside the home in Europe, with more equitable workloads at home between males and females. In contrast, Jewish and Italian immigrants preferred married women to avoid working outside the home if possible. Southern European women had to adjust to taking care of housework and their children alone in the United States, resulting in feeling isolated and confined by their household duties. Southern European women were used to communal working situations for doing household duties, such as laundry and baking bread, and for taking care of children. In southern Europe, children were cared for by relatives and neighbors, as they distrusted institutions. Because of this cultural experience, southern European immigrants were suspicious of nurseries in the United States; they feared losing control over their children's custody and the degree of instilled cultural assimilation. As pointed out by Weatherford (1975), "women feared the damage that nurseries might do to children's souls . . . [since] . . . too many natives thought Protestantism and Americanism were synonymous" (p. 175); and "when parents sometimes did voluntarily place children in the care of Americans, their offspring grew up in a culture so alien from their own that future healthy family relationships became impossible" (p. 177). In fact, it was certainly true that most U.S. institutions had as a major goal to Americanize immigrants, and the younger the better. As stated by Weatherford (1995), "Women who placed children in such facilities [nurseries] were rarely allowed any input into their children's lives. Because Protestant expressions of faith were mandatory in most, they were avoided by Catholic and Jewish immigrants" (p. 174). Thus, immigrant women had to adapt to different cultural values and lifestyles affecting their roles of taking care of their children and working outside the home.

Immigrants Returning to Europe

The immigrants who could not adapt to the new American culture and language might decide to return to their countries of origin. In general, out of eight arrivals in the United States, three would return to Europe in the period between 1908 and 1930, especially during the Great Depression of the 1930s and even during some years of the WWI era. Most returning immigrants would stay permanently in Europe; they were not simply following seasonal migratory patterns.

However, there was a difference in the rate of returnees in relation to the national or ethnic origin of immigrants. The groups with lower numbers of returnees were the Scottish, Irish, and Jews who had some specific motivation not to return to Europe. The Jewish immigrants, for instance, were escaping religious or ethnic persecution during the pogroms and wars that bound them to the United States. These three groups (i.e., Scottish, Irish, and Jews) also had a larger percentage of women immigrants, who either came by themselves, like the Irish single young women looking for jobs, or emigrated as families looking for better economic situations and opportunities. In contrast, Swedish immigrants had a higher tendency to return permanent by to their country of origin because the economy in sweden was more prosperous than their Irish and Scottish counterparts. In addition, the adaptation of Swedish immigrants to the English language and mainstream American culture was more difficult than their Irish and Scottish counterparts.

Finally, another reason to decide to return home or stay in the United States may be associated with an interface between gender and family obligations. In general, women immigrating alone perceived immigration as a permanent change, and were more likely to be young and single; whereas men coming by themselves could be married, with a family waiting for them in Europe, and considered immigration more as a fortune-seeking, temporay adventure. However, there were also single women who came to the United States to work with the ultimate goal of gaining a dowry to be able to get married in Europe. Once exposed to American values and the higher economic and social status of women, however, some immigrant women changed their plans and decided to stay permanently in the United States.

During the early 1900s, the passage between the United States and Europe became shorter, easier, and less risky. Many homesick immigrants were able to return to their home countries and visit relatives and old familiar places. Some of these trips helped immigrants to confirm that they had made the right decision, and also to realize how much their cultural values and behaviors had changed. Ets describes an aging Italian immigrant as being proud of her cultural adaptation to her new American identity and her ability to speak English: "Now I speak English good like an American, I could go anywhere" (cited in Weatherford, 1995, p. 37). Thus, the majority of immigrants decided to stay for good and adopt the United States as their home country.

Housing Conditions

With the turn of the century, southern and eastern European immigrant families experienced some rent discrimination because available housing was scarce. This rent discrimination problem resulted in overcrowded "ghettos" well into the 1930s and 1940s. Abbott (1936) referred to ethnic neighborhoods in large urban areas, such as Chicago, inhabited entirely by immigrants, even as late as the 1930s (cited in Weatherford, 1995, p. 160). Indeed, the public infrastructure and the buildings' exterior appearance were shabby and interiors were dilapidated; however, many immigrant families managed to keep their homes clean and their children neat and cared for.

Political consciousness, economic power, and voting rights were lacking for many immigrants. Even though this lack of political power pushed immigrant families into ghetto home conditions, they considered this situation temporary and saved every cent, aspiring to pursue their American dream: to become homeowners. Immigrant families could only afford cheap rents and wanted to save money to buy their own home. As stated by Weatherford (1995), "Even before World War I, twice as many foreign-born employees owned their homes compared to their native co-workers" (p. 160). Especially in small towns, such as silk-mill towns in Pennsylvania, immigrants could afford to buy their homes rather quickly. Once they owned their home, it was common for immigrant women to become landladies and to make arrangements for renting space and providing meals for immigrant male or female workers who came to the United States by themselves. Thus, part of making their "American dream" a reality was for immigrants to own their own home and improve their family's living conditions.

Working Conditions: Impact on Economic Status

For most immigrant families, income was below their necessity level, requiring immigrants to have managerial skills to balance their budgets. Following European culture, it was the women who were given their husband's paychecks and were expected to handle the budget in their households. The task of buying goods such as food and clothing was not easy for immigrant women because they had to learn and adapt to the American lifestyle and the comparative cost of goods in the market.

In addition to their contribution to the family's well-being by handling and balancing budgets, many married women also contributed with earnings. In fact, during the industrial era in the United States, women could get jobs more easily; and even if women stayed home they made some money by engaging in homebound work such as sewing, knitting, making flowers or cigars, or by becoming landladies. In addition, older women, or younger women who had too many children, and could not get factory jobs, engaged in selling goods in open-air markets in the cities. For instance, during the decade of the 1910s, "the average Italian family received 48% of its income from male wage earners and 44% from female wage earners" (Odencrantz, 1919). As pointed out by Weatherford (1995), "The only ethnic group . . . that received substantially more than half of its income from the father was the long-resident Irish" (p. 193). Most recent immigrants during the early 1900s would make a living by adding the contributions of both spouses to balance their family budget. Many times, the occupations of male breadwinners who had recently emigrated from Europe were not relevant in the United States. For instance, skills in handcrafting wood became useless because of the effect of machinery on making goods. Other men suffered from seasonable jobs, such as immigrants in the building trade who were out of work during winters, many of whom refused to work on other odd and lower paying jobs.

Older children usually contributed to their family household incomes by working once they were teenagers. Many young women delayed marriage so that they could help their family to earn a living. The difference in wages between males and females meant many immigrant families were poorer just because their older children were girls, who earned lower wages than boys. Many immigrants were unmarried women coming alone to the United States, motivated to seek their own fortunes by the European system of primogeniture for male siblings, who would be the sole beneficiaries of family inheritance. For instance, Irish women between the ages of 15 and 35 were 85 percent of all Irish immigrants during 1885 to 1890, and this figure increased to 90 percent during 1908. For the same kind of laboring work, immigrants were paid much more in the United States than in their home countries. Because of the emphasis on young women to work, many daughters of immigrant families married much later than their mothers. In addition, many immigrants were trying to save money to support relatives in Europe or to pay for passage of newcomers to the United States.

In general, the living conditions of immigrant workers were not easy; most of them lacked health insurance and their wages were below standards, particularly in the case of immigrant women. As stated by Weatherford (1995), "The protection of exploited workers was a high priority of activists in the Progressive Era, and . . . several states undertook to determine what salary was needed for a decent lifestyle" (p. 195, information based on Hutchinson, 1919). Even though immigrants could find jobs in the industrialized America of the early 1900s, they had to endure difficult working conditions and long hours, yet could make a better life for their families here than in their countries of origin. A similar job situation is found today by many Asian and Latin American immigrants, who still work in large numbers in manufacturing and service industries, hard manual labor for which most middle-class, mainstream Americans are overqualified.

The Internal Migration of African Americans: Schooling Conditions

The African American population was settled primarily in the southern region of the United States before WWI, and therefore was not mentioned in Liberal Progressive philosophers' thinking and writings, living as they did in the north, such as Dewey. Schools serving African American children were rigorously segregated and underfunded in the South, and few survived into the twentieth century. Elementary education was only sporadically available for the southern African American population, and high school education was absent or present in restrictive forms in very few cities during the 1920s.

The years preceding and following WWI mark a historical event in U.S. history, the "great migration" of African Americans from the rural, agricultural areas of the South to industrialized cities in the south and north, such as Chicago, Philadelphia, Detroit, and New York City. Schooling conditions in the city environments were not far removed from the negative situation in the south. As explained by Urban and Wagoner (1996),

> Conditions for black students in Philadelphia and other northern cities deteriorated during the 1920s as their growing black populations were crowded into ghetto areas that could not be escaped. These large concentrations of blacks enabled northern school boards to use a neighborhood school concept to segregate black children almost as effectively as laws segregated them in the South. (p. 236)

THIRD AND FOURTH IMMIGRATION WAVES

The interwar period between WWI and WWII began in 1918 and ended in 1939, and is called in the United States the Age of Normalcy. Americans wanted to return to the policy of isolationism and neutrality that was partly responsible for limitations on immigration that began in the 1920s. In addition, the economy was suffering from the nation-and worldwide Great Depression, meaning there were fewer jobs for immigrants. In contrast to the 1920s, during which production rose and people were working hard to improve their lives, the 1930s brought economic hardship due to high tariffs that prevented foreign countries and American people from buying U.S. goods. In addition, the Industrial Revolution had introduced new machinery that reduced the number of unskilled manufacturing jobs available. On Black Tuesday, October 29, 1929, the stock market crashed, upsetting the economy and triggering the depression era in the United States and the world. By 1932, the depth of the depression had caused over 12 million people in the United States, or one-fourth of the workforce, to be out of work. Many businesses, banks, and factories had to shut down and many individuals who were still employed had their wages reduced.

Franklin D. Roosevelt became president in 1932, with Americans expecting optimistically that he would be able to help the unemployed poor people. Roosevelt had as a philosophy the famous three R's: relief, recovery, and reform. Relief measures meant to provide direct money payments or jobs to the unemployed, and to provide mortgage loans to help farmers and homeowners in danger of losing their property. Recovery meant to provide aid to farmers, business owners, and workers to help get people back to work. About 5 million people became government employees by building roads, highways, public buildings, dams, and parks. Reform meant to develop measures to prevent a repeat of the economic depression such as to regulate businesses and banks; and to protect bank depositors, investors, consumers, the aged, children, and the unemployed. These measures restored confidence and stimulated the economy in a timely manner.

Before the start of WWII, Congress passed Neutrality Acts in 1935, 1936, and 1937. The war in Europe began on September 1, 1939, when Adolf Hitler ordered the German army to invade Poland. The major Axis countries that fought with Germany were Italy and Japan. The Allied countries, initially comprised of France and Great Britain, opposed them and later were joined by the Soviet Union and the United States. By 1940, France had been defeated by Germany, and England stood alone against the Axis powers. Public opinion in the United States began to favor intervention to help the Allies. Congress passed the Selective Service Act in 1940, and led the government to start drafting men into the army. In 1941, substantial help to England had been given already with the lend-lease of war materials. On Sunday, December 7, 1941, the Japanese attacked Pearl Harbor in Hawaii, and President Roosevelt, with the support of Congress, declared war on Japan the next day. The Allies had also received the support of the Soviet Union earlier in 1941, resulting in three strong powers. By September 1943, Italy had surrendered unconditionally. By early May 1945, Germany surrendered unconditionally. Even when faced with defeat by the stronger Allied navy, the Japanese refused to surrender unconditionally. The new U.S. president, Harry S. Truman, decided to use the powerful atomic bomb, newly developed in the United States, which resulted in Japan finally surrendering.

As a result of WWII, the United States and the Soviet Union became the two major world powers because Germany, Italy, and Japan suffered nearly complete defeat, and Great Britain and France lost large parts of their colonies and were no longer world powers. During WWII the United States started to act on giving civil rights to minority people, such as African Americans suffering from discrimination, especially in the South. Major areas of segregation limited still the right to vote, resulting in segregated schools and job discrimination for African American people. President Roosevelt established the Fair Employment Practices Committee in order to prevent discrimination by the defense industries against anyone because of "race, creed, color, or national origin." The states and some private organizations started to apply some job training programs and their own fair-employment policies.

Once WWII ended, President Truman continued the development of policy for achieving equality by appointing the Committee on Civil Rights. The committee's most important finding was that discrimination on the basis of race or religion prevents achievement of the American ideal of democracy. A major milestone was achieved in

1954 when the Supreme Court ruled in favor in the case of *Brown v. Board of Education of Topeka* (Kansas). The ruling stated "separate educational facilities are inherently unequal." In general, the court's rule was that segregated public schools were unconstitutional. The ruling was followed in 1955 by a court order to desegregate public schools. The most widely known leader of the civil rights movement was Reverend Martin Luther King, Jr., who advocated for nonviolent, or peaceful, demonstrations for changing society and its laws. He led the famous March on Washington in 1963, when both African Americans and whites marched to Washington, D.C., to try to get civil rights legislation passed. Reverend King's approach of advocating peacefully for equality of civil rights gained the support of many citizens and made it possible for the movement to become successful. The federal government passed Civil Rights Acts in 1957, 1960, 1964, and 1968 in order to guarantee equality for blacks. It passed the Voting Rights Act in 1970 to try to stop discrimination against black voters in southern states.

President John F. Kennedy supported legislation advocated by the civil rights movement, including such measures as housing, funding for education, and efforts to rid the country of poverty. President Lyndon Johnson, Kennedy's successor, continued the effort with his War on Poverty and increased the amount of money the federal government spent on social programs with the objective of forming the Great Society with equality and opportunities for everyone. In general, the decade of the 1960s brought many social changes, led by the **civil rights movement** that caused turmoil and protest and resulted in legislative and social action.

The Civil Rights Era: 1960s–1980s

The 1964 Civil Rights Act contained several important titles mandating enforcement of civil rights of minority groups. One famous social science report, the Coleman Report (1966), documented the lack of educational opportunities for the poor, and therefore served as a substantial support for the 1964 Civil Rights Act. Coleman led a research team at Johns Hopkins University in the study of the relation between economic resources in the schools and majority and minority students' academic achievement. This study found that differences in school resources were not directly connected to differences in majority and minority students' achievement per se, but were mediated to the educational backgrounds and aspirations of peer groups. Findings reported that poor minority students' academic performance improved when placed in classes with high-achieving, economically advantaged students. Thus, the Coleman Report provided data-based support for the use of desegregation as a tool to achieve educational equality opportunity for poor minority students. The most important contribution of the Coleman Report was not to offer a tangible solution to the civil rights social problem, but to open an area of social scientific inquiry for the study of the interaction of socioeconomic, racial, and academic achievement factors.

One of the civil rights being sought was achieving equality in education through desegregation, enforced through Title VI. Since the late 1960s and early 1970s, school districts were mandated to enforce this law because of its provision to withdraw federal funds from segregated school districts by the Lyndon B. Johnson administration.

Segregation in Public Schools: 1960s to the Present

Segregation in the public schools has been a social problem that continued through the 1960s, a period in which, under the influence of the civil rights movement, schools were mandated to integrate the education of mainstream and minority students, and to use "busing" as a strategy for serving both groups within the same school buildings. In this way, it was thought that the neighborhood in which the student lived would not dictate the school that the student attended; instead, students with a diverse array of ethnic and economic backgrounds could attend the same school. In reality, until today, we can see that desegregation never occurred because mainstream populations left inner-city school districts and moved to wealthier suburban school districts. Then, during the 1970s, the different minority groups representing lower SES moved to the inner-city school districts and they were offered a choice of enrolling in "magnet" schools that presented some special thematic curriculum. The schools could not solve the social problem of a disintegrating America, with its division of SES levels by ethnic, cultural, linguistic, and racial groups, of which new immigrant groups are now a part.

Following a recent visit to a magnet school, I could attest to this phenomenon of failed desegregation even as late as the current decade. This magnet school is located in the inner-city school district of a middle-size, midwestern metropolitan area and offers voluntary enrollment and busing as strategies for opening their classrooms to minority and mainstream populations.

Even though there are some capsules of wealthy and middle-income mainstream neighborhoods in this inner-city school district, the practice of neighborhood schools still prevails in conjunction with magnet schools. This particular magnet school offers several foreign language classes to students as an enticing, special thematic curriculum. However, when I visited the classrooms, I could see a majority of African American students, with a large group of other low-SES, language-minority students, some U.S.-born and others foreign-born. This latter group represents 100-plus countries and first languages other than English. However, one of the prevailing groups are the Hispanic poor new immigrants who are in need of ESL instructional programs.

When I walked through the hallways I could see a dilapidated, poorly funded school, in the remains of an old well-to-do neighborhood school, that once served middle-class mainstream students, but is now abandoned in the middle of the inner city. I left the magnet school with the uneasy sentiment that nothing has changed since the 1960s—that the history of immigrants and minority poor groups in the United States recreates itself.

In contrast, I had a rather different experience when I visited a suburban public elementary school located in a well-to-do, upper-middle-class neighborhood in the same midwestern middle-size metropolitan area. The building was brand-new, with large classrooms, a well-equipped gym, cafeteria, library, and computer laboratory; and educational materials, furniture, and computers were plentiful in each classroom. The ideal infrastructure was set up for children to learn; however, as I started visiting classrooms it was obvious to me that the ratio between teachers and students was very far from ideal. Even though personnel seemed to be experienced and highly qual-ified, teachers' aides were almost absent, and primary-level single-classroom teachers had large classrooms: they were teaching the maximum number of children allowed by the federal and state regulations. The kindergarten rooms not only had the same high ratio of students to teachers, but here to the age of students resulted in a more acute situation not conducive to learning. I found experienced and qualified kindergarten teachers who were required to teach a morning shift of 20-plus students and an afternoon shift of another group of 20-plus students, all by themselves! In this half-day kindergarten setting, 5-and-6-year-olds can receive smaller group attention from their teacher perhaps once a week, if they are lucky, during a small-group reading activity.

In this classroom environment, the physical setting was ideal, but there was not enough personnel, or a full-day program, to complement the educational experience, resulting in lowered the quality of instruction. Young children developing language and social abilities as prerequisites for high literacy skills and academic achievement across subject areas, need developmental time provided in a full-day program, as well as individualized instruction that can only be provided by a 7 or 8:1 child: teacher ratio. I observed children working on their own at smaller group tables doing "busy work" from workbooks, with no individual contact with a teacher, and disjointed from a meaningful and developmentally appropriate activity. I also observed children gathering around a teacher reading from a big book, but about half of the children were so far from the teacher that some were falling asleep and never had the chance to participate in a meaningful way. Thus, I left the school with mixed feelings: I could see plenty of economic resources invested in developing infrastructure, but this brightness was shadowed by a desperate need for increasing the number of qualified personnel. It was very painful for me to see overworked teachers trying to stretch their attention among a very large number of young children. Learning occurs within the context of human interaction, with nurturing role models and mentors acting as facilitators of learning. Learning and development cannot take place in the absence of meaningful human and social interaction.

As I reflect about my visits to the magnet public school and the suburban school in a midwest city, I realize that social problems have in reality never, ever, changed. Poverty and distance between racial and cultural groups still prevails, and reflects itself in their access to education. It does not matter how profound and long is the history of U.S. education in trying to infuse change and reform. The issue of social justice will never permeate schools unless the broader society assumes responsibility for providing access to high-quality life conditions and education to all U.S.-born and new immigrant students. In order for minority and new immigrant children to achieve in schools, U.S. society first needs to improve the life conditions in their homes, neighborhoods, and communities so they can be ready to learn and become resilient academic achievers.

Equal Educational Opportunity for the Poor

A renowned scholar, James Conant, published in 1959 a study of U.S. high schools in relation to educational opportunities for potentially gifted and talented students in the areas of science, mathematics, and English and foreign languages. In 1961,

Conant published another study of the educational needs of economically disadvantaged students in inner-city schools and economically advantaged students in suburban schools. Conant advocated for separating social class and economic background from academic ability and talent in students in both inner-city and suburban school settings. He recommended that both types of school districts offer an enriched academic track for academically talented students, and a vocational track for students of average and below-average academic ability. However, Conant's argument failed to follow the Social Rights movement philosophy, when he found that more academically talented students were found in suburban schools, and that higher dropout rates and many more low achievers prone to vocational tracks populated inner-city schools. Clearly, socioeconomic background of students was tied with their academic achievement.

This same issue of the negative effect of poverty on academic achievement was the focus of Michael Harrington's book, published in 1963, *The Other America: Poverty in the United States.* Harrington discussed the tremendous increase of poverty during the 1950s and made obvious for mainstream America the concentration of poverty among the old, African Americans, and other minority groups. In addition, Harrington highlighted the connection between poverty and differences in values and expectations for long-term economic and social improvement, resulting in a "culture of poverty." In contrast to earlier new immigrant and white mainstream poor groups who used education for their children (and even themselves) as a way out of poverty, the minority poor of the 1950s perceived themselves to be trapped in their social situation, with no hope to use education as a tool for climbing the socioeconomic ladder. The minority poor of the 1950s considerd the school system as one more social institution used to validate their inability to access mainstream society. The minority poor's experience with the school system was colored by a high dropout rate and low-quality instructional environments. As already discussed in relation to the civil rights movement, and responding to this call to attention of mainstream America made by Harrington, Lyndon B. Johnson declared a War on Poverty with the Economic Opportunity Act of 1964. One of the most important consequences of this Act was the creation of the Head Start educational programs. In this section only a brief overview of most prominent legislation affecting the education of ESL immigrant populations will be made (see Chapter 2 for further discussion).

Head Start.   The Head Start program was created with federal surplus moneys of metropolitan school districts not complying with desegregation mandates supported by Title VI of the Civil Rights Act. From its inception, Head Start had a mission to prevent school underachievement and developmental delays by providing an equal educational opportunity for poor children to enhance their cognitive, social, and physical development. Readiness for schooling through development of social competence for economically disadvantaged children is the focus of contemporary Head Start programs. Parents are supported to become competent social agents who nurture their children's development. According to Urban and Wagoner (1996), "The parent focus of the Head Start program, however, appealed to the urban poor and captured their political support . . ." (p. 311).

Elementary and Secondary Education Act. The Elementary and Secondary Education Act (ESEA) of 1965 has been the most comprehensive, influential, and costly federal education law in U.S. history. The targeted population for this federal fund was the economically disadvantaged children who were underachieving in public schools. Most of these students at risk of underachievement and dropping-out of school were concentrated in large metropolitan areas and came from minority groups, with large representations of African Americans and ESL groups. These disadvantaged, under-achieving children should be served through Title I funds, specifically allocated for serving the needs of the "educationally deprived children." The educational needs of these poor minority children could be served with Title I funds through nutrition programs, social and medical services, innovations in teaching practices, and "cultural and social enrichment" programs.

However, the urban, minority, and poor population rejected the negative connotations of terminology used and philosophy endorsed by the programs institutionalized by Title I funds. Terminology (e.g., "economically disadvantaged" and "the culture of poverty") was perceived as culturally biased by minority groups. Given its negative political response, and other redirection of federal educational funding, support for Title I programs has not been as consistent as support for Head Start program.

Bilingual Education Act of 1968 and No Child Left Behind Act of 2001: Equal Educational Opportunity for ESL Learners. The Bilingual Education Act of 1968 started the legitimization of the need to provide native-language instruction for ESL learners in order to provide equal educational opportunities for them. The Supreme Court case, *Lau v. Nichols*, resulted in a ruling for the support of bilingual education for ESL learners. This suit validated the case of unequal educational opportunities suffered by Chinese American students in a public school district in San Francisco that offered only English instruction. This social problem still persists today, with the political debate of offering non-English-language instruction for new immigrant ESL students in public schools. Many Americans still view schools as the traditional social institutions to "Americanize" or assimilate new immigrants. Minority leaders and contemporary educational data-based studies support maintenance of cultural and linguistic diversity in new immigrant and minority students, as part of the rich multicultural, multilingual, multiracial "new mainstream America." Thus, for the ESL population, the educational dilemma of reducing the achievement gap in minority students is also colored by a social and political debate.

During December 2001, the Bilingual Education Act became the No Child Left Behind (NCLB) Act for Title III. The NCLB comes as the product of 30 years of policy started under the civil rights movement of the late 1960s with the Bilingual Education Act, as a comprehensive, complete, and pervasive system that meets the needs of English-language learner (ELL) students. The NCLB Act mandate is for ELLs to learn academic English in order to achieve at grade level in all content areas. The NCLB Act also mandates that in order to measure ELLs' progress accurately in academic achievement, assessments need to be aligned with state standards. Therefore, assessment instruments need to be more discrete, and the curriculum and instruction needs to be linked with annual measurable achievement objectives, English-language proficiency assessments, and English-language proficiency standards. That is, language proficiency needs to be measured in five domains: the acquisition of language in reading, writing, speaking, listening, and comprehension. In addition, the NCLB Act for Title I requirements include the use of academic content standards that are aligned with academic achievement standards and annual measurable objectives. Both Title III and Title I requirements together enforce the need for ELLs to be immersed in English-language proficiency and academic achievement standards and annual measurable achievement objectives.

Overall, the NCLB Act for Title III offers a framework of school reform for teachers to meet the educational needs of ELLs, and *not* for children to meet the instructional needs of teachers. Title III also mandates the assessment of all limited English proficient (LEP) students in K–12 grades in U.S. public schools, with the use of an annual English language proficiency assessment for all students identified as LEP. However, states need to set technical criteria for using multiple assessments that are valid and reliable for the ELLs, and provide accommodations for the valid use of assessments with this population for a specific educational purpose. Some examples of common accommodations enforced by states are allocation of extra time for testing, small group administration, flexible scheduling, use of dictionaries, providing audio-taped instructions in the native language, providing clarifying information and simplified instructions (e.g., synonyms for unclear or idiomatic words and phrases, simplifying the language, but not "simple language"). Most important, native language testing can be used—the point for content assessment is to get to what students know in a valid and reliable way. In this manner, when evaluating our ELL students, they can be successful in learning English and another language, and in using English as an academic tool for learning content. Thus, when properly implemented by school districts, the NCLB has the potential for enforcing the proper use of valid and reliable assessments for all, and higher academic achievement and educational success for ESL immigrant students coming from low socioeconomic backgrounds.

THE NEW IMMIGRANTS OF THE 1980s, 1990s, AND 2000s

"The recognition that many big-city schools, particularly the schools that serve poor children, have become failures for almost all students has given particular urgency to the issue of school reform" (National Research Council, 1999b, p. 1). During the late 1800s, "as waves of newcomers filled the land, schooling was promoted as the way to make them American, to knit together a nation of immigrants" (p. 10). Education is still seen during the twenty-first century as a major social agent to "Americanize" immigrants, either through cultural integration or adaptation. "Since the time of the Revolution . . . the idea of improving education in order to improve society has been a powerful force" (p. 10).

The public school system has experienced an influx of different large groups of new immigrant students, first during the late 1800s and early 1900s with eastern and southern Europeans, during the Ellis Island years, and more recently since the 1980s until the present with Asians and Hispanics. From a historical perspective, Urban and Wagoner (1996) compared these two immigration trends and found

> the public schools of the late nineteenth century were not uniformly successful in assimilating immigrant children. Historically, the educational success or failure of immigrant groups is best understood by considering the cultural characteristics that made different groups more or less receptive to the culture of the school and the larger society. (p. 348)

Different cultural groups of ESL children during the Ellis Island years, such as the Jewish students, and more recently certain groups of Asian immigrant children, have had success integrating into the school culture and becoming high achievers. This is possible because the value of educational achievement is part of the cultural background of Jewish and some Asian communities. For other minority groups, this emphasis on school attainment is foreign to their rural and illiterate backgrounds, and completely off-limits to the social and educational history and realities of their home countries.

For instance, Mexican immigrant parents who are illiterate in their native and only language, Spanish, have not had access to educational opportunities in their home country. However, they may be mentored to believe in the importance of early childhood and first-language instruction for their children to achieve success in the U.S. public school system, even though it is outside of their own educational experience. Many new immigrant parents, coming from low SES groups in their home countries, may not have any prior knowledge and experience of how education may be linked to social and economic mobility for their children. In fact, among many Hispanic rural communities in Latin American, the value of hard work in agricultural and menial jobs may continue to be instilled and enforced in young boys, whereas the cultural expectation of becoming mothers and housewives remains in place for young girls. These strong cultural beliefs and expectations can provide a rationale for why teenage pregnancy is the most important factor connected to a high dropout rate in Hispanic girls in the United States.

Many young, immigrant, poor, Hispanic mothers are secluded in their homes, completely dependent on their husbands for communication and contact with the outside world. These young women have very low literacy levels in their only language, Spanish, to the point that filling out registration forms in Spanish for their preschool Head Start children becomes a very demanding task. Most of these Hispanic mothers start having children at very young ages, and continue with several pregnancies very close together. They are secluded in their homes because they cannot drive or take a drivers' exam; their level of reading skills in Spanish also tends to be very low; they are not familiar with driving on U.S. highways; and are pregnant frequently or have to care for young infants and toddlers. Several times I have experienced their desperate need to communicate with a cultural mediator, who can offer some social contact and communicate in their own native language. When I have reached out to them, either at recruitment fairs, or by following up and calling them to offer bilingual preschool services for their young children, they quickly bond and open up and do not want to hang up the phone. They call me back and are eager to come to the bilingual preschool with their children, they ask desperately for classes to help them learn English, and they are eager to learn about community resources for improving their life situations (e.g., health care, church services, school services, nonprofit organizations, etc.).

The social and economic condition of female immigrants of today is not that different from the experiences of immigrant women who came through Ellis Island. High dependency on husbands is very marked among today's immigrant Hispanic women. Because of the more culturally accepted role of men as breadwinners among rural and low SES-background immigrant Hispanics, men's contact with mainstream society through their jobs is more common. Wives rely heavily on their husbands to negotiate contact, communication, and decision making in social situations. For instance, because men typically are the only drivers in the family, they will be asked to help their wives to register the children in school, find locations on maps, learn bus routes, and so on. Even now, after the women's rights movement and legislation of the 1960s, which formed part of the civil rights movement, the gap between mainstream U.S.-born and immigrant poor women is even wider.

It takes the effort of mentors, acting as mediators between the mainstream and minority cultural value systems, for minority parents to become aware of the need for cultural adaptation. Parents' awareness of cultural values endorsed by the mainstream school culture provides a genuine opportunity for their children to become achievers, access higher education, and gain social and economic mobility.

SUMMARY AND CONCLUSIONS: OVERVIEW OF THE BOOK THEME AND RECOMMENDATIONS FOR EDUCATORS FOR BETTER SERVING ESL STUDENTS

Chapter 1 introduced the book theme by providing readers with a historical overview of the role of ESL immigrant groups in the U.S. public school system as a major cultural institution. We explored patterns of sociohistorical similarities and differences between the ESL immigrants of the Ellis Island years, primarily eastern and southern Europeans, and of contemporary Asian and Hispanic groups. Our intention was to help educators perceive the continuity of the challenges faced by serving ESL immigrant students in the past and today within a mainstream cultural institution: the school culture, which may not be responsive to the diverse cultural and linguistic educational needs of ESL students. This continuity is also present for the historical underachievement of ESL students, which is also directly connected with their lower SES backgrounds and lower degree of cultural adaptation to mainstream American society.

Our recommendations for better serving ESL students presently in the U.S. public school system are presented throughout the chapters of this book, and follow the ethnic educator philosophy endorsed by the theme of the book. We encourage educators to develop a personal connection and become empathic role models, committed advocates, and mentors for bridging the mainstream school experience and the home and community ethnic experiences of ESL students and their families. This personal connection can begin by looking into our own family or a colleague's or a friend's history, and most likely finding a connection with an ancestor who was an ESL immigrant to the United States. This personal connection is necessary for educators to establish a trusting friendship with ESL students and their families, to help them develop transcultural identities, bicognitive and bilingual minds, and bicultural souls; and most important, to become achieving productive minority (or new mainstream diverse) citizens of the United States. In fact, the ultimate realization of the "American dream" is for educators to realize that most of us are part of this dream, the creation of a country of immigrants and for immigrants. We enthusiastically invite you to join us in the following chapters, to celebrate the diversity of Americans.

REVIEW QUESTIONS

1. Identify the four immigration waves in the U.S. history, and discuss the similarities and differences of these immigration waves in terms of the social, economic, cultural adaptation, and academic achievement factors experienced by ESL immigrant students in U.S. public schools.

2. What can educators do to increase their awareness and knowledge levels of the cultural and linguistic backgrounds of their ESL immigrant students? How can making a personal connection to the large number of ESL immigrants in the history of U.S. education make a difference for teachers' expectations and attitudes toward today's ESL students?

3. How can educators help ESL students' increase their cultural adaptation to the school culture and their academic achievement? How can regular and ESL teachers collaborate to help ESL immigrant students in the mainstream classrooms?

4. Provide three examples of how poverty can affect academic achievement among ESL immigrant students. In your opinion, what is the relationship between poverty, cultural adaptation, and academic achievement among today's ESL immigrant students?

5. Do Asian and Hispanic ESL immigrant students achieve at the same levels in today's U.S. public schools? Discuss the similarities and differences in relation to cultural factors.

CRITICAL THINKING QUESTIONS

1. The concepts of *integration* and *assimilation* are key to understanding similarities and differences in the sociohistorical experiences of Ellis Island and today's Asian and Hispanic ESL immigrant's cultural adaptation experiences. Reflect about the position of the school culture in your community and whether assimilation and or integration is expected of ESL students and their families today.

2. Using Table 1.2 as a source of information, compare and identify similarities and differences between cultural expectations of U.S. public school educators during the immigration Ellis Island years and the reality of ESL students and their families today. Use the concepts of *assimilation* and *transculturation* reviewed earlier in this chapter for analyzing the expectations of educators during the Ellis Island years and of today

regarding the cultural adaptation of ESL immigrants.

3. The *Chinese Exclusionary Act of 1882* was one of the first immigration acts that restricted and prohibited the legal immigration of Asians. See Table 1.3 for other acts that followed and continued to restrict the number of Asian immigrants to the United States during the 1900s. Using the information provided in Table 1.3 and in the section on immigration quotas, reflect on the following issues: What legislated act triggered the larger numbers of Asian immigrants during the 1980s? Is that immigration trend still bringing in large numbers of ESL Asian students to the U.S. public schools? What is the number of ESL Asian students in your local community schools, in your state, in your region, in the nation? Is the number of Asian students increasing during the present decade? What are the most common countries of origin and languages spoken by Asian ESL students today?

4. After reading Cubberley's quote published in 1919 (page 00), reflect on similarities and differences between the traditional cultural assimilation of immigrants position held by defenders of the Conservative Progressive movement during the early 1900s and the schooling practices held today toward Asian and Hispanic ESL students. After reading the former section on the Conservative side of the Progressive movement and the following section on the Liberal side of the Progressive movement, think about your school building and school district's philosophy, position, and instructional practices when serving ESL students. Does this school district and building endorse cultural assimilation (Americanization through mainstream culture and language instruction—similar to the Conservative side of the Progressive movement) or transculturation (maintenance of bilingualism and biculturalism—similar to the Liberal side of the Progressive movement)?

    In addition, think about other social institutions besides the school district.

Think about the philosophical position endorsed by public media and by society. What is the message that the general public receives from U.S. public media (television programs and ads, newspapers, magazines, movies) about the influence of Asian and Hispanic immigrants on contemporary U.S. culture, economy, and institutions, such as public schools? Is the media supporting cultural *assimilation* or *transculturation*? Pay attention to public media and share with your classmates two examples of images of contemporary ESL immigrant groups portrayed by media (such as newspaper articles or a television program—for example, *The Brothers Garcia* or *Dora The Explorer*).

5. An illustration of the specific case of cultural and economic factors affecting school performance among immigrant children in Chicago during the 1850s through the 1930s is presented in Chapter 1. This case provides an example of a series of educational reform movements and crises that have persisted in the history of U.S. education, in relation to the major challenge of educating the ESL students since the 1800s until the present. Think about ways in which you can use the summary of research studies and historical information presented in Chapter 1 to dispel the myth that former European immigrant groups with ESL backgrounds did well in the U.S. public school system. Identify the most commonly held myths held by educators about former ESL immigrant students, in relation to how long it took for them to learn English and how difficult their cultural adaptation experience was to the American school culture. Are these myths in touch with the historical reality presented in Chapter 1? How can educators help to dispel these myths about the cultural adaptation experiences of former ESL immigrants, and help the general public gain a more realistic view? How can educators help ESL students to perform at high levels in school?

6. Use the example of the preschool Hispanic girl provided in the text to reflect about different cultural adaptation patterns

experienced by immigrant ESL parents and their children. How are ESL children's experiences in the school setting similar or different from situations experienced at home, while interacting with their mother, father, and younger and older siblings? Think of some specific examples of similarities and differences between home and school experiences, such as language use, feeding habits, childrearing values, religious practices, and so on. Do first-born and/or single ESL children have different home experiences than children with older siblings? How can educators help ESL children bridge the cultural

and linguistic gap experienced between school and home settings?

7. Read the comparison of the lower- and middle-class public schools presented by the authors, and reflect on your own experience with the influence of students' backgrounds such as social class, socioeconomic status, and cultural and linguistic diversity on their public education experience. Think of some specific examples of ESL students and the kind of educational resources and personnel available to them in their public school experience.

ACTIVITIES

Visit the companion Web site, www.ablongman.com/ gonzalez1e, for additional information and activities.

1. The quotes presented in Box 1.1 are excerpts from an interview conducted with a female international graduate student from Taiwan, who was majoring in educational psychology at a large state university in the Southwest. Kim (pseudonym) participated in a case study reported by Gonzalez (in 2004). Read the quotes presented in Box 1.1 and discuss whether Kim's experiences represent *assimilation* and/or *transculturation* as a cultural adaptation process to the American culture. Explain the rationale for your choice of cultural adaptation process.

2. In order to gain awareness and make a personal connection with the sociohistorical reality of the presence of ESL students in the U.S. public education, interview an educator (e.g., a colleague teacher or a classmate), a family member (e.g., a parent, aunt or uncle, or grandparent), a neighbor, or a friend who has an ancestor who came through Ellis Island. Questions need to focus on their linguistic and cultural background, their education prior to and after immigration to the United States, their economic situation, living conditions, and

family situation. The questions in Box 1.1 can be used for the interview activity. Bring the interview information to class and draw some patterns by comparing the stories compiled by your classmates about Ellis Island immigrants. If possible also gather pictures, documents, media in formation, or other objects that represents the social, cultural, and linguistic situation of Ellis Island and today's immigrants.

3. Visit the companion Web site which provides some biographies of famous Ellis Island immigrants, and continue your search for other supporting documents that you can find online and/or in your local library, such as biographies and history books, magazines and newspapers of the time, pictures, and so on. Study the lives of these gifted immigrants and identify three patterns of social, cultural, and economic contributions made by these Ellis Island immigrants. Discuss how the United States as a nation benefited from the talents of these eastern and southern European immigrants, and how their cultural background contributed to create some uniquely American cultural traits.

4. Using the Ellis Island Web site <http:// www.internationalchannel.com/education/

ellis/mentalinspection.htm>, or our companion Web site, reflect on some parallels between the "survival of the fittest" philosophy of the social Darwinism era of the early 1900s represented in the mental testing performed in Ellis Island and today's standardized testing used for ESL students in the U.S. public school system. What may be some cultural and linguistic flaws in testing that make ESL students perform poorly in academic achievement and intelligence areas? Are these cultural and linguistic flaws in testing related to the higher incidence of ESL students in special education placements, especially among learning disabilities and language disorders categories? How can classroom teachers help prevent these problems in testing flaws and overrepresentation of ESL students in special education?

5. Some interview quotes from international graduate students in a large southwestern state university (Gonzalez, 2001) are provided in Box 1.2 as illustrations of *cognitive dissonance* in the adaptation process to American culture, and the experience of living "between two value systems." In Box 1.2, quotes from four case studies have been selected. Victor, the first case, illustrates the supporting role of their children in their cultural adaptation process to U.S. college culture. Alejandra, the second case, provides an example of advantages and disadvantages of academic cultures perceived in the United States and her home country. Job provides an example of gaining cultural awareness through exposure to diverse cultural value systems. Finally, Leonardo can identify the source of challenges as the conflict in behaviors and values between American and his original cultures.

    As you read the quotes in Box 1.2, identify some of the challenges these international students went through during their cultural adaptation process. Discuss the particular behaviors and cultural values that they identified as the source of cognitive dissonance and what coping strategies they used to help them adapt to the American way of life.

6. Some recorded interviews with high school students, conducted by the first author in a public school located in a mixed suburban neighborhood in a metropolitan area of the Midwest, are provided in the companion Web site for the book. In Box 1.3, we provide some quotes for illustrating the cultural adaptation process of a Hispanic high school student, Melissa (pseudonym), as she experienced some *cognitive dissonance* when comparing some cultural values of her home country, Peru, with behaviors and values perceived in the U.S. school culture and her classmates.

    Read the summary of Melissa's interview provided in Box 1.3 and use it as an example for reflecting on the challenges she encountered as she was trying to learn academic and social English and to adapt to the American school culture. Think about the sources of the cognitive dissonance that she experienced. What were some of the school experiences that puzzled her? What were the educational needs that she felt went unfulfilled? Think about how teachers can help ESL students better cope with their adaptation process. How can teachers reduce the level of cognitive dissonance that ESL students may experience?

7. Enlist one of the high school ESL students in your community, or a neighbor or friend who is a recent ESL immigrant to the United States for a brief interview. Ask him or her some questions about the reasons to immigrate, and his or her perceptions about the advantages and disadvantages of living in the United States versus his or her former home country's lifestyle. Also, ask questions about whether they go back and visit their home country and, if so, how they feel during their reentry experience in their home country and then back to the United States. Some questions you can ask about their cultural identity include: Have they experienced any changes in how they feel about the values, beliefs, habits, traditions, food, dress style, and general lifestyle of their country of origin? Have they adopted new ways of thinking and acting? Do they feel

comfortable when visiting their country of origin? Do they feel as though they "belong" when they come back to the United States? How have their cultural identities changed from when they first came to the United States in comparison to their present self? Share the summary of your interview with classmates and come up with some patterns of changes of cultural identities among ESL immigrants.

GLOSSARY

advocate or advocacy   When a person represents the best interests of a protégé, or in this case an ESL student, in order to help him or her to achieve maximum potential and enjoy the right for an equal educational opportunity. Advocates, such as educators, can become role models and show commitment to nurture and support the learning process of ESL students within and outside the school setting, such as also providing support for their family and home lives.

assimilation or Americanization   The process of adoption of the language and cultural practices of the place of immigration (if the United States, then the term *Americanization* is applied) by newcomers. Assimilation means to internalize or assimilate new behavioral and thinking patterns from the new cultural and linguistic models experienced in the new setting.

civil rights movement era   The decade of the 1960s brought tremendous public interest and protest, resulting in major policy changes representing the civil rights of minority groups in the United States, such as African Americans, Hispanics, Asians, and Native Americans. Some of these policy changes enforced educational rights for minority students, resulting in the Bilingual Education Act during the late 1960s.

cultural adaptation process   The process of becoming familiar with new cultural and linguistic practices and behaviors, lifestyles, and value and belief systems. The ability to change behavioral and thinking patterns to become part of a new society or community, such as a school or neighborhood. Cultural adaptation can result in assimilation or transculturation processes.

Ellis Island years   The period between the 1850s and 1950s when millions of Eastern and Southern Europeans entered the United States as immigrants through Ellis Island, the gateway and processing center established in front of the port of New York City. After its closure, Ellis Island was designated as a National Park, and became a museum during the early 1990s, which preserves and exhibits immigration documents as part of U.S. history. See link to Ellis Island Museum in the companion Web site for the book.

integration   *See* transculturalism

personal connection   The book theme presented in Chapter 1 encourages educators to develop a "personal connection," meaning to gain awareness of the United States as a country founded by immigrants, many of whom have learned English as a second language (ESL). More than one third of today's U.S. citizens are descendants of at least one ancestor who was an ESL immigrant, who came through Ellis Island within the period of the 1850s until the 1950s. By making a personal connection with the sociohistorical reality of the presence of ESL students in U.S. public education, educators can build rapport and become empathic and committed advocates for better serving and meeting the culturally and linguistically diverse needs of ESL students and their families.

school culture   The particular set of expectations and value and belief systems, expressed in behavior styles endorsed by administrators and educators at a school system, which is the result of mainstream society's views about the objective of education as a social institution. School culture also affects training programs for educators in higher education, and how mainstream parents socialize their young children to show school-readiness behaviors (e.g., socialization skills such as the values of assertiveness and independence, and particular academic skills such as traditional nursery songs and stories).

sociohistorical conditions   Conditions in society that characterize certain time periods, such as historical events in certain decades (e.g., Civil War, WWI, depression era, civil rights movement, etc.). Conditions in society within certain time periods are also characterized by economic, social, cultural, and technological factors (e.g., WWII changing the role of women in society and generating social power for them as breadwinners).

transculturation   The process of integrating new cultural and linguistic behaviors and ways of thinking into previous cultural identities. The idea of transculturation for new eastern and southern European immigrants of the time was endorsed by John Dewey during the 1920s as a part of the Cultural Pluralism and social justice movement. This book also endorses Pluralism because the result is a stronger and well-adapted individual who knows when and in what social contexts to use his or her home culture and language, and when to show the new cultural and linguistic patterns learned. The new, emerging identity is stronger because the individual can continue developing and using his or her language and culture and origin, and in addition he or she learns new cultural concepts and ways of thinking, becoming bicognitive; develops new cultural behaviors, becoming bicultural; and learns a second language (L2), becoming bilingual.

REFERENCES

Abbott, E. (1924). *Immigration: Select documents and case records*. Chicago: University of Chicago; reissued by Arno Press and the *New York Times*, American Immigration Collection, 1969.

Abbott, E. (1936). *The tenements of Chicago, 1908–1935*. Chicago: University of Chicago.

American Federationist. (1916). *American foreign workers*, XXIII, August, pp. 690.

Bayles, E. E. (1961). Sketch for a study of the growth of American educational thought and practice. *History of Education Quarterly, 1*(3), 43–49.

Bureau of Citizenship and Immigration Services (2003). www.immigration.gov/graphics/services/natz/natzsamp.htm

Carlson, R. A. (1970). Americanization as an early twentieth-century adult education movement. History of Education Quarterly, 10(4), 440–464.

Cohen, D. K. (1970). Immigrants and the schools. *Review of Educational Research, 40*, 13–27.

Cole, D. B. (1963). *Immigrant city: Lawrence, Massachusetts, 1845–1921*. Chapel Hill: University of South Carolina Press.

Coleman, J. S., Campbell, E. Q., Hobson, C. J., McPortland, J., Mood, A. M., Weinfeld, F. D., & York, R. L. (1966). *Equality of educational opportunity*. Washington, D.C.: U.S. Government Printing Office.

Conant, J. B. (1959). *The American high school today: A first report to interested citizens*. New York: McGraw-Hill.

Conant, J. B. (1961). *Slums and suburbs: A commentary on schools in metropolitan areas*. New York: McGraw-Hill.

Cubberley, E. P. (1919). *Public education in the United States*. Boston: Houghton Mifflin.

Daniels, R. (1990). *Coming to America: A history of immigrants and ethnicity in American life*. New York: HarperCollins.

Drake, W. E. (1961). Some implications of the institutionalization of American education. *History of Education Quarterly, 1*(1), 41–47.

Ellwood, C. A. (1913). *Sociology and modern social problems*. New York: American Book Company.

Ernst, R. (1965). *Immigrant life in New York City: 1825–1863.* Port Washington, NY: Ira J. Friedman, 1949, first published, reissued by same publisher 1965.

Ferrie, J. P. (1994). The wealth accumulation of Antebellum European immigrants to the U.S.: 1840–1860. *Journal of Economic History, 54*(12), 145–167.

Galenson, D. W. (1995). Determinants of the school attendance of boys in early Chicago. *History of Education Quarterly, 35*(4), 371–400.

Gans, H. (1962). *The urban villagers.* New York: Random House Vintage Books.

Gonzalez, V. (2004). *Second language learning and cultural adaptation processes in graduate international students in U.S. universities.* New York: University Press of America.

Gonzalez, V. (2001a). Immigration: Education's story past, present, and future. *College Board Review, 193,* 24–31.

Gonzalez, V. (2001b). The role of socioeconomic and sociocultural factors in language-minority children's development: An ecological research view. *Bilingual Research Journal, 25*(1, 2), 1–30 (adapted and reprinted by the College Board, available in their Web page www.collegeboard.com/about/association/academic/2000_2001_scholars.html#gonzalez)

Hampel, R. L., Johnson, W. R., Plank, D. N., Ravitch, D., Tyach, D., & Cuban, L. (1996). Forum: History and education reform. *History of Education Quarterly, 36*(4), 473–502.

Handlin, O. (1951). *The uprooted.* New York: Grosset & Dunlap.

Harrington, M. (1963). *The other America: Poverty in the United States.* Baltimore, MD: Penguin Books.

Heffron, J. M. (1991). Intelligence testing and its pitfalls: The making of an American tradition. *History of Education Quarterly, 31*(1), 81–88.

Hodge, G. B. (1912). *Association educational work for men and boys.* New York: Association Press.

Hughes, G. S. (1925). Mothers in industry: Wage earning by mothers in Philadelphia. New York: New Republic.

Kellor, F. A. (1914). Who is responsible for the immigrant? *The Outlook, CVI,* April 25, pp. 912–913.

Kohn, M. (1969). *Class and conformity: A study in values.* Homewood, IL: Irwin.

More, L. B. (1907). *Wage earner's budgets: A study of standards and costs of living in New York City.* New York: Henry Holt and Co.

National Research Council. (1999b). *Improving student learning.* Washington, D.C.: National Academy Press.

Odencrantz, L. C. (1919). *Italian women in industry.* New York: Russell Sage Foundation.

Olneck, M. R., & Lazerson, M. (1974). The school achievement of immigrant children: 1900–1930. *History of Education Quarterly, 14*(4), 453–482.

Perlmann, J. (1988). *Ethnic differences and social structure among Irish, Italians, Jews, and Blacks in an American city, 1880–1935.* New York: Cambridge University Press.

Piper, T. (1998). *Language and learning: The home and school years.* Upper Saddle River. NJ: Prentice Hall.

Pope, C. L. (1989). Household on the American frontier: The distribution of income and wealth in Utah: 1850–1900. In D. W. Galenson (Ed.), *Markets in history: Economics studies of the past* (pp. 168–172). Cambridge, England: Cambridge University Press.

Psathas, G. (1957). Ethnicity, social class, and adolescent independence. *American Sociological Review, 22*(3), 415–423.

Rosen, B. (1956). The achievement syndrome: A psychocultural dimension of social stratification. *American Psychological Review, 21*(1), 123–137.

Safford, V. (1925). *Immigration problems: Personal experiences of an official.* New York: Dood, Mead, & Co.

Senate Document. (1912). *History of women in trade unions, Vol. 10.*

Senate Documents. (1912). *Infant mortality and its relation to the employment of mothers, 645,* Vol. 12.

Thomas, W. I., & Znaniecki, F. (1958). *The Polish peasant in Europe and America.* Reissued by Dover Publications (originally published by Chicago: University of Chicago Press, 1918).

Urban, W., & Wagoner, J. (1996). *American education: A history.* New York: McGraw-Hill.

U.S. Immigration Commission. (1911). *Reports, vol. 1,* p. 761; vol. 26, pp. 226, 318, 404, 423, 577.

Weatherford, D. (1995). *Foreign and female: Immigrant women in America (1840–1939).* New York: Facts on File.

Whyte, W. F. (1943). *Street-corner society.* Chicago: Chicago University Press.

UNDERSTANDING THE DEMOGRAPHICS AND POLICIES OF LANGUAGE DIVERSITY IN THE UNITED STATES

LEARNING OBJECTIVES

1. Understand the role of the demographic increase within the social, historical, linguistic, cultural, and educational realities
2. Identify the legal and policy implications of the demographic changes for teacher qualifications and curriculum standards
3. Recognize the sociocultural, historical, and policy background of language contact and language attitudes

PREVIEW QUESTIONS

1. What are the most important demographic trends?
2. Which federal policies have been recognized as the most significant for the education of English-as-a-second language (ESL) students?
3. How do transitional bilingual education programs compare with two-way bilingual programs?
4. What are the most important issues of the No Child Left Behind legislation in terms of accountability and teacher quality?
5. How can you implement the TESOL standards in a content area of your choice? Provide a detailed description.

Chapter 2 provides an overall view of demographics for ESL students in the United States based on recent census figures with emphasis on sociocultural, historical, linguistic, and economic factors documented as important contributors in educational outcomes by demographic data, as well as by previous research and practice.

The first section emphasizes the role of external factors on ESL students' learning, development, and academic achievement to understand the effect of educational structure factors. It examines the latest U.S. census demographics, which include a majority of "minorities" within the decade in the most populated states. It presents desegregated demographic information in relation to ESL students' educational, social, economic, cultural, and linguistic realities. It examines specific demographics in the education of ESL students—enrollment, language backgrounds, academic achievement, language of instruction.

The second section discusses the historical perspective and examines the educational response to the demographic increase of the ESL student population nationwide and the implications for policy and practice. It provides an overview of legislation and focuses on legal aspects, the kinds of instructional programs to serve ESL students, policy mandates and their implementation, teacher quality issues such as certification, and content area and language standards and benchmarks to serve this student population.

The third section is twofold; it examines recent socioeconomic, educational research and demographics on the Hispanic population growth, the largest minority group in the nation: first, second, and third generations; language status; socioeconomic status; and cultural traits. This section also addresses the sociocultural and historical background of language contact and language attitudes toward the ESL students' native languages in education and the implications of its long-term effect in U.S. society.

The position and perspective of Chapter 2 and the entire book is access and equity in education for linguistically and culturally diverse students. We want to stimulate all educators and policy makers to recognize the demographic imperative and attend to the needs of ESL students. Many ESL students need to learn not only English, but also a new culture and school system. We want to encourage sensitization and acceptance of the multilingual and multicultural reality extant in the United States, and to value and celebrate diversity.

Therefore, Chapter 2 is connected to the second theme of the book because it aims to increase teachers' understanding in (1) the most recent demographics on ESL students affecting the way schools and programs are being implemented, and (2) ways to respond to the demographic imperative. By increasing educators' and policy makers' understanding, we also intend to infuse awareness and sensitivity to the socioeducational reality in classrooms with ESL students. We aim to encourage and support their efforts to attend to ESL students' needs and to become advocates for these students.

THE DEMOGRAPHIC SHIFT AND PERSPECTIVE: GROWTH OF THE LINGUISTICALLY AND CULTURALLY DIVERSE POPULATION

Public school enrollments are being transformed by an increase in the number of ESL students who bring a richness of linguistic and cultural diversity with them to school (Garcia, 1999). The U.S. population grew at a rate of 17 percent from 1980 to 2000. Hispanics are the fastest-growing group and represented 11.7 percent of the U.S. population in 2000 and is projected to double to 24.3 percent by 2050 (National Clearinghouse for Bilingual Education, 1999). Asia, Latin America, and Africa have replaced Europe as the main source of newcomers (Ovando, Collier, & Combs, 2003). The educational significance of this demographic shift is that many immigrants are children, or are adults who give birth to children, who enter schools speaking little or no English. An estimated 9.9 million of the total 45 million school-aged children live in households in which languages other than English are spoken (National Center for Education Statistics, 2003).

The number of 5- to 24-year-olds who were reported speaking a language other than English at home has increased dramatically in the past twenty years—from 6.3 million in 1979 to 13.7 million in 1999 (NCES, 2003). Thus, in 1979, 8 percent of all 5- to 24-year-olds spoke a language other than English at home, compared with 17 percent in 1999. Of those who spoke a language other than English at home in 1979, 2.2 million (or 3 percent of the total population) spoke English with difficulty, compared with 4.5 million (6 percent of the total population) in 1999. From 1979 to 1998, the population of 5- to 24-year-olds increased by 6 percent, whereas the population of those who spoke another language at home increased by 118 percent during this period; those who spoke a language other than English at home and spoke English with difficulty increased by 110 percent.

INCREASE OF THE FOREIGN-BORN POPULATION

The United States has become increasingly multicultural since the middle of the twentieth century. Prior to 1965, when Congress abolished the national-origins quota system, Europe was the major source of immigrants to the country. However, by the 1980s about 85 percent of immigrants were coming from Third World countries—Latin America, Asia, and Africa (Crawford, 1999). Since 1970 the foreign-born population has increased rapidly due to large-scale immigration, mainly from Latin America and Asia. Table 2.1 illustrates this increase, from 9.6 million in 1970 to 14.1 million in 1980, and from 19.8 million in 1990 to 28.4 million in 2000 (U.S. Census Bureau, 2001).

Immigrants have continued to flow rapidly into the United States By 2000, the Census Bureau estimated the nation's total foreign-born population at 30 million, or roughly 11 percent of the 281 million residents. That count included 35.5 million Hispanics nationwide. The continued influx of Asian immigrants, reported at

TABLE 2.1   U.S. Total and Foreign-Born Population: 1970–2000

YEAR	U.S. TOTAL	U.S. FOREIGN-BORN
1970	203,210	9,619 (4.7%)
1980	226,546	14,079 (6.2%)
1990	248,791	19,767 (7.9%)
2000	281,421	28,379 (10.1%)

**TABLE 2.2   Ethnic Composition of U.S.
Foreign-Born Populations**

YEAR	HISPANICS	ASIANS	EUROPEANS
1970	1,803 (18.7%)	24,887* (0.26%)	5,740 (59.6%)
1980	4,372 (31%)	2,539 (18%)	5,149 (36.6%)
1990	8,407 (42.5%)	4,979 (25.1%)	4,350 (22%)
2000	14,477 (51%)	7,246 (25.5%)	4,255 (15.3%)

*In hundreds

25.5 percent of the total foreign-born population (Lollock, 2001) led the Census Bureau to project that San Francisco would soon become the second major U.S. city, after Honolulu, with a higher Asian than white population (McCormick, 2000). Table 2.2 illustrates the ethnic compositions of the foreign-born populations and the percentages of increases during the last four decades of Hispanics, Asians, and Europeans.

ESL STUDENTS' PUBLIC SCHOOL ENROLLMENT LEVELS

Kindler (2002) has reported that ESL enrollment levels in the United States continued to increase in 2000–2001, both in absolute numbers and as a percentage of the total student enrollment. She estimates that 4,584,946 ESL students were enrolled in public schools, representing approximately 9.6 percent of the total school enrollment of students in the nation (47,665,483) in pre-kindergarten (Pre-K) though grade 12 (NCES, 2002a). Over 67 percent of all ESL students were enrolled at the elementary level, where they accounted for 11.7 percent of the total school enrollment. Table 2.3 presents the ESL students enrollment as compared to the total enrollment in the elementary and secondary school levels and the percentages of ESL students for each level.

The reported number of ESL students enrolled grew by 3.8 percent from the 1999–2000 school year, and their representation as a percentage of total school enrollment increased by 3.1 percent. Since the 1990–1991 school year, the ESL students

**TABLE 2.3   Summary of ESL Students' Enrollment by Levels
of Schooling: 2000–2001**

LEVEL OF SCHOOL	ESL STUDENTS' ENROLLMENT	TOTAL ENROLLMENT	% ESL STUDENTS
Elementary (Pre-K–Grade 6)	3,086,204	26,365,875	11.7%
Secondary (Grades 7–12)	1,424,329	20,780,160	6.9%
Other, Not Specified	74,413	519,448	14.3%
Total	4,584,946	47,665,483	9.6%

population has burgeoned approximately 105 percent, while the general school popu-lation has grown only 12 percent (Kindler, 2002; NCES, 2003).

Numbers of ESL Students in the United States

California has the largest number of ESL students enrolled in public schools and repre-sents one third of the national ESL students enrollment, with 1,511,646, followed by Puerto Rico (598,063), Texas (570,022), Florida (254,517), Illinois (140,528), and Arizona (135,248). California alone represents one fourth of the total national ESL stu-dents enrollment. The states with the highest percentages of total enrollments of ESL students are California (25 percent), New Mexico (19.9 percent), Arizona (15.4 percent), Alaska (15 percent), Texas (14 percent), and Nevada (11.8 percent) (Kindler, 2002).

Numbers of ESL Students by Grade

The ESL students enrollment in the nation is concentrated in the early elementary grades. Over 44 percent of all ESL students are enrolled in Pre-K through grade 3, with a decreasing number of ESL students in the succeeding grades. Over a third (35 percent) of ESL students are enrolled in the middle grades (4–8), and only 19 percent are enrolled at the high school level.

ESL Students' Language Backgrounds

There are 460 languages spoken by ESL students nationwide (Kindler, 2002). Spanish is the first language of the great majority of ESL students (79.2 percent), followed by Vietnamese (2 percent), Hmong (1.6 percent), Cantonese (1 percent), and Korean (1 percent). All other groups each represented less than 1 percent of the ESL students' population. Languages with more than 10,000 speakers include Arabic, Armenian, Chuukese, French, Haitian Creole, Hindi, Japanese, Khmer, Lao, Mandarin, Marshallese, Navajo, Polish, Portuguese, Punjabi, Russian, Serbo-Croatian, Tagalog, and Urdu. ESL students identified as "Chinese" and "Native American" also numbered over 10,000 each. Table 2.4 illustrates the estimated rank of the language spoken by ESL students with the numbers and percentages for the five top groups.

TABLE 2.4   Estimated Language Backgrounds of ESL Students: 2000–2001

RANK	LANGUAGE	PERCENTAGES OF ESL STUDENTS
1	Spanish	79.045%
2	Vietnamese	1.953%
3	Hmong	1.555%
4	Chinese, Cantonese	1.021%
5	Korean	0.966%

TABLE 2.5   ESL Student Population Changes in Five States: 1991–1992 and 2001–2002

NO.	STATE	1991–1992 NUMBER OF ESL STUDENTS	2001–2002 NUMBER OF ESL STUDENTS	PERCENTAGE CHANGE
1	Georgia	7,955	61,307	671%
2	North Carolina	7,026	52,835	652%
3	Nebraska	1,856	12,451	571%
4	South Carolina	1,466	7,004	378%
5	Tennessee	2,636	12,422	371%

The percentages of the ESL students population have tripled in 24 states in a ten-year span. Table 2.5 describes the five states with the largest ESL students' population percentage increase from the 1991–1992 to the 2001–2002 school years.

How Do ESL Students Fare in School?

Policies and regulations regarding ESL students' retention, classification, and assessment can vary greatly across states and school districts (Kindler, 2002). Therefore, generalizing to the nation is very difficult. Kindler's data come from 45 states that reported retention data in Grades 7 to 12 to the U.S. Department of Education in 2000–2001, and reveal that, for the most part, ESL students do not fare well in school.

Retention of ESL Students.   In the 2000–2001 school years, approximately 9.1 percent of secondary school ESL students, Grades 7 to 12, was not promoted to the next grade. Table 2.6 summarizes the numbers and percentages of ESL students retained and reclassified across the nation.

According to Kindler (2002), Oregon reported the highest retention rate at nearly 21 percent. Other states retaining over 10 percent ESL students include Florida (18.2 percent), Hawaii (17.9 percent), North Carolina (15 percent), Virginia (14.6 percent), Nevada (12 percent), Pennsylvania (10.7 percent), Texas (10.4 percent), and Illinois (10.4 percent).

TABLE 2.6   Summary of Retention of ESL Students at the Secondary Level—Grades 7–12, 2000–2001

INDICATOR	RESULTS FROM 41 STATES	PERCENTAGE
Students Retained	48,060	9.1%
Students Reclassified	363,720	10.4%

Reclassification of ESL Students.   In 2002–2001, more than one out of every ten ESL students was determined (reclassified) to possess the English proficiency to participate fully in the regular all-English, mainstream program. States and districts relied on several methods and tests to assess a student's readiness to enter the regular all-English program. Kindler (2002) points to the following criteria: student records and grades, teacher observation, informal assessment, formal assessment tests (e.g., LAS, Woodcock-Muñoz, and SAT9), state achievement tests, teacher interviews, parent information, referrals, and home language surveys.

Reclassification rates vary by grade (Kindler, 2002). Rates are lowest in Grades K-2 and in Grade 9 when ESL students are entering school systems and may have little or no experience with academic English. Rates are highest in Grades 3 and 5. One out of every 6 ESL students is reclassified. For the most part reclassification rates are high from upper elementary grades through Grade 12, with the exception of Grade 9. Maryland reported the greatest proportion of ESL students reclassified, at over 31 percent. States with high classification rates of 15 percent or more include Hawaii, Iowa, Kansas, New Jersey, New Mexico, and Virginia. States with low classification rates of 5 percent or less include Idaho, Mississippi, Montana, Oklahoma, Vermont, West Virginia, and Wisconsin.

ESL Students' Reading Comprehension.   Kindler (2002) reiterates that there are very little data available with respect to reading assessment in the native language. Only thirteen states were able to report on native language assessment. The variability of assessment measures used by states make it difficult to interpret available data and impossible to make a cross-state comparison. Since states only conduct assessments in selected grades and are not required to specify which grades are tested, it is impossible to define the ESL population eligible for assessment. Kindler calculates that approximately 45 percent ESL students are tested in English and 4.3 percent are tested in the native language.

Only 18.7 percent of the ESL students assessed scored above the state-established norm in English reading comprehension. Of the 13 states that were able to report on ESL students' success in native language reading comprehension assessments, 57.4 percent of ESL students assessed scored above the state-established norm. Commonly used tests administered to assess English reading comprehension were the Language Assessment Scales (LAS) and Terra Nova. Three states reported native language reading comprehension tests: Spanish LAS and Spanish Assessment of Basic Education (SABE). States also reported they used state-designed tests.

Language of Instruction.   According to Kindler (2002), 22.7 percent of ESL students are receiving native language instruction compared to 54 percent of ESL students receiving English-only instruction. As expected, the use of the native language for instruction is most frequently incorporated at the early elementary levels with English becoming most prevalent in the upper elementary and secondary schools. Table 2.7 presents a summary of the language of instruction based on Kindler's survey. It includes the ESL students enrollment by grade level, the language of instruction—either native language instruction or English-only instruction—for ESL students and the percentages.

TABLE 2.7   Language of Instruction for ESL Students by Grade: 2000–2001

GRADE	ESL STUDENTS ENROLLMENT	NATIVE LANGUAGE INSTRUCTION	ENGLISH-ONLY INSTRUCTION	NOT REPORTED
Pre-Kindergarten	70,591	41,254 (58.4%)	21,214 (30.1%)	8,123 (11.5%)
Kindergarten	233,122	114,331 (49%)	105,318 (45.2%)	13,473 (5.8%)
Grade 1	246,939	123,738 (50.1%)	108,723 (44%)	14,478 (5.9%)
Grade 2	224,455	112,731 (50.2%)	98,473 (43.9%)	13,251 (5.9%)
Grade 3	201,008	100,925 (50.2)	88,321 (43.9%)	11,762 (5.9)
Grade 4	169,421	78,069 (46.1%)	81,037 (47.8%)	10,315 (6.1%)
Grade 5	144,778	63,190 (43.6%)	72,826 (50.3%)	8,762 (6.1%)
Grade 6	123,543	37,366 (30.2%)	76,778 (62.1%)	9,399 (7.6%)
Grade 7	118,618	30,683 (25.9%)	74,972 (63.2%)	12,963 (10.9%)
Grade 8	108,994	28,140 (25.8%)	68,542 (62.9%)	12,312 (11.3%)
Grade 9	133,124	30,970 (23.3%)	84,800 (63.7%)	17,354 (13%)
Grade 10	100,451	24,782 (24.7%)	61,407 (61.1%)	14,262 (14.2%)
Grade 11	69,570	17,018 (24.5%)	43,722 (62.8%)	8,830 (12.7%)
Grade 12	55,820	13,639 (24.4%)	33,177 (59.4%)	9,004 (16.1%)
Ungraded	22,274	4,405 (19.8%)	11,811 (53%)	6,058 (27.2%)
Unspecified	2,562,238	218,467 (8.5%)	1,439,463 (56.2%)	904,308 (35.3%)
Total	5,584,946	1,039,708 (22.7%)	2,470,584 (53.9%)	1,074,654 (23.4%)

Policy decisions relating to the language of instruction are made at the national, state and district/school levels. In the following eight states more than half of ESL students receive instruction incorporating the native language: Connecticut, Idaho, Illinois, Kansas, Massachusetts, Michigan, New Jersey, and New Mexico. In the following 10 states English is the exclusive language of instruction for more than 95 percent of ESL students: Alabama, Georgia, Maryland, Missouri, Nebraska, Oklahoma, South Carolina, Vermont, Virginia, and West Virginia.

THE DEMOGRAPHIC IMPERATIVE AND EDUCATIONAL RESPONSE: LEGAL FRAMEWORKS AND POLICIES TO MEET THE NEEDS OF ESL STUDENTS

The legal frameworks and policies of the federal government and states reflect deliberate efforts to affect language education and the functions of the non-English languages spoken in the country. Although there have been scattered historical instances—usually private but occasionally public—of bilingual education programs in bilingual communities, the initial sanction for such programs came through the **Bilingual Education Act** of 1968 under the Title VII of the Elementary and Secondary Education Act (Crawford, 1999). This act had been stimulated by the court challenges brought by citizens or citizens' groups claiming discrimination on the basis of the 1964 Civil Rights Act. The 1964 Civil Rights Act, in turn, had been engendered by court decisions brought by plaintiffs claiming discrimination on the basis of violations of their rights to equal educational opportunities as guaranteed by the Fourteenth Amendment to the Constitution.

In other words, there would be no bilingual education policies and practices and probably only private or miniscule public bilingual education programs in the United States were it not for the individual efforts of private citizens challenging an existing state of social affairs in relation to an abstract principle voiced in the Constitution (Minaya-Rowe, 1988). Furthermore, it is evident that not just one challenge and not just one precedent-setting decision would have been sufficient to establish bilingual education policies and programs nationally. The process has had to be repeated in the various localities where **bilingualism** or non-English **monolingualism** (e.g., Spanish monolingualism or Chinese monolingualism) is present. The first court decisions led Congress to pass the Education Act that directed the establishment of bilingual education programs. However, even with the law on the books, subsequent actions have been necessary to get programs started in specific localities or to challenge the validity of the program of a specific school district as conforming to the aims of the court-directed mandate. States have also implemented policies and their own bilingual education programs.

The Title VII reauthorizations of the Bilingual Education Act of 1974, 1978, 1984, and 1988 for bilingual program funding purposes reviewed and expanded the definitions for the eligibility of all children of limited-English-speaking ability. The Title VII reauthorization of 1994 made important contributions to school reform efforts to attend to the needs of ESL students through the Improving America's Schools Act (IASA) and its companion legislation, Goals 2000: Educate America Act. IASA broke with the compensatory, remedial mind-set in serving ESL students endorsed by previous legislations. For the first time, it gave priority in federal funding to ESL students programs whose goals included proficient bilingualism and **biliteracy** along with academic achievement in English. The law reflected research findings demonstrating that the most effective approaches seek to develop rather than replace the ESL students' native-language skills, while teaching English through academic content rather than through instruction in discrete language skills (Crawford, 1999; Tse, 2001).

The 2001 No Child Left Behind (NCLB) federal legislation stresses greater accountability for results. NCLB aims to close the achievement gap by measuring adequate yearly progress on test scores. Under this new law, Title VII becomes Title III and the Bilingual Education Act has been renamed as the English Language Acquisition, Language Enhancement, and Academic Achievement Act. The pedagogical emphasis is on English acquisition and academic achievement in English—not the promotion of bilingualism, biliteracy, or native language instruction as stressed in the Improving America's Schools Act of 1994. NCLB penalizes states and districts if "benchmarks" for English language acquisition have not been met (Abedi, 2004).

The National Association for Bilingual Education (NABE) has criticized NCLB's approach to school accountability as "overly rigid, punitive, unscientific, and likely to do more harm than good for students who are . . . English language learners" (Crawford,

2004, p. 1). NABE contends that the law misguides accountability and that after just two years it is failing to meet its goals. NCLB has set arbitrary and unrealistic targets for student achievement. This accountability system cannot distinguish between schools that are neglecting ESL students and those that are making improvements. Concerned about making adequate yearly progress on English-language achievement tests, school districts often disrupt their bilingual programs and mandate additional hours of, for example, English reading. These pressures are guiding local policymakers not to use the research-based practices that benefit **ESL students**.

A summary of NABE recommendations for reforming NCLB as it applies to ESL students follows.

1. Do not use invalid and unreliable assessments to make high-stakes decisions for students, educators, or schools.
2. Do not calculate adequate yearly progress for an ESL students subgroup; instead, track the progress of ESL students toward English proficiency and high academic standards on a longitudinal and cohort basis.
3. Measure ESL students' achievement using multiple indicators, including grades, graduation and dropout rates, and alternate forms of assessment. The most important goal of assessment is to help educators improve instruction and students achieve long-term academic success.
4. Accountability should focus on building schools' capacity to serve ESL students, not on stigmatizing labels or punitive sanctions.
5. Accountability for serving ESL students should consider whether: (i) schools are providing sound programs of instruction; (ii) programs are supported with qualified teachers, sufficient funding, adequate materials, and appropriate assessment and placement; (iii) programs are evaluated comprehensively for effectiveness; and, (iv) programs are being restructured when needed to ensure that students are acquiring high levels of English proficiency and academic achievement.

Program Models

The increase of ESL students across the nation has resulted in large numbers of students whose first language is not English and in schools that are unprepared to attend to their educational needs. Stringfield, Datnow, Ross, and Snively (1998) have pointed out that none of the popular comprehensive school reform models have been designed specifically with ESL students in mind. Only recently have these models been adjusted to serve this clientele. However, these models do not include guidelines regarding the education of ESL students and educators have to make adaptations in their schools (Datnow, Borman, Stringfield, Rachuba, & Castellano, 2004). All in all, the academic success of ESL students involves concerted efforts at school, district, state and federal levels.

The program models of instruction for ESL students have been influenced by federal, state, and local policies. These are the most common instructional programs currently serving ESL students (Genesee, 1999).

1. *Transitional bilingual education (TBE) programs.* The nation's most common bilingual education model and most widely supported by federal and state funding. TBE is a compensatory or remedial model designed to prepare ESL students to enter mainstream all-English classes. The overall instruction includes the student's native language in all subject areas as well as instruction in English as a second language (ESL), but only for two to three years. Students receive bilingual instruction until they are proficient enough in English to achieve academically in their second language at the same level as native English speakers. ESL is an integral component of the TBE program. During the English instructional time, ESL teachers provide ESL students with access to English and academic content using the standards-based curriculum, taught with second-language strategies. After a period of time, usually three years, students are "transitioned" into the mainstream curriculum. TBE programs have as their aim facilitating a transition from monolingualism in a non-English language through bilingualism on an individual level to ultimate English monolingualism on the community level. Bilingualism is seen as transitional, with the ideal goal being English monolingualism for the entire curriculum and instruction (Baker & Prys Jones, 1998). Language Transition Support Services programs of about a year long are sometimes organized within the district to receive TBE program students who have not achieved high levels of language proficiency during the three years. The problems with the TBE model are: (i) it is perceived as remedial, segregated and compensatory education, as a low ability track program for slow students; (ii) it is based on the erroneous assumption that two or three years is sufficient time to learn both social and academic English; and (iii) students who are not yet proficient in English score very low on the tests in English, become frustrated with their program and potential dropouts (Crawford, 2004).

2. *ESL Pullout.* This program is taught by extra resource teachers who are trained in second-language teaching methodology. The teacher may have a resource room where ESL students of diverse levels of language proficiency, ages, and grade levels may come and go during the day, some staying longer than others. The main problem with this model is of no access for ESL students to: (i) schooling in their native language; (ii) the full standards-based curriculum; (iii) curriculum articulation with mainstream classroom teachers; and (iv) full school participation with English-speaking peers.

3. *Sheltered English Instruction.* A program of instruction in which English and academic content are taught together. It is an effective program when content area teachers are properly trained to use effective second-language teaching strategies and who accomplish language and content objectives in each lesson (Echevarria, Vogt, & Short, 2000). Some of the curriculum content (science, math, social studies) lends itself to experiments and hands-on experiences that are part of second-language acquisition methods (using visual aids, gestures, body language, realia, cooperative learning groups) to help ESL students learn English and the standards-based curriculum. The ESL students' native language is not used in the classroom. **Sheltered English instruction** is more effective than ESL pullout because ESL students have access to the standards-based curriculum while they are learning English. Sheltered English instruction is often a component of TBE programs and serves as a bridge between the bilingual program and the regular mainstream program.

4. *Two-way, dual-language, or bilingual immersion programs.* An additive or enrichment model designed to achieve bilingualism in minority and majority language, ESL students, and English speakers. The model cultivates the native-language skills of speakers of a minority language (e.g., Spanish, Korean, Navajo) and English speakers (Calderón & Minaya-Rowe, 2003). These programs provide a minimum of six years of bilingual instruction in which students from the two language backgrounds are integrated in most or all of their content instruction. Both languages are separated for instruction and the use of the minority language at least 50 percent of the instructional time and as much as 90 percent in the early grades. ESL students are exposed to the standards-based curriculum, which leads to full language proficiency and mastery of content. **Two-way bilingual programs** are inclusive and integrated education for all the students in contrast with the segregated, exclusive education offered in TBE or ESL pullout programs (Thomas & Collier, 2003). Two-way programs are considered equitable educational programs that treat all students as equal members of the school community. They can also become educational reform tools as school become transformed by increases in the numbers of ESL students who bring the richness of linguistic and cultural diversity with them to school. As whole-school reform tools, two-way program goals are to: (i) promote native-language literacy skills and balanced bilingualism; (ii) enrich with a quality program design for standards-based education; (iii) educate first-class students to achieve at the highest levels; (iv) do justice to the two languages and cultures based on a well-designed infrastructure; and (v) dispel the myth and mindset as an enrichment, rather than a remedial, bilingual program before and during program implementation. Recent research evidence points to two-way bilingual programs as beneficial in the reading achievement of ESL students (Slavin & Cheung, 2004).

TEACHER QUALITY AND CERTIFICATION GUIDELINES

ESL students' academic success depends on teachers' knowledge and applications of effective pedagogy in the classroom. As we have seen in the previous pages, the numbers of ESL students have increased and will continue to rise steadily, and schools require instructional programs to teach them not only English but also to compete academically with English-speaking peers. The provision of educational services to ESL students is one of the most important challenges confronting teacher education today. Although teacher training has lagged behind new and effective pedagogy, the ESL students' demographic increase creates a wider gap between what teachers have been trained to do and the skills they need to teach them (Riley, 2000). The professional development of teachers of ESL students is the most unexamined and overlooked area of preservice and in-service teacher education.

To date, much of the professional development in schools on language and academic needs of ESL students has been addressed to bilingual and/or ESL teachers. Universities have developed undergraduate and graduate programs with curricula and courses to prepare these professionals. In turn, school systems have addressed professional development programs for furthering the continuing education of in-service teachers. However, comparatively little attention has been focused on main-stream teachers who have or will have ESL students in their classrooms (Menken & Antúnez, 2001). This is a cause for concern if we consider that the numbers of ESL students in the regular mainstream classroom are increasing, and will continue to increase at a very rapid pace, if demographic projections hold true (NCES, 2003).

A number of states have legislation and specific policies to assist school districts with implementation of educational programs for ESL students. An important level of implementation is teacher certification. Menken and Antúnez (2001) surveyed state education agencies and found that 41 states and the District of Columbia offered either bilingual or ESL teacher certification or endorsements; 17 states required that teachers placed in bilingual classrooms must have bilingual certification. Twenty-three states required teachers placed in ESL classrooms must have ESL certification. The following 10 states did not provide them the bilingual or ESL certification or endorsements: Alaska, Idaho, Louisiana, Mississippi, Oklahoma, Pennsylvania, Rhode Island, South Carolina, South Dakota, and Vermont.

No Child Left Behind Requirements for Highly Qualified Teachers

According to the No Child Left Behind (NCLB) legislation, all new teachers hired must be **highly qualified**. Teachers teaching a core academic subject are required to have a valid Standard Professional Certificate, Advanced Professional Certificate, or Resident Teacher Certificate. In order for new elementary school teachers to be "highly qualified," they need a minimum of a bachelor's degree and must pass a state certification test showing knowledge of and teaching skill in reading, writing, math, and any other basic elementary school curriculum area. New middle and secondary school teachers need a minimum of a bachelor's degree and must show competence in each of the academic subjects taught by passing one or more state certification tests, or having completed an academic major, coursework equivalent to a major, graduate degree, or advanced certification in each subject taught. Teacher evaluations include the following methods of demonstrating competence in an academic subject: evidence of satisfactory teaching performance, academic coursework, curriculum committee assignments, work on content standards development, work on content assessment, and service as a teacher mentor.

States must determine in conjunction with the school districts professional development strategies and activities grounded in scientifically based research and to ensure that the districts are using the scientifically based professional development strategies. States are responsible to identify ways to meet grade-appropriate subject knowledge and teaching skills; be aligned with the state's content and performance standards and developed in accordance with core content specialists, principals, and other school administrators; give objective information about the teacher's core content knowledge in the academic subject(s) taught; be applied consistently to all teachers in the same subject and the same grade throughout the state; take into consideration how long the teacher has been teaching the subject; involve multiple measures of teacher competence; and be made available to the public on request.

STANDARDS FOR INSTRUCTION

The publication of "Nation At Risk," a 1983 report to the National Science Board Commission on Pre-college Education in Math, Science and Technology, set the tone for establishing national goals or standards in all disciplines of instruction (Bracey, 1996). Several professional organizations posed their own sets of teaching standards to improve academic achievement. The National Committee on Science Education Standards (NCSES, 1994) advocates "more science as a process, in which students learn such skills as observing, inferring, and experimenting" (p. 2). The National Council of Teachers of Mathematics (NCTM) also supports educational opportunities for students to "understand mathematics and its applications when teacher and student view the same phenomena from various mathematical perspectives" (2000, p. 3). By the same token, the National Council for the Social Studies (NCSS) focuses on powerful social studies teaching and learning that is "meaningful, integrative, value-based, challenging and active" (1997, p. 214). Furthermore, the standards proposed by the Teachers of English to Speakers of Other Languages (**TESOL**) stipulate that ESL students need to become proficient in English to have unrestricted access to grade-appropriate instruction in challenging academic subjects (TESOL, 1997).

The content areas can provide an important context in which ESL students can develop their second language, their own identity, learn about the world, and exercise their roles as productive citizens (Robles-Rivas, 2001). However, science, mathematics, and social studies have the potential to create frustration for ESL students who have yet to develop an academic vocabulary and sentence complexity or are struggling readers in English in need of instructional support.

Content Area Textbooks and ESL Students

Content area textbooks also add to the degree of difficulty in content classes for ESL students. Current problems in existing textbooks are:

1. Textbooks are written for English speakers with no adaptations or provisions to attend to language and academic needs of ESL students. They use an expository style of writing that contradicts the narrative style found in ESL classes and textbooks. They also contain a great deal of complex sentence structure (Chamot & O'Malley, 1994). Textbooks are written for English speakers with no adaptations or provisions to attend to language and academic needs of diverse students. Textbooks focus on specialized Tier 3 words, those low-frequency words limited to the content area domains (Beck, McKeown, & Kugan, 2002).

2. Textbooks include large amounts of standards-driven contents with hundreds and hundreds of pages to cover during the year. They do not attend to the ESL students' background knowledge. They leave teachers of ESL students with the task of parsing or selecting portions of extensive textbooks to teach ESL students. Textbooks contain large amounts of specialized vocabulary. Very few textbooks provide guidance to teach ESL students.

3. Most textbooks are limited in or do not include hands-on activities. Textbooks rely heavily on advanced literacy skills and academic vocabulary. They may or may not include science experiments. They may or may not include hands-on social studies activities. They may or may not represent the diversity of students in American schools.

4. Textbooks include mostly questions that are fact oriented. Textbook contents and presentations do not motivate or promote students' critical thinking skill development. Teachers have the added task to generate Bloom-type questions and activities to develop these skills.

The resulting difficulties in English-language learners' language and content learning are summarized below.

- Students are unable to comprehend academic and context-reduced language text because the lack contextual clues—such as realia, concrete objects.
- Students are pressed to learn through diminished simulation or without real life experiences. They are often forced to focus on rote memorization of specific curriculum content in context or alone in an attempt to participate in class.
- Students become unmotivated and have the feeling of not being welcome or of not belonging. Their frustrations may lead to inappropriate behavior.
- Students are overwhelmed with the large amounts of content material in English that does not correlate with their levels of English language acquisition.
- The specialized vocabulary is extensive and does not acknowledge the student's background knowledge.
- Students' self-esteem is lowered and they become reluctant or unmotivated to participate in class or to follow a passive curriculum.
- Students may not have the chance to integrate with English-speaking peers in instructional activities using the textbooks because they cannot comprehend them.
- Students do not practice their critical thinking skills in a challenging but comprehensible context.
- Students often become unmotivated and reluctant to follow a passive curriculum.

A number of strategies can assist the teachers to address this problem. They are beyond the scope of Chapter 2. However, they will be addressed in the second part of the book.

National Science Education Standards and the ESL Students

The main goal of NCES is scientific literacy for all students. It promotes the teaching of science in a way that will accommodate the linguistic needs of ESL students in achieving scientific goals (Lee & Fradd, 1998; Ortiz, 2000). ESL students must be able to make sense of what they see, say, read, and hear in order to be scientifically literate

(Rosebery, Warren, Conant, & Hudicourt-Barnes, 1992). The National Science Teachers Association (NSTA) has advocated inquiry-based science lessons and activities that mirror NSES goals. The lessons aim at developing the abilities and understanding of students to:

1. Ask questions about objects, organisms, and events in the environment
2. Plan and conduct a simple investigation
3. Employ simple equipment and tools to gather data and extend the senses
4. Use data to construct a reasonable explanation; and, most important
5. Communicate investigations and explanations to others

Science as inquiry is an endeavor that demands a deep and highly cognitive effort from all students. Students engaging in inquiry-based activities ". . . must actually use the cognitive and manipulative skills associated with the formulation of scientific explanations" (NSTA, 1995, p. 1). In Grades 9–12, students should be able to achieve certain level of sophistication in their abilities and understanding about doing science as inquiry (NSTA, 1994). This constitutes a challenge to ESL students who are learning English and the science curriculum at the same time; they are at a disadvantage when competing with their monolingual English-speaking counterparts (Ortiz, 2000; Ovando, Collier, & Combs, 2003). A brief description and summary of one NSTA goals of Content Standard A is presented next.

NSTA CONTENT STANDARD A
Goal 1—Abilities necessary to do scientific inquiry
a. Identify questions and concepts that guide scientific investigations. Students will be able to:
   ■ Formulate testable hypotheses and demonstrate logical connections between scientific concepts and the design of an experiment
   ■ Demonstrate appropriate procedures, a knowledge base, and conceptual understanding of scientific investigations
b. Design and conduct scientific investigations. Scientific investigations require:
   ■ Introduction to the major areas being investigated, proper equipment, safety precautions, assistance with methodological problems, recommendations for use of technologies, clarification of ideas that guide inquiry, and scientific knowledge obtained from sources other than the actual investigation
   ■ Student clarification of the question, methods, controls, and variables; student organization and data display; student revision of methods and explanations; and a public presentation of the results with a critical response from their peers
   ■ Student use of evidence to apply logic and construct an argument for their proposed explanations
c. Use of technology and mathematics to improve investigations and communication. Students' scientific investigations should include:
   ■ The use of a variety of technologies such as hand tools, measuring instruments, and calculators

- The use of computers for the collection, analysis, and data display
- The use of mathematics in all aspects of inquiry (e.g., use of charts and graphs to communicate results)

d. Formulate and revise scientific explanations and models using logic and evidence. Students and their products should:
- Culminate in the formulation of an explanation or model
- Be physical, conceptual, and mathematical
- Answer questions by presenting a basis of scientific knowledge, logic, and evidence

e. Recognize and analyze alternative explanations and models. Students should be able to:
- Use scientific criteria to find the best explanation for the experiments' findings and conclusions
- Revise their scientific understanding by weighing the evidence and questioning the logic of their experiments in order to choose the best explanation or model

f. Communicate and defend a scientific argument. Students' abilities should include:
- Accurate and effective communication
- Highly cognitive procedures such as expressing scientific concepts, reviewing information, summarizing data, using language appropriately, developing diagrams and charts, explaining statistical analysis, speaking clearly and logically, constructing a reasonable argument, and responding appropriately to critical comments

The NSES standards do not make provisions for ESL students who need to learn language and content at the same time and who are at disadvantage with their English-speaking peers. Although the standards focus on real world experiences for all students engaging in significant and authentic work, they need to be considered within the ESL students' educational needs and without watering down its content. Curriculum and methodological opportunities are needed to engage ESL students on a kind of learning that enables them to learn English and to understand scientific concepts and develop abilities of inquiry, investigate and analyze science questions; use multiple process skills in context; use evidence and strategies to develop and revise an explanation; analyze and synthesize data and defend conclusions; conduct investigations to develop understanding, ability, values of inquiry, and knowledge of science content and communication with peers.

National Council of Teachers of Mathematics Standards and the ESL Students

NCTM has issued standards and evaluation frameworks that emphasize mathematics classrooms where problem solving, concept development, and the construction of learners-generated solutions. The standards describe the foundation of mathematical ideas and applications intended for all grade levels for students (Romberg & Wilson, 1995). NCTM's 2000 Principles and Standards for School Mathematics describe the content and process standards for curriculum development and instruction. A summary of these standards as they relate to Grades Pre-K through 12 follows.

NCTM CONTENT STANDARDS

1. *Number and operation.* Instructional programs Pre-K through 12 should enable students to:
   i. Understand numbers, ways of representing them, relationships among them, and number systems
   ii. Understand the meanings of operations and how they relate to one another
   iii. Compute fluently and make reasonable estimates
2. *Algebra.* Instructional programs Pre-K–12 should enable students to:
   i. Understand patterns, relations, and functions
   ii. Represent and analyze mathematical situations and structures using algebraic symbols
   iii. Use mathematical models to represent and understand quantitative relationships
   iv. Analyze change in various contexts
3. *Geometry.* Instructional programs should enable students to:
   i. Analyze characteristics and properties of two- and three-dimensional geometric shapes and develop mathematical arguments about geometric relationships
   ii. Specify locations and describe spatial relationships using coordinate geometry and other representational systems
   iii. Apply transformations and use symmetry to analyze mathematical situations
4. *Measurement.* Instructional programs should enable students to:
   i. Understand measurable attributes of objects and the units, systems and processes of measurement
   ii. Apply appropriate techniques, tools, and formulas to determine measurements
5. *Data analysis and probability.* Instructional programs should enable students to:
   i. Formulate questions that can be answered with data and collect, organize, and display relevant data to answer them
   ii. Select and use appropriate statistical methods to analyze data
   iii. Develop and evaluate inferences and predictions that are based on data
   iv. Understand and apply basic concepts of probability

NCTM also recommends the following means to accomplish these standards:

   i. Problem solving where students engage in a task with an unknown solution method
   ii. Reasoning and proof when students explain particular kinds of reasoning and justification in a formal way
   iii. Communication for students to share ideas and clarify understandings
   iv. Connections in which students explore the interrelatedness of mathematical ideas

   v. Representation when students use present mathematical ideas to model physical, social, and mathematical phenomena

In the same trend as with the NSES standards, the NCTM standards do not make provisions for ESL students who need to learn language and content at the same time and who are at a disadvantage with their English-speaking peers. Although the standards focus on real-world experiences for all students engaging in significant and authentic work, they need to be considered within the ESL students' educational needs and level of English-language proficiency without watering down its content. Curriculum and methodological opportunities are needed to engage ESL students on a kind of learning that enables them to learn English and to:

   i. Create and use representations to organize, record, and communicate mathematical ideas

   ii. Select, apply, and translate among mathematical representations to solve problems

   iii. Use representations to model and interpret physical, social, and mathematical phenomena

National Council for Social Studies Standards and the ESL Students

The NCSS (1997) standards for K–12 education suggest a holistic framework for curriculum and instruction with the goal to help students ". . . develop the ability to make informed and reasoned decisions for the public good as citizens of a culturally diverse . . . society . . ." (p. 213), and to offer students a curriculum that is ". . . meaningful, integrative, value-based, challenging and active . . ." (p. 214). Ovando, Collier, and Combs (2003) link these five terms to the instruction of ESL students; their contribution is summarized here:

- *Meaningful.* ESL students have the opportunity to bring their own cultural experiences to the classroom and to apply social studies themes to their real-life experiences. The focus is on the development of big ideas that allow students to develop schema from broad social studies concepts.

- *Integrative.* The integration of social studies across the curriculum involves use of new technology; it also integrates own values, traditions, ways of life that ESL students can express orally or in writing into the curriculum.

- *Value-based.* ESL students have the opportunity to think critically, to learn to deal with social issues, social values, and policy implications. All students practice mutual respect, become sensitive to multiculturalism and accept social responsibility in a forum for discussion in which all points of view are heard and respected.

- *Challenging.* ESL students receive the same standards- and age-appropriate curriculum that their English-speaking peers receive. Critical and creative thinking skills are developed and practiced through debates, position statements, and dialogue.

■ *Active*. ESL students become active social studies learners with genuine and authentic hands-on and experiential activities that make English comprehensible to their level of second-language development.

In the same trend as with the NSES and NCTM standards, the NCSS standards do not make provisions for ESL students who need to learn language and content at the same time and who are at a disadvantage with their English-speaking peers. Efforts like the one summarized here are needed. These standards also focus on real-world experiences for students to engage in significant and authentic work, but they need to be considered within the ESL students' linguistic and academic needs and without diminishing its content (Villar, 1999). Curriculum and methodological opportunities need to consider that ESL students may not: (i) have studied formal social studies in their home country and may not possess the background knowledge or the complex vocabulary terminology; (ii) be familiar with the social studies textbooks, their formats, mode of presentation, volumes; (iii) know the word meanings for concepts if their own languages use representations to model and interpret physical, social, and mathematical phenomena; and (iv) possess the advanced literacy skills assumed to understand complex text, making the subject difficult.

TESOL Standards for Pre-K–12 Students

TESOL standards advocate language development for ESL students across grade levels and to promote English language development with reinforcement of subject matter teaching (Peregoy & Boyle, 2001). The three TESOL goals cover the spectrum of language proficiency required of ESL students to succeed in school.

Goal 1: To use English to communicate in social settings
  Standard 1: Students will use English to communicate in social interactions.
  Standard 2: Students will interact in, through, and with spoken and written English for personal expression and enjoyment.
  Standard 3: Students will use learning strategies to extend their communicative competence.
Goal 2: To use English to achieve academically in all content areas
  Standard 1: Students will use English to interact in the classroom.
  Standard 2: Students will use English to obtain, process, construct, and provide subject matter information in spoken and written form.
  Standard 3: Students will use appropriate learning strategies to construct and apply academic knowledge.
Goal 3: To use English in socially and culturally appropriate ways
  Standard 1: Students will choose a language variety, register, and genre according to audience, purpose, and setting.
  Standard 2: Students will use nonverbal communication appropriate to audience, purpose, and setting.
  Standard 3: Students will use appropriate learning strategies to extend their sociolinguistic and sociocultural competence.

THE HISPANIC POPULATION GROWTH

The Hispanic population continues to grow as it did last decade and the states in the South and West continue to show the largest numbers. Hispanics have higher birth rates and a continued influx of new immigrants looking for jobs (NCES, 2003). Georgia topped the list of states with the fastest-growing Hispanic populations, adding nearly 17 percent between July 2000 and July 2002 to reach 516,000 residents. North Carolina's Hispanic population grew by 16 percent, while Nevada, Kentucky and South Carolina were next. California still has the largest number of Hispanics with 11.9 million, about one-third of its total population, followed by Texas, New York, Florida, and Illinois. Los Angeles County had the largest population of Hispanics among counties (4.5 million), and Webb County, Texas, on the U.S.–Mexico border, which includes Laredo, was the county in which Hispanics comprised the highest proportion of the population (95 percent).

Hispanics are the nation's largest minority group (NCES, 2003). The Hispanic population stood at 38.8 million, an increase of almost 9 percent in the two years ending July 2002. That was four times the growth rate for the U.S. population overall and about 14 times greater than the rate for non-Hispanic whites. Between 2000 and 2002, the Hispanic population had an annual growth rate of 4.1 percent, slightly lower than the 4.6 percent annual rate of the 1990s. New Hispanic immigrants continue to be drawn beyond traditional gateway states like California, New York, and Texas and into places in the fast-growing South and West, as well as rural parts of the Midwest where jobs on farms and in meatpacking plants are available.

Although Spanish speakers are by far the largest group of language-minority students, Spanish is not the dominant language in several states. For example, according to Kindler (2002), Blackfoot was the top second language in Montana, French in Maine, Hmong in Minnesota, Ilocano in Hawaii, Lakota in South Dakota, "Native American" in North Dakota, Serbo-Croatian in Vermont, and Yupik in Alaska.

Patterns in Hispanic Population Growth

The composition of the Hispanic population is undergoing a fundamental change as it continues to grow. Suro and Passel (2003) define three generations in order to frame projections of the Hispanic population growth in the nation from 2000 to 2050.

- *First Generation:* Hispanics who are born outside the United States, its territories, or possessions. They can be naturalized U.S. citizens, legal immigrants, or undocumented immigrants
- *Second Generation:* Hispanics who are born in the United States with at least one foreign-born parent. They are U.S. citizens by birth
- *Third-plus Generations:* Born in the United States with both parents also born in the United States. They are also U.S. citizens by birth

Births in the United States are outpacing immigration as the key source of growth. Over the next twenty years this population increase will produce an important shift in the makeup of the Hispanic population with second-generation Hispanics—the U.S.-born children of immigrants—emerging as the largest component of that population.

As stated in Table 2.2, immigration has represented by far the fastest and the largest source of Hispanic population growth since the 1970s, and, as a result, the first generation—the foreign born—has become more numerous than the second and third generations—those born in the United States to U.S.-born parents. This demographic equation is changing rapidly in important ways: Mainly, that in the next 20 years the number of second-generation Hispanics in U.S. schools will double, from 35.3 million to 60.4 million (Suro & Passel, 2003). Table 2.8 illustrates the growth of the Hispanic population in thousands, percentages, and share of total growth from 2000 with projections to 2020.

The growth of the second generation accelerated in the 1990s and reached 63 percent for the decade, up from 53 percent in the 1980s, surpassing the growth due to immigration (55 percent in the 1990s and 78 percent in the 1980s) even as the nation experienced a record influx from Latin America. This pattern was the legacy of the high levels of immigration in the 1970s and 1980s. The median age of first-generation Hispanics in 2000 was 33.4 years old compared to 38.5 in the non-Hispanic white population overall. Fertility rates are higher among Hispanic immigrants than in any other segment of the U.S. population. In 2000 the fertility rate was 3.51 births per woman for first-generation Hispanics compared to 1.84 for non-Hispanic whites overall. It was higher even than the fertility rates among black (2.53) and Asian (2.60) immigrants (Edmonston, Lee, & Passel, 2003). Parallel trends of high fertility rates for foreign-born women among Ellis Island immigrants can be found in Chapter 1 of this book.

Although the Hispanic immigrant population can be expected to continue increasing, the growth rate for the second generation has already gained sufficient momentum that it will remain higher than the first generation's even if immigration flows of Hispanics accelerate. Second-generation births are a demographic echo of immigration and the high fertility among immigrants. Consequently, larger numbers of Hispanic immigrants will simply produce larger numbers of second-generation Hispanics (Suro & Passel, 2003). Using a mid-range estimate of immigration flows, the Hispanic population will grow by 25 million people between 2000 and 2020. During that time the second generation accounts for 47 percent of the increase compared to 25 percent for the first as illustrated in Table 2.8. Moreover, the second generation more than doubles in size, increasing from 9.8 million in 2000 to 21.7 million in 2020.

TABLE 2.8 Second-Generation Change in the Hispanic Population: 2000–2020

2000–2020	GROWTH (IN THOUSANDS)	GROWTH (IN %)	SHARE OF TOTAL GROWTH
Total Hispanic Population	25,118	71%	100%
First Generation	6,398	45%	25%
Second Generation	11,771	119%	47%
Third+ Generations	6,949	62%	28%

TABLE 2.9   Language Dominance among Hispanics: 2002

GENERATIONS	SPANISH-DOMINANT	BILINGUAL	ENGLISH-DOMINANT
First	72%	24%	4%
Second	7%	47%	46%
Third Plus	0%	22%	78%

Language Status across Generations

Changes in the generational composition of the Hispanic population will have broad consequences because of important differences among the three generations in a number of characteristics. Table 2.9 illustrates an important consequence in language dominance due to the changes in the generational composition of Hispanics (Pew Hispanic Center & the Kaiser Family Foundation, 2002). Spanish-speakers make up most of the first generation. The second generation is substantially Spanish–English bilingual, and the third-plus generations are primarily English speakers.

Levels of Education across Generations

Native-born Hispanics have distinctly higher levels of education than their immigrant counterparts. This means that change in the generational composition alone—without any change in attainment—will significantly lift the educational profile of the Hispanic population. For example, in 2000 more than half of the first generation lacked a high school diploma compared to a quarter or less of the native-born generations. Similarly, there are significantly higher levels of college attendance among native born and higher rates of college graduation (Suro & Passel, 2003). Table 2.10 summarizes the 2000 educational attainment (with or without high school diploma, some college studies and graduates with a bachelor's degree or more) for Hispanics, aged 25 to 64 by generation.

Income

Not surprisingly, given the differences in language and education, native-born Hispanics earn more than the first generation. First-generation Hispanics have mean weekly earnings of $457. The second generation was earning $535 per week, and the third $550 (Suro & Passel, 2003).

TABLE 2.10   Educational Attainment for Hispanics Aged 25 to 64, by Generation: 2000

GENERATION	< H.S. GRAD.	H.S. GRAD.	SOME COLL.	B.A. OR MORE
First	54%	24%	13%	9%
Second	23%	33%	29%	15%
Third	25%	24%	15%	13%

Intermarriage

First-generation Hispanics tend to marry within their ethnic/racial group (Suro & Passel, 2003). This is a pattern for immigrants in general. However, this pattern does not hold true for the second and third generations of Hispanics. According to Edmonston, Lee, and Passel (2003), only 8 percent of foreign-born Hispanics intermarry within their racial/ethnic group, compared to 32 percent of the second generation and 57 percent of the third-plus generation. Similar trends of marriages within ethnic/racial group among Ellis Island immigrants are discussed in Chapter 1 of this book.

Regardless of whether immigration flows from Latin America increase, decrease, or stay the same, a great change in the composition of the Hispanic population is underway. The rise of the second generation is the result of births and immigration that have already taken place, and it is now an inexorable, undeniable demographic fact. These Hispanics are U.S. citizens by birth and will be the products of U.S. schools and they will present a different character and have a different impact on the nation and their immigrant parents. The Hispanic second generation is still very young—nearly two-thirds is under the age of 18 years old. Much is uncertain about these young people emerging from immigrant households:

- How much will the second generation resemble the older generation? Or the third-plus generation?
- Will their cultural and political identities respond to their parents' experiences?
- Will they respond to contemporary influences or past immigrant generations, like the Ellis Island immigrants discussed in Chapter 1 of this book, that are different from those that shaped past Hispanic generations?
- Will the present educational system change at almost every level to serve this generation?

One prediction about second-generation Hispanics seems to be certain: Given their numbers and projected population increases, their future will be a matter of national interest.

SOCIOCULTURAL AND HISTORICAL OVERVIEW OF LANGUAGE ATTITUDES IN THE UNITED STATES

We have discussed the demographic imperative, the policies of language diversity and the program models to meet the imperative. Since these policies and programs do not exist in a vacuum (i.e., unrelated to any sociocultural matters), we would like to provide a sociocultural and historical background of language contact and attitudes out of which these programs grew and that each, of course, reflects. If we look more closely at the sociocultural contents in U.S. society, we will see how the history of the languages and their speakers produced both the situations toward which policies and instructional programs now respond and the thinking behind them (Minaya-Rowe, 1988).

The language distribution and contact in North America corresponding roughly to the geographical boundaries of the United States from the initial stages of European immigration through the present would look something like the following.

1. We would see a stage of intrusive European language communities—English, Spanish, French, Dutch, and so on—during the seventeenth and eighteenth centuries in contact with American Indian languages in various, often widely separate, locations.

2. We would later see a stage from the eighteenth through the nineteenth centuries, during the first part of which English becomes the national language of the newly formed political entity occupying the Eastern seaboard and extending increasingly inland (Crawford, 1999). During this period we can see three important processes occurring:

a. The American Indian languages in contact with English continue to disappear from an ever expanding area. Most simply cease to be spoken, though a few, like Cherokee, move westward to escape the inevitable results of the contact

b. Formation continues on a large scale of what is to become the only major variant of English, Black English. The emergence of Black English can be observed throughout the southern half of the United States

c. A third process taking place during this time is the gradual yielding of other European language communities to the pervasiveness of English as those communities become increasingly incorporated into the U.S. government. This process can be seen in areas such as Florida, the southern parts of the Louisiana Purchase, and the Dutch-speaking portions of New York.

3. A new kind of contact situation intensifies during the late nineteenth and early twentieth centuries between established communities of English speakers and groups of newly arrived speakers of other languages—Norwegian, Italian, German, Swedish, Polish, Yiddish, Chinese, Japanese, and so on. Details about living conditions of Ellis Island immigrants can be found in Chapter 1. In these cases, we can see initially non-English monolingualism usually shifting to one-and-a-half generational bilingualism and finally to English monolingualism. However, the languages of certain groups of immigrants (e.g., Chinese speakers and some Yiddish speakers), who had continuous migration and a localized community, remain in a stage of rather more stable bilingualism (Crawford, 1999).

4. The westward expansion of the late nineteenth century continues the eradicatory contact with American Indian languages and brings new contact with older, long-established communities of Spanish speakers of the West and the Southwest.

5. The continued and present influx of immigrants from Asia and Latin America has continued to flow rapidly to almost all states.

Thus, currently, we have not one, but a large number of different social processes reflected in the various bilingual situations extant in the United States:

- The English–Black English contact situation
- The contact with the remaining American Indian language communities

- Contact situations such as the English–Spanish or English–Chinese contact in which the nonofficial language is represented by a long history within the United States and in which there is a wide range of dialects and speech styles in which each is spoken
- The current contact situation between and among immigrants from Latin America speakers of Spanish and English in widely scattered geographical areas

In understanding the reshaping of processes of change in the United States' language-contact scene over the last 3 centuries, we need to review the attitudes about language that reflect social concepts of "humanness" on the part of members of, especially, the sociopolitically dominant English-speaking community.

We have seen that historically in U.S. society there has been an almost entirely one-way dominance of English in language use. This may be due to at least three factors:

1. There has been great sensitivity toward language use; that is, there is no casualness toward which language one uses in the United States. It is very important to speak the "proper" language
2. This attitude has been supported by the feeling that there is only one acceptable language—English. Monolingualism is accepted as a normal situation in the United States. Being a non-English-speaker in U.S. society has meant socially being not quite as acceptable as the native-English speakers
3. There is, and has been historically, almost no structural effect on English of the various languages involved in the different kinds of contact situations just described

Table 2.1 illustrates the ethnic categories of U.S. society and the language identities corresponding to those categories. It describes the position or thinking about the relation of language to the nature of social-person. The first column lists some of the terms for socioethnic categories of persons, and, in the second column, the way in which they correspond to language identities. The term *American* has two meanings;

1. One of national identity
2. A second one of the ethnic category of citizens who are tokens par excellence of the identity, that is, not members of any other of the many "foreign" groups. The national language, English, is the language identity of this group

Implications for Long-Term Effects or Results of the Policies of Language Diversity and the Instructional Programs

We will consider these results in terms of the following three dimensions:

1. The final linguistic state of U.S. society, in terms of whether it is to be bilingual or monolingual. We have seen that most legislations have passed programs that aim at facilitating a transition from monolingualism in a non-English language through

TABLE 2.11   Taxonomy of Ethnic Categories of Social-Person in the United States in Conjunction with Language Identities*

ETHNIC IDENTITY	LANGUAGE
1. American (National Identity)	English
1.1 American	English
1.2 Mexican American	Spanish (+/− English)
1.3 Chinese American	Chinese (+/− English)
1.4 Italian American	Italian (+/− English)
1.5 Japanese American	Japanese (+/− English)
1.6 —etc.	
1.8 American Indians	
1.8.1 Navajo	Navajo (+/− English)
1.8.2 Apache	Apache (+/− English)
1.8.3 —etc.	

*According to LaFontaine, Persky, and Golubchick (1978), the ethnic category *Puerto Rican* can stand on its own, that is, it is used unattached to the term *American* and there is no ethnic identity for Puerto Rican American

bilingualism on an individual level to ultimate English monolingualism on the community level. Bilingualism has been seen as transitional with the ideal goal being English monolingualism for the entire population. The policies have been implemented based on the assumption that one can only be a "real" member of U.S. society by becoming a monolingual English speaker, thus giving up one's **native language** and ethnic identity.

2. The degree of mutual versus unidirectional influence of the languages involved. Historically, the non-English languages in the various contact situations have had almost no influence on English. This has been because of the attitudes toward language use in conjunction with the direction of bilingualism (i.e., monolingual English speakers in contact with bilingual speakers of a native language plus English).

3. It is yet to be proved whether legislation would support two-way bilingual programs. We have seen that, as school reform innovations, two-way programs can promote access and equity and improved minority–majority relations in which where both languages and cultures are truly valued and used for instruction.

SUMMARY AND CONCLUSIONS: EQUITY AND ACCESS FOR ENGLISH LANGUAGE LEARNERS

The chapter provides a view of demographic imperatives for ESL students in the nation. The position of this chapter and the entire book is pluralism and the chapter provides sufficient information to point out the dire need for policies and practices that make education of English-language learners a reality. Demographics and policies can be in agreement to serve ESL students. They are considered important to serve all students; but for ESL students, who are mostly at risk of educational failure, effective attention to these policies is vital.

In the first major section of Chapter 2, we reviewed the latest demographics, projected growth, and distributions of ESL students in the nation. Particular demographic information in relation to ESL students' educational, social, economic, cultural, and linguistic realities is emphasized. For example, the chapter contributes to our knowledge of how ESL students fare at school, how they fare in reading, what language is used for instruction, and how many drop out of school.

In the second section of Chapter 2, we explore legislation and policies that respond to the demographic imperative in order to meet the educational needs of ESL students in the nation. The discussion and supporting demographics discussed above point to a number of issues for language policies and implementation to promote quality schooling of ESL students. They require an understanding of the legislation and policies that influence language and academic learning to promote equity, access, and effective schooling of ESL students. We explore in realistic fashion the most significant legislation since the first bilingual education act was passed by Congress. We see here that policy implementation often has meant depriving the ESL students of using the only language they bring with them to school for instruction to pave the way to learning English. We learn about the kinds of programs that reflect the political thinking behind those programs in terms of compensatory verses enrichment programs. We learn that professional development is a priority in school reform and that proper teacher training can make a difference to help ESL students succeed.

In the third section, we examined the patterns of the Hispanic population growth and the projected changes. We learned about the characteristics of first-, second-, and third-generation Hispanics in terms of the language dominance patterns for each group. We also learned about the one-way dominance of English in the nation historically and that English monolingualism has been the norm for centuries.

In sum, this foundational chapter provides new insights about the demographics of and language policies used in educating ESL students. It documents their usefulness in program models, teacher education, content area standards, and second-language teaching to promote access and equity in education.

REVIEW QUESTIONS

1. How would you explain the demographic increases of ESL students? How are they affecting the way schools and programs are implemented?

2. What is your personal position about two-way bilingual programs? Would you enroll your child(ren) in a two-way program? If so, how will it benefit your child(ren)? If not, what other program do you have in mind?

3. Do you consider that the legislation in your state and its policies to implement instructional programs for ESL students is a fair one? How would you modify them to serve the districts' ESL students?

4. Do you believe that standards-based instruction will improve the quality of teaching and learning for all students, including ESL students? Can we truly improve the educational services for ESL students?

5. Provide three characteristics about the Hispanic population growth in the United States that have impressed you while reading the chapter. Describe your thinking behind each characteristic.

6. Trace your own sociocultural, historical, and language profile. Go as for back as you can: your great-grandparents (Where did they come from? What language(s) did they speak?) or even farther.

CRITICAL THINKING QUESTIONS

1. Think of two examples in which you as a teacher can use the demographic data and projections to plan your curriculum and lessons for ESL students and/or for making a case about the best program of instruction for your students. How can these figures be interpreted and used in the school/classroom?

2. Two-way bilingual programs are becoming more popular and implemented according to the unique characteristics of ESL students being served. Visit a two-way bilingual program in a nearby school district or choose a program on the Web (e.g., www.cal.org). Describe its components. If possible examine annual evaluation reports of the program and look for strengths, areas that need improvement, and so forth.

3. Design a cross-content area standard comparison of two or more standards; select one from each content area. Delve deeper into the contents and processes for each standard chosen. Identify the technical vocabularies. Ask yourself the following question: How can the language of mathematics compare with the language of social studies? Of science? As much as possible, relate your answer to an earlier examination of a content area textbook to strengthen your project.

4. Identify the Hispanic group(s) in your neighborhood school and find out as much as possible about their backgrounds. Come up with a profile. Are they mostly first-, second-, or third-generation Hispanics? Make projections and discuss them with your classmates in terms of language status, educational attainment, income, and intermarriage.

ACTIVITIES

1. Select a school and review its existing data on numbers of ESL students; examine data on the state Web site, reports, newspaper stories, and so on, and compare your findings with the nationwide data you just reviewed. Organize your data by grade, language backgrounds, ethnic composition, and so on. Construct a table and share it with classmates; identify similarities and differences resulting from your data results; make projections using selected variables.

2. Kindler's 2002 survey is the most recent and comprehensive document on the status of ESL students, their growth and their academic achievement. Identify the strengths and weaknesses of the data. In what ways would you use the data? In your opinion, what else is needed to have a clearer picture of the status of ESL students? Provide specific examples.

3. Examine the NCLB legislation and compare it to NABE's proposals for review and improvement. Discuss with your classmates the advantages and disadvantages of NCLB. Do NABE's proposals make sense? Are they realistic? How can ESL students be better served? Explain your opinion.

4. You have been asked to recommend and provide a rationale for an appropriate instructional program for a group of ESL students at your school. Include in your recommendation: (a) a definition of the program you propose; (b) a description of the

group in terms of its numbers, native language, educational background, language(s) spoken in the home, literacy in the first language; (c) identification of resources, the availability of appropriate curriculum, textbooks, trained teachers, building, and so on. Base your recommendation on what is the best and the most practical.

5. Select a content area textbook and the grade level of your choice. Use the four descriptors for the problems encountered with textbooks and examine your textbook for degree of complexity, technical vocabulary, contextual cues, and so forth. Describe the possible difficulties ESL students might encounter when using such a textbook.

6. Select a content-areas standard and grade level and incorporate elements of the TESOL standards, goals, and objectives to make the curriculum content more ESL student-friendly. Discuss with your classmates ways to combine language and content instruction and give specific examples.

7. Review the data about the second-generation Hispanics and their project population growth. Why is this group so important? How do you foresee this group impacting the national scene? Linguistically? Culturally? Politically? Economically? Educationally? Give rationales for your answers.

GLOSSARY

Bilingual Education Act   The 1968 Bilingual Education Act was the first attempt of the federal government to address the educational needs of ESL students (Crawford, 1999).

bilingualism   A person's ability to use two languages in communication. There are many degrees of bilingualism and a number of dimensions to consider: ability in language and use of language; proficiency across the four language skills of listening, speaking, reading, and writing; dominant language (Baker & Prys Jones, 1998).

Biliteracy   A person's ability to read and write in two languages (Baker & Prys Jones, 1998).

ESL students   English-as-a-second-language (ESL) student is a preferred term instead of *limited English proficient* (LEP). In this book, we have chosen the term *ESL student* over LEP for it conveys that the student is in the process of learning English, without having the connotation that the student is in some way defective until full English proficiency is attained (Ovando, Collier, & Combs, 2003).

ESL instruction   English-as-a-second-language is a component of a transitional bilingual program; it is also a program in itself in districts with no bilingual education.

highly qualified teacher   The No Child Left Behind legislation considers teacher quality as one of the most important components of the law. Teachers must have a bachelor's degree, demonstrate competence in content area, and pass a state certification test.

monolingualism   The opposite of bilingualism; a person's ability to use just one language.

native language   The language spoken in the home; the language in which the ESL student was raised.

Sheltered English instruction   It refers to the concept of comprehensible subject-matter teaching (math, science, social studies, etc.) with English, the second language, as the medium of instruction. Sheltered English differs from what native English speakers receive in the regular all-English program (subject-matter instruction in English) in that sheltered English is aimed at providing both language (listening, speaking, reading, and writing) and academic instruction to ESL students.

TESOL   The Teachers of English to Speakers of Other Languages organization has set forth standards to develop English proficiency.

Transitional Bilingual Education Program   TBE is a compensatory instructional program in which the native language and English are used as medium of instruction. Its duration is about three years.

Two-Way Bilingual Education Program   TWB is an enrichment instructional program designed to achieve bilingualism and biliteracy in ESL students and English speakers. Students are integrated in one class for all or most of their instruction. Its duration is from 6 years onwards (Calderón & Minaya-Rowe, 2003).

REFERENCES

Abedi, J. (2004). The No Child Left Behind Act and English language learners: Assessment and accountability issues. *Educational Researcher, 33*(1), 1–14.

Baker, C., & Prys Jones, S. (1998). *Encyclopedia of bilingualism and bilingual education.* Clevedon, England: Multilingual Matters.

Banks, J. A., & McGee Banks, C. A. (2001). *Multicultural education: Issues and perspectives* (4th ed.). New York: John Wiley & Sons.

Beck, I. L., McKeown, M. G., & Kugan, L. (2002). *Bringing words to life: Robust vocabulary instruction.* New York: Guilford.

Bracey, G. W. (1996). International comparisons and the condition of American education. *Educational Researcher, 21*(1), 5–11.

Calderón, M. E., & Minaya-Rowe, L. (2003). *Designing and implementing two-way bilingual programs: A step-by step guide for administrators, teachers and parents.* Thousand Oaks, CA: Corwin.

Chamot, A. U., & O'Malley, J. M. (1994). *The CALLA handbook: Implementing the Cognitive Academic Language Learning Approach.* Reading, MA: Addison-Wesley.

Crawford, J. (1999). *Bilingual education: History, politics, theory, and practice* (4th ed.). Los Angeles: Bilingual Educational Services.

Crawford, J. (2004). *No Child Left Behind: Misguided approach to school accountability for English language learners.* Washington, DC: National Association for Bilingual Education.

Darling-Hammond, L., & Sykes, G. (Eds.). (1999). *Teaching as the learning profession: Handbook of policy and practice.* San Francisco: Jossey-Bass.

Datnow, A., Borman, G. D., Stringfield, S., Rachuba, L. T., & Castellano, M. (2004). Comprehensive school reform in culturally and linguistically diverse contexts: Implementation and outcomes from a 4-year study. *Educational Evaluation and Policy Analysis, 25*(2), pp. 149–172.

Echevarria, J., Vogt, M., & Short, D. (2000). *Making content comprehensible for English language learners.* Boston: Allyn & Bacon.

Edmonston, B., Lee, S. M., & Passel, J. S. (2003). Recent trends in intermarriage and immigration and their effects on the future racial composition of the U.S. population. In *The new race question: How the census counts multiracial individuals,* pp. 59–87. Washington, DC: Russell Sage Foundation and the Levy Institute of Bard College.

Garcia, E. (1999). *Student cultural diversity: Understanding and meeting the challenge* (2nd ed.). Boston: Houghton Mifflin.

Genesee, F. (1999). *Program alternatives for linguistically diverse students.* Santa Cruz, CA: Center for Research in Education, Diversity, & Excellence.

Kindler, A. L. (2002). *Survey of the states' limited English proficient students and available educational programs and services. 2000–2001 summary report.* Washington, DC: National Clearinghouse for English Language Acquisition and Language Instruction Educational Programs.

LaFontaine, H., Persky, B., & Golubchick, L. (Eds.) (1978). *Bilingual education.* Wayne, NJ: Avery.

Lee, O., & Fradd, S. H. (1998). Science for all, including students from non-English language backgrounds. *Educational Researchers, 27*(4), 12–21.

Lollock, L. (2001, January). The foreign-born population of the United States: March 2000. Current population reports (P20–534). Retrieved September 20, 2002, from the World Wide Web: www.census.gov/prod/2000/pubs/p20-534

McCormick, E. (2000, September 3). Asians will soon be biggest S. F. group. *San Francisco Examiner,* A1, A12.

Menken, K., & Antúnez, B. (2001). *An overview of the preparation and certification of teachers working with low English proficiency students.* Washington, DC: National Clearinghouse for Bilingual Education.

Minaya-Rowe, L. (1988). A comparison of bilingual education policies and practices in Perú and the United States. In. H. S. Garcia & R. Chávez Chávez (Eds.), *Ethnolinguistic issues in education* (pp. 100–116) Lubbock: Texas Tech University.

National Center for Education Statistics (NCES). (2003). *The condition of education.* Washington, DC: Author.

National Center for Education Statistics (NCES). (2002a). *Public school student, staff, and graduate counts by state, school year 2000–2001.* Washington, DC: Author.

National Center for Education Statistics (NCES). (2002b). *Core of Common Data, 1998–1999 through 2001–2002.* Washington, DC: Author.

National Clearinghouse for Bilingual Education (NCBE). (1999). *The growing numbers of limited English proficient students.* Washington, DC: Author.

National Committee on Science Education Standards (NCSES). (1994). *National science education standards.* Washington, DC: National Academy Press.

National Council for the Social Studies (NCSS). (1997). *A sampler of curriculum standards for social studies: Expectations of excellence.* Upper Saddle River, NJ: Prentice-Hall.

National Council of Teachers of Mathematics (NCTM). (2000). *Principles and standards for school mathematics.* Reston, VA: Author.

National Science Teachers Association (NSTA). (1995). *A high school framework for national science education standards: Scope, sequence, and coordination of secondary school science.* Arlington, VA: Author.

Ortiz, J. A. (2000). *English language learners developing academic language through sheltered instruction.* Storrs: University of Connecticut Press.

Ovando, C. J., Collier, V. P., & Combs, M. C. (2003). *Bilingual and ESL classrooms: Teaching in multicultural contexts* (3rd ed.). Boston: McGraw Hill.

Peregoy, S. F., & Boyle, O. F. (2001). *Reading, writing, and learning in ESL* (3rd ed.). White Plains, NY: Longman.

Pew Hispanic Center and the Kaiser Family Foundation. (2002). *National survey of Latinos.* Washington, DC: Author.

Riley, R. W. (2000). *Remarks as prepared for delivery by the U.S. Secretary of Education: Web-Based Education Commission.* Retrieved December 10, 2000, from the World Wide Web: www.ed.gov/Speeches/02–2000/20000202.html

Robles-Rivas, E. (2001). *An examination of standards for effective pedagogy in a high school bilingual setting.* Storrs: University of Connecticut Press.

Romberg, T., & Wilson, L. (1995). Issues related to the development of an authentic assessment system for school mathematics. In T. Romberg (Ed.), *Reforming in school mathematics and authentic assessment* (pp. 1–18). Albany: State University of New York Press.

Rosebery, A. S., Warren, B., Conant, F. R., & Hudicourt-Barnes, J. (1992). Cheche Konen: Scientific sense making in bilingual education. *Hands-on Math and Science Learning, 15*(1), 1–16.

Slavin, R., & Cheung, A. (2004). How do English language learners learn to read? *Educational Leadership 61*(6), 52–57.

Stringfield, S., Datnow, A., Ross, S. M., & Snively, F. (1998). Scaling up school restructuring in multicultural, multilingual contexts: Early observation from Sunland county. *Education and Urban Society, 30*(3), 326–357.

Suro, R., & Passel, J. S. (2003). *The rise of the second generation: Changing patterns in Hispanic population growth.* Retrieved November 1, 2003 from the World Wide Web: www.pewhispanic.org

Teachers of English to Speakers of Other Languages (TESOL). (1997). *ESL standards for pre-K–12 students.* Alexandria, VA: Author.

Thomas, W. P., & Collier, V. P. (2003). The multiple benefits of dual language. *Educational Leadership, 61*(2), 61–64.

Tse, L. (2001). *"Why don't they learn English?" Separating fact from fallacy in the U.S. language debate.* New York: Teachers College Press.

Villar, J. A. (1999). *A model for developing academic language proficiency in English language learners through instructional conversations.* Storrs: University of Connecticut Press.

U.S. Bureau of the Census. (2001). *Census 2000 briefs* [Online]. Available: www.census.gov/population /html

FROM THEORY TO PRACTICE WITH ESL AND *ALL* STUDENTS

LEARNING OBJECTIVES

1. Understand the role of language on cognitive development and learning
2. Recognize which are the research-based principles and strategies in learning and teaching
3. Understand the role of language on affective, emotional, and social development
4. Identify learning and teaching principles derived from affective, emotional, and social factors

PREVIEW QUESTIONS

1. What are the internal and external factors affecting the ESL learning process? List and explain.
2. How can educators nurture the natural functions of second-language (L2) learning? Explain.
3. What is the role of prior and conceptual knowledge for learning? Why is it important for educators to use prior and conceptual knowledge for stimulating L2 learning?
4. How can educators link assessment and instruction for ESL student?
5. Why do educators need to know different approaches for L2 teaching?

Chapter 3 provides a socioconstructivistic theoretical framework for understanding conceptually the process of first- and-second-language (L1 and L2) learning and the derived educational principles for English-as-a-second-language (ESL) learners and *all* students, taking into consideration a research-based knowledge perspective.

The first major section discusses cognitive aspects of learning and teaching, bringing research-based knowledge from cognitive and developmental psychology, and its applications in educational psychology. The second subsection discusses educational principles derived from research-based knowledge in learning and teaching, with an emphasis on expectations, effort, and motivation.

The second major section presents best educational approaches and classroom teaching strategies for ESL teaching and learning, with an emphasis on examining the L2 learning process. In this second major section, two main ESL approaches (stemming from behavioristic and socioconstructivistic theories) are discussed, taking a pluralistic approach to ESL teaching and learning. This second major section encompasses two subsections presenting the following ESL approaches to educational applications of teaching and learning in the classroom: (1) behavioristic language approaches, embedding the grammar translation and the direct approach, and (2) socioconstructivistic approaches embedding the communicative competence and the conceptual learning approaches. These two subsections discuss examples of what to teach and how to teach it by demonstrating best educational approaches using a mix of theory, ESL teaching skills or strategies, and adaptations or individualization of instruction for responding to the diverse and individual educational needs of ESL students.

The position or perspective of Chapter 3 and this entire book is one of **pluralism,** and not **eclecticism.** In other words, we want to stimulate ESL teachers to develop conceptual knowledge about ESL approaches and their underlying theoretical principles and research-based knowledge, so that they can learn how to make informed decisions about the selection and use of ESL instructional strategies derived from these L2 approaches in order to match the particular strengths and weaknesses that diverse ESL students have. In contrast, we want to discourage ESL teachers from choosing only an eclectic position, because their instructional decisions would be based solely on teacher-felt needs for ESL students at particular points in time, with little regard for principles or methods and theories on which good ESL teaching is based.

Therefore, Chapter 3 connects with the second theme of the book because it aims to increase teachers' understanding of: (1) the theoretical principles and research-based knowledge affecting the ESL learning process, and (2) best educational strategies to link assessment and instruction to serve ESL learners. By increasing teachers' understanding, we also aim to infuse cultural awareness and therefore make their attitudes toward ESL students more positive. In turn, by aiming to make teachers' attitudes more sensitive and encourage them to value and celebrate diversity, we also aim to increase their motivation, commitment, and advocacy levels for better serving ESL students.

THE ROLE OF LANGUAGE ON COGNITIVE DEVELOPMENT AND LEARNING: A SOCIOCONSTRUCTIVISTIC PERSPECTIVE

In a natural sociocultural environment, such as a home, children learn language and concepts simultaneously, with language providing a symbolic tool for expressing nonverbal and verbal thoughts. Language is added to nonverbal thinking and concepts during the second year of life, providing children the ability to move from more concrete and perceptual ideas to more abstract and metacognitive ways of thinking during the preschool years. Language provides the capacity of abstraction and displacement from the immediate time and space, allowing the individual to communicate ideas at a distance via media (*written:* e.g., books, messages, newspapers, magazines, computers; *oral:*

e.g., phone, radio; *visual:* e.g., videos, photos, drawings, graphs, figures, realia, symbolic play, art crafts). Then, educators need to nurture the natural function of language by using concrete and developmentally appropriate materials to think and talk about in relation to subject areas and topic knowledge.

With the onset of language, toddlers and preschoolers can start manipulating real-life experiences, by using language to shape, categorize, store, and recreate experiences. Young children can recall and transform past experiences from memory through their symbolic play and other forms of representation (e.g., drawings, dialogue, questions, dreams, and recollection of previous experiences through language, role playing, and acting out). Infants and toddlers develop awareness of the onset of language and become sensitive to how language provides for them conventional mapping for verbal expression of thoughts, so they can engage in the communication of their verbal and nonverbal ideas through an intentional and observable mean: words. Preschool children have the newly acquired ability to develop labels and verbal networks for better developing and communicating their thoughts. An example of this language awareness and sensitivity gained during the toddler and preschool years is provided below.

EXAMPLE OF LANGUAGE AWARENESS AND SENSITIVITY GAINED DURING THE TODDLER AND PRESCHOOL YEARS

It is interesting to observe young toddlers before or around 1 and 2 years of age trying to utter some sounds to call the attention of adults, resulting in "conversational babbling." The first author could observe a monolingual Spanish 2-and-a-half-year-old child interacting with a bilingual English/Spanish 5-and-a-half-year-old, as they were playing. The context of the observation was a Latin American country in which the Spanish monolingual child lived, and his bilingual cousin was just visiting, as he was born and lived in the United States. The bilingual child would use code switching for communicating, resulting in some English and some Spanish sentences. The monolingual Spanish toddler would react to the English utterances with conversational babbling, that is, he would imitate the sounds he had "heard" as he could perceive them: as sounds with no meaning at all! It is important to notice that this monolingual Spanish-speaking toddler had a very advanced Spanish language development for his age. This monolingual Spanish-speaking toddler had also learned some sociolinguistic rules, such as that conversations need to be maintained by responding and taking turns when engaging in a dialogue, and he would apply this pragmatic rule regardless of whether meaning was present or not.

More recently, I could observe these two young boys playing again, after about a year and a half, when the monolingual Spanish-speaking child had just turned 4, and the bilingual English/Spanish child was almost 7 years old. Both children had advanced significantly in their language development; however, the progress that the younger child had made was much more dramatic, going from an emergent language stage during his toddler years to an established oral language proficiency during his preschool years. Other important factors were that the 4-year-old recently had spent about 3 weeks in the United States and that the observation setting was the US, country in which the now 7-year-old was born and had always lived. Because the 4-year-old had been exposed to the English language in its natural cultural setting during his visit, he had become very aware and sensitive to this new linguistic code used by most speakers. This sensitivity had made the 4-year-old adopt some memorized English phrases that he would use when interacting with his 7-year-old bilingual cousin. Even though the 4-year-old's repertoire in English was very limited, he pretended (symbolic play) that he could understand all English phrases uttered by his bilingual cousin by responding with "Yes," "O.K," and "Yes, we can do it" (he had memorized and borrowed the latter phrase from the TV show *Bob the Builder*).

Besides the cultural awareness gained and his strong identification with an English-speaking cartoon character, the 4-year-old was creatively using symbolic play to enact his newly acquired "English identity." He wanted his 7-year-old cousin and all adults in the household to call him Bob. It is interesting to note that the 4-year-old Spanish phonemic discrimination and pronunciation was interfering with his perception of the word as *Buk* instead of *Bob*. This latter issue aroused some heated debate between the cousins, both insisting on their perceived pronunciations. After a lot of modeling the word *Bob* the 7-year-old bilingual child wrote down the word and read it aloud to his preschool cousin several times—"Bob, Bob, Bob!"—to no avail. Each boy continued to pronounce the word as their Spanish or English auditory discrimination and pronunciation skills would allow them: the bilingual English/Spanish child as "Bob" and the monolingual Spanish child as "Buk." Finally some peace and quiet returned to the household of the aunt and mother, who also happened to be the first author of this book and an avid psycholinguist. You can also use any classroom or daily life or family experience to find examples of language development in bilingual and monolingual children.

The example provided above illustrates the tremendous progress occurring in oral language development during the toddler and preschool years. Besides the acquisition of oral language that naturally occurs at home, children need to be socialized both at home and at school in order to establish a solid foundation for developing preliteracy and literacy skills. Children need a high degree of literacy as an abstract tool for succeeding in learning at school. Oral, preliteracy, and literacy, skills need to be established in L1 and then transferred to the L2 for children to become bilingual and biliterate. A strong foundation in oral language is a prerequisite for developing preliteracy and literacy skills, and social language proficiency up to age level is needed to develop academic language in L1 and ultimately L2 proficiency in social and academic areas.

Piaget was the founder of cognitive developmental psychology, generating a constructivistic approach for exploring cognitive development in young children as nonverbal and abstract processes that precede language development. From the 1940s through the 1960s, Piaget (1964, 1967, 1970) conducted a series of qualitative studies to demonstrate that abstract operational (or conceptual nonverbal) thinking is deeper (and more mature) than semantic (or verbal) and semiotic (figurative or perceptual, such as drawings, imitation, play, nonverbal motor behaviors such as play, and language) functions. A more contemporary socioconstructivistic approach adds a third and central component, culture, to the interaction between cognition and language. That is, the specific sociocultural context influences how children construct concepts and map words into meanings (semantic development). As ESL children learn the similarities and differences across L1 and L2 concepts across abstract, symbolic, and verbal domains, they understand how some concepts are culturally and linguistically bound, and how other concepts are more universal and can be transferred across languages (for further discussion of this topic see Gonzalez & Schallert, 1999).

Within the school contexts language becomes the most important method for instruction. Schools use language as a tool for learning; it is a prerequisite for the study of all other subjects or content areas (e.g., math, science, social studies). Therefore, during the primary grades, language becomes a cognitive process when used for learning and thinking about concepts and content. Therefore, language becomes the foundation to thinking about learning (metalearning) because it is used by schools as a metacognitive tool for learning. During the later early childhood years (5 to 8 years of age), language can help the young child to make cognitive connections at three levels: (1) concrete via recalling and transforming direct experiences with objects at a manipulative or motor level, (2) perceptual or figurative via recalling and transforming experiences with drawings and graphic representations, and (3) conceptual or constructive via recalling and transforming experiences at a more abstract nonverbal or verbal level.

Language also makes it possible for the young child to establish relations to other cognitive processes such as attention, perception, problem solving, creativity, symbolic representations, analogical reasoning, formation of verbal concepts and networks, verbal creativity, and cognitive operations (e.g., classification, conservation, seriation, number, space). Memory grows from a nonverbal stage in infants and young toddlers to incorporating a verbal encoding process in older toddlers and preschoolers. Thus, language influences automatic memory cognitive processes such as storage, retrieval, and recalling (i.e., recognition, association) strategies. In addition, language influences constructive or semantic memory processes, such as metacognition, including monitoring and content knowledge (i.e., using prior knowledge as advance organizers to facilitate storage and recalling of information, helping in the recall of details and reconstruction of sequences of events experienced; organizing networks that integrate new information resulting in assimilation processes, and forming new concepts or categories resulting in accommodation processes). Some memory strategies using cognitive and metacognitive verbal labels and verbal conceptual processes include: rehearsal, organization, categorization (i.e., use of constructive semantic or verbal memory to link labels and verbal experiences with verbal and nonverbal new and prior concepts), and elaboration (i.e., using verbal and nonverbal images and mnemonics as a strategy for connecting information in a meaningful manner).

For example, children use organization processes for identifying prototypical objects that can be used as core examples or exemplar-based representations for learning concepts. Identifying content knowledge distinctions help children organize new information learned (and first stored in automatic short-term memory) into conceptual knowledge (later stored in semantic or constructive, long-term memory). A child may learn that birds fly and have wings as prototypical characteristics for organizing new labels for animals such as birds or mammals.

An example of children using categorization is forming thematic connections, based on functions of objects, perceptual or figurative characteristics of objects (e.g., shape, size, color, parts, smell), or more concrete concepts (e.g., number, kind—mammals, birds, furniture) or abstract features (e.g., linguistic characteristics such as first letter of labels—all fruits that start with consonants—or analogical reasoning that compares across conceptual domains—"my stomach makes noises like a piano"—resulting in the use of metalinguistic and metacognitive processes).

Language becomes a semantic tool for conveying meaning and for representing ideas and events through symbols that can be communicated. Language also provides flexibility and creativity for expressing unique ideas with a system that offers an infinite number of possible combinations. Thus, language stimulates problem solving, concept formation, and active learning because children can create and recreate dynamically their ideas through a language system that can help them to think via internal verbal thoughts or in a social context through group brainstorming, instructional conversations, inquiry-based learning, and dialogue.

A higher difficulty level is imposed by school language in comparison to natural social contexts, such as home settings. School language tends to be more abstract as it presents verbal content in a decontextualized manner. School language uses logical and expository verbal communication is used for presenting subject areas and topics. That is why ESL children tend to have more learning difficulties when literacy skills in L2 are used for learning content areas. During the primary grades, reading and writing and oral language become more abstract and decontextualized because logically organized linguistic input is mostly used for communicating content.

Thus, because schools emphasize using language as a method of instruction, teachers are practicing psycholinguists because they use language as a tool for developing thinking and for learning. For example, assessment of children's cognitive skills is done primarily through verbal stimuli, which present some methodological difficulties for assessing LEP students. Reading requires active processing of written language, and thus is a good example of the interaction between cognition and language. Teachers are good users of language learning strategies because they need to communicate with young children who are at various developmental levels of language competence and literacy skills.

Following a socioconstructivistic perspective, the role of language on cognitive development and school learning discussed in the previous section, can be better understood in relation to educational principles derived from research-based knowledge. Based on the National Research Council document on *How People Learn* (1999a), a core set of three major learning principles derived from contemporary research on learning and teaching are a powerful tool for understanding that the selection of teaching and learning strategies is mediated by subject matter, grade level, and purpose of education. A single panacea cannot solve every learning and teaching situation, especially in relation to the unique needs of diverse ESL students, but a more wholistic perspective of using teaching and learning principles can help design and evaluate classroom environments that are optimal learning settings. These three major learning principles encompass: (1) the central role of prior knowledge for learning, (2) the development of a conceptual competence in topic and content knowledge, and (3) the endorsement of a metacognitive approach to teaching and learning.

Central Role of Prior Knowledge for Learning

Teachers need to tap into students' use of prior knowledge, skills, and attitudes for developing an understanding of concepts within specific topic and content knowledge. As stated by the National Research Council (1999a), "only by probing for and identifying students' prior knowledge, including misconceptions and misunderstandings, can teachers use instruction to move their students on to more accurate and more sophisticated levels of understanding" (p. 25). This means that classrooms need to be more learner-centered, and learn about students' preconceptions, cultural differences, values and beliefs about educationally relevant concepts (e.g., how intelligence develops, what is the role of effort and luck in learning, and expectations from the school system and instructors), their personal interests (to maintain their task engagement) and individual progress, and developmental growth and maturation.

According to the National Research Council (1999a), "Students come to the classroom with preconceptions about how the world works. . . . A critical feature of effective teaching is that it elicits from students their pre-existing understanding of the subject matter to be taught and provides opportunities to build on—or challenge—the initial understanding" (p. 10). New information and concepts that contradict preexisting beliefs and real-world experiences or naïve understandings are more difficult to learn. As well stated by the National Research Council (1999a), "Teachers need to make time to hear their students' ideas and questions. . . . [and]. . . be prepared to assess children's thinking abilities, to decide when to make connections between existing knowledge and school learning" (p. 25).

According to the National Research Council (1999a), extensive research evidence stemming from studies conducted during the 1980s and1990s (e.g., Bruner, 1990; Cole, 1996; Tobin, Wu, & Davidson, 1989) showed that learning, both in terms of acquisition and use of knowledge, is the result of the interaction between internal variables such as individual cognitive processes and external factors such as the context of cultural and social norms and expectations. The implications of these research findings about learning are many. Teachers need to provide opportunities for students to reveal their thinking in the classroom. For instance, teachers need to use instructional tasks and formative assessments (i.e., ongoing evaluations designed to make students' thinking explicit to both learners and teachers) that tap students' beliefs, pre-conceptions, thinking, and real-world and subject matter knowledge and understanding. By using formative assessments or ongoing evaluations, teachers can make students' thinking explicit to themselves, their peers, and their students. In this way, students can receive constructive feedback from teachers conducive to modifying and refining their thinking in light of new concepts and information. These "reflective" assessments can help students monitor their development throughout the inquiry process and show developmental progress resulting in the creation of motivation for learning. "The exercise is less a test than an indicator of where inquiry and instruction should focus" (National Research Council, 1999a, p. 22). Thus, formative assessments help students and teachers identify problems and progress toward educational goals (which can be self-imposed based on reflections). **Summative assessments** will be final evaluations, typically a posttest or end-of-the-school-year testing, that help teachers and students understand the level of success at reaching the goal. Both formative and summative assessments, need to be closely connected and linked with instructional activities and curriculum design.

Moreover, following research findings about learning, teachers need to infuse in their classroom environments a community-centered approach, in which classroom norms and connections to the external world supports core learning values. Students can use collaboration and cooperation to develop knowledge and help each other to solve problems. Through engaging in dialogue and inquiry, students and teachers can contribute to the creation of new ideas and knowledge, which can establish clear connections to their real-world experiences at home and in their family and communities. Guided learning can also occur at home and in other real-life settings (e.g., a visit to the mall or a shopping experience at the supermarket) for allowing students to make connections between real-life experiences and schoolwork and classroom learning.

Development of Conceptual Competence in Topic and Content Knowledge

In order to learn at a conceptual level, students need to develop a deep foundation of **factual knowledge** and a strong conceptual framework for transforming information into meaningful knowledge. **Conceptual knowledge** is defined as a network of meaningful patterns that can be retrieved for problem solving and transference of learning (National Research Council, 1999a). Students also need to learn how to organize knowledge into hierarchical conceptual networks through cognitive and metacognitive strategies. Developing hierarchical conceptual networks can facilitate for ESL students the retrieval of information and knowledge for problem-solving applications and transference to other knowledge domains.

Research comparing competence in experts and novices and on learning transference, shows that developing expert competence in any area of inquiry is connected to developing conceptual and factual knowledge, and well-organized knowledge that supports understanding. Students must have opportunities to develop deep understanding of subject matter so that they can transform factual knowledge into usable knowledge. ESL students must develop and use a conceptual structure for becoming able to identify patterns and relationships, extract underlying meaning at an abstract level, generate arguments and explanations, and draw analogies to other problems and knowledge domains. Thus, students' abilities to acquire organized sets of facts and skills are actually enhanced when "they are connected to meaningful problem-solving activities, and when students are helped to understand why, when, and how those facts and skills are relevant" (National Research Council, 1999a, p. 19).

According to the National Research Council (1999a),

> The enterprise of education can be viewed as moving students in the direction of more formal understanding (or greater expertise). This will require both a deepening of the information base and the development of a conceptual framework for that subject matter . . . organizing information into a conceptual framework allows for greater 'transfer'; that is, it allows the student to apply what was learned in new situations and to learn related information more quickly. (p. 13)

That is, it is a much better teaching strategy to just focus lesson plans throughout the school year (and even across school years) on in-depth coverage of fewer topics, making available multiple applications of concepts in relation to factual knowledge for stimulating students to further develop their thinking skills. Thus, it is a much better teaching practice to stimulate students to develop conceptual knowledge and metacognitive skills, such as learning skills and thinking and problem-solving abilities at an abstract level; and to apply them to well selected topics or content across subject areas.

Finally, the same educational principles used by teachers stimulating their ESL students to develop conceptual competence and topic and content knowledge should be used in higher education teacher training and professional development programs. As stated by the National Research Council (1999a), the development of this deeper conceptual knowledge should also be part of teachers' professional development and education training programs.

> Teachers must come to teaching with the experience of in-depth study of the subject area themselves. Before a teacher can develop powerful pedagogical tools, he or she must be familiar with the progress of inquiry and the terms of discourse in the discipline, as well as understanding the relationship between information and the concepts that help organize that information in the discipline. (p. 16)

Then, teachers need to integrate three critical elements for deep understanding: (1) in-depth knowledge of content and topic knowledge (subject matter), (2) conceptual understanding in order to gain awareness of the structure of knowledge in a discipline, and (3) critical thinking skills to be able to engage in metacognitive strategies to self-monitor learning (i.e., learning how to learn—metalearning—and how to think and problem solve—metacognition).

Thus, both ESL teachers and their ESL students need to develop and use conceptual competence in topic and content knowledge, leading them to become better instructors and learners: to learn how to learn and how to think and problem solve at an abstract or metacognitive level as well as at a topic or content level for specific segments of information across subject areas. Indeed, experts identify similarities among problems on the basis of major principles, so students need to learn that domains of knowledge are embedded into frameworks that have a coherent structure based on principles. Understanding these frameworks provides students with conceptual knowledge that they can transfer to other theoretical and applied domains. As very well said by the National Research Council (1999a), "Helping students to recognize and build on knowledge structures is a crucial goal of teaching" (p. 26). Learning through multiple examples, practicing application of concepts to multiple real-life problems connected to subject matter, and making connections between prior and new knowledge, help students to develop topic and content knowledge as well as problem-solving skills and critical-thinking skills, all leading to metacognitive abilities. Engaging in multiple cognitive processes can help the learner, such as "processes of comparison, evaluating same/different distinctions, categorizing the new problem in terms of what seems familiar or unfamiliar . . . evaluating feedback" (National Research Council, 1999a, p. 27).

A Metacognitive Approach to Teaching and Learning

Learning and thinking strategies can be modeled and acquired by students to monitor their understanding and progress in learning. In other words, teachers will facilitate and mediate learning by becoming models for learning how to learn (i.e., metalearning) and how to think and problemsolve (i.e., **metacognition**). That is, by developing metalearning and metacognitive abilities, "students can take control of their own learning by self-defining goals and monitoring their progress in achieving them" (National Research Council, 1999a, p. 13). For instance, teachers and students can engage in meaningful instructional conversations that teach them explicitly how to use strategies for problem solving, such as using thinking aloud for articulating observations and making deductions and elaborations.

Relatedly, the development of "adaptive expertise," according to Hatano and Inagaki (1986), involves learning how to use metacognitive strategies for monitoring learning activities, such as drawing analogies with prior knowledge. By developing metacognitive strategies, students learn how to generate alternative approaches to critical-thinking and problem-solving situations more effectively. Class discussions can be used by teachers for modeling alternative thinking, with the ultimate goal of learners becoming independent thinkers with self-regulation. That is, as stated by the National Research Council (1999a), content or subject matter needs to be used by teachers to exercise their students' minds and encourage them to talk, write and think about content in collaboration with their peers.

> By talking and listening to each others' thinking, learners gain vocabulary, syntax, and rhetoric—the discourse—needed to understand and describe the knowledge structures associated with specific subjects and specific problems. They can gain greater capacity for metacognition—thinking about and gaining insight into their own thinking and learning processes. (p. 26)

Learning has a social dimension and cognitive processes can be stimulated by a supportive social environment that provides intellectual tools such as the transmission of language and other cultural representational symbolic systems. The presence of other minds to interact with and learn from can result in the transmission of cultural frameworks that help build meaningful knowledge. Then, students internalize social processes and mental tools (i.e., metacognitive and metalearning processes) when learning. Because social and cultural factors are so important for learning, they can alter the quality of learning among cultural groups of individuals, such as minority students. The National Research Council (1999a) also recognizes sociocultural factors' influence in relation to the cultural and linguistic diverse characteristics of ESL students: "The social perspective of learning has also focused scholarly attention on understanding populations of learners and revealed learning differences among children of different social class and learning variations associated with race and ethnicity" (p. 28).

Because learning has an important social and cultural dimension, the use of active learning and discovery of concepts for developing higher level critical-thinking skills needs to be modeled by teachers. For instance, internal dialogue is an important mental tool for metacognition that initially needs to be modeled explicitly by teachers. However, in order for strategies to be useful for learning they need to be modeled within specific subject matters, because strategies are not transferable across subject matters; they are not generic. According to the National Research Council (1999a), "Integration of metacognitive instruction with discipline-based learning can enhance student achievement and develop in students the ability to learn independently" (p. 21). Relatedly, professors in teacher education programs, and in professional development programs, at the higher education level also need to model and prepare teachers for designing and implementing curriculums that improve students' conceptual learning and critical-thinking skills.

Teachers need to be involved in sustained learning through professional development opportunities, that model for them translation of learning and teaching principles into as many inquiry-based strategies as possible. For instance, teacher preparation programs need to model for teachers: curriculum examples, real-life case studies, practice problem solving within specific situations, self-study and reflection, cooperative learning involving practicing metacognitive strategies (such as thinking aloud), simulations and role-playing, videos of their own teaching, **formative assessment** linked with instruction, diversity in learners, and so on. Teachers themselves need to develop strong metacognitive strategies, applied to specific subject matter, and then learn how to model and how to teach these strategies to their students. Teachers must be knowledgeable about content or subject matter in addition to understanding how children think about this subject matter across developmental stages.

Thus, in general, using educational implications of the three learning principles discussed in this chapter, school curricula needs to stimulate students to develop a conceptual knowledge framework as a mental tool for learning factual knowledge and higher level critical-thinking skills (i.e., cognitive and metacognitive and metalinguistic strategies). In the following section the role of language as a cognitive learning tool and the derived three learning principles will be integrated with the role of language as a tool for affective/emotional and social development.

THE ROLE OF LANGUAGE ON AFFECTIVE/EMOTIONAL AND SOCIAL DEVELOPMENT: A SOCIOCONSTRUCTIVISTIC PERSPECTIVE

Learning a language also has an impact on the affective/emotional and social development of a child. Language learning also involves understanding the culture, and thinking culturally in an appropriate manner. Language has a socialization function: to become part of a family, a community, and the larger social group. Within a socioconstructivistic approach, social and cultural mediators (i.e., teachers, parents, and caregivers) use language to interact with children within the social environment in order to develop social skills in children. Communicative interaction, which is social interaction that uses language for communicating meaning, has a central role in developing language and social skills. The child acquires language within a social interactive environment by using social imitation and active learning. According to a socioconstructivistic perspective, language and social abilities are developed by children in an interactive manner. That is, social interaction mediates exposure to language models following meaningful semantic and cultural conventions. In this manner, language learning provides for children a tool for experiencing social interactions within a natural cultural environment.

Relatedly, as language is a tool for socialization, the degree of acculturation of language-minority families and their children is reflected in three ways: (1) in their home language use, (2) in their daily cultural practices, and (3) in the particular values socially communicated—verbally and nonverbally—by parents to their children. That is, the particular language used at home helps parents to socialize their children as they transmit implicitly cultural values to their children. According to Ovando, Collier, and Combs (2003), socialization relates to religious and spiritual cultural styles and to cultural abstractions such as social constructs. Some examples of cultural values and social constructs are independence, freedom, individual choice, conformity, idealism, respect for authority, morality, the concept of time, achievement orientation, work ethic, extended family, and so forth. Learning these cultural values as social constructs is accomplished primarily through adults using language as a socialization tool for educating children.

Socialization also relates to styles of nonverbal communication, such as paralinguistic aspects (e.g., body movements, spatial distance, eye contact, emotional tone). Identity is also a central part of socialization, providing for individuals with personal choice in relation to assuming a cultural identity. Some ESL students chose to become bicultural, other may be more ambivalent about their cultural identity choice, and yet others may choose to become monocultural. In countless instances the first author has heard undergraduate students painfully acknowledging that they are not comfortable in the mainstream American society but neither are they in their minority group, and others yet may choose to become monocultural and monolingual and identify with the mainstream culture only.

It is also important to understand that different cultures have different styles of social interactions and therefore caretakers model different language patterns across different cultures. For instance, the construct of "motherese" has been studied and demonstrated that caretakers use a simplified language when communicating with youngsters. Moreover, different cultures emphasize different social uses of language, as caretakers need to model for youngsters the social conventions and cultural styles of communication and social interaction. Thus, the way in which language is used at home also reflects different cultural ways of socializing children: what Shatz refers to as "communicative modes" or styles, related to cultural content transmitted such as social values.

Educators should provide a good model of standard English, but understand and respect the dialect and/or language that children learn at home because language and cultural identity is connected to their children's ethnic and social identity (i.e., linked to their SES and cultural heritage). Thus, educators should nurture ESL children's ability to master the mainstream academic English language in order to develop a tool for learning conceptual and content knowledge and for becoming affective/emotionally and socially competent, and ultimately achievers in the mainstream school culture and society at large. Some educational principles on the role of language within a sociocon-structivistic perspective on affective/emotional and social development in ESL children are reviewed next.

EDUCATIONAL PRINCIPLES DERIVED FROM RESEARCH-BASED KNOWLEDGE IN AFFECTIVE AND EMOTIONAL FACTORS: EXPECTATIONS, EFFORT, AND MOTIVATION

According to the National Research Council (1999b),

> For school-age children, motivation to achieve is strongly related to their beliefs about the nature of intelligence, and how it is acquired. If they believe in the malleability of intelligence and some internal locus of control (rather than fixed aptitude and luck or the actions of others), children will try and keep trying. (p. 31)

Cross-cultural research, comparing China, Japan, and the United States (e.g., Tobin et al., 1989), has revealed the powerful effect of beliefs on students' academic achievement, such as the belief in effort. The Carnegie Task Force on Learning in the Primary Grades (1996) revealed that students' expectation about their academic achievement tend to be set up during the early grades and respond to perceptions of peers, school, family, and community explicit and overt messages. These expectations can be damaging not only to mainstream, but especially to minority students, because "societal messages about fixed aptitude associated with groups (by race, ethnicity, or gender) can be particularly oppressive" (cited in the National Research Council, 1999b, p. 31). According to the U.S. Department of Education (1996, cited in the National Research Council, 1999b), "Students who live in high-poverty and culturally diverse areas experience conditions at home, at school, and in the community that correlate with low academic achievement" (p. 48).

Unfortunately, demographic growth in these at-risk urban areas will show a much higher growth index, resulting in a major challenge for educators to educate every child to high academic standards. As asserted by the National Research Council (1999b), the level of socioeconomic status is a very significant factor negatively affecting academic achievement in minority students,

> The conditions endemic in many urban areas—high concentrations of poverty, family instability, crime, unemployment—complicate the process of education enormously. . . . Once a school has more than 40 percent low-income students, there are few programs that have a significant effect on achievement levels" (p. 48).

Even though teaching ESL students exposed to at-risk SES conditions can be challenging, high-quality teaching can help students to increase their intrinsic motivation for learning. As suggested by the National Research Council (1999b), "intrinsic motivation can be enhanced through involvement in activities that are varied, engaging, social, and 'authentic' (that is related to real-world 'purposes' or uses)" (p. 34), such as project learning, cooperative learning, and discovery learning. According to the Carnegie Task Force on Learning in the Primary Grades (1996), "Drawing on theory and practice in developmental psychology and cognitive science . . . children learn best in the context of caring and collaborative relationships" (p. 40). Socializing students to understand that intelligence is also connected to effort spent on multiple trials and practice, spending time and energy in improving skills and abilities and acquiring new knowledge, will promote intrinsic motivation and higher achievement levels (Resnick & Kolper, 1989). Comparing students' performance to their own individual gains can also rewarding them to improve their learning outcome, and has been proved to be an effective external motivation (Natriello, 1987; Slavin, 1980). The focus of instruction needs to be on developing competence, on developing a sense of belonging to a learning community so that students participate actively in all learning activities. According to Simon (1996, cited in the National Research Council, 1999b),

> Research indicates that in order to be effective, discovery learning experiences must strike the right balance between simplicity and complexity, build on the previous knowledge and experience of the learner, and offer opportunities for discovery at a pace that sustains student interest. (p. 37)

When students lose intrinsic motivation for learning, they disengage from learning, resulting in negative outcomes such as underachievement, dropping out of school, and, ultimately, problems in transitioning to work and a productive life. Based on a large body of research studies (see e.g., Ensminger & Slusarcick, 1992; Felner, Kasak, Mulhall, & Flowers, 1997; Kaplan & Luck, 1977; Lloyd, 1978; Sheperd & Smith, 1992; Stroup & Robins, 1972), the higher risk for dropping out of school has been associated with absenteeism in the primary grades, a history of poor academic achievement in the primary grades, history of tracking and grade retention, problems with school adjustment mainly due to a mismatch between the home and school culture and expectations, and tracking.

Applying the same knowledge base, for teachers to perform at higher levels they need to belong to a professional community of colleagues. The sense of collegiality can support and encourage teachers to share values, engage in collaborative decision making, have access to continuous professional developmental activities, and take collective responsibility for students' learning (National Research Council, 1999b). Thus, in the first two sections we have discussed the important role of language for learning and development across cognitive, affective/emotional, and social areas. The use of language at home and school by adults as a tool for learning and socialization can be understood and improved to help ESL students learn how to think and problem solve and, ultimately, how to become members of a family, a community, and a social group. See Box 3.1 for the case of a Hispanic 10th-grade ESL student. Higher education teacher training and professional development programs can also benefit from applying these same educational principles derived from research. For teachers to become role models and to apply high-quality educational principles, they also need to learn from instructors and mentors or role models how to learn and how to think and problem solve when serving and catering to the educational needs of the diverse group of ESL students.

BOX 3.1

SUMMARY OF AN INTERVIEW WITH A 10TH-GRADE, HISPANIC ESL STUDENT

The interview was conducted in Spanish by the first author of the book. The actual digital recording of the interview is available in the companion Web site for the book.

BACKGROUND

Sonia (pseudonym) was a 16-year-old, Hispanic female ELS student, who was finishing grade in a suburban high school within a mixed neighborhood of a metropolitan area in the Midwest region of the United States. Sonia was born and raised in Mexico, a city Morelia, located in the southern province of Michoacan. She had finished up to seventh grade in Mexico and then had relocated with her family to the United States about 2 years before the time of the interview.

Sonia had moved to the United States with her family, consisting of her father and mother and her three younger sisters. She was the first-born, and had three younger sisters (ages 11, 9, and 3). The family spoke primarily Spanish at home, with the siblings using also some words in English. Sonia considered that her father spoke some English, but he could not write or read English. Her father had finished up to sixth grade in Mexico and could read and write in Spanish. Her father worked in a warehouse helping to load merchandize. Sonia considered that her mother could not speak English at all, but she had finished up to sixth grade in Mexico and could read and write in Spanish. Her mother worked in a sausage factory.

SCHOOL EXPERIENCE IN THE UNITED STATES AND ESL HISTORY

Sonia was finishing up her second year of schooling in the United States by the time of the interview. She had come to the United States with very little knowledge of English; as she explained, "I could say only a few words." When asked to rate her ability to speak English, Sonia thought that her abilities were intermediate by the time of the interview. She explained that, "I have improved a lot in the last 2 years, but still need to learn to conjugate verbs and improve my punctuation and spelling." Sonia acknowledged that she had had some difficulties adapting to school in the United States because of her lack of adequate English skills that made her feel embarrassed. She considered that English pronunciation was her most difficult area, and writing was easier for her. Sonia also had experienced some difficulty in math, but could manage to get As in all other subject areas. Even though Sonia had experienced some academic difficulties due to her limited English skills, she still maintained a positive attitude toward the opportunity to study in the United States. She explained that her parents decided to come to the United States because she and her sisters could study and have a career, and enjoy better job and economic opportunities for their future. Her goal was to study photography or computer skills at the university after graduating from high school. She wanted to make her parents happy and feel proud of her by becoming a high school and university graduate. She had visited a nearby university with a Hispanic support group at school, but still needed some help with information about scholarships.

Sonia, however, also could see some disadvantages of being in the United States. She explained that, "I cannot be with my family [meaning her relatives and extended

(continued)

BOX 3.1 CONTINUED

family members] in special events such as birthdays. I cannot go out by myself because I do not have a car, back in Mexico everything was closer [since she used to live in a much smaller town in Mexico than in the United States], I cannot finish learning how to write in Spanish." Thus, Sonia could perceive some advantages in terms of academic, job, and economic opportunities opening for herself in the United States, but also could see some disadvantages in terms of missing contact with her extended family and native language. Contrasting pros and cons created some cognitive dissonance for Sonia, resulting in feeling puzzled by what she had to lose in affective and emotional ties with her family, culture, and language that she used to enjoy in Mexico in order to gain some educational, professional, and economic opportunities in the United States.

Sonia considered that participating in a pullout ESL program for the past 2 years had been helpful because a Spanish-speaking teacher could explain to her the instructions for homework, projects, and exams she could not understand. She believed that her grades had improved, and she could even get As in most subject matters because of the support she received in the ESL program. This help was especially necessary in math, an area in which she used ESL teachers to explain concepts, and also was provided with extra time to complete projects and exams.

EXTRACURRICULAR ACTIVITIES IN ENGLISH INFLUENCING SOCIAL LANGUAGE AND SOCIALIZATION ABILITIES
Sonia explained that she could talk with some students at school and also with some teachers outside classroom situations, such as in the cafeteria or during recess. However, some other students and teachers do not talk to her at all outside classroom situations. She continued, explaining that she had a best friend, also a Hispanic ESL student, who sat with her at the cafeteria and they enjoyed speaking in Spanish.

Sonia used the help of classmates to explain to her words or instructions she could not understand. She also received help from some teachers such as the science, math, and ESL teachers, who elaborated instructions and content by using easier words in English.

PROCESS OF SECOND-LANGUAGE LEARNING: BEST EDUCATIONAL APPROACHES AND CLASSROOM TEACHING STRATEGIES FOR ESL TEACHING AND LEARNING

In this book, we are taking a pluralistic approach to ESL teaching and learning. The term *approach* in general ESL terms relates to or references particular research perspectives, paradigms, or models (Celce-Murcia, 1991). So, approach in an ESL and text context means examining sets of assumptions made in L2 learning concerning how language is learned. In this sense, then, an approach makes a common set of assumptions that are implicit in L2 teaching and learning (Celce-Murcia, 1991; Ovando, Collier, & Combs, 2003).

In turn, **pluralism** in these contexts refers to two or more approaches or multiple models of ESL. An example of using a pluralistic approach clarifies these terms. For instance, a teacher understands and diagnoses the ESL students' level of English-language acquisition and production. In turn, this teacher plans the additional series of lessons for this and other ESL students. In using a pluralistic approach, the teacher matches major ESL theoretical perspectives with the ESL skills to be taught to the ESL student. On the other hand, the eclectic approach takes advantage of previous years of ESL teacher experiences and personal hunches as to what to teach (i.e., ESL skill/s) and how to teach it (i.e., approach or perspective). However, the eclectic approach may become unfruitful if it lacks explicit use of theory and research-based information to make informed decisions about the underlying rationale for the selection of ESL instructional strategies. True to the meaning conveyed by the phrase "There is nothing more practical than a good theory," theoretical principles and research-based information can be translated by knowledgeable teachers into very useful ESL instructional strategies, and ultimately into tremendous benefits for the academic and social English-language skills and academic achievement of ESL students.

The pluralistic or "best practices" approach is based on a best match between theory, ESL skill/s, and ESL students' characteristics. In the following sections, we demonstrate this best practices approach using this mix of theory, ESL skills, and students' characteristics. The five major approaches chosen for explanation follow: grammar translation, direct, audiolingual, cognitive, and communicative competence approaches. A discussion of each perspective follows and major instructional strategies are identified for each perspective with examples of how these strategies can be used. This discussion gives examples of the pluralistic approach and the mix of theory, ESL skill, and the ESL students' level of growth, acquisition and production of English. In Chapter 4 of this book these best educational approaches and classroom teaching strategies are further expanded into educational applications.

BEHAVIORISTIC LANGUAGE APPROACHES

Grammar Translation Approach

The use of the grammar translation approach predates the twentieth century and continues to the present day. As the authors teach and work with American and international ESL teachers in the United States and from other countries, our data suggest that the **grammar translation approach** is not only alive and well but used extensively worldwide, including in the United States. Notable examples from the Renaissance period include using grammar translation to teach Classical Greek, from the Old Testament Greek, and Classic Latin. Currently, in the United States this grammar translation approach is still used to teach modern world languages. It has declined in use in the United States since the 1960s; however, at a worldwide level this approach is very much in vogue. The grammar translation approach in ESL methods and as a teaching technique emphasizes understanding of the language form or structure and its meanings.

Clearly, the focus or major concern is emphasizing reading content materials in the L2 and in writing in L2 (Ovando, Collier, & Combs, 2003). Learning oral language or its use in communicating meaningfully is not of great concern to either the teacher instructing the class or the students. This method can be successful in moving the students to learn to read and write the target L2 but its main emphases is on translations from L2 to L1. For example, in Latin courses and other world language courses, the students are given some important texts written in the target L2 and then spend much time in translating the content to L1.

For example, one of the authors was required to take Latin to graduate from high school. The first of four years of Latin focused on translating a rather difficult text narrating Julius Ceasar's Gallic Wars. Long lists of vocabulary words were put to memory with no context except that provided by the text, and equally long verb conjugations also were committed to memory. These vocabulary words and verb conjugations were converted to drills that were learned automatically. It is clear in working with and teaching international students, that the method of choice for teaching English as an L2 is grammar translation. The international students in English as a Foreign Language (EFL) from Korea or Taiwan, for example, do much translation of L2 textbooks and reading materials. In turn, L1 is discussed extensively, as it is used to identify themes, respond to questions over L2 content, and, ultimately, translate the L2 texts and materials. As one can imagine, reading levels of the majority of these EFL students tend to be high, especially with an 8 to 10 year use of this approach. Writing levels are a distant third or fourth in proficiency, however, and oral language and listening require much more dedicated usage and meaningful learning in classroom social contexts. So, the content in this approach became the grammatical structure emphasized in L2 translating of text and reading materials (Celce-Murcia, 1991).

The ESL or EFL teacher using the grammar translation approach uses the L1, not L2, in teaching. The popularity of this method rests with several facts (Brown, 1994). These include: little skill requirements on the part of the teacher and the development of tests for content items are easy to score and make, such as tests for grammar rules and translations from L2 to L1. Freeman and Freeman (1998) give a template for the grammar translation approach; notice the emphasis on steps or procedures.

1. First, a text or portion of a text is assigned to be read and translated from L2 to L1. Freeman and Freeman note that the texts usually focus on L2 heroes or heroines.
2. Next, vocabulary words from the text are listed and memorized.
3. Some questions follow about the content of the narrative, which then are answered in L1 writing or in oral discussion.
4. Following the questions, formal study occurs of grammar such as predicates, subjects, and verb conjugations.
5. Finally, the students receive practice with aspects of grammar and verb tenses covered in Step 4. Here, the students complete the worksheets and exercises and translate from L1 to L2 or L2 to L1.

This template points out the fact that there is no need for oral communication, pronunciation, and comprehension. With some mental gymnastics, a benefit of this approach is learning grammar of L1, that is, the native language. The students learn verb tenses and conjugations, transitive and intransitive verbs and many exceptions to the grammar rules. Brown (1994, p. 53) characterized this approach as "theorylessness" because there is no empirical and research support that this approach is effective in teaching L2 acquisition. This approach may be used in part or in toto in world languages and in learning L2. However, this approach is still very much used and in vogue in the United States and worldwide.

Direct Approach

Celce-Murcia (1991) said that the **direct approach** arose as a direct reaction to the grammar translation approach and its perceived problems. The specific criticisms of the grammar translation approach that were addressed in the direct approach included three main issues:

1. Emphasis on the analyses of L2 language/s
2. Use of the L1 and the medium of instruction for L2
3. Focus on translations of L2 content to L1 using difficult texts for grammar analyses

Instead, according to Celce-Murcia (1191), the direct approach provided some advantages over the grammar translation approach because it included three main characteristics:

1. Emphasis on the uses of L2 in conversations and other natural language situations
2. Use of L2 in teaching and instructing and providing modeling of L2 language use in natural contexts
3. Focus on recreational readings and materials written in L2 without the heavy emphases on grammar and grammatical parsing (the process that studies inflections and forms of grammar)

With the swing of the pendulum, the direct approach was billed as a natural way to learn language because its emphases is on use in situational contexts rather than on grammar, tenses, and so forth emphasized in translating L2 texts. The term *naturalistic way* was associated with the direct approach because its language learning was thought to parallel or simulate the way children learned their L1 (Brown, 1994).

The naturalistic way, with its parallels to L1 development, shows spontaneous use of words and phrases, much oral dialogue and conversational interactions between individuals, and no focus on or concern with grammatical rules and parsing. This approach, like the grammar translation approach, predates the twentieth century and continues to the present. However, its popularity too experiences pendulum swings in terms of increasing and decreasing importance and usage in selected schools and universities.

Freeman and Freeman (1998) emphasized that all instruction uses L2 even from the very beginning. With no translations to L1 permitted, the focus is on the developing L2 language users who could actually use the language in dialogues and in conversations that they were studying. For the direct approach, the teacher must demonstrate native fluency or near native fluency and proficiency in L2 because the entire class, every activity and in all situations is carried out in L2 contexts. In introducing new words or phrases, the teacher uses actions, gestures, pantomime, and other communicative forms to demonstrate meanings of these new terms and phrases. In addition, pictures, miniature objects, and authentic realia are used to illustrate the meanings of these phrases and terms. Although the emphasis is on listening and speaking, students also write L2 sentences, words, and paragraphs as soon as instruction begins. (Freeman & Freeman, 1998). Because of the total use of L2 in classrooms, the direct approach commonly is called *immersion* or immersion without support from L1.

However, Ovando, Collier, and Combs (2003) qualified this statement by differentiating immersion in the direct approach from the Canadian form of bilingual immersion. In the latter approach, immersion in L2 is the focus but L1 is used as well in classroom programs. The direct approach uses L2 only with no L1 support. In addition, Ovando, Collier, and Combs (2003), in similar contexts of immersion, make other sound points by distinguishing the direct and ESL approaches: "ESL classes with students from mixed language backgrounds automatically become immersion classes taught completely in a second language" (p. 72). They qualified this statement, however, by saying that not all ESL classes use the direct approach because of the variability of content and sequencing choices and of different teaching strategies and materials used by ESL teachers.

The students are immersed in L2 and learn culture and grammar structures such as pronunciation and grammatical rules inductively by actually experiencing and living the L2. Teacher corrections of oral pronunciations of words and phrases, for example, are done by modeling and imitating, which signals that students are to listen and imitate the teacher to the best of their abilities (Celce-Murcia & Goodwin, 1991). In classroom settings, teachers using the direct approach bring materials such as real objects or miniatures into the classroom. These materials become tools for students around which they converse and respond naturally and spontaneously and in open-ended conversations. The L2 conversations are not scripted or sequenced beforehand; instead, they mirror real-life experiences within L2 cultural settings.

Freeman and Freeman (1998) developed a highly flexible general template for teaching and developing lessons and activities for use in the classroom based on the direct approach:

1. It uses organizers such as themes or topics around which instruction is focused. As examples, themes can be foods, clothing items, family work schedules and body parts, and so forth.

2. With L2 language proficiency, cultural aspects are added and provide more in-depth understandings as foundations for L2 learning. Examples of these themes include: heroes/heroines, holiday calendars of the culture, cultural customs and other aspects of history, sociology, geography, the arts, music and other themes relevant to these L2 foundations.

3. Across these topics, inductive approaches to learning L2 grammar are used so that the students experience L2 grammar within related, focused contexts. This use of themes and contexts are thought to be meaningful because of L2 utility. Adding meaningful cultural contexts can be done with videos, musical selections, readings, real objects, and other authentic materials, cultural and country-specific posters, and other travel and vacation support materials that provide situational and contextual settings.

4. Students and teachers interact and work with each other by asking questions and answering in L2 and using new vocabulary and standard grammar.

5. Pronunciation is also part of the picture. In ideal form, students help each other correct and self-correct pronunciation through modeling and imitating one another and the teacher.

6. Role playing and demonstrations are used for stressing communication of expressions, words, and statements through the development of speaking, listening, reading, and writing skills. Sequencing of L2 grammar occurs within these communicative situations that use dialogue activities and anecdotes. The latter become the organizers that arise from grammar sequences

7. Students' levels of L2 proficiency are assessed and in turn evaluated using communicative situations such as actual discussions, oral interviews, situational activities; and also through the usual written exercises, assignments, and tests.

The direct approach is widely accepted and used extensively as the L2 approach of choice in numerous private academic and language schools throughout the United States. Also, this approach is used quite successfully in universities and special institutes across the United States. For example, in summer terms, immersion world-language institutes are offered during six- and eight-week terms at two of the authors' universities. The students taking these special immersion language institutes live together in campus dormitories, have classes together, eat and socialize and do recreational things together. However, across these activities, the students use L2 exclusively. And, at the end of the six or eight weeks, the graduates show a sound mastery of social L2 to enable them to conduct activities and in some cases, business, in L2 languages. Commonly, the languages of choice for these university and college language immersion institutes include: Russian, Chinese, Spanish and select languages of interest such as Italian. Finally, Freeman and Freeman (1998) stated that the direct approach is used by Berlitz Schools. The Berlitz method is actually the direct approach. Begun by founder Maximillian Berlitz, the Berlitz Schools use the direct approach and are found worldwide, such as in Puerto Rico and Taiwan.

In public schools in the United States, the direct approach requires small class size, supportive budgets, instructors thoroughly knowledgeable in target languages, and large blocks of subject-focused time. Because of these requirements, public schools in the United States do not make extensive use of this approach (Brown, 1994). In fact, Brown said that the success of the direct approach is more a function of enthusiastic and high-energy-oriented personalities and the skills of the teachers than the approach itself. In Europe, the use of the direct approach is another matter because of geographic proximity. For example, France, Germany, Spain, Holland, Belgium, Denmark, and other countries produce living language laboratories for contextual learning of multiple

L2s. It is not uncommon for Europeans to demonstrate L2 competencies and fluencies in multiple world languages.

Audiolingual Approach

With pendulums swing in terms of emphasis on various world-language teaching approaches, the **audiolingual approach** emerged as the teaching method of choice. The audiolingual approach goes by several names, including: audiolingual method (ALM), the Army Specialized Training Program (ASTP), and the Army method (AM). Initially, the colloquial AM or more formal ASTP emerged from large amounts of U.S. Army funding at the onset of World War II to develop intensive world-language courses that emphasized oral and, more specifically, communicative (not-reading) approaches to L2 acquisition and training. The AM or ASTP of the 1940s became the audiolingual approach in the 1950s.

This approach of oral-aural learning of languages was a backlash against and reaction to the perceived failures of the direct translation approach, so renamed as the "handmaiden of reading" approach (Bowen, Madsen & Hilferty, 1985; cited in Brown, 1994) and especially its lack of focused oral skills in L2 teaching. Although the audiolingual approach took many characteristics from the direct translation approach, these attributes and others became more structured and sequenced and spun around the current theories of behavioral psychology and structural linguistics. In the next section, the attributes of behavioral psychology are examined that characterize the audiolingual and related theoretical language approaches.

With the audiolingual approach, L2 learning begins with dialogues and new learning is introduced via dialogue form. In dialogue form, new structural patterns are introduced and taught through continual repetition that in a sense, become manipulative drills. Ovando, Collier, and Combs (2003, p. 73) called this characteristic *mim-mem*, meaning teaching L2 through much mimicry and memorization. These structural grammar patterns, from simple to more complex ones, are taught one at a time and reinforced through manipulative student drills. These procedures are thought to control and essentially reduce student L2 errors. To determine the structural grammar patterns, contrastive analyses were used. Here, L2 and L1 languages are contrasted and differences between them provide the bases for determining and sequencing these teaching points found within these patterns (Ovando, Collier, & Combs, 2003). These structures, through dialogue, produce grammar teaching that is inductive rather than deductive. So, teaching grammar didactically is almost nonexistent and is not recommended in this approach.

Listening, speaking, reading, and writing are emphasized. In this particular sequence or order, the language skills are taught. Exact pronunciations characteristic of native speakers of L2 are stressed. So, in a sense, the speaker's pronunciations need to match the criterion of native speakers. Needless to say, a great emphasis on pronunciation is critical to this approach. In a sense, the attempt is for pronunciation that is L2 error-free. To get error-free utterances with native fluency, many types of media are used with teaching. These technical media creating somewhat of a psychological reality include: audiotapes, many visual aids, language laboratories with ear phones, microphones and speakers, computer software and related hardware, and so forth

(Brinton, 1991). Nontechnical media used actively in this approach include: blackboards and whiteboards, realia, posters and maps, and so forth (Brinton, 1991).

In the audiolingual approach, the total use of L2 in classroom settings is recommended strongly for explanations, descriptions, directions, or instructions. However, there is some acknowledgement to and at limited times of L1 uses. Correct use of L2 by the students is rewarded and reinforced immediately following behavioral language traditions.

Freeman and Freeman (1998) provided a specific template that is highly structured and sequenced. This template gives sound examples for L2 teaching in the classroom using the audiolingual approach. In describing a typical audiolingual lesson, Freeman and Freeman, as well as other authors such as Celce-Murcia (1991), said that the students begin with the teacher handing them a dialogue. This dialog focuses on a specific structural pattern. An example from Celce-Murcia and Goodwin (1991, p.141) follows; the specific structural pattern in this dialog is intonation and its importance in oral speaking and questioning.

A: "I've just read a book"

B: "What?"

This short dialogue is read aloud many times and read purposefully in several different ways. Depending on the intonation, Celce-Murcia and Goodwin (1991) said that many different meanings arise from B's "What?" Here, B's "What?" might mean: "What did you say?" or "What book was it?" or "What! You actually read a book?" (p. 141). As a reminder, this structural pattern practices varieties of intonations with many varieties of interpretation characterizing this patterned, focused dialogue and not others.

The audiolingual approach emphasizes nurturing oral language and, in this example, derives meanings from varieties of intonations, thereby developing oral language. Consequently, there is much time spent in class going through and saying the dialogue many times. Language drills can be substituted for dialogues. Freeman and Freeman (1998) gave an example of a single-slot substitution drill. For example, in holding up and showing a pencil the teachers says: "This is a pencil!" (Freeman & Freeman, 1998, p. 11). After this is mastered and repeated, the teacher moves on and prompts the students by saying "pen" while holding up the pen. Again, the students respond, "This is a pen!" Freeman and Freeman (1998) gave a more complicated drill called two-slot substitution drill. Here, the students would listen to two-slot substitutions: "Tom, plumber," putting both words into the drill and replacing "Julio, principal" after practicing the original drill, "Julio is a principal!", many times.

Meanings of the structural patterns fundamental to these dialogues and drills rather than simply understanding the words, are of primary concern. For example, in rephrasing the question in the above dialogue from "What did you say?" to "What book was it?" the student's understandings or meanings of these questions may not be understood but he or she gets the structural or syntactic patterns.

There are many types and kinds of language drills for many practice skills such as stresses, reduced speech, rhymes, and so forth. An example of a language drill sequenced for rhythm is the following "jazz chant" from Celce-Murcia and Goodwin (1991, p. 141):

A: What's your name and where are you from? What's your name and where are you from?

B: My name is Mei and I am from Taiwan! My name is Mei and I am from Taiwan!

A: Been here long? Been here long?

B: Not too long. Just a few months! Not too long. Just a few months!

The reader of the stanzas of the jazz chant can feel the oral pronunciation demands on the speaker as well as the rhythms of the various stanzas.

Celce-Murcia and Goodwin (1991, p. 142) listed some procedures for the teacher for further thought as she or he works with dialogue using the audiolingual approach.

1. Have students listen and make stressed words. (As an additional clue, you may want to tell students how many words are stressed in each line.)
2. Have students mark each line (e.g., rise, fall, rise-fall).
3. Read certain lines with various intonations and ask the students to decide which mood is being express (e.g., anger, sadness, amazement).
4. Ask students to read or act out the entire dialogue in one particular mood and to note the variations in intonation patterns.

The audiolingual approach is the philosophy many public schools and universities follow today, both in the United States and worldwide. In its audiolingual rather than AM form, this approach is of 1960s vintage with great *emphases* on oral pronunciation and precise, native speech. Whether in public schools or universities, this approach does not produce fluent students who communicate well in L2 (Freeman & Freeman, 1998). This particular problem with audiolingual approach plus its heavy emphases on structure and sequence and reliance on repetition and mimicry leave much to be desired as an approach of choice in L2 language development. Rephrasing a frequent outcome of audiolingual use, Freeman and Freeman (1998) pointed out that after many years of L2, students say they do not use their L2 knowledge because they don't come across dialogue situations (e.g., "At the Railroad Station," "While at the Beach") in which they were trained or the cues they have studied are not provided. The end result is that they are not able to respond. Nonetheless, the audiolingual approach continues to enjoy widespread use in high schools, colleges, and universities.

BEHAVIORISTIC LANGUAGE THEORY OR MODEL: FROM APPROACH TO CLASSROOM TECHNIQUES

The term *approach* as defined and used in the previous section means examining sets of assumptions made in L2 learning and teaching. In other words, as we ESL teachers work with ESL students we use certain classroom techniques or activities to develop English language growth. These techniques then have and show some common methodological elements that document and demonstrate the "whys" and "hows" of L2 teaching and ESL students' learning of L2. In a sense then, an approach has a common, similar set of assumptions that tie together the methods and that are implicit and document assumptions in L2 teaching and learning (Celce-Murcia, 1991; Ovando, Collier, & Combs, 2003). The closest step to the classroom application or actual work directly with ESL students then is technique. Techniques are actual strategies or instructional pedagogies that anchor the approach in the classroom. Let's now examine further the three approaches previously discussed (e.g., grammar translation, direct approach, and audiolingual approach) to see common assumptions and identify examples of some instructional classroom techniques or teaching strategies derived from these common assumptions.

The grammar translation, and the direct and audiolingual approaches have a number of common characteristics that suggest and imply how L2 is learned and taught. In surveying these three approaches, there are several assumptions that tie them together broadly under the umbrella representing behavioristic language theory or model. A major, basic assumption seen in varying degrees across these three approaches show their behavioristic frameworks. Initially, learning language is viewed as habit formation. More recently, with the advent of the Audiolingual Approach, learning language is viewed through operant conditioning models or theories (Celce-Murcia, 1991; Freeman & Freeman, 1998).

LEARNING LANGUAGE: FROM HABIT FORMATION TO OPERANT CONDITIONING

According to habit formation, the primary objective or goal of L2 learning was "learning the language." Historically, habit formation is part of behavioristic language theory and a psychological relative of more current behavioristic language views. Behavioristic language theory views language as a unified "system of rule-governed structures" that are sequenced or ordered in serial and hierarchical fashion (Celce-Murcia, 1991, p. 70). So, L2 with its structure is teaching L2 rather than teaching *about* L2 (Freeman & Feeman, 1998). Here, language becomes a set of habits that are strengthened as L2 skills are learned. Emphasis is first on oral (aural-oral) language and then on written language.

Although the grammar translation approach stresses exclusively written language, it is nonetheless included within the behavioristic language tradition because of its strong control of sequencing of content in translations, evaluating the translated content to correct structural, grammatical form, and so forth (Gonzalez, Brusca-Vega, & Yawkey, 1997). In addition, the direct approach uses open-ended responses to authentic materials brought into classroom settings rather than manipulative exercises. However, these materials are controlled and sequenced on selected skills, categorized by degree of difficulty, from easiest to most difficult. Both grammar translation and direct approaches fit with early forms of behavoristic language perspectives. The most contemporary forms of behavioristic language theory include the audiolingual approach.

So, in more current behavioristic language theory, language learning moves historically from a set of habits as analogies to stimulus-response associations or connections (e.g., operant conditioning). For example, the audiolingual approach emphasis is on correct structural patterns, first beginning with oral-aural, and then moving to written structural forms. So, the emphasis on form (or morphology) and order (or syntax) is preceded by sound patterns or philology in the audiolingual approach, and then followed by form and order. These patterns were reinforced by automaticity via drills and exercises. The earlier section on audiolingual approach gave examples of drills and exercises. In addition, these patterns were stimulus-response associated by means of memorizing dialogues heavily relying on mimicry and memorization or simply in mim-mem fashion (Ovando, Collier, & Combs, 2003). Within more current behavioristic language theory, for example, in audiolingual approach, the sequence of skills is precisely followed from listening to speaking and then to reading and writing.

Behavioristic language theory structures tight control of language sounds, their forms in learning processes, and of course their order. So, the lessons become graded from simple to complex with the product or outcome intended to demonstrate a native-like command of L2. Within the lessons' structure, the L2 learner is guided through this sequence of learning to produce responses whose criteria demonstrate and reflect native-like proficiencies. Along with the internal structure of the lessons, the L2 teacher also plays a very active and directive role because he or she becomes the model for native-language response correctness. In addition, the L2 teacher within behavioristic language theory sets the pace or speed of the lessons and moves the students toward specific objectives, goals, and directed endpoints. In the following section, examples are given of particular methods and classroom techniques for mainstream behavioristic language theories.

Methods and Classroom Techniques

Behavioristic language methods show selected procedures of teaching and learning L2. These procedural methods can fit with several approaches grouped within the behavioristic language paradigm (e.g., grammar translation approach, and direct and audiolingual approaches). Some examples of these methods or principles are provided here in relation to classroom techniques (see also Yawkey, in preparation).

Language Words.   Language words, statements and concepts are seen as discrete, measurable, and overt (observable) actions (see Gonzalez, Brusca-Vega, & Yawkey, 1997). As stated by this methodological principle, observable actions become discrete behaviors and therefore keys to perceiving objectively if the L2 learner acquires language statements, words, and so forth. Classroom techniques that fit this method include form- and order-fashioned learning materials with slots for nouns, followed by verbs and then objects. For example, the L2 learner finds noun cards, pronounces the noun and puts word card into the "noun" slot. The L2 learner continues and builds nouns learned into the three-word sentence/s, and so forth.

Language Practice.   Another method is: the more the oral or written language is practiced correctly, the more strongly language is learned (Yawkey, in preparation). Here, this principle focuses on practice and repetition—essentially, habits are reinforced appropriately after responses are made to stimuli. There are many classroom techniques that show this method. For example, "jazz chants," in which L2 learners repeat oral language patterns that show word stress, intonation, rhyming, and other grammatical elements. These are repeated to demonstrate comprehension, with language emerging as a communicative tool. Other techniques include dictation, cloze activities, conjugating verbs in oral and written fashion, and so forth.

Language as Operants.   An example of the language-as-operants method is that language results from actions in the environment on the L2 learner (Yawkey, in preparation). Oral and written language are viewed as "operants" or sets of responses demonstrated or emitted and governed by stimulus consequences that result because of these response sets. In a sense, L2 learners demonstrate native-like proficiency because of the consequences received or applied after showing appropriate oral or written statements, and so forth. There are many classroom techniques that apply this method in classroom applications. Examples include: computer interactive programs for L2 acquisition, simple spell checks, language tapes used with picture dictionaries and computer L2 narratives in which responses are immediately identified as incorrect (in which case cueing and prompting are used) or correct (in this case, the L2 learner knows that correct responses are made).

Language as Ordered/Sequenced Elements.   An example of language as ordered or sequenced elements follows: For language learning and mastery, we break language down into smaller units of learning and then arrange or order them into a hierarchy of difficulty (Yawkey, in preparation). This method drives teaching techniques as well. The assumption here is that concrete behaviors as main or specific behaviors can be subdivided into smaller and more easily learned units and then quantitatively measured through structured observations and task analyses (Gonzalez, Brusca-Vega, & Yawkey, 1997). Gonzalez, Brusca-Vega, and Yawkey (1997) provided some important examples of this fourth method and asked teachers to analyze specific concepts for teaching by asking four questions. In turn, these questions help the teacher greatly to develop techniques and classroom activities. One system for determining levels of difficulty asks the teacher the following questions:

1. What concepts must children know in order to complete the task?
2. What kinds of attention skills must they have?
3. What kinds of physical movements are necessary (to learn the task)?
4. What behavior consequences must children perform (to learn the task)?

Answers to these questions define L2 language elements, and after survey of the elements the order and sequence emerge for planning for classroom techniques. There are other systems available for assisting the ESL teacher with analyzing language into smaller units. For example, Brown (1997) considered the Prator system (in Brown, pp. 209–210), which presented the ESL teachers with six categories of language difficulty, ranging from Level 0 (Transfer) to Level 5 (Split) and gave an example of another system (in Brown, pp. 78–79) that breaks down L2 language tasks into a four-step process ranging from entry behavior to training methods.

In applying this method of language as ordered or sequenced elements, several techniques used in the classroom come to mind. An initial example is the ESL teacher making predictions about difficulties of particular L2 language concepts for teaching and then ordering or sequencing them for ESL mastery. Another example is the classroom use of error correction. Here, the ESL teacher compares L1 and L2 and tries to establish beforehand areas of difficulty that may arise in L2 learning. These items are then built into the activities in a sequenced and ordered manner.

Language and Discriminative Stimuli.   The fifth method, making and using discriminative stimuli, facilitates language learning because these discriminative stimuli encourage appropriate language behaviors (Yawkey, in preparation). This method uses a variety of prompts, ranging from concrete to social prompts, as discriminative stimuli that accelerate responses of the learner to act in particular ways. Discriminative stimuli tend to elicit or accelerate L2 learning in desired ways. The basic underlying premise is the creation of opportunities for ESL students to elicit appropriate responses. With classroom techniques, many activities are developed that focus on L2 language and discriminative stimuli. For example, when the child produces a response, "school," to the stimulus picture and the question, "What is this building called?" the appropriate language label, *school*, was given. In the following example, L2 language and discriminative stimuli are increased in difficulty. An ESL teacher can take this L2 learning to another level by finding four pictures of schools; each school is different by way of size, location, and color of building material. The teacher again holds up the pictures and requests the name for these buildings. If the L2 student says, "school," it shows he is able to recognize similarly structured buildings regardless of size, location, and color. With this method, discriminative stimuli can be any objects or materials that produce appropriate responses for any given L2 language task using these objects.

CONSTRUCTIVISTIC THEORY OR MODEL: FROM APPROACH TO CLASSROOM TECHNIQUES

From behavioristic language theory that stresses form and analyses of language as key ingredients of L2 learning and teaching, the pendulum of L2 learning moved toward the constructivistic theory that emphasizes the use of thinking and communicating in social contexts and of experiential learning rather than memory and exercises and extensive drills (as stressed by the behavioristic approach). During the early 1960s, Dr. Wilga Rivers pioneered this shift in L2 theory and method. Rivers (1964) criticized major assumptions of behavioristic language theory as represented in the audiolingual approach, which included: overemphasis on habit formation, overlearning, error avoidance, and memorization because these elements did not produce long- (or for that matter, short-) term communication in L2. These criticisms increased rapidly in the 1970s through the works of anthropological linguists such as Hymes and Halliday. Both

Hymes (1972) and Halliday (1973) felt that the outcomes of L2 language teaching and learning were being able to communicate in social contexts. To be able to communicate from the perspectives of Rivers, Hymes, and Halliday meant to be understood, rather than to be a native-like speaker in L2. These and other criticisms added fuel to the communicative competence approach that shared some common assumptions with constructivist theory of psychology. Among the latter, for example, significance of processes rather than products and use of meaningful and real-life contexts for developing thinking and communicating rather than memory and rote drill in isolation (Yawkey, in preparation). So, with the connections to constructivist theory and the growing emphases that the purposes of L2 are communicating, the communicative competence approach was born during the 1970s. Later, during the late 1970s, and also following a constructivistic perspective, the schema theory approach was applied to L2 learning through a conceptual L2 learning approach.

Communicative Competence Approach

In addition to communicating in social contexts, several factors become important. Here, trial and error in L2 language becomes important. Through trial and error, L2 language is produced creatively. And, L2 language is determined by the context and not by criterion of native-speaker perfection. So, in a sense, fluency is important in the **communicative competence approach.** From context, trial and error, and fluency in social contexts, the L2 learner becomes motivated through her successful communication with others (Brown, 1994).

Further, the communicative competence approach gives great credence to four components within this approach: sociolinguistic, grammatical, strategic, and discourse competencies. Sociolinguistic competence focuses on appropriate cultural rules of when to use L2 and under what specific circumstances, learning styles, registers, and so forth (see Ovando, Collier, & Combs, 2003). Grammatical competence stresses rules and knowledge of syntax, semantics, and so forth (see Ovando, Collier, & Combs, 2003). Added to communicative competence, strategic competence is knowledge of verbal and nonverbal ways to bridge potential shutdowns and breakdowns in L2 communicating. These shutdowns and breakdowns are common in learning and mastering L2 and for that matter L1 as well (see Swain & Canale, 1982). The final competence critical to communicative competence is discourse competence. The latter is defined as knowledge of the "hows" of maintaining communication with an individual that is coherent and cohesive (see Canale, 1983; Cummins, 1981; Ovando, Collier, & Combs, 2003). So, within the communicative competence approach, these four competencies play a major role in developing communication abilities.

Its view of teaching pronunciation also is characteristic of the communicative competence approach. The emphasis on pronunciation is just the opposite of the audiolingual approach. With communicative competence, the goal of making the L2 learner pronounce words and phrases similar to a native speaker is not necessary. In fact, Celce-Murcia and Goodwin (1991) considered the goal of native-like proficiency as unrealistic. In a word, the push in pronunciation is for comprehensibility.

Freeman and Freeman (1998) provided several characteristics of using the communicative competence approach in classroom settings. These major characteristics provide a window to develop a picture of using this approach with L2s.

1. The native language is not used in the classroom. In fact, Freeman and Freeman (1998) noted a purposeful exclusion of L1 in communicative competence approach. Other authors such as Brown (1994) disagreed and noted that native language is used when and where feasible. However, both researchers would agree that using L2, the target language, provides more approaches to learning to communicate—which is the ultimate goal of the communicative competence approach.

2. In encouraging communication, the ESL teacher wants to build and develop understandings by associating new vocabulary with their meanings in context. So attempts to communicate are honored and supported in L2 rather than to translate these same terms into L1 (Freeman & Freeman, 1998). Translation is used by L2 students to develop communicative competence (Brown, 1994) in L2 learning.

3. Oral language using L2 is stressed from the beginning of the course. In addition, writing and reading in L2 can also be used and stressed at the beginning of the course. These become interrelated and assist L2 learning and teaching.

4. Cultural and sociocultural knowledge is a part of the communicative competence approach. Here, through readings about culture and discussions, L2 popular culture comes alive and becomes a foundation for language learning and teaching. Assuming continued interest in reading about L2 culture, this activity continues. So, in a sense, interest in L2 culture in this instance determines the sequence of reading and discussion.

The communicative competence approach is the most current approach to L2 teaching and learning in the United States, and continues to gain popularity. In many schools and universities nationwide, this approach is replacing the audiolingual approach because of its emphases on developing L2 communication abilities in meaningful social contexts.

Methods and Classroom Techniques of the Communicative Competence Approach

The communicative competence approach has a theory base that we reviewed briefly in the previous sections. In the following section, selected examples of communicative competence methods or principles and classroom techniques provide additional in-depth understandings of the functionality of this approach. Behavioristic language methods show selected procedures of teaching and learning L2 (Yawkey, in preparation).

Authentic Events.   Learners construct L2 using real materials, and authentic events and situations (Gonzalez, Brusca-Vega, & Yawkey, 1997). This method shows clearly that L2 develops by engaging learners in functional and pragmatic uses of language having meaningful goals and purposes. L2 becomes used in actual dialogues and unrehearsed contexts with real materials and in authentic situations. With this method, interconnectedness is emphasized using L2, authentic events, and real materials and situations. In using these real materials, authentic events, and so forth, this method implies that L2 is task-based learning (Brown, 1995). In following examples of this method, notice the problem solving involved, set within real-world contexts to encourage communication outcomes.

As examples of this method, L2 learners plan a birthday party for one of their peers. And in planning, L2 students need to use real-life language for writing invitations, listing types of foods, making seating arrangements, creating prizes, and developing other elements of a birthday party. In this way, L2 is used as a vehicle for meaningful communication. Other examples of authentic events using L2 are: placing a telephone call for information about cultural holiday, using a bus schedule, getting on and off the bus and paying for the ride, ordering food at a restaurant, and so forth.

Group Work.   Recall that in the communicative competence approach, the focus on the L2 learner is to develop communication abilities. This second method extends this same focus or goal by using small group structures to assist with this goal. The number of students in small groups ranges from two to four members to maximize opportunities for L2 interactions. These work groups, such as cooperative learning groups, extend students' L2 because they are pushed to use L2 appropriately and precisely to convey ideas. Group work becomes L2 learner controlled, and not adult controlled, which is motivating (Yawkey, in preparation).

Small group work also has other advantages for the L2 as learner and for the ESL teacher. Small group work permits learners to use communication to negotiate roles and responsibilities among their peers. This negotiation requires concentration and making L2 errors in small groups, and is less anxiety producing than in larger groups. The L2 and non-L2 learners also have opportunities to correct "talk" in these small work groups. In addition, from a cultural perspective, L2 members working in small groups also learn about cultural nuances as their peers communicate (e.g., use of body movements, hands/head, and eyes). Moreover, the ESL teacher can use a variety of roles in small group work including: helping to plan dialogue, facilitating L2 roles they develop for themselves, using directive teaching and nondirective guidance (Brown, 1994).

Classroom techniques using this method abound. L2 students working in groups of two members can interview each other and write down ideas and put them into paragraphs. During the interview process, ESL students question each other as bases for information. Older or more advanced L2s can work in small groups to find main ideas in the paragraphs, underlining them and then checking each other's understandings. In small group work, L2s can discuss and list two or three things they like to eat, or to do, or games they enjoy and so forth. They can talk about their likes, and this classroom technique can be turned around to list two or three things they dislike. Thus, small group interactions produce meaningful forums for interaction and socially mediated communication, both of which are highly effective in developing L2.

L2 Adjustments.   Using role-playing, dramatization, pantomime, and other vehicles to provide for interactive L2 language learning is a third method highly useful in the communicative competence approach. Using a variety of these interactive language learning techniques provides students with many real-life opportunities to adjust and design their language for different social contexts and to learn a variety of linguistic rules (Brown, 1995). In addition, students develop language capacities to respond to open-ended questions—without set or pat answers. Here, ESL students have to adjust their discourse to open-ended questions, and practice with expressing their opinions provides ample, rich opportunities for interactive language learning.

Within role-playing activities and other forms of interactive language learning, the ESL students can express themselves and share self-feelings about ideas, situations, and so forth. Developing a sense of relationships between self and others becomes critical in developing meaningful L2 (Brown, 1994). In a sense, trying to infer and understand their classmates' thoughts produces effective learning outcomes. This method suggests many classroom techniques that can be used to actualize and capitalize on its effectiveness.

Using the "What if?" phrase and providing a situation brings much interactive language learning opportunities for ESL students. For example, "What if you were going to a movie? And, what might you say to the movie cashier to buy your ticket?" These same "What if?" situations can be dramatized and used in role-playing for additional L2 benefits. Another example of a classroom technique using this method is with teacher and student modeling. The ESL teacher and L2 student or native-speaking student can use role-playing in any situation ("Ordering at the Restaurant," "Buying a Bus Ticket at the Window," "Returning a Purchase for a Refund"). The other students observe the dramatization and in turn they model the teacher and fellow student. Guidance suggestions and adjustments come from the teacher and observers.

Integrated Language.   It demonstrates a communicative competence approach method where classroom techniques and activities purposefully involve reading, speaking, listening, and writing. This method perceives integration, rather than isolation of skills, from the beginning of L2 learning and teaching as primary to its success. In linking this method with communicative competence approach, there are a number of rationales. Initially, integrating speaking, listening, reading, and writing provides a solid base for L2 and interlinking these areas for L2 extensions via different modalities (Celce-Murcia & McIntosh, 1979). This form of integration was the primary view of ESL specialists of the 1960s and 1970s (Celce-Murcia & McIntosh, 1979). With this rationale is also found that the integration of visual, auditory, kinesthetic, and tactile sense that provide extensions, expansions, and encouragement for L2 learning.

From Celce-Murcia's and McIntosh's (1979) perspectives, the rationale for this method is also found when integration is viewed as meshing content areas of the curriculum. Meshing and integrating primary content areas of instruction for ESL students provide sound and beneficial L2 teaching across integrated content areas. And, in the 1990s, integrating is likewise accomplished at the beginning of L2 learning and teaching. This gives a final answer, in a sense, to the big question of "When does integration begin?" Here, a highly effective way or mode of integrating content areas is using a theme or thematic approach. Integrating science and mathematics are examples of this perspective of integration. In addition, attempts to integrate literacy areas (e.g., reading, language arts) with science, or mathematics with social studies are also fruitful and beneficial L2 possibilities. This higher level and more contemporary form of L2 subject/content integration is being accomplished successfully in many school agencies for the benefit of L2 learners (Yawkey, in preparation). However, one of the biggest problems with subject fields' integration is educating subject specialists that they too are language-content teachers, regardless of content areas or age of student they teach, and that their responsibilities (as well as the ESL teacher) are to teach L2 and *all* students (Yawkey, in preparation).

Lastly, Collier (1994) used another rationale and provides another perspective to support this method of communication competence approach. She perceived integration benefiting the L2 student as well if academic, cognitive, and language development approaches are integrated within and become parts of social and cultural processes. This rationale also is critical to L2 learning because it supports the interplay among growth or developmental areas and intersects with cultural and social processes.

Classroom techniques to anchor this method abound. Storytelling is one example: Here, the ESL teacher, in going through a picture book, asks L2 students to: (1) look at the pictures, (2) tell about the pictures, (3) predict "What might happen next?," and (4) asks questions about the story/picture content. The ESL teacher can return to this book later, read the entire text, and again ask similar questions about content, characters, story line, and ending points. After the teacher modeling, one or two L2 students working together models and retells the story with the text, and so on. This is one of many classroom techniques that integrates the skills of speaking, listening, reading, and writing. In addition to integrating content fields' subjects, a theme might be run across combined language arts, social studies, and science. The theme might be called, for example, "Lives of Prairie Animals." A theme can be made as well with different locations and can likewise have and show L2 foci. With the theme "Lives of Prairie Animals," stories can be written about life on farms. Types of animals and their feeding habits can be examined. Mathematics can be added as an additional content field: weights of these animals are used to calculate amounts of food needed and ratios of weight, height, and life expectancies compared with humans. Appropriate books can be read as well as gathering information on each of these areas for this or other themes. See Chapter 5 in this book for an extended discussion of the use of thematic curriculums for ESL students.

CONCEPTUAL APPROACH

In 1978, Bialystock presented a model of L2 learning called, the **conceptual approach,** that explained discrepancies in individual achievement in different semantic domains in terms of learning processes and strategies that are organized in three levels: input, knowledge, and output. The knowledge level refers to L2 learners representing information about a language in three ways: (1) explicit linguistic knowledge (i.e., conscious factual information that has been internalized by the L2 learner and can be expressed verbally), (2) implicit linguistic knowledge (i.e., intuitive information the L2 learner has for producing or comprehending a language), and (3) other knowledge (i.e., implicit or explicit knowledge of the culture of the L2 and other knowledge of the world, such as specific cultural aspects of meanings-connotative meanings).

Karmiloff-Smith (1979, 1985, 1986) advanced earlier dichotomies for explaining the nature of cognitive processes involved in L2 learning (i.e., dichotomies such as implicit and explicit knowledge). She conceptualized knowledge as modules, each representing a knowledge domain (or continuum of codes of degrees of accessibility, with verbal higher representations and nonverbal lower representations at each end). Language was considered to be the highest and most abstract representational system for cognition, giving access to higher order concepts, prepositional thinking, logical reasoning, and metaknowledge. She presented (Karmiloff-Smith, 1986) a three-phase multidimensional model that applies to specific domains and is loosely age related. She proposed that L2 learning is a sequential rather than a simultaneous process of rule learning, which consists of recurrent cycles of processes that are repeated as the different aspects of the linguistic system develop. Thus, L2 learning is a sequential process of rule learning that is influenced by recurrent transformations of knowledge in different domains. In the first phase, linguistic knowledge is encoded through one-to-one mapping of form and function without rules or access to consciousness. In the second phase, the L2 learner forms networks of semantic representations of linguistic information in different contexts. Cognitive processes involved in L2 learning can be conceptualized as strategies of rule learning. Robinett and Schachter (1983) proposed some developmental errors of L2 rule learning that can be applied to the second phase proposed by Karmiloff-Smith, such as overgeneralization, ignorance of rule restrictions, incomplete application of rules, and false concepts. In the third phase, Karmiloff-Smith (1986) proposed that the L2 learner can transform or re-represent nonverbal into verbal codes and to connect abstract codes with verbal and explicit metaknowledge. The L2 learner in the third phase can have access to a very flexible cognitive system that consists of semantic networks of explicit access.

O'Malley and colleagues (1988) presented three types of learning strategies applied to L2 learning: (1) metacognitive (i.e., conscious access to cognitive processes such as attention, memory, or higher level thought processes—creativity, problem solving, concept formation), (2) cognitive (i.e., internal mental processes that are used automatically for learning), and (3) social-affective (i.e., internal emotional processes that are learned within a particular sociocultural reality).

Gonzalez, Schallert, de Rivera, Flores, and Perrodin (1999) and Gonzalez and de Rivera (1999) integrated Bialystock's forms of knowledge, Karmiloff-Smith's developmental phases, and O'Malley and colleagues' learning strategies into cognitive processes used for concept construction. That is, Gonzalez and colleagues argued that the language learning processes used by L2 learners vary according to idiosyncratic preferences and developmental level, and also according to the linguistic and cultural content being learned. They proposed that the learner develops cognitively through internalization, transformation, and concept re-representations in terms of cognitive, cultural, and linguistic factors. That is, they proposed that the interface of linguistic structures, nonverbal concepts, and cultural concepts influences the formation of concepts in L2 learning at four levels: (1) conceptual knowledge about linguistic structures that can be expressed at both implicit and explicit levels, (2) knowledge of cultural conventions for using linguistic structures that is expressed as language proficiency at the pragmatic level, (3) knowledge of nonverbal sociocultural symbolic meanings that is expressed as cultural nonverbal concepts used at the pragmatic level, and (4) the multidimensional interaction of language, cognition, and culture when constructing new concepts in a L2 language. Gonzalez and colleagues further explained that the process of L2 concept construction varies depending on the conceptual complexity and the symbolic sociocultural context in which linguistic structures are used. Whether a specific concept is represented with a linguistic structure and marker and its corresponding symbolic meaning depends on the cultural value that it carries, and might also reflect the sociohistorical development of the language. Languages differ in what aspects of meaning they represent directly in their linguistic structures, and this fact influences the formation of symbolic meanings and semantic categories of concepts. A modified and more advanced model is presented in Chapter 5 of this book in relation to L2 learning in K–12 students' curriculum and assessment processes.

Methods and Classroom Techniques of the Conceptual Approach

Because L2 learning of rules is explained through the formation of cognitive processes, such as concept formation and problem solving, the conceptual approach provides the L2 learner with the direct exposure to a wide variety of cognitive, metacognitive, and social-affective learning and thinking strategies. The aim of the L2 teacher is to provide his or her students with algorithms or direct instruction through modeling and role playing of cognitive procedures for how to think (metacognitive learning strategies) and how to learn (cognitive learning strategies) within a specific way of thinking culturally in a specific social environment (social-affective learning strategies). The aim is *not* on specific information or content of linguistic rules to memorize (*not* on learning *what* and *how*), but instead on learning ways of thinking and studying strategies for understanding the rationale (or *why*) underlying linguistic rules and cultural connotations of meanings. The next sections provide some examples of metacognitive, cognitive, and social-affective strategies that can be use by L2 teachers and learners.

Metacognitive Strategies. O'Malley and colleagues (1988) presented nine metacognitive strategies:

1. *Advanced organizers:* Making a general but comprehensive preview of the concept or principle in an anticipated learning activity
2. *Directed attention:* Deciding in advance to attend in general to a learning task
3. *Selective attention:* Deciding in advance to attend to specific details of a learning task

4. *Self-management:* Understanding the conditions that help one learn and arranging for the presence of those conditions
5. *Functional planning:* Planning for and rehearsing linguistic components necessary to carry out an upcoming language task
6. *Delayed production:* Consciously deciding to postpone speaking to learn initially through listening comprehension
7. *Self-evaluation:* Checking the outcomes of one's own language learning against an internal measure of completeness and accuracy
8. *Monitoring:* Bringing explicit knowledge of word meanings and structures to a language task for examining or correcting the response
9. *Inferencing:* Generating an explicit linguistic hypothesis about a previously unknown linguistic structure

Cognitive Strategies.   O'Malley and colleagues categorized 14 cognitive strategies:

1. *Repetition:* Initiating a language model, including overt practice and silent rehearsal
2. *Directed physical response:* Relating new information to physical actions used as directives
3. *Imagery:* Relating new information to visual concepts in memory by familiar and easily retrievable visualizations
4. *Auditory representation:* Retaining the sound of a linguistic sequence
5. *Key word:* Remembering a new word by linking it with a familiar linguistic sequence, image, or concept
6. *Resourcing:* Expanding a word or concept through the use of the target language reference materials
7. *Translation:* Using the L1 as a basis for understanding or producing the target language
8. *Grouping:* Reclassifying and labeling the new linguistic material based on common attributes
9. *Note taking:* Writing down the main ideas, outlining, or summarizing target language materials in a written or oral form
10. *Deduction:* Consciously applying rule to produce or understand the L2
11. *Recombination:* Constructing a meaningful language sequence by combining known elements in a new way
12. *Contextualization:* Placing a word or phrase in a meaningful language sequence
13. *Elaboration:* Relating new information to other concepts in memory
14. *Transfer:* Using previously acquired linguistic and/or conceptual knowledge to facilitate a language-learning task

Social-Affective Strategies.   O'Malley and colleagues categorized four social-affective strategies:

1. *Cooperation:* Working with peers to obtain feedback, look for information, or model a language activity

2. *Question for clarification:* Asking an instructor or other native-speaker for repetition paraphrasing, explanation, and/or examples
3. *Formal practice:* Attempting to increase exposure to the target language or asking for information about the rules of the linguistic structures and markers to represent meaning
4. *Functional practice:* using the target language in communicative situations

In addition, Robinett and Schachter (1983) proposed four social-affective L2 learning strategies:

1. *Overgeneralization:* Creating a deviant structure on the basis of experience with other linguistic structures in the target language in order to avoid redundancy
2. *Ignorance of rule restriction:* Failing to observe the restrictions of existing linguistic structures when applying them to new concepts
3. *Incomplete application of rules:* Lacking accurate and complete knowledge of linguistic rules
4. *False concepts hypothesized:* Making developmental errors resulting from faulty comprehension, distinctions, or contrast in the target language

In sum, by L2 teachers stimulating their students to form concepts, the L2 learning process will be enhanced by providing metacognitive, cognitive, and social-affective strategies as mental tools for learning, as a method for instruction and learning. L2 students can learn how to think about learning by exposure to instructors who model how to elevate the L2 learning process to higher and more abstract levels through teaching explicitly algorithms or strategies for understanding and developing concepts or meanings within the target cultural and social context. These L2 conceptual strategies can be used at different levels and across content domains and subject areas. The conceptual learning approach can be used for L2 learning situations in relation to reading comprehension, listening comprehension, speaking, writing, or any other language arts activities, or other activities across subject areas (i.e., as an instructional method for teaching mathematical concepts, social science concepts, science concepts, etc.). See Boxes 3.2 and 3.3 for interviews of ESL students.

SUMMARY AND CONCLUSIONS: PLURALISM FOR L2 LEARNING

This chapter presents perspectives of L2 learning and teaching from psychological, linguistic, and developmental perspectives. The position or perspective of Chapter 3 and this entire book is one of pluralism, not eclecticism. In other words, particular ESL theories are used because they emphasize particular strengths that ESL students have, in order to increase their L2 capacities. For example, behavioristic theory and the audiolingual approach, with its stress on dialogue generate methods or principles to bridge to the classroom from which ESL teachers can generate classroom techniques and activities.

BOX 3.2

SUMMARY OF AN INTERVIEW WITH A 9TH-GRADE, CHINESE ESL STUDENT

The interview was conducted in English by the first author of the book. The actual digital recording of the interview is available in the companion Web site for the book.

BACKGROUND

Toni (pseudonym) was a 15-year-old, Chinese male ELS student, who was finishing ninth grade in a suburban high school within a mixed neighborhood of a metropolitan area in the Midwest region of the United States. Toni was born and raised in mainland China, and had come to the United States 4 years ago. He was an only child and had come to New York City with her father and mother, and had first settled in a Chinese ethnic neighborhood (Chinatown) where he lived for 2 years. He had then moved to a middle-size metropolitan area in the Midwest and was finishing his second year of schooling by the time of the interview.

The family spoke primarily Cantonese at home. Toni considered that his father spoke very little English, and he could say some words only but could not understand English for daily use such as when shopping at stores. His father had finished up to the fourth grade in China. Toni considered that his mother had an intermediate level of English skills, and had been learning English at school for 1 year. Her mother had a higher level of education; she had finished up to junior high school in China. However, both his parents had to quit school because they were from a poor background and needed to work. His father and mother used to raise poultry in China and had come to the United States looking for better jobs. His mother worked in a restaurant as a waitress.

SCHOOL EXPERIENCE IN THE UNITED STATES AND ESL HISTORY

Toni explained that he did not need to use much English during the 2 years that he lived in Chinatown in New York City. During his first 2 years in the United States, he had attended a seventh grade and an eighth grade bilingual Chinese/English school in Chinatown where he had continued to learn Chinese-Cantonese and also had started to learn English. Two years ago, after moving to the Midwest, he was placed in a regular ninth grade classroom with the support of an ESL pullout program, placement that he was in by the time of the interview.

Toni had come to the United States with very little knowledge of English, as he explained, "I could say only very little words because I did not need any English in China." When he had moved to the Midwest he started to learn English faster. When asked to rate his ability to speak English, Toni thought that his abilities were intermediate when he moved to the Midwest, and two years later, by the time of the interview, he had made progress to a good command of writing and understanding in English, but his speaking and reading had remained at the intermediate level. Toni explained that, "I have mostly A's because I can understand my teachers, but still need help with spelling." His strength was social studies, a subject area in which he could achieve because he paid close attention to the words that the teachers said. He explained "I pay attention to my teacher in class and listen to the new words, like American history." He considered that his weakness was math because "the content was hard and my background is not good."

Toni perceived that the ESL pullout program helped him to improve his pronunciation and writing skills by providing some basic rules. He also had been in summer ESL programs at his school, where he had improved his reading comprehension skills.

EXTRACURRICULAR ACTIVITIES IN ENGLISH INFLUENCING SOCIAL LANGUAGE AND SOCIALIZATION ABILITIES

Toni explained that while he lived in Chinatown in New York City he did not need to speak English much because everybody spoke Chinese in his neighborhood and also at school. However, when he moved to the Midwest, all his neighbors spoke only English, even some friends at the Chinese restaurant where his mother worked. Only recently the number of Chinese students at school, who also lived close to his home, had started to increase, providing him some peers to interact with who shared his bilingual background. Toni seemed well-adjusted to school and had been able to participate and identify with some extracurricular activities. He had taken some Navy Junior Reserve Officer Training courses. He shared proudly with the interviewer that he was getting a purple-heart medal by the end of the school year (which was very close in time to the interview). He had been selected as the chief of a company (leader of a training group) and was very aware that his participation in these activities could very well open an opportunity for a college scholarship.

He also liked to participate in sports, such as football and basketball. But he felt the need to learn the specific idioms and rule related to these sports that he was not yet familiar with. In addition, Toni also participated in the chess club, in which he had won the first prize when he was in junior high school. He still played for the chess team while in ninth grade, where most of his team members were Chinese or Vietnamese students. He felt that other afterschool activities could also help him to improve his English skills, such as Advancement Placement Courses (APC) for ESL students, like the ones available for mainstream students where content was harder, such as math that could help with the Scholastic Aptitude Test (SAT) scores.

Following American tradition, Toni had been told by his mother that he needed to work during the following summer because he was already 16 years old. His parents considered that Toni needed to start saving money for college, because he needed to pay for it by himself (and hopefully with the assistance of a scholarship). His parents had advised him to study in college so that he could get an easy job after graduation.

① grammar rule   (Reading writting, speaking)
②

BOX 3.3

SUMMARY OF AN INTERVIEW WITH A 12TH GRADE, CHINESE ESL STUDENT

The interview was conducted in English by the first author of the book. The actual digital recording of the interview is available in the companion Web site for the book.

BACKGROUND

Chris (pseudonym) was a 19-year-old, Chinese male ELS student, who was graduating from high school in a suburban high school within a mixed neighborhood of a metropolitan area in the Midwest region of the United States. Chris was born and raised in Taipei, Taiwan, and had come to the United States 6 years ago. He was the first-born child and

(continued)

■ ■ ■ ■ ■

BOX 3.3   CONTINUED

had a younger sister, who was 16 years old. His parents mainly speak Mandarin at home with some words of English, and he and his sibling speak in English at home.

Chris considered that his father spoke an intermediate level of English, and he had started college in Taiwan but did not finish. His father worked in the food industry in the United States. Chris considered that his mother had a good level of English-speaking skills, and an intermediate level of writing English skills. Her mother had studied English in Taiwan at school and had completed high school in Taiwan. His mother worked in a restaurant as a waitress in the United States. Chris believed that his 16-year-old sister had a better command of the English language than he did across areas.

SCHOOL EXPERIENCE IN THE UNITED STATES AND ESL HISTORY

Chris and his family came to the United States looking for better job and economic opportunities, and also because his parents wanted their children to learn English. Chris self-perceived his English skills to be good, with speaking, listening, and reading as his strength areas, and writing as the area in which he still experienced some difficulty. He came to the United States with no knowledge of English at all, as he had never learned English before. He received the help of cousins when he first arrived in the United States; he considered his cousins as his friends and teachers because they helped him a lot at home. His ESL teachers had also helped him with reading and writing, and he felt that he had made progress in these areas, especially during his last high school year.

Chris considered that the advantages of living in the United States were many, starting with better schooling conditions. He stated that "physical punishment was used in Taiwan, and in the United States teachers are very nice, they use detention but also help you." He considered that his strengths were in science and math. He explained these academic areas of strength as the result of prior knowledge developed in Taiwan. History was somewhat difficult for him because he was not familiar with the topic; as he stated, "I was not born here."

**EXTRACURRICULAR ACTIVITIES IN ENGLISH INFLUENCING
SOCIAL LANGUAGE AND SOCIALIZATION ABILITIES**

Chris had taken some Advanced Placement Courses (APC) during the past summer to help increase his Scholastic Aptitude Test (SAT) for the areas of reading and writing so that he could get into college. He was planning to work for a year before applying for college, so that he could make some money. He was planning to study in college to become an artist because he liked to paint and do drawings.

He considered that ESL students needed to talk more with mainstream students, and not with ESL peers only, so that they could improve their English-speaking skills. Maybe, he suggested, that this interaction between ESL and mainstream students could occur through clubs and summer programs.

In contrast, making ESL teaching decisions from eclectic theory is generally done solely on the basis of teacher-felt needs for ESL students at particular points in time with little regard for principles or methods and theories on which good ESL teaching is based.

In the first major section of Chapter 3, a socioconstructivistic framework lays the foundations for viewing L2 teaching and learning from developmental, cultural, and learning perspectives. Particular types of language and relevance at developmental ages are emphasized. For example, the relevance of oral language at infant and toddler levels develop solid benchmarks for not only cognitive language but also emotional language supports and connectors with culture/s.

In the second major section, we explored basic educational principles that cut across the major language and cognitive theories such as prior knowledge. And, particular learning and teaching strategies were explained for ESL teaching and learning. We also explored in realistic fashion the roles of language on affective/emotional and social development of ESL students, in particular in relation to their family, neighborhood, and community. We see here that language in its various forms become important tools for interactions. We learned the various roles language plays in developing social skills of ESL and *all* students and see how specific educational principles relating to affective, emotional, and social factors are used effectively in ESL teaching and learning.

Finally, the processes and products of L2 learning are viewed in terms of two predominant theoretical clusters in contemporary ESL: Behavioristic and constructivistic language theories and research paradigms. Within the behavioristic language cluster, three predominant approaches were examined in depth: grammar translation, and direct and audiolingual approaches. Within the constructivistic theory, we examined in depth the communicative competence and conceptual learning approaches. With the investigation of each of these L2 approaches generated from major theory, we see how each language approach is tied to and interrelated with methods and principles that provide windows to jump to classroom techniques focusing on ESL activities for ESL students. And examples of classroom techniques and activities illustrate how methods and principles are generated from theories and serve as fuel for pluralistic approaches. In sum, this foundational chapter provides new insights within the exciting world of ESL teaching. And, it documents the usefulness and gives examples of "Pluralistic" perspectives in classroom work and use with ESL and *all* students.

REVIEW QUESTIONS

1. What is your position about the interaction of internal and external factors in L2 learning? Discuss your position in relation to examples of ESL students that you have observed.

2. What is your personal position about the interaction of cognitive, affective, and social development on L2 learning? Explain your position in relation to examples of ESL students that you have observed.

3. Can you identify an application of Piaget's theory in L2 teaching? What is the practical educational value of theoretical principles and strategies derived from research for educators? Can this research-based knowledge of

educational principles and strategies enhance educators' pedagogical applications when serving ESL students? Explain your educational practice with ESL students: Is it related to research-based pedagogical principles, such as the role of prior knowledge in learning?

4. Do you believe that your assessment practice is related to your teaching practice? How can you improve the link between assessment and instruction to better serve ESL students?

5. In your opinion, is there any application of different approaches and strategies for L2 learning? Provide three examples of applications of different approaches and strategies for L2 learning that can improve ESL students' performance.

6. Do you belong to any professional community of colleagues? Why is it important to join a professional community?

CRITICAL THINKING QUESTIONS

1. Think of two examples in which you as a teacher use language as a tool or method of instruction in your classroom. Discuss with your classmates how these instructional experiences in which language of instruction is used can be different for mainstream and ESL students. How is language used as an instructional tool in the classroom setting similar or different from using language as a socialization tool within a natural environment, such as home or the recess period?

2. Using the recommendations for developing topic and content knowledge, and problem-solving and critical-thinking skills of the National Research Council (1999a, p. 27) quoted in the text, provide two examples in which a teacher can help ESL students to "learn how to learn" and "learn how to think" (metacognitive skills). Think of the following examples as an inspiration or model. An example can make use of very simple instructional materials for developing observation skills related to learning how to learn in science. For instance, an ESL teacher is using a sensory table full of water and some familiar objects (e.g., a plastic toy boat, a small towel, a metal spoon, and a wood spoon) to make preschoolers experiment with flotation. She is modeling how to guess based on the weight and material from which the object is made, experimenting and seeing what happens, and understanding why it happened. Through modeling and questioning the children, the teacher is showing her students how to use observation as a mode of inquiry and language as a tool for learning the concept of flotation in science. What other examples can you think of for ESL students from Pre-K to Grade 12?

3. Think of some observed situations that you have experienced as a teacher that illustrate the use of language as a socialization tool. Are you, as a teacher or a colleague, using any phrases that transmit some cultural values without becoming conscious of it? An example is provided as an illustration; a first-grader comes home one day and announces to his amused parents that he chooses not to clean up after himself because "this is a free country." When asked about the meaning of his statement, the first-grader replies that his teacher said today that America is a free country and Americans are free to make choices. This 7-year-old youngster had become empowered by language to think that freedom means to make choices in life, and his parents wondered if that was the "true" meaning of the teacher's phrase. Think about, How was the teacher intentionally or not influencing the social development of her students through the use of language? What is the power of language as a socialization tool?

4. After reading the descriptions of the grammar translation, direct, and audiolingual approaches, identify the similarities and

differences among them in terms of its theoretical principles and use of instructional strategies for helping L2 learners. After finishing contrasting these three approaches, think about their underlying assumptions about how a L2 is learned. Are ESL teachers aware of these assumption and theoretical differences when they use instructional approaches? Why is it important for ESL teachers to become aware of the theoretical differences between L2 instructional approaches?

5. After reading about most important L2 learning and teaching approaches, principles, and strategies, reflect about your own personal choice for your pluralistic approach for helping ESL students learn English faster and at higher levels. Authors of this book encourage ESL teachers to become knowledgeable of research-based educational applications, and to develop their own personal teaching style and repertoire of instructional strategies for ESL students. We want to encourage ESL teachers to develop their own pluralistic approach for L2 learning and teaching, which is anchored in conceptual understanding of theory and research. In contrast, we want to discourage ESL teachers to have an eclectic approach only, which is based on intuition and is not rooted in theoretical understanding. Develop some rationales, based on research-based principles, for the instructional approaches and strategies chosen.

ACTIVITIES

1. Related to example on language awareness and sensitivity gained during the toddler and preschool years. Interview the mother or father, teacher, or caretaker of a toddler or preschooler (ages between 1 1/2 and 5 and 1/2) in relation to language development in L1 and/or L2 (the child can be exposed to a monolingual or bilingual environment). Focus the brief phone or face-to-face interview on questions about the history of L1 and/or L2 learning, such as first words learned, first typical sentences, speed at which vocabulary is increasing, type of words learned, grammar and syntax use (e.g., conjugation of verbs, use of word order), concepts learned in school (e.g., color, shapes, numbers), and social and communication skills developed in relation to language. Share the information collected during the interview with classmates and identify some patterns (similarities and differences) resulting from individual differences and bilingual or monolingual settings.

2. Related to the section on the role of language on cognitive development and learning: a socioconstructivistic perspective. Think about the following scenario. A preschool teacher is explaining to her 3-to-5-year-old ESL and mainstream students the classroom rules during the first week of classes. The teacher is reading from the blackboard the five classroom rules that need to be used and learned by the preschoolers. The first rule refers to how and when to use the restroom, the second to sharing, the third to using words, the fourth to cleaning up after finishing playing, and the fifth to procedures for family-style eating during lunchtime. Is the teacher using language as a learning tool and/or as a socialization tool? Explain the rationale for your response.

3. Related to the section on the role of language on affective/emotional and social development: a socioconstructivistic perspective. Initiate a dialogue with your classmates about different cultural styles for childrearing, and particularly of using language for socializing young children. Perhaps some of your classmates are international students themselves, or you or they can interview some international mothers and find out about typical phrases used for communicating with

their children while taking care of their primary needs (e.g., feeding, dressing, bathing). Compare and contrast the use of different languages as socialization tools, and analyze what cultural values underlie these language uses. For instance, when the first author's child was a toddler, his nursery school teacher told her that "He *chose* not to drink his milk," to which she replied "But, he did not have any *choice*. He is supposed to just have his milk." What are the cultural value connotations of this mainstream teacher's statement and the Hispanic mother's response? Does the word "choice" carries different cultural expectations for the mainstream teacher and the Hispanic mother?

4. Share with a classmate your newly developed ESL teaching position about approaches, principles, and strategies. Identify similarities and differences between your ESL teaching positions, and interview each other using the two questions below.

    Do you think different ESL instructional strategies can be used for teaching different content or subject areas? Do you think that different instructional ESL strategies can be used for matching the diverse cultural and linguistic backgrounds and idiosyncratic or individual needs of ESL students? Is there diversity also between teachers about their instructional position? What are the factors to which you attribute this diversity in teaching positions? Is this diversity in teaching positions also part of the pluralism that we refer to in this chapter?

5. Read carefully the interview with a Hispanic ESL female student, presented in Box 3.1. As you read, think about how ESL teachers can collaborate with mainstream teachers to help Sonia improve her academic language English skills and academic achievement in math. Sonia explained, during the course of the interview, that she is still weak in pronunciation and writing skills in English, and that mathematics is still a difficult subject area. In addition, think about how ESL and mainstream teachers can help Sonia not "to feel embarrassed" about her difficulties in pronouncing new words in English, and help her to develop self-confidence and better skills through effort in order to increase her intrinsic motivation. Finally, brainstorm about how ESL and mainstream teachers can help Sonia achieve her expectations of entering college, pursuing a career, and becoming a professional after graduating from high school. Explain how intrinsic motivation is for learning, related to effort and expectations, and ultimately to increased academic achievement. How can this principle of the role of language on affective, emotional, and social development be applied to the case of Sonia? What kind of messages can ESL and mainstream teachers deliver to Sonia to support her affective, emotional, and social development and, ultimately, her L2 learning and academic achievement?

6. Read carefully Boxes 3.2. and 3.3. providing a summary of interviews with two ESL Asian high school students. As you read these interviews pay attention to these ESL students' L2 history, their schooling experiences in the United States, and their resulting academic achievement and cultural adaptation. After reading, complete three tasks. First, analyze the similarities and differences that these two Asian ESL students are presenting in terms of these three factors (i.e., L2 history, their schooling experiences in the United States, and their resulting academic achievement and cultural adaptation). Second, think about the educational needs of these two Asian ESL students, and determine what L2 approach (or combination of approaches) and derived instructional strategies would be most beneficial for them to improve their academic English proficiency and their academic achievement. While completing this second task, take into consideration all five L2 approaches discussed in this chapter, from the grammar translation, to the direct, to the audiolingual, and cognitive and communicative competence approaches. Third, analyze what advantages and disadvantages the selected instructional strategies derived from these five L2 Approaches can offer for these two ESL Asian students.

GLOSSARY

approach   Within an ESL and text context, approach means examining sets of assumptions made in L2 learning concerning how it is learned. In a sense, then, an approach makes a common set of assumptions that are implicit in L2 teaching and learning (Celce-Murcia, 1991; Ovando, Collier, & Combs, 2003).

audiolingual approach   New structural patterns in L2 are introduced and taught to ESL students through continual repetition of dialogue forms.

communicative competence approach   Focuses on teaching ESL learners through trial and error for communicating in social contexts.

conceptual approach   This method stimulates ESL learners' learning processes and strategies across different domains and taking into consideration individual differences. Stimulation for concept formation is organized in three levels: input, knowledge, and output.

conceptual knowledge   It is a network of meaningful patterns that can be retrieved for problem solving and transference of learning (National Research Council, 1999a).

direct approach   It is one of the behavioristic language approaches. A teaching technique that emphasizes analyses of a L2 language, and the use of L1 as the method of instruction for L2.

eclecticism   The eclectic approach takes advantage of previous years of ESL teacher experiences and personal hunches as to what to teach (i.e., ESL skill/s) and how to teach it (i.e., approach or perspective). However, ESL teachers lack conceptual knowledge of underlying theoretical and research-based information that can help them make informed decisions about how to best match theoretical principles of most important L2 approaches, with selected ESL instructional strategies, and the diverse and idiosyncratic educational needs of each ESL student.

factual knowledge   These are facts or information that a student retrieves from books, people, and other experiences and internalizes and stores in memory (e.g., reading about Piaget's stages of cognitive development and memorizing them as sensorimotor, preoperational, concrete operations, and formal operations).

formative assessment   It is the ongoing evaluations designed to make students' thinking explicit to both learners and teachers. These ongoing evaluations can help students monitor their development throughout the inquiry process and show developmental progress resulting in the creation of motivation for learning.

grammar translation approach   It is one of the behavioristic language approaches. A teaching technique that emphasizes understanding of the language form or structure and its meanings.

metacognition   A higher conceptual process that makes learners aware of what they are thinking.

pluralism   It refers to the adoption of two or more approaches or multiple models of ESL theory and instructional practice. An example of using a pluralistic approach clarifies these terms. For instance, a teacher understands and diagnoses the ESL students' level of English language acquisition and production. In turn, this teacher plans the additional series of lessons for this and other ESL students. In using a pluralistic approach, the teacher matches major theoretical perspectives in ESL with the ESL skills to be developed by the ELL student. The pluralistic or best practices approach is based on a best match between theory, ESL skill/s, and ESL students' characteristics.

summative assessment   It is the final evaluation, usually a posttest at the end of a semester or a school year. This final evaluation helps teachers and students understand the level of success at reaching the goal.

REFERENCES

Bialystock, E. (1978). A theoretical model of second language learning. *Language Learning, 28*(1), 69–83.

Bowen, J. D., Madsen, H., & Hilferty, A. (1985). *TESOL techniques and procedures.* New York: Newbury House.

Brinton, M. (1991). The use of media in language teaching. In M. Celce-Murcia (Ed.), *Teaching English as a second or foreign language* (pp. 454–472). Boston: Heinle & Heinle.

Brown, H. D. (1994). *Teaching by principles: An interactive approach to language pedagogy.* Upper Saddle River, NJ: Prentice-Hall/Pearson.

Bruner, J. (1990). *Acts of meaning.* Cambridge, MA: Harvard University Press.

Canale, M. (1983). From communicative competence to communicative language pedagogy. In J. Richard & R. Schmidt (Eds.), *Language and communication* (pp. 2–27). New York: Longman.

Carnegie Task Force on Learning in the Primary Grades. (1996). *Years of promise: A comprehensive learning strategy for America's children.* New York: Carnegie Corporation of New York.

Celce-Murcia, M. (Ed.). (1991). *Teaching English as a second or foreign language.* Boston: Heinle & Heinle.

Celce-Murcia, M., & Goodwin, J. M. (1991). Teaching pronunciation. In M. Celce-Murcia (Ed.), *Teaching English as a second or foreign language* (pp.136–153). Boston: Heinle & Heinle.

Celce-Murcia, M., & McIntosh, L. (Eds.). (1979). *Teaching English as a second language or foreign language.* Rowley, MA: Newberry.

Cole, M. (1996). *Cultural psychology: A once and future discipline.* Cambridge, MA: Harvard University Press.

Collier, V. (1994). *Promoting academic success.* Washington, DC: TESOL.

Cummins, J. (1981). The role of primary language development in promoting educational successes for language minority students. In California State Department of Education, *Schooling and language minority students: A theoretical framework* (pp. 3–49). Los Angeles: National Evaluation, Dissemination, and Assessment Center, California State University, Los Angeles.

Ensminger, M. E., & Slusarcick, A. L. (1992). Paths to high school graduation or dropout: A longitudinal study of first-grade cohort. *Sociology of Education, 65*(2), 95–113.

Felner, R. D., Kasak, D., Mulhall, P., & Flowers, N. (1997). The project on high performance learning communities: Applying the land-grant model to school reform. *Phi Delta Kappan, March,* 520–527. www.pdkintl.org/kappan/k_v78/k9703fel.htm

Freeman, Y. S., & Freeman, D. E. (1998). *ESL/EFL teaching: Principles for success.* Portsmith, NH: Heinemann.

Gonzalez, V., Brusca-Vega, R., & Yawkey, T. D. (1997). *Assessment and instruction of culturally and linguistically diverse students with or at-risk of learning problems: From theory to practice.* Needham Heights, MA: Allyn & Bacon.

Gonzalez, V., & Schallert, D. L. (1999). An integrative analysis of the cognitive development of bilingual and bicultural children and adults. In V. Gonzalez (Ed.), *Language and cognitive development in second-language learning: Educational implications for children and adults* (pp. 19–55). Needham Heights, MA: Allyn & Bacon.

Gonzalez, V., Schallert, D. L., de Rivera, S., Flores, M., & Perrodin, L. M. (1999). Influence of linguistic and cultural variables on conceptual learning in second-language situations. In V. Gonzalez (Ed.), *Language and cognitive development in second-language learning: Educational implications for children and adults* (pp. 104–155). Needham Heights, MA: Allyn & Bacon.

Gonzalez, V., & de Rivera, S. (1999). Conceptualizations of *ser* and *estar* by college students learning Spanish as a second language and adult Spanish native speakers. In V. Gonzalez (Ed.), *Language and cognitive development in second-language learning: Educational implications for children and adults* (pp. 156–189). Needham Heights, MA: Allyn & Bacon.

Halliday, M. A. K.(1973). *Explorations in the functions of language.* London: Edward Arnold.

Hatano, G., & Inagaki, K. (1986). Two courses of expertise. In H. Stevenson, H. Azuma, & K. Hakuta (Eds.). *Child development and education in Japan* (pp. 56–89). New York: Freedman.

Hymes, D. (1972). On communicative competence. In J. B. Pride & J. Holmes (Eds.), *Sociolinguistics: Selected readings* (pp. 269–293). Harmondsworth, England: Penguin.

Kaplan, J. L., & Luck, E. C. (1977). The dropout phenomenon as a social problem. *Educational Forum, 42*(1), 41–56.

Karmiloff-Smith, A. (1979). Micro- and macrodevelopmental changes in language acquisition and other representational systems. *Cognitive Science, 3*, 91–118.

Karmiloff-Smith, A. (1985). Language and cognitive processes from a developmental perspective. *Language and Cognitive Processes, 1*(1), 61–85.

Karmiloff-Smith, A. (1986). From meta-processes to conscious access: Evidence from children's metalinguistic and repair data. *Cognition, 23*, 95–147.

Lloyd, D. N. (1978). Prediction of school failure from third-grade data. *Educational and Psychological Measurement, 38*, 1193–1200.

National Research Council. (1999a). *How people learn.* Washington, DC: National Academy Press.

National Research Council. (1999b). *Improving student learning.* Washington, DC: National Academy Press.

Natriello, G. (1987). The impact of evaluation processes on students. *Educational Psychologist, 22*, 155–175.

O'Malley, J. M., Russo, R. P., Chamot, J. M., & Stewner-Manzanares, G. (1988). Applications of learning strategies by students learning English as a second language. In C. Weinstein, E. T. Goetz, & P. Alexander (Eds.), *Learning and study strategies: Issues in assessment, instruction, and evaluation* (pp. 215–231). San Diego, CA: Academic Press.

Ovando, C. J., Collier, V. P., & Combs, M. C. (2003). *Bilingual and ESL classrooms: Teaching in multicultural contexts* (3rd Ed.). New York: McGraw-Hill.

Piaget, J. (1964). *The early growth of logic in the child, classification, and seriation.* New York: Columbia University Press.

Piaget, J. (1967). *Mental imagery in the child, a study of the development of imaginal representation.* New York: Oxford University Press.

Piaget, J. (1970). Piaget's theory. In P. Mussen (Ed.), *Carmichael's manual of child's psychology* (Vol. 1, pp. 703–732). New York: Wiley.

Piper, T. (1998). *Language and learning: The home and school years.* Upper Saddle River, NJ: Prentice Hall.

Read, J. M. (Ed.) (1995). *Learning styles in the ESL/EFL classroom.* New York: Heinle & Heinle.

Resnick, L. B., & Kolper, L. E. (1989). Toward the thinking curriculum: Current cognitive research. *Yearbook of the Association for Supervision and Curriculum Development.* Alexandria, VA: Association for Supervision and Curriculum Development.

Rivers, W. M. (1964). *The psychologist and the foreign language teacher.* Chicago: University of Chicago Press.

Robinett, B. W., & Schachter, J. (1983). *Second-language learning: Contrastive analysis, error analysis, and related aspects.* Ann Arbor: University of Michigan Press.

Sheperd, L. A., & Smith, M. L. (1992). *Flunking grades: Research and policies on retention.* New York: Felner.

Slavin, R. E. (1980). Effects of individual learning expectations on student achievement. *Journal of Educational Psychology, 72* (4), 520–524.

Stigler, J. R., Shweder, R., & Herdt, G. (1989). *Cultural psychology: The Chicago symposia on culture and development.* New York: Cambridge University Press.

Stroup, A. L., & Robins, L. N. (1972). Elementary school predictors of high school dropouts among black males. *Sociology of Education, 45*(2), 212–212.

Swain, M., & Canale, M. (1982). The role of grammar in a communicative approach to second language teaching and testing. In S. S. Seidner (Ed.), *Issues of language assessment, Volume 1: Foundations and research* (pp.45–72). Evanston: Illinois State Board of Education.

Tobin, J. J., Wu, D., & Davidson, D. (1989). *Preschool in three cultures: China, Japan, and the United States.* New Haven, CT: Yale University Press.

Yawkey, T. D. (in preparlation). Retraining of inservice teachers for culturally and linguistically diverse ESL and All students. [Research Monograph]. University Park: Pennsylvania State University Press.

AN HISTORICAL AND CONTEMPORARY VIEW OF BEST INSTRUCTIONAL APPROACHES FOR ESL AND *ALL* STUDENTS

LEARNING OBJECTIVES

1. Recognize theoretical models and principles and their implementation in the classroom
2. Understand historical changes in language-teaching methodology based on theoretical developments in the fields of linguistics, psycholinguistics, and sociolinguistics
3. Identify the role of meaning-based methods in present-day ESL instruction at all grade levels
4. Understand implications of sheltered instruction, its protocol and instrument, strategies and delivery for the standards-based curriculum

PREVIEW QUESTIONS

1. How does Vygosty's theory compare with Krashen's theory in terms of methods of second-language (L2) instruction?
2. What is the role of Krashen's five hypotheses of language acquisition? Categorize each hypothesis based on its usefulness in the classroom
3. Which are the main similarities and differences between the natural approach and sheltered instruction?
4. What are the main components of a sheltered English lesson?
5. How applicable is the SIOP for use by mainstream, ESL, and bilingual teachers?
6. How can you use graphic organizers to teach ESL students?

Chapter 4 focuses on educational approaches and teaching strategies from the 1960s until the present. It expands on the theoretical models, philosophical, educational approaches, and teaching strategies presented in Chapter 3 with a focus on best service delivery for ESL students and all students.

The first major section discusses the state-of-the-art educational **approaches** for instructing English-as-a-second-language (ESL) students and all students to improve their four language skills (listening, speaking, reading, and writing) in English at the social and academic levels, which in turn would pave the way for their academic achievement. The chapter presents a spectrum of approaches from traditional grammar-based perspectives to current meaning-based approaches. These educational strategies use dual-language or two-way immersion and transitional bilingual educational models in the United States, ESL, and English as a foreign language (EFL), which help ESL students learn English in a contextually and culturally appropriate manner. Different degrees of English-language competence, derived from ESL and EFL instructional approaches, will be discussed and illustrated in one chapter section in relation to stages or levels of language development.

The second major section presents a historical perspective of teaching approaches and strategies from the 1960s until the present, from a disadvantaged model to an advantaged model with the goal in mind to help ESL students learn in a contextually, linguistically, and culturally appropriate manner. This section also includes real-life scenarios of needs of ESL students' and model experienced teachers for illustrating how: (1) L1 and L2 academic skills are developed in successful ESL and dual-language programs, (2) to translate concepts and principles into best instructional strategies and practices and educational programs, and (3) to integrate best instructional practices with performance-based assessments in order to evaluate teaching and learning continuously.

The position or perspective of Chapter 4 and this entire book is one of pluralism. Our intention is to assist teachers, teacher trainers, and staff developers to strengthen or develop their own perspectives on existing methods and strategies, how they have proved to be successful in two-way bilingual, ESL, and EFL settings for the benefit of the teaching-learning process. Therefore, Chapter 4 is connected to the second theme of the book because it (1) expands on theoretical models, the behavioral, maturational, constructivist paradigms; (2) addresses a philosophical and pluralistic view of the ethnic educator approach; and, (3) it relates to educational approaches and strategies presented in Chapter 3. Chapter 4 aims to provide an understanding of the historical perspective of language-teaching methodology. By providing this historical view, we intend to assist educators in their efforts to teach ESL students and to help them succeed academically.

THEORETICAL BACKGROUND

The accumulation of knowledge about the best instructional approaches to teach second-(L2) and foreign language (FL) learners, English-as-a-second-language (ESL) students, and *all* students during the past five decades has paved the way for a promising new millennium in terms of the applications of this knowledge to help build a global society. By the middle of last century, language educators witnessed the emergence of one field of L2 teaching with instructional approaches based on sound applied linguistics research on the nature of language learning and the successful acquisition of L2 and FL in the classrooms.

The theoretical groundwork for Chapter 4 is based on **socioconstructivism,** current theories on L2 methodology, the five standards for effective pedagogy, and the Language Across the Curriculum (LAC) movement. Pedagogy in L2 learning emphasizes language and content instruction, fostering personally and academically meaningful language development (Collier & Thomas, 2001). The four language modes (i.e., listening, speaking, reading, and writing) are taught as an integrated whole, lessons are learner-centered and meaningful to the students, and social interaction and collaborative learning are emphasized (Krashen, Candin, & Terrell, 1996). Furthermore, the philosophy of learning movement calls for a reduction in the amount of teacher talk in order to expose students to more opportunities for using language in creative, useful, and motivating ways (Schifini, 2000).

Socioconstructivism

Research on learning processes in social contexts (e.g., schooling and professional development) has provided an explanation of how interaction impacts cognition. According to Shotter (1997), the learning process involves self and others in an exchange of ideas to deepen individual understanding. Vygotsky (1986) contends that learning is a sociocultural practice and that language gives and receives meaning from social activity. In other words, thought develops from undergoing changes produced by social interactions. Vygotsky's theory assumes that cognitive development arises as a result of social interactions between individuals and that learning is a dynamic social process in which dialogue between the novice and the expert leads to the development of higher cognitive levels. His **"zone of proximal development" (ZPD)** is defined as the distance between the actual developmental level (as determined by individual problem solving) and the level of potential development (as determined through problem solving in collaboration with more capable peers). The ZPD is the level of performance at which a learner is capable of functioning when there is support from interaction with a more capable individual. Interactions in the "zone" are those that use speech, visual representations such as modeling and feedback (Bull, Kimball, & Montgomery, 2000). Although the writings of Vygotsky were not directly related to L2 learning, the relationship drawn between learning and cognitive development offers valuable insights into the role of social interaction in language acquisition. Vygotsky (1978) reiterated that ". . . language and consciousness are both lodged within a matrix of social activity, and that this activity system, rather than the isolated individual, should be the primary focus of study" (p. 21). Krashen's Input Hypothesis is reminiscent of Vygotsky's ZPD (John-Steiner, 2000). According to Krashen (1985, 1989), comprehensible input is a key factor in acquiring a L2. Acquisition occurs when learners understand language that is slightly beyond their current level of competence through input that is made comprehensible by the context or a simplified linguistic message in a way that is meaningful. Krashen (1989) stated that learners ". . . move from i (their current level), to $+ 1$ (the next level along the natural order), by understanding input containing $i + 1$" (p. 2) as illustrated in Figure 4.1.

Theories of L2 Acquisition and Methodology

Language teaching methodologies have undergone a radical shift from the behaviorist methods of the 1960s to an interactive instructional approach in which the student takes an active (intrinsic) role. The process of developing L2 proficiency is an essential part of both learning and instruction (Tharp, Estrada, Dalton, & Yamauchi, 2000). Learning a L2 depends on access to and participation in legitimate social activities in which students use multiple forms and functions of language. Ovando, Collier, and Combs (2003) posed a model with four major components to explain the process of L2 learning in the classroom:

1. Sociocultural, in which students learn the L2 in situations that occur in their everyday lives
2. Language development, through the subconscious and conscious aspects of language learning
3. Academic development, by learning academic knowledge and conceptual development in all content areas of the curriculum; and
4. Cognitive development, which is the subconscious, natural process that occurs developmentally from birth to schooling and beyond

These theories of L2 acquisition have served to develop and implement a number of important programs and methodological trends. They are discussed below.

The Five Standards for Effective Pedagogy

Researchers from the Center for Research in Education, Diversity and Excellence (CREDE) have proposed five standards to provide teachers with tools to enact best teaching practices (Dalton, 1998). They are:

1. Joint productive activity, when experts and novices work together for a common product or goal
2. Language development, fostered best through meaningful use and purposeful conversation between teachers and students
3. Contextualization, which utilizes students' knowledge and skills as a foundation for new knowledge
4. Challenging activity; ESL students are not often challenged academically on the erroneous assumption that they are of limited ability
5. Instructional conversation, promoted through dialogue, by questioning and sharing ideas and knowledge.

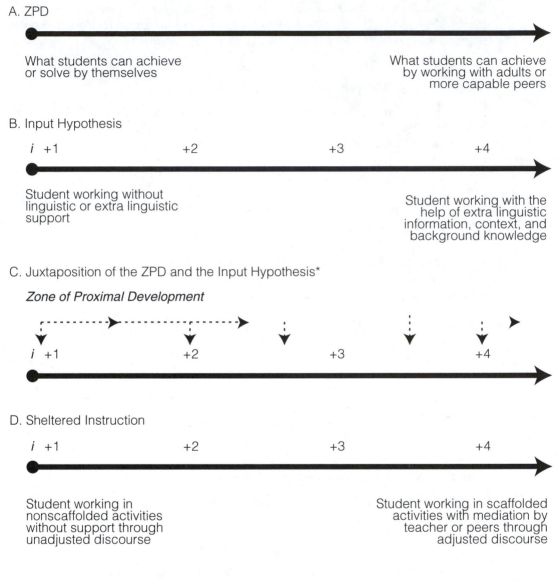

A. ZPD

What students can achieve or solve by themselves

What students can achieve by working with adults or more capable peers

B. Input Hypothesis

i +1   +2   +3   +4

Student working without linguistic or extra linguistic support

Student working with the help of extra linguistic information, context, and background knowledge

C. Juxtaposition of the ZPD and the Input Hypothesis*

Zone of Proximal Development

i +1   +2   +3   +4

D. Sheltered Instruction

i +1   +2   +3   +4

Student working in nonscaffolded activities without support through unadjusted discourse

Student working in scaffolded activities with mediation by teacher or peers through adjusted discourse

*There is a basis for comparison between Vygotsky's ZPD (dotted line) and Krashen's (*i* +1) theories (solid line). Both emphasize the distance between what a child does by himself/herself and what he/she can achieve by working in collaboration with an adult or more capable peer. In addition, sheltered instruction merges both concepts into a representation that describes properties that portray teacher behavior in the planning and delivery of effective lessons for L2 learners.

FIGURE 4.1   The Input Hypothesis and the Zone of Proximal Development

CREDE's researchers conclude that these five standards have the potential to give all students the opportunity to obtain the language and the content necessary to succeed in school (Waxman & Padrón, 2002). The standards have been designed to generate activity patterns of collaboration, reflection, and active involvement of teachers and students during classroom instruction (Tharp et al., 2000). These five principles went through a consensus defining process in which researchers, teachers, parents, administrators, and policymakers had the opportunity to alter them when necessary. Tharp (1999) suggests that these standards are recommendations on which literature is in agreement, across all cultural, racial, and linguistic groups in the United States, at all age levels, and in all subject matters. He posed that ". . . for mainstream students, the standards describe the ideal conditions for instruction; but for students at-risk of educational failure, effective classroom implementation of the standards is vital" (p. 5). Furthermore, Rueda (1998) believed that the five standards also can be applied to professional development: [I] the principles that describe effective teaching and learning for students in classrooms should not differ from those of adults in general and teachers in particular" (p. 1).

The five educational principles proposed by CREDE can be applied to both instruction of ESL students and to the professional development of ESL teachers. They are explained further below.

The Language across the Curriculum (LAC) Movement

The LAC movement follows the example set by sheltered instruction (SI), which seeks to use content as the central learning tool in L2 classes. LAC has emerged as a means to improve cross-cultural knowledge and purpose-specific multilingual and intercultural skills of postsecondary students. Rather than relegating content instruction to subject-matter instruction, LAC works with university and/or college faculty to identify the specific vocabulary and genres students need in order to function effectively in another language in their respective disciplines (Straight, 1998). LAC aims to facilitate the use of languages in a variety of meaningful contexts and to motivate and reward students for using their multilingual skills in every class they take at each level in the university curriculum (Stryker & Leaver, 1997). In short, students who learn languages for a purpose, learn it better (Fichera & Straight, 1997).

HISTORICAL OVERVIEW OF INSTRUCTIONAL APPROACHES

A glance through the past four decades or so of ESL and EFL teaching has given varied interpretations on how to best teach a language. Fed by education-related disciplines—linguistics, psycholinguistics, sociolinguistics, and so on, some language-teaching methods have risen to the top as the most popular and others have fallen as the most unpopular. The ensuing description of instructional approaches is not an exhaustive one, but includes the most commonly used methods of teaching English to nonnative speakers as reflected in the research literature and in practice. They have been organized following the broad definitions set forth by the Teachers of English to Speakers of Other Languages (TESOL, 1997) standards as instruction that aims to teach students to communicate in social settings, engage in academic tasks, and use language in socially and culturally appropriate ways. The three common groupings or subdivisions are as follows.

INSTRUCTIONAL APPROACHES

- *Grammar-Based Approaches.* Instruction that teaches *about* the language, including its structure, functions, and vocabulary
- *Communication-Based Approaches.* Instruction that emphasizes *using* the language skillfully in meaningful contexts
- *Content-Based Approaches.* Instruction that attempts to develop language skills and prepare students to study grade-level material in ESL and EFL

The first part includes grammar-based methods, those methods that promote knowledge of the language, including its structure, functions, and vocabulary. The second section includes communication-based methods, those methods that emphasize using the language skillfully and in meaningful contexts. The third section includes content-based methods and refers to methods that attempt to develop the four language skills and prepare students to study grade-level material in the L2 or FL. The overview of grammar-based methods addresses the grammar translation method, the audiolingual method, the cognitive code approach, and the direct method. The overview of communication-based methods includes the total physical response method and the natural approach method. The overview of the content-based methods includes SI and the cognitive academic language learning approach.

Grammar-Based Instructional Approaches

The following methods discussed are as follows:

- the grammar translation method
- the audiolingual method
- the cognitive code approach
- the direct method

The Grammar Translation Method.   This was the most popular method from about the mid-nineteenth to the mid-twentieth century. It focuses on grammatical rules, memorization of vocabulary and conjugations, translations of texts, and doing written exercises (Richard-Amato, 1996). The major characteristics of the grammar translation method are presented in Table 4.1 below.

The Audiolingual Method.   Also known as the Army method used during World War II, the **audiolingual approach** is based on behaviorism (Skinner, 1957). Its

TABLE 4.1   Characteristics of the Grammar Translation Method

FEATURES	DESCRIPTIONS
• Language of instruction	• L2 and FL classes are taught in the student's L1 with very little use of the L2
• Vocabulary instruction	• Taught in the form of lists of isolated words in the L2 along with definitions in the L1
• Grammar instruction	• Focuses on the form and the inflection of words via extensive explanations of grammar in the student's L1. Instruction of the rules for putting words together in strings of unrelated sentences to demonstrate how the "rule of the day" works.
• Reading	• Rules and new words are included in the reading, which is usually beyond the level of comprehension and proficiency of L2 learners (e.g. a trip by train, a shopping expedition)
• Lessons contents	• Lessons are grammatically sequenced and students are expected to produce perfect translations of stilted or literary prose from the beginning
• Oral language	• Little or no attempt is made to communicate orally in the L2 and pronunciation is not a key feature
• L2 instructions	• Directions and explanations are given in the student's L1

theory is based on habit formation and stimulus/response association. Learning a L2 is a matter of fighting off the habits of the L1 through mimicry drills and pattern practices. Audiolingualism is also grounded in structural linguistics and focuses on the teaching of linguistic patterns (Brown, 2001). The characteristics of the audiolingual method are presented in Table 4.2.

The Cognitive Code Approach.   The Cognitive Code Approach is not a method per se and does not prescribe steps to teach a L2 or a FL. It reflects the Chomskyan revolution in linguistics and advocates for the "deep structure" of language and generative transformational grammar. It allows for meaningful practice around a grammatical syllabus while allowing for meaningful practice (Richards & Rogers, 1986). It has elements of the audiolingual and the grammar translation methods; it uses the pattern drilling of the audiolingual method but adds rule explanations and reliance on grammatical sequencing of materials.

TABLE 4.2   Characteristics of the Audiolingual Method

FEATURES	DESCRIPTIONS
• Lessons	• Language material is presented in dialogue form
• Grammar	• Structures of the L2 are carefully ordered in dialogues and students repeat in an attempt to develop correct habits of speaking
• Instruction	• Emphasis is placed on mimicry, memorization of set phrases, and overlearning of L2
• Grammar drills	• Grammar structures are taught using repetitive drills. Sentences in the substitution, mim-mem (mimicry-memorization), and other drills are often related only syntactically (e.g., I go to the movies, You go to the movies, He goes to the movies). Often these structures have nothing to do with what is actually happening. However, these structures can resemble real communication in that the situational scenarios to be memorized include greetings and idiomatic expressions
• Inductive teaching	• Rules are presented but not formally explained. Grammar is taught by inductive analogy rather than by deductive explanation. Activities such as minimal pairs (e.g., feet-fit; cat-cut) are used to overcome the negative transfer or interference of sounds of the student's L1
• Vocabulary	• Vocabulary is presented and learned in context
• Language skills	• Listening and speaking skills take precedence over reading and writing skills. Pronunciation sessions often take place in fully equipped language laboratories. Attention is paid to correct pronunciation and error-free sentences
• L1 use	• Teachers use the L2 only and allow little or no use of the student's L1
• Reinforcement	• Successful responses are immediately and positively reinforced
• Language focus	• The focus is on language accuracy and not on content

The characteristics of the Cognitive Code Approach follow:

■ Students need to master subskills in listening, speaking, reading, and writing (e.g., sound discrimination, pronunciation of specific elements, letter discrimination, etc.) before participation in real communication activities

■ Phonemes need to be learned before words, words before phrases and sentences, simple sentences before more complicated ones, and so forth

- Highly structured through a deductive process, and the "rule of the day" is practiced
- Emphasizes a conscious awareness of rules and their applications to the learning of a L2
- Students are expected to produce correct language from the start
- Creative language is used during the practice of the L2

The Direct Method.   The direct method is currently known as the Berlitz approach. Its earlier version was called the natural method in the mid-nineteenth century. It is natural because it attempts to immerse L2 learners in the target language. Teacher monologues, formal questions and answers, and direct repetition are frequent activities. The topic of the lesson is grammar; the students inductively discover the rules of the language (Richard-Amato, 1996).

The direct method has the following characteristics.

- Grammar is the foundation on which language should be taught. Conscious awareness of the rules and their application to L2 learning is emphasized.
- Sentences are taught in isolation, without a temporal or logical sequence. The purpose is to demonstrate the use of a predetermined grammatical structure in an effort to develop linguistic competence.

Communication-Based Instructional Approaches: The Total Physical Response and the Natural Approach

Research on ESL/EFL suggests that effective language learning is best accomplished under conditions that stimulate natural communication and minimize the formal instruction of linguistic structures (Murphy, 1997). The methods previously described focus on the grammatical structures of the language. The teacher's role is to transmit knowledge and the ESL/EFL student's role is to passively receive and internalize the knowledge. Effective ESL/EFL approaches that emphasize the development of communicative skills allow students to use the new language for meaningful communication rather than for rote repetition (Savignon, 1999).

Socioconstructivism provides for teacher and student to have an ample role in the way they teach and learn and embraces concepts such as situated learning, scaffolding, and modeling. Knowledge is situated and is partly a product of the activity, context, and culture in which it is used (Doughty & Williams, 1998). ESL/EFL students need to be guided to construct their own language ability and develop communicative proficiency. Scaffolding allows students to move from what they presently know to what they need to learn.

Socioconstructivism attaches great importance to teaching ESL/EFL. The meaningful use of the target language moves teachers and students away from treating the language as an object, but rather practicing it as a medium of communication in a socially meaningful context (John-Steiner & Mahn, 1997). Thus, language acquisition becomes interesting, meaningful, and natural. Social interaction is important because the expert can model the appropriate solution, assist in finding the solution, and monitor student's progress (Tharp & Gallimore, 1998). Communication-based instructional approaches and content-based instructional approaches are based on the Monitor model of L2 acquisition (Krashen, 2000a). The model is comprised by five hypotheses that form the theoretical tenets of the NA and sheltered instruction. A summary is presented in Table 4.3 below.

The Total Physical Response Method (TPR).   The total physical response method emphasizes the use of physical activity to increase meaningful learning opportunities and language retention (Asher, 2000). It is based on principles of child language acquisition and on the relationship between language and its physical representation or execution. TPR emphasizes the use of physical activity to increase meaningful learning opportunities and language retention (Asher, 1977). It is a successful beginning language teaching method because students are allowed to demonstrate comprehension through nonverbal means, such as actions and gestures, while developing receptive ability (Ovando, Collier, & Combs, 2003). TPR allows for ESL and all students to acquire language in a manner similar to their first language because language input is immediately comprehensible (Krashen, 1999). It is especially effective in the beginning levels of language proficiency. A TPR lesson involves a detailed series of consecutive actions accompanied by a series of commands

TABLE 4.3   Krashen's Monitor Model of L2 Acquisition

HYPOTHESES	CHARACTERISTICS
1. The Acquisition Order Hypothesis	There are two ways of developing a L2. *Acquisition* is a subconscious process and *learning* a conscious process that results in 'knowing about' the language.
2. The Monitor Hypothesis	Acquisition and learning are used in producing language. Acquired competence (subconscious knowledge) allows the learner to produce utterances while learned language (conscious language) serves as a monitor. The monitor allows correction of the language.
3. The Natural Order Hypothesis	The rules of the language are acquired in a predictable order, some rules tending to come early and others later.
4. The Affective Filter Hypothesis	It consists of the affective filter, a mental block that prevents the acquirer from fully utilizing the comprehensible input they receive for language acquisition.
5. The Input Hypothesis	Humans acquire language by understanding messages, or by receiving comprehensible input.

or instructions given by the teacher. Students respond by listening and performing the appropriate actions.

The TPR method has the following characteristics:

- Lessons focus on meaning and comprehension to build receptive vocabulary
- Students do a great deal of listening and acting. Its appeal to the dramatic or theatrical nature of language learning makes it attractive
- The teacher directs or orchestrates a performance in which the students are actors
- It uses commands as a way to get learners to move about and to loosen up: *Open the door, Stand up, Go to the chalkboard,* and so on
- No verbal response is necessary. Students respond by listening and performing the appropriate actions
- More complex syntax could be incorporated in commands: *Stand up, walk quickly to the window and open it,* and so on
- Humor is easy to introduce: *Put your pen on Rosa's head*
- Questions can also be used and students can point to the response: *Where is your backpack?* (Student points to the backpack). *Who is your best friend?* (Student points to a friend)
- Eventually, students would feel comfortable enough to give verbal responses to questions, then to ask questions themselves and to continue the process
- The teacher always uses the target language
- When students overcome the fear of speaking out, they proceed with classroom conversations
- Reading and writing activities spin off from the oral work in the classroom

The Natural Approach (NA).   The goal of the natural approach is the development of basic oral and written communication skills or everyday language situations (Bonnet, Kahl, & Krashen, 2000). Like TPR, the students must acquire the L2 in natural situations (ibid.). The NA provides comprehensible input in the L2 or FL in a low-anxiety environment and aims to fulfill the requirements for learning and acquisition. The NA assumes that ESL/EFL students acquire the target language in stages, in much the same way that they acquire a first language (Echevarria & Graves, 1998). The NA uses a series of topics that students find interesting and that can be discussed in a comprehensible way, supplemented by games, tasks, and other activities that provide comprehensible input (ibid.). The NA teacher speaks only the target language and class time is committed to providing input for acquisition. Students may use either the target language or their first language.

The NA is designed to (1) help beginning ESL/EFL students achieve intermediate proficiency, and (2) depend on the learners' needs (Lightbown & Spada, 1999). Students have more receptive ability than expressive ability during the early stages of L2 acquisition (Walqui, 2000). The NA rests on four principles:

- *Principle One: Comprehension precedes production.* Listening comprehension precedes oral production or speaking. It is the silent period that allows ESL/EFL students to build up competence by active listening, because they are not ready to produce language (Krashen, 2000b).

Teaching Application: Lessons focus on listening comprehension to build receptive vocabulary (Walqui, 2000). Comprehensible input is presented in the target language, using techniques such as TPR, gestures, and mime. The teacher always uses the target language. The focus of the communication is on a topic of interest for the students, and the teacher strives at all times to help students understand. TPR is used during this phase as a beginning teaching method that allows students to acquire language in a manner similar to their first language, because input is immediately comprehensible. Through comprehensible input, ESL/EFL students proceed with natural language acquisition and fluency is promoted. The level of stress (low affective filter) enhances participation and increases the motivation to learn the L2 or FL (Asher, 2000).

■ *Principle Two: Production emerges in stages.* Oral production is very low in the early speech emergence stages and slowly increases to more complex discourse where students do not feel pressured to produce the language. The development of comprehension and the silent period are crucial: (1) the ESL/FL students' anxiety levels are lower and (2) their comprehension in their target language develops faster.

Teaching Application. The use of TPR is recommended when teaching all students who are the first stage (preproduction). Songs, single words, gestures, and realia can be used to provide comprehensible input. Students begin producing the target language by simply using words and short phrases before they use complex discourse. At the speech emergence stage, the ESL/FL students are able to produce longer sentences. The NA blends strategies and techniques so that concepts are recycled in many different ways in order for the students to master them (Ellis, 1997).

■ *Principle Three: Content must be comprehensible and based on communicative goals.* Communicative goals are the basis of L2/FL teaching. Input must be comprehensible. The focus of activities is organized by topics that are understandable to the ESL or EFL learner and not by grammatical structures. Grammar can be effectively acquired if goals are communicative. If goals are grammatical, some grammar will be learned and very little acquired. Communicative ability and not grammatical accuracy is emphasized in beginning comprehension and production stages.

Teaching Application. The focus of classroom activities should be organized by topic, not by grammatical structure.

■ *Principle Four: Activities and classroom environment must work together to produce a lowered affective filter.* The learning environment must be one of low-anxiety that encourages participation. The affective filter must be kept low in order for input to take effect. A low affective filter means that the L2 or FL learner is more open to the input and that the input strikes deeper (Burt, Dulay, & Krashen, 1990). Having a low affective filter encourages all students to try to get more input and to be more receptive to the input (Krashen, 2000b).

Teaching Application. Classroom activities should provide comprehensible input in a low-anxiety natural environment.

The NA depends heavily on active learning and social interactions (Tharp, et al., 2000). All students develop oral L2/FL communication skills as they interact and collaborate with each other (Krashen, 1981). It recognizes that students construct their knowledge naturally and socially regardless of background, ethnicity, or social class (Cummins, 2000).

Stages of ESL/EFL Acquisition.   According to the natural approach, ESL/EFL students move through a series of five predictable stages as they progress in their language development toward native-like fluency in the L2 or FL (Krashen, 2000b).

> Stage I: Preproduction
> Stage II: Early Production
> Stage III: Speech Emergence
> Stage IV: Intermediate Fluency
> Stage V: Advanced Fluency

The characteristics of ESL/EFL learners at each of their L2 stages are described in Table 4.4. Students can move quickly through the beginning stages of language acquisition and must be provided with ample opportunities that will help them move them toward the Advanced Fluency Stage (Birdsong, 2000).

Appropriate instructional strategies and techniques need to be utilized to help ESL/EFL students move toward the Advanced Fluency stage (Schifini, 2000). Table 4.5 summarizes the natural approach teaching strategies that should be utilized in order to assist students through their language acquisition stages.

The natural approach stresses that ESL/EFL students must expand their oral language proficiency before they acquire the grammatical structures of the target language. Students acquire their L2/FL quickly and easily when they use it for meaningful communication (Mora, 2000).

A Content-Based Approach: Sheltered Instruction

Sheltered English Instruction.   The integration of L2 acquisition and standards-based content area learning has been given considerable attention in the fields of psycholinguistics and pedagogy in the last two decades. Research continues to point out the following:

1. A L2 is not learned by direct instruction in the rules of the language, but by using language in meaningful contexts.
2. Students will learn a L2 only if they receive comprehensible input in it; talk becomes comprehensible to students through context and reference to background knowledge.
3. Talk is not enough; ESL students need more than conversational fluency, they need to develop higher order thinking skills and the academic technical language required for learning the content areas in order to succeed in school.

The aim of school is to teach students the content areas (e.g., math, science, social studies, literature). This also applies to ESL students. From the early grades, ESL students

TABLE 4.4   The Natural Approach Stages of Language Acquisition

STAGES	STUDENT BEHAVIORS AT EACH STAGE
Stage I Preproduction	Responds to oral commands and cues • Begins to name basic vocabulary and use greetings • May respond with one-word answers • Speech errors are normal part of the language acquisition process • Produces two-word strings
Stage II Early Production	Expresses self in short 3–5 word phrases or sentences • Produces questions/answers and limited conversations • Responds and interacts in conversation including class discussions • Repeats, recites memorable language • Listens with greater understanding • Identifies people, places, and objects
Stage III Speech Emergence	Speaks with less hesitation and demonstrates increasing understanding • Produces longer phrases or sentences with grammatical inaccuracy • Uses new receptive vocabulary to experiment and form messages • Participates more fully in discussions • Explains, describes, compares and ESL students in response to literature • Engages in independent reading based on oral fluency and prior experience with print • Uses writing for a variety of purposes
Stage IV Intermediate Fluency	Engages in conversation and produces connected narratives • Level of comprehension is high • Makes inferences and defends ideas • Has difficulty expressing abstract concepts of academically demanding tasks
Stage V Advanced Fluency	Comprehends most conversation and academic discourse • Uses vocabulary, grammar, and idioms appropriately • Uses listening/oral strategies similar to first-language peers • Uses receptive vocabulary comparable to first-language peers

need to have a good head start toward gaining **academic language**, with an emphasis on what things mean. There are several aspects of what makes content areas so hard for ESL students. Vocabulary, the most common aspect of the language of these domains, gives good examples for the need to properly address content areas while teaching the L2.

TABLE 4.5   Natural Approach Stages and Teaching Strategies

STAGES	TEACHING STRATEGIES
Stage I Preproduction	• Provide abundant opportunities for active listening, utilizeprops, visuals, and real objects • Surround students with language—chants, songs, and simple poems • Avoid forcing students to speak prematurely • Group students with more advanced ESL/EFL peers • Conduct shared reading and storytelling with ample visual support and the incorporation of prior knowledge • Use physical movement in language activities • Encourages use of art, mime, music and other forms of creative expression to represent meaning and increase student's sense of aesthetics.
Stage II Early Production	• Continue to provide ample opportunities for listening comprehension with contextual support • Ask yes/no questions • Require students to answer using two-word answers • Expose students to a variety of experiences with understandable tests • Introduce interactive dialogue journals
Stage III Speech Emergence	• Focus on communication in meaningful contexts in which students express themselves orally and in writing for a wide range of purposes and audiences. • Ask open-ended questions; model, express, restate and enrich student's language • Have students describe personal experiences, objects, and so on • Conduct shared reading, guided reading, and storytelling, especially with patterned and predictable text • Use puppets, flannel board to aid in retelling or role-plays • Promote conceptual development in the content area through trade books, newspapers • Help students create books through language experiences
Stage IV Intermediate Fluency	• Structure group discussion and provide opportunities for students to create oral and written narratives • Guide use of reference material for research and facilitate more advanced literature studies • Provide for a variety of realistic writing experiences: creative innovations or stories, newsletters, pen pals, business letters, and so on • Publish student-authored stories, newsletters, bulletins • Encourage drama, art, music and other forms of creative expression to represent meaning and increase students' sense of aesthetics
Stage V Advanced Fluency	• Continue to provide ongoing language development through integrated language arts and content area activities

1. Mathematics has many ways to say the same thing—students need to know that addition can be signaled by any of these words: *add, plus, combine, sum,* and *increased by.* Similarly subtraction can be signaled by these words: *subtract from, decrease by, less, take away, minus, differ, or less than.*

2. In science, logical connectors such as "because," "however," "consequently," and "for example," indicate the nature of the relationship between the parts of a text or experiment. An experiment itself is formulaic, and language is used to express it: *hypothesis, experiment, results, conclusion.*

3. For social studies it is not only the vocabulary but the background knowledge many ESL students do not have. For example, the Fourth of July may bring thoughts to an American English speaker of the founding of this country, the Declaration of Independence, the Revolutionary War, and so forth. For an ESL student it may mean very little.

Added to these constraints are the semantics and discourse features of language, and the vocabulary in different contexts. Vocabulary differences can be overwhelming to many ESL students (e.g., the word *power* as in "the electric power company"; or *power* as in "the powers of the president"; or *power* as in "4 to the highest power").

Sheltered English Instruction (SEI) methodology provides ESL/EFL learners with a medium to develop the academic and linguistic demands in their L2 (Parker, 1985; Shaw, Echevarria, & Short, 1999; Short, 1999). SEI is based on research findings that the L2 is learned effectively when it is a vehicle of instruction, not the object; ESL students can reach a high level of L2 development while mastering subject matter. Academic language is made comprehensible through a variety of means: demonstrations, visual aids, graphic organizers, hands-on materials, and manipulation of content. Schema or background knowledge is built before a topic is introduced, so ESL students are able to process material from the "top down," having general knowledge of the broad picture before studying the details (ESCORT, 2003).

The key components of SEI are lesson preparation, comprehensibility, lesson delivery, and interaction (Echevarria, Vogt, & Short, 2000). SEI is scaffolded and mediated to provide refuge from the linguistic demands of L2/FL discourse that is beyond the current level of comprehension of the students. The theoretical underpinning of the model is that language acquisition is enhanced through meaningful use and interaction. SEI can be described as a melding of elements of language acquisition principles and elements of quality teaching (Echevarria & Graves, 1998). It is also influenced by sociocultural theory because it occurs within social and cultural contexts. This approach facilitates a high level of student involvement and interaction in the classroom. Teachers present material in patterns related to their students' language and culture as well as that of the school. Through this approach, students learn new material through the lens of their own language and culture (Valdes, 1996).

The sheltered instruction methodology fits well in socioconstructivism. According to Vygotsky (1978), learning is a social construct mediated by language via social discourse. He contends that a child's cultural development appears twice: first, on the social level between people, and second, on the individual level inside the child. Consequently, full development of the "zone of proximal development" (ZPD) depends on full social interaction. For a ZPD to be created, there must be a joint activity that promotes a context for ESL/EFL students and experts' interaction (Tharp, 1997). It is the stage in the student's life when he or she is ready to learn a particular piece of information but does not have all the prerequisites or other information without assistance. Furthermore, the ZPD varies according to the student's culture, society, and experiences (Tharp & Gallimore, 1998). Figure 4.2 illustrates the sociocultural contexts of sheltered instruction.

SEI (often called "Specially Designed Academic Instruction in English" or SDAIE) involves the teaching of grade-level subject matter in English in ways that are comprehensible and engage students academically, while also promoting English language development. Sheltered instruction is designed for ESL and EFL students who have reached at least intermediate proficiency and who possess basic literacy skills. This method requires significant teacher skill in English language development and subject-specific instruction; clearly defined language and content objectives; modified curriculum; supplementary materials; and alternative assessments. This instructional method is often used as a bridge between primary language instruction and placement in a mainstream classroom.

Sheltered instruction refers to the concept of comprehensible subject-matter teaching (math, science, social studies, etc.), with the L2 as the medium of instruction. Sheltered instruction can function in two-way bilingual (TWB) programs as a bridge or transition between the first and L2 class as a means of facilitating comprehension of and responses to content instruction. In TWB programs, the aim is to provide both language (listening, speaking, reading, and writing) and academic instruction to students so that they do not fall behind in grade-level content learning.

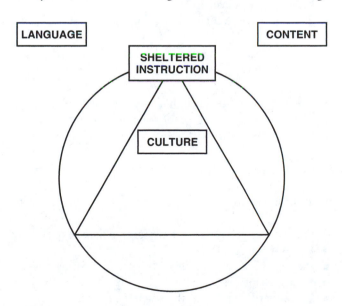

FIGURE 4.2   Sociocultural Contexts of Sheltered Instruction

Strategies for Sheltered Instructional Delivery

The teacher's delivery of instruction can be made comprehensible despite the difficulty or complexity of the reading material, the information being presented, and/or the instructional model being used. The instructional strategies/techniques proposed here will complement any instructional approach used by the teachers (Calderón & Minaya-Rowe, 2003; Echevarria & Graves, 1998). They can be used to teach any content: math, science, social studies, or language arts, reading, and writing.

Teacher Speech.   Teachers can facilitate comprehension, regardless of the difficulty of the text or subject matter. Teachers can use a combination of the following strategies to help second-language learners comprehend without having to resort to translation:

- Slower but natural rate of speech and clear enunciation, being careful not to raise volume
- Simpler and shorter sentences to explain a process or a concept, use more pauses between phrases
- Frequent communication strategies such as rephrasing, repetition, and clarification when presenting new material, explaining tasks, or conducting interactive reading of literature books, communicate the same idea repeatedly using different words
- Verbal emphasis or writing new vocabulary, idioms, or abstract concepts on the board to facilitate comprehension during interactive reading or provide explanations to students who are at the beginning stages of comprehension in the target language, use consistent vocabulary and reinforce vocabulary, language structures and intonation
- Use appropriate repetition or natural redundancy, clarify terms and vocabulary

Modeling.   Teachers can model what is expected of the students, that is, before students begin solving word problems in math, the teacher

- Takes the student through a word problem step-by-step
- Models useful strategies for solving such problems
- Presents procedures in a clear, explicit manner

Contextualization.   Teachers can make abstract concepts more concrete by using examples that are already well known or can be easily understood when providing visual reinforcement. Meaning becomes clearer when teachers use:

- Pantomime, gestures, or exaggerated facial expressions
- Props, realia (real objects)
- Pictures of the objects or sets of pictures for a concept
- Songs, chants, raps, patterned stories
- Blackboard sketches as the teacher explains
- Films, filmstrips, videotapes, slides, and transparencies before, during, and after reading complex text

- Bulletin board for reference (e.g., visual representation of lesson information)
- Demonstrations and role-plays (for social studies or science)
- Hands-on interactive tasks during an explanation or afterwards to check for understanding
- Real-life activities with lots of opportunities for listening, speaking, reading, and writing
- Use of graphic organizers on the board, such as story maps and word webs during storytelling or retelling
- Computer graphics by the teacher and students
- Computer vocabulary activities as a follow-up to sustain vocabulary development

Giving Directions.   Teachers have found the following techniques useful for giving directions in ESL or SSL that will avoid translating, mixing languages, or doing preview-review in the other language:

- Break down complex tasks into simpler steps with specific instructions such as, "Look at the story map. Point to the author box. Now point to the first event box. . . . "
- Interrupt the lesson with questions to the students. This is a natural way to check for comprehension throughout the lesson. This can be done individually or by asking group questions

Ample Opportunities for Student Interaction.   One of the benefits of SEI is that ESL students are exposed to good models of English language and to practice using English in academic settings. ESL students need to practice their new language in meaningful ways. Cooperative learning groupings are critical with ESL students with different levels of language proficiency. Heterogeneous groupings help increase language proficiency and academic skill level; one student's strength compensates for a classmate's weakness. ESL students have the opportunity to use their first language to clarify key concepts as needed. Teacher talk needs to be balanced with student talk; no matter how limited the students might be in L2. One way is to stop every few minutes and ask students a question, who then turn to their partners and "buddy buzz" until they come up with a good answer. The types of questions to ask students periodically are as follows:

- What do you think will happen?
- Do you have any questions so far?
- Please summarize up to here.
- Please clarify for your partner. . . .
- Teach each other. . . .
- Ask students to "buddy buzz" or "put your heads together and see if you have any questions," "summarize," "clarify," "tell me more," and "teach each other" as frequently as possible.

Checking for Understanding.   The teacher should verify comprehension of each instructional unit by checking for understanding frequently. This will help students start their tasks right away, because they understand the "what and how" of their task. Some checking for understanding techniques are as follows:

- "Tell us the first step, Laura. What is the second step, John?"
- "Wh__" questions (who, what, where, when, whose)
- "Proof" questions ("How do you know that?")
- "Funny" questions ("So, the head of the United States is called a king, right?")
- Confirmation checks ("Do you mean . . . ?")
- "Tell me more" (when clarification is needed)

Error Correction.   To prevent students from withdrawing or feeling embarrassed and thus refusing to "try to use the L2," teachers and student partners should use the following guidelines:

- Error correction must be minimal at the beginning. Let the student feel safe in the new environment.
- Teacher and student peers should recognize that language errors are a necessary part of second-language acquisition.
- Teacher and student peers should concentrate on the message the students communicate, not the correctness of the message (function before form).
- When correction is done, a "restatement" form (positive modeling technique) can be used:
  - Student: "Does she has a pet?"
  - Teacher: "Does she have a pet? Yes, she does. She has a pet."

Interdependent Dialogue.   To foster conversation, teachers should use a rich discussion instead of a straight lecture or instructions because this builds comprehension and fluency. Dialogue in which meaning is negotiated works best. Teachers can foster conversations with and between L2 learners by asking referential (open-ended questions) rather than display (closed-ended) questions; in the former, the teacher seeks new information ("What do you think this looks like?"), but in the latter, the teacher already knows the answer ("Where is the boy?"). Teachers should give examples that are personalized rather than impersonal (e.g., "Let's say that Juan took that trip into the jungle" rather than "We took a trip into the jungle").

In the SEI Classroom.   Teachers need to remember that their ESL students are learning English, the content areas, and the style of the American educational system and should present information as clearly and systematically as possible. In addition to the eight strategies describe above, there are some daily reminders that not only apply to SEI classes, but may be of assistance to all teachers (ESCORT, 2003).

a. Announce the lesson objectives and activities. Write the objectives on the board and review them orally before class begins. Place the lesson in the context of its broader theme and preview upcoming lessons.
b. Write legibly. Remember that many ESL students have low levels of literacy; some are even unaccustomed to the Roman alphabet.

   c. Develop and maintain routines. Routines help ESL students anticipate what will happen (e.g., types of assignments, ways of giving instructions); in this way, ESL students do not rely only on language cues.

   d. List instructions step-by-step. Familiarize ESL students with each step individually when teaching them to solve math and science word problems; do not require them to find the answer or complete the whole process from the start.

   e. Present information in varied ways. Use multiple media in the classroom to reduce the reliance on language and to place the information in a context that is more comprehensible to ESL students.

   f. Provide frequent summations of the salient point of the lesson. Try to use visual reviews with lists and charts; paraphrase the points where needed; and encourage students to provide oral summaries themselves.

Mapping and Graphic Organizers

Semantic maps and graphic organizers are very effective in building language and content knowledge and of importance in a SEI classroom. They also engage the ESL students in a mental activity that activates prior knowledge and provides multidimensional clues to the new concepts and technical academic vocabulary. It also gives students more vocabulary and concepts for talking and writing about new knowledge or new words (Calderón & Minaya-Rowe, 2003). The teacher can use graphic organizers in at least two ways:

1. Model on the board techniques for mapping
2. Have small groups of students work on their maps—this preliminary practice provides the students with patterns to replicate. In as much as possible encourage students to use drawings for those content words not yet in their repertoire

Figures 4.3, 4.4, and 4.5 describe and illustrate some graphic organizers used with science, social studies, and literature contents at the upper elementary and secondary levels.

GENERAL PRINCIPLES FOR TEACHING ESL/EFL STUDENTS

Based on the review of Chapter 4's grammar, meaning, and content-based methods, we can summarize and point out the following three general principles for ESL/EFL teachers that draw directly on socioconstructivism and language-teaching methodology (Jameson, 1998).

   1. *Increase Comprehensibility:* This principle involves the ways in which ESL/EFL teachers can make content more understandable to their students. With early to intermediate ESL students, these strategies include providing many nonverbal clues such as pictures, objects, demonstrations, gestures, and intonation cues. As competency develops, other strategies include building from language that is already understood, using graphic organizers, hands-on learning opportunities, and cooperative or student-explaining-to-student techniques.

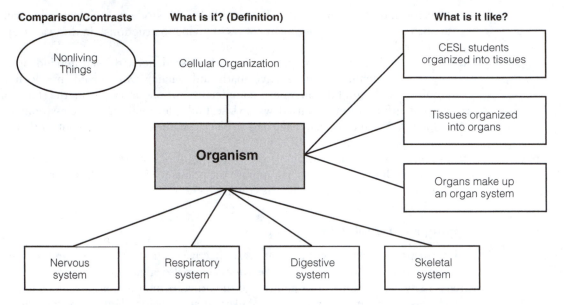

FIGURE 4.3   Concept Definition Mapping

Description: Concept definition maps are graphic organizers for teaching students the meaning of key concepts. Students can *explain* their understanding and *elaborate* by citing examples from their own experiences.

2. *Increase Interaction:* This principle involves a number of methods, strategies and techniques that increase students' opportunities to use their language skills in direct communication and for the purpose of "negotiating meaning" in real-life situations. These include total physical response, the natural approach, sheltered instruction, study buddies, project-based learning, and one-on-one teacher/student interactions.

3. *Increase thinking/study skills:* This principle suggests ways to develop more advanced, higher order thinking skills as student competency increases. Sheltered instruction attempts to promote the development of these skills. These include asking students higher order thinking questions. Use Bloom-type questions and the following sample questions' stems:

- Knowledge—can you tell me why . . . ?
- Comprehension—can you write in your own words . . . ?
- Application—what things would you change if . . . ?
- Analysis—what was the problem with . . . ?
- Synthesis—how would you write a song about . . . ?
- Evaluation—how would you feel if . . . ?

Strategies also include: Modeling "thinking language" by thinking aloud, explicitly teaching and reinforcing study skills and test-taking skills, and holding high expectations for all students.

SOCIAL STUDIES CONTENT: SPANISH EXPLORATIONS

Textbook Section	*Queries*
Montezuma tried to bribe Cortés to stay away from Tenochtitlán. However, the gifts only encouraged Cortés, who arrived in Tenochtitlán on November 8, 1519. One conquistador recorded his impressions of the city, which sat in the middle of a great lake: "We were astounded. These great towns and temples and buildings rising from the water, all made of stone, seemed like an enchanted vision."	What is the author telling us about Cortés? *Follow-up queries if needed:* What does the author mean by saying that Tenochtitlán "seemed like an enchanted vision"? "Montezuma tried to bribe Cortés to stay away from Tenochtitlán." What is that all about? How does that fit into what we've learned about the conquistadores?
California was one of the last borderland areas settled by the Spanish. In 1769 missionary Junípero Serra established a mission at San Diego. Serra led his friars and local American Indians in building San Francisco and eight other missions along the Pacific coast. Yet few settlers wanted to move to this faraway part of the empire, particularly when there seemed to be better opportunities in México and Perú. By 1790 there were fewer than 1,000 settlers in California of the some 100,000 Europeans in the whole New Spain.	What do your think the author is telling us about the eighteenth-century settlers? What would it mean for people to settle in California? *Follow-up queries if needed:* What does that tell us about the conquistadores?

FIGURE 4.4   Questioning the Author (QtA)

Description: QtA is designed to assist students in their efforts to understand text as they read. It provides students with an opportunity to increase their understanding of topics, ideas, and themes as they read.

SUMMARY AND CONCLUSIONS: BEST INSTRUCTIONAL APPROACHES FOR ESL AND *ALL* STUDENTS

The chapter provides a view of educational research-based approaches and teaching strategies from the 1960s until the present. It presents an overview of the theoretical models, philosophical, educational approaches and teaching strategies with a focus on quality of instruction for all students in the nation's schools. The position of this chapter and the entire book is of pluralism and access and the chapter provides sufficient information to point out what works in the education of ESL students. Teacher delivery is very important to serve all students; but for ESL students who are mostly at-risk of educational failure, effective instruction is crucial in their schooling.

The first major section discusses the most significant educational approaches for instructing ESL and all students to improve their listening, speaking, reading, and writing

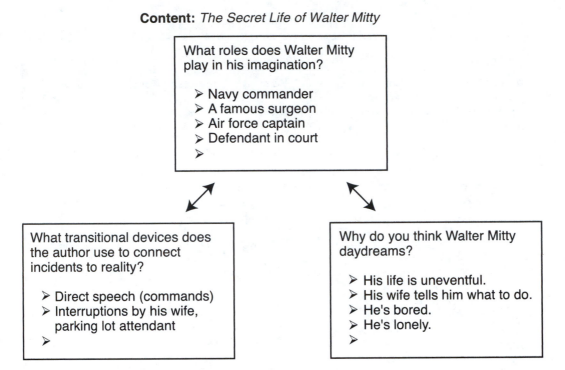

Content: *The Secret Life of Walter Mitty*

What roles does Walter Mitty play in his imagination?

➢ Navy commander
➢ A famous surgeon
➢ Air force captain
➢ Defendant in court
➢

What transitional devices does the author use to connect incidents to reality?

➢ Direct speech (commands)
➢ Interruptions by his wife, parking lot attendant
➢

Why do you think Walter Mitty daydreams?

➢ His life is uneventful.
➢ His wife tells him what to do.
➢ He's bored.
➢ He's lonely.
➢

FIGURE 4.5   Graphic Organizer for Structured Note Taking

Description: Structured note taking provides the graphic organizers for students to be able to arrange their notes in the same way that the content is structured in the text. It assists students in recall and retention of information.

skills in English at the social and academic levels. The chapter presents a spectrum of approaches from traditional grammar-based perspectives to current meaning-based approaches. It also includes theoretical overviews of language acquisition models. It discusses different degrees of English-language competence, derived from ESL and EFL instructional approaches with descriptions of the stages or levels of language development.

REVIEW QUESTIONS

1. How would you compare methods of instruction within the historical perspective? Which are the ones you have been exposed to as a student of ESL or EFL? What worked and/or did not work for you?

2. What is your personal position about the natural approach? Would you use it to teach ESL and all students in your classroom? If so, how will it benefit your students? If not, what other method(s) would you use?

3. Do you consider that sheltered English instruction can replace bilingual or two-way bilingual programs? What, in your opinion, is best for your students? How would you modify SEI to serve your school's ESL students?

4. How and when would you use graphic organizers in your classroom? In your experience what kinds of semantic maps do your students need to develop academic language?

Learn technical content vocabulary? Identify multiple meanings for one word?

5. Provide three characteristics about the total physical response that have been incorporated into the natural approach and SEI? Describe your thinking behind each characteristic.

6. How would you use the stages of language development described in this chapter to assess your students' levels of proficiency in English? What would you add? Delete? Construct a language-stages template for use with specific students.

CRITICAL THINKING QUESTIONS

1. Think of two examples in which you as a teacher can use the Comprehensible Input Hypothesis and the ZPD to develop a curriculum plan for ESL students and/or for explaining the special attention they need in instruction. How can Figure 4.1 be interpreted and used in the school/classroom?

2. The five standards proposed are common-sense strategies and can apply not only to ESL students but also to all classrooms. Visit a classroom and use the five standards as a template; identify each as you observe a content lesson. Describe your observations; give examples of each standard being practiced. Interview the teacher briefly: what does she or he call the standards? Do they have a different name? Why does she use them?

3. Design a cross-hypotheses comparison of two or more principles of the natural approach;

explain how the hypotheses can help understand the principles. Design a mini-training module to explain the principles to a partially trained audience. Identify the sophisticated terminology and find a simpler more understandable language, use visual, graphic organizers, and so on to make your presentation clearer. In as much detail as possible, relate your presentation to the immediate needs of ESL students.

4. Come up with a profile of ESL students' needs to learn the content areas. Relate to their stage(s) of language proficiency. Select one area and design a graphic organizer for one level of language development and one content area. Include language and content issues that need to be addressed and how SEI can be of use.

ACTIVITIES

1. Related to the section on the existing methods used since the 1960s. Use the information and the format to devise an approach that meets ESL students with the following variables: language at home, literacy, and print-rich environment at home. Select from one of the following groups: (1) a group of ESL students who bring language and literacy development, who speak, read and write in their home language; or, (2) a group of ESL students who have oral skills in their home language only but who do not know how to read or write. Plan your approach and be as specific as possible and write it for a partially trained audience.

2. Related to the stages of language development and the vocabulary. Devise a plan to

increase the vocabulary for ESL students who are at the speech emergence or intermediate fluency stages. Make a list of words and expressions that might be difficult for the students; for example, multiple meaning words (e.g., *power*, *trunk*) and idiomatic expressions ("pull one's leg," "hit the road"). Include effective strategies to teach these words and phrases to ESL students.

3. Related to socioconstructivism. Design a graphic organizer with methods of instruction that draw directly or fit well with the philosophy of socioconstructivism. Explain your selection in simple terms to a partially trained audience.

4. Related to existing sheltered English instruction. Examine a standards-based curriculum in a content area of your choice and grade level. Determine the language level of the ESL students. Select and describe the appropriate SEI strategies that need to: (1) develop language, (2) content, and (3) higher order thinking skills.

5. Related to the section of the natural approach. Often, listening, speaking, reading, and writing are treated as isolated skills by language teachers. How would you integrate them using the natural approach. Give some specific examples.

6. Related to section on the meaning-based methods. How can these methods lower the anxiety in ESL students when trying to learn English? What do you think of the role of the teacher as language models and facilitators?

GLOSSARY

academic language A dimension of language proficiency connected with literacy and subject-matter contents; it is the language used in the formal contexts of academic subjects (Ovando, Collier, & Combs, 2003).

content-based approaches Instructional methods used to teach ESL students English with standards-based subject-matter content (Echevarria, Vogt, & Short, 2000).

content standards Descriptions of what content areas (e.g. science, social studies, math, etc.) instruction should enable the students to know and do.

ESL students A term used to describe students who are learning English as their second or additional language; it encompasses proficiencies in listening, speaking, reading, and writing (Calderón & Minaya-Rowe, 2003).

grammar-based approaches Instructional methods used to teach about the language, including its structure, functions, and vocabulary.

home language The language spoken by people who live in the ESL student's home. Other terms used are native language, primary language and first language.

meaning-based approaches Instructional methods used to teach emphasizing using the language skillfully in meaningful contexts.

socioconstructivism Cognitive development arises as a result of social interactions between individuals in a dynamic and social learning process (Vygotsky, 1986).

strategies Mental processes that people use to comprehend, learn, and retain new information. There are three kinds of strategies that people adapt and monitor during reading, writing, and learning: cognitive strategies, metacognitive strategies and socio affective strategies (Echevarria, Vogt, & Short, 2000).

ZPD The "zone of proximal development" is the distance between the actual developmental level (as determined by individual problem solving) and the level of potential development (as determined through problem solving in collaboration with more capable peers). The ZPD is the level of performance at which a learner is capable of functioning when there is support from interaction with a more capable individual (Bull, Kimball, & Montgomery, 2000).

REFERENCES

Asher, J. J. (1977). *Learning another language through actions: The complete teacher's guidebook.* Los Gatos, CA: Sky Oaks Productions.

Asher, J. J. (2000). *Year 2000 update for the total physical response known worldwide as TPR.* Los Gatos, CA: Sky Oaks Productions.

Birdsong, D. (2000). *Second language acquisition and the critical period hypothesis: The second language acquisition research series, theoretical and methodological issues.* Mahwah, NJ: Lawrence Erlbaum Associates.

Bonnet, A., Kahl, P., & Krashen, S. D. (Eds.). (2000). The comprehensible input hypothesis and second language acquisition. In *Innovation und Tradition im Englischunterricht*, pp. 166–201. Stuttgart: Klett Verlag.

Brown, H. D. (2001). *Teaching by principles: An interactive approach to language pedagogy.* White Plains, NY: Addison Wesley Longman.

Bull, K. S., Kimball, S. L., & Montgomery, D. L. (2000). Designing instructional content: Constructivist instructional design. In K. S. Bull, D. L. Montgomery, and S. L. Kimball (Eds.) *Quality university instruction online: An advanced teaching effectiveness training program—an instructional hypertext.* Stillwater: Oklahoma State University Press.

Burt, M., Dulay, H., & Krashen, D. (1990). *Language two.* Oxford: Oxford University Press.

Calderón, M., & Minaya-Rowe, L. (2003). *Designing and implementing two-way bilingual programs: A step-by-step guide for administrators, teachers, and parents.* Thousand Oaks, CA: Corwin.

Collier, V., & Thomas, W. P. (2001, February). *Reforming schools for English language learners: Achievement gap closure.* Feature speech delivered at the annual meeting of the National Association for Bilingual Education, Phoenix, AZ.

Cummins, J. (2000). *Language, power, and pedagogy: Bilingual children in the crossfire.* Bristol, PA: Multilingual Matters.

Cummins, J., & Fillmore, L. W. (2000). *Language and education: What every teacher (and administrator) needs to know.* (Casette Recording No. NABE00-FS10A). Dallas, TX: CopyCats.

Dalton, S. S. (1998). *Pedagogy matters: Standards for effective teaching practice.* Santa Cruz, CA: Center for Research on Education, Diversity and Excellence.

DiSpezio, M., Lisowski, M., Skoog, G., Linner-Luebe, M., & Sparks, B. (1999). *Exploring living things.* Menlo Park, CA: Addison Wesley.

Donnell, H., Miller, J. E., & Hogan, R. J. (1989). *Traditions in literature.* Sunnyvale, CA: Scott, Foresman and Company.

Doty, J. K., Cameron, G. N., & Barton, M. L. (2003). *Teaching reading in social studies.* Alexandria, VA: Association for Supervision and Curriculum Development.

Doughty, C., & Williams, J. (1998). *Focus on form in classroom second language acquisition.* New York: Cambridge University Press.

Echevarria, J., & Graves, M. (1998). *Sheltered content instruction: Teaching English language learners with diverse abilities.* Needham Heights, MA: Allyn & Bacon.

Echevarria, J., Vogt, M. E., & Short, D. J. (2000). *Making content comprehensible for English-language learners: The SIOP model.* Needham Heights, MA: Allyn & Bacon.

Ellis, R. (1997). *The study of second language acquisition.* Oxford: Oxford University Press.

Eastern Stream Center on Resources and Training. (ESCORT). (2003). *Help! They don't speak English. Starter kit.* Oneonta, NY: Author.

Fichera, V. M., & Straight, H. S. (Eds.). (1997). *Using languages across the curriculum: Diverse disciplinary perspectives.* Binghamton: State University of New York.

Genesee, F. (1994). *Integrating language and content: Lessons from immersion.* Santa Cruz, CA: National Center for Research on National Diversity and Second Language Learning.

Genesee, F. (1999). *Program alternatives for linguistically diverse students.* Santa Cruz, CA: Center for Research in Education, Diversity, & Excellence.

Jameson, J. (1998). Three principles for success: English language learners in mainstream content classes. In *From theory to practice (issue No. 6).* Tampa, FL: Region XIV Comprehensive Center at ETS, Center for Applied Linguistics.

John-Steiner, V. (2000). *Creative collaboration.* Oxford: Oxford University Press.

John-Steiner, V., & Mahn, H. (1997). *Sociocultural approaches to learning and development: A Vygotskian framework.* [On-line] members.home.net/vygotsky/johnsteiner.html

Krashen, S. D. (2000b). What does it take to acquire language? *ESL Magazine 3*(3), 22–23.

Krashen, S. D. (2000a). An interactive view of the Natural Approach. [On-line] www.greenheart.com/jrmenlel/krashenpick.htm

Krashen, S. D. (1999). TPR: Still a very good idea. [On-line] ipisun.jpte.hu/~joe/novelty/

Krashen, S. D., Candin, C. N., & Terrell, T. D. (1996). *The natural approach: Language acquisition in the classroom.* New York: Simon & Schuster.

Krashen, S. D. (1985). *The input hypothesis: Issues and implications.* New York: Longman.

Lightbown, P. M., & Spada, N. (1999). *How languages are learned* (rev. ed.). New York: Oxford University Press.

Mora, R. (2000). *Identity conflicts and literacy development in first and second languages.* New York: Teachers College Press.

Murphy, E. (1997). Characteristics of constructivist learning & teaching. [On-line] www.stemnet. nf.ca/~elmurphy/emurphy/cle3.html

Orr, J. (2001). Standards for bilingual and dual-language classrooms. *Nabe News 24*(6), 4–7.

Ovando, C. J., Collier, V. P., & Combs, M. C. (2003). *Bilingual and ESL classrooms: Teaching in multicultural contexts* (3rd ed.). Boston: McGraw Hill.

Parker, D. (1985). *Sheltered English: Theory to practice.* Sacramento: California State Department of Education.

Richard-Amato, P. A. (1996). *Making it happen: Interaction in the second language classroom.* White Plains, NY: Longman.

Richards, J., & Rodgers, T. (1986). *Approaches and methods in language teaching: A description and analysis.* New York: Cambridge University Press.

Rueda, R. (1998). Defining mild disabilities with language-minority students. *Exceptional Children, 56*(2), 121–128

Savignon, S. J. (1999). *Communicative competence: Theory and classroom practice* (2nd ed.). New York: McGraw-Hill.

Schifini, A. (2000). *Second language learning at its best: The stages of language acquisition.* Carmel, CA: Hampton Brown.

Shaw, J. M., Echevarria, J., & Short, D. J. (1999, April). *Sheltered instruction: Bridging diverse cultures for academic success.* Paper presented at the annual meeting of the American Educational Research Association, Montreal.

Short, D. J. (1999). Integrating language and content for effective sheltered instruction programs. In C. Faltis & P. Wolfe (Eds.), *So much to say: Adolescents, bilingualism, and ESL in secondary schools* (pp. 105–137). New York: Teachers College Press.

Shotter, J. (1997). *Talk of saying, showing, gesturing, and feeling in Wittgenstein and Vygotsky.* [On-line].

Available: www.massey.sc.nz/~Alock/virtual/wittvyg.htm

Straight, H. S. (1998). *Languages across the curriculum.* ERIC Digest. [On-line]. Available: www.cal.org/ericcll/digest/lacdigest.html

Stryker, S. B., & Leaver, B. L. (Eds.). (1997). *Content-based instruction for the foreign language classroom: Models and methods.* Washington, DC: Georgetown University Press.

Teachers of English to Speakers of Other Languages (TESOL). (1997). *ESL standards for pre-K–12 students.* Alexandria, VA: Author.

Tharp, R. G. (1997). *From at-risk to excellence: Research theory and principles for practice.* Santa Cruz, CA: Center for Research on Education, Diversity, and Excellence.

Tharp, R. G. (1999). *Proofs and evidence: Effectiveness of the five standards for effective teaching.* Santa Cruz, CA: Center for Research in Education, Diversity, & Excellence.

Tharp, R. G., Estrada, P., Dalton, S. S., & Yamauchi, L. A. (2000). *Teaching transformed: Achieving excellence, fairness, inclusion, and harmony.* Boulder, CO: Westview.

Tharp, R. G., & Gallimore, R. (1998). *Rousing minds to life: Teaching, learning, and schooling in social context.* New York: Cambridge University Press.

Valdes, G. (1996). *Con respeto: Bridging the distances between culturally diverse families and schools. An ethnographic portrait.* New York: Teachers College Press.

Vygotsky, L. S. (1986). *Thought and language.* Cambridge, MA: MIT Press.

Vygotsky, L. S. (1978). *Mind in society: The development of higher psychological processes.* Cambridge, MA: Harvard University Press.

Walqui, A. (2000). *Contextual factors in second language acquisition.* [On-line]. www.cal.org/ericcll/digest/0005contextual.html

Waxman, H. C., & Padrón, Y. N. (2002). Research-based teaching practices that improve the education of English language learners. In L. Minaya-Rowe (Ed.), *Teacher training and effective pedagogy in the context of student diversity* (pp. 3–38). Greenwich, CT: Information Age.

CHAPTER 5

A BILINGUAL DEVELOPMENTAL MODEL AND CURRICULUM FOR INCREASING ESL AND MAINSTREAM YOUNG CHILDREN'S ACADEMIC ACHIEVEMENT

LEARNING OBJECTIVES

1. Develop social and moral responsibility when serving ESL students
2. Understand research supporting the bilingual developmental model and its derived philosophical, theoretical, and pedagogical principles
3. Understand ESL standards and its interface with the bilingual developmental model
4. Identify educational principles, goals and objectives, and pedagogical strategies of the bilingual developmental curriculum

PREVIEW QUESTIONS

1. Why is it important for educators serving ESL students at-risk of underachievement to develop social and moral responsibility?
2. Which research trends, and philosophical, theoretical, and pedagogical principles endorsed by socioconstructivistic perspective and the bilingual developmental model can be useful for educators to increase the academic achievement of ESL students?
3. Why is it important for ESL teachers to understand and apply TESOL Standards in their educational practice?

Chapter 5 presents a bilingual developmental model and curriculum that represents best educational practices derived from contemporary socioconstructivistic and developmental research. This bilingual developmental model and curriculum can effectively stimulate cognitive, linguistic, and socioemotional development and academic achievement in young, at-risk, low socioeconomic (SES), English-as-a-second-language (ESL) students and mainstream students. The objective of Chapter 5 connects to the first theme of this book: to infuse an ethnic educator philosophy in order for school personnel to develop cultural awareness of the powerful effect of their attitudes and educational practices on ESL and majority, low SES, young learners' development and academic achievement.

In a first major section, encompassing three subsections, the bilingual developmental model is presented, with its derived philosophical, theoretical, and pedagogical principles. Two bodies of research are interconnected as a theoretical framework for the bilingual developmental model proposed in this chapter, including:

1. Mainstream studies in cognitive and developmental psychology and cognitive science, following a traditional paradigm, resulting in educationally applied recommendations made by the National Research Council (1999a, 1999b)
2. Studies in the area of bilingual education and ESL, following an "Ethnic Educator" philosophical paradigm (the latter term first presented by the authors in Gonzalez, Brusca-Vega, & Yawkey, 1997), resulting in educationally applied recommendations that are interfaced with *ESL Standards* developed by the Teaching English as a Second Language (TESOL, 1997) professional organization

A second major section, with two subsections, presents a bilingual developmental curriculum with goals and objectives, and pedagogical strategies that stem from a socioconstructivistic and ethnic educator perspective. An extended collection of instructional activities and lesson plans are presented in the companion Web site, www.ablongman.com/Gonzalez1e for the book. The curriculum presented has been pilot tested and is in the process of program evaluation by the first author of the book (for more information please see our Web page at www.uc.edu/bpdc).

BILINGUAL DEVELOPMENTAL EDUCATIONAL MODEL

In the United States the bilingual developmental education model is considered an enrichment program that can positively enhance the holistic development and long-term academic achievement of young language-minority, as well as mainstream, children. The current underachievement of ESL students may be attributed to educational programs that focus only on the linguistic aspects of the developmental process, ignoring the influence of cognitive, affective, and sociocultural factors in the process of first-and-second-language (L1 and L2) learning. The bilingual developmental educational model and curriculum proposed here considers that cognitive and linguistic development in the L1 is needed in order to acquire the L2 and be able to use both languages as methods for teaching and learning. The bilingual developmental educational model proposed has an epistemological orientation that considers learning as an active process in which concepts are constructed through cognitive, affective, and sociocultural symbols that are represented verbally in L1 and L2 and nonverbally in both cultures.

Bilingual developmental programs are also called two-way bilingual programs because they use native-speaking peers as social and cultural role models for developing native-like linguistic, cognitive, and cultural competency in a L2. Monolingual Spanish and English children participate in the program, and their presence provides peer native-speakers models that motivate L2 learning, positive attitudes, and higher academic achievement.

Positive development and achievement outcomes are possible due to the presence of an additive bilingual environment that stimulates L1 and L2, academic achievement, and conceptual development. According to the Center for Research on Education, Diversity, and Excellence (CREDE, 2002), this additive bilingual environment can use three approaches to initial literacy development: (1) native language first with the classic 90/10 model, (2) both languages simultaneously, with the classic 50/50 model, and (3) the second language first approach that also applies the 90/10 model. The bilingual developmental model proposed in this chapter endorses the classic 50/50 model that uses both languages simultaneously as methods of instruction for both language-minority and mainstream students.

The bilingual developmental model endorses a socioconstructivistic philosophy and theoretical framework. Therefore, this instructional approach uses both languages as methods of instruction, as tools for thinking, as symbolic representations for content knowledge and experiences, and as communication and socialization tools. The curriculum focuses on subject matter and developmental objectives with a holistic perspective, so that children are developing simultaneously complementary concepts in L1 and L2. Therefore, children are enriching their intelligence ability by creating more verbal and nonverbal (or culturally loaded) symbolic representations that can enhance their cognitive, metacognitive, and metalinguistic processes (e.g., concept formation, phonological awareness, creativity, problem solving, analogical reasoning, convergent and divergent abilities, etc.).

Bilingual developmental programs meet the conditions for successful L2 acquisition in school, such as the provision of meaningful and purposeful language. That is, to use L1 and L2 within genuine or authentic social and academic communication settings (see Gonzalez et al., 1997). For instance, some appropriate instructional strategies for ESL students to improve their L1 and L2 skills include the communication of experiences or observations on a field trip, retelling a story, asking for questions, communicating in a cooperative or symbolic playing activity, doing a cooking recipe, communicating feelings or emotions or needs, and so forth. These successful strategies will be developed further in the curriculum presented below.

In sum, bilingual developmental educational programs provide a high-quality learning environment that can stimulate at-risk, low SES, ESL students to develop higher level cognitive, metacognitive, and metalinguistic abilities and learning strategies that result in sustained progress in academic achievement across content areas. Research-based knowledge about the effectiveness of bilingual developmental programs demonstrates that a holistic developmental curriculum, based on a socioconstructivistic perspective, develops higher levels of L1 and L2 academic and social competence by using both languages as methods of teaching and learning, which in turn increases developmental potential and abilities, and translates into academic competence.

Thus, the sociocultural mediation of advocates and empathic teachers, and a supportive school culture that endorses high-quality teaching, can help ESL at-risk students to actualize their developmental potential into resiliency and successful social adaptation and academic competency. Successful learners also have developed sociocultural adaptive expertise through the help of role models and mentors who transmit social and cultural learning.

EDUCATIONAL APPLICATION OF CORE PHILOSOPHICAL AND THEORETICAL PRINCIPLES FOR THE STIMULATION OF ACADEMIC ACHIEVEMENT IN BOTH ESL AND MAINSTREAM, LOW SES STUDENTS

The National Research Council published two important documents, entitled *How People Learn* (1999a) and *Improving Student Learning* (1999b), that identify major principles for teaching and learning, derived from contemporary research in cognitive and developmental psychology and cognitive science, which can improve our educational practice. The philosophical and theoretical principles listed and discussed below integrate mainstream (National Research Council, 1999a, 199b) and ESL (TESOL, 1997) research within a socioconstructivistic perspective for developmental, learning, and teaching processes.

The integration done in Chapter 5 identifies three core **philosophical** and **theoretical principles,** recommended by the National Research Council (1999a, 1999b), which are listed in Table 5.1. These three core philosophical and theoretical principles are derived from contemporary mainstream research in cognitive and developmental psychology and cognitive science, including:

1. A holistic developmental perspective for learning and teaching. That is, the importance of educating the whole child by stimulating learning across cognitive, linguistic, and socioemotional developmental and academic areas. In reference to teaching, we emphasize the importance of developing in teachers a holistic vision of education that responds to children's individual psychological and sociocultural differences (including their ethnic, language, and ESL background)
2. The interaction of internal and external factors in L1 and L2 learning; cognitive, literacy, and socioemotional development; and academic competence
3. The important role of teachers as sociocultural instructional mediators to develop cultural adaptation and higher learning and achievement levels in at-risk ESL and

TABLE 5.1   Three Core Philosophical and Theoretical Principles for Development and Academic Achievement for ESL and Mainstream, Low SES Students

GENERAL PRINCIPLES	SPECIFIC PRINCIPLES
PRINCIPLE 1	
Holistic developmental perspective *In reference to children's learning:*	
A holistic developmental perspective for learning across cognitive, linguistic, andsociocultural developmental and academic areas.	• L1 and L2 learning follows a simultaneous and complex developmental process
In reference to teachers' approach to instruction:	
A holistic developmental perspective in teachers who can respond to children's individual's psychological and sociocultural differences (i.e., ethnic, linguistic, cultural, and SES backgrounds)	• Use of holistic principles for selecting subject-matter content in relation to grade level and purpose of instruction
PRINCIPLE 2	
Interaction of internal and external factors in first- and second-language learning; and cognitive, literacy, and sociocultural development and academic achievement	
Cognitive development	• Learning L1 and L2 is affected by internal factors (i.e., maturational, psychological, and biological) and external factors (i.e., cultural, social, schooling, and family settings) • Powerful effect of external factors, such as at-risk conditions for developmental delays and underachievement, should not be confounded with, and differentiated from, genuine handicap ping conditions and disabilities (linked with internal factors)
Language and literacy development	• L1 and L2 learning is a process that takes developmental time and effort (BICS** develops in 2–3 years, and CALPS*** develop in 5–8 years) • Languages vary in relation to external or sociocultural factors (i.e., social class, ethnicity, topic, purpose, etc.)
Socioemotional development	• Learning and academic achievement is influenced by external family, community, and school conditions

(continued)

TABLE 5.1   Continued

PRINCIPLE 3	
Role of teachers as sociocultural mediators for learning, and committed advocates and mentors for linking school and family environments	• Teachers need to develop nurturing learning communities in which ESL students can maintain collaborative relations, participate actively, and have a sense of belonging and intrinsic motivation. • Teachers need to act as mentors between the mainstream school culture and the minority home and family cultural environments. • Teachers need to act as mentors for developing rapport or a friendship relation that offer ESL students mutual trust and respect for cultural and linguistic diversity and idiosyncratic differences. • Teachers need to help ESL students to develop abstract learning principles (or conceptual frameworks) that can be transformed and become relevant to other knowledge and problem domains.

* Adapted and expanded for the case of ESL students from documents developed by the National Research Council (1999a, 1999b)

** BICS = Bilingual Interpersonal Communicative Skills

*** CALPS = Cognitive Academic Language Proficiency Skills

mainstream, poor, young students. Teachers also have another important role as mentors and as committed and empathic advocates. That is, teachers can become powerful social agents who can help at-risk ESL and mainstream, low SES students to become resilient learners and achievers in the U.S. public school system

The three core philosophical and theoretical principles are discussed here in relation to cognitive, language and literacy, and socioemotional developmental areas. Each principle is described and discussed in relation to L1 and L2 learning processes.

CORE PHILOSOPHICAL AND THEORETICAL PRINCIPLES

A Holistic Developmental Perspective

1. Use of a holistic perspective for selecting teaching and learning principles in relation to subject matter, grade level, and purpose of instruction
2. Language processes develop independently and form a holistic competence. Divisions of language proficiency areas into pronunciation, vocabulary, syntax, and grammar; and of literacy development into speaking, listening, reading, and writing skills is a methodological artifact to study and stimulate sequentially a complex

and simultaneous process. In real life, authentic language uses simultaneously different language processes. That is the rationale underlying more simultaneous, than sequential processes, in natural L1 and L2 learning

Core Philosophical and Theoretical Principles: Internal and External Factors Influencing L1 and L2 Learning

Cognitive Development

1. For all students, including language-minority and majority, learning is the result of the interaction of internal and external factors. Among the most important factors are: (i) maturational and psychological individual differences in cognition, linguistic, and affective/emotional developmental areas; and (ii) biological factors such as idiosyncratic characteristics in temperament and physical growth rates. Among the most important external factors are cultural, social, school, and family settings; resulting in idiosyncratic characteristics that need to be respected and nurtured in the learner-centered classroom environment
2. It is important that the powerful effect of external factors (e.g., nutrition, level of income of parents, etc.) is not confounded with biological, developmental, or psychological genuine differences (such as disabilities or handicapping conditions). Developmental delays resulting from external factors need to be differentiated from genuine learning disabilities or mental retardation, especially among language-minority and majority students (for a more extended discussion of this topic, see Gonzalez [2001])

Language and Literacy Development

1. Language acquisition for both monolingual and bilingual students is a long-term process that takes time and effort to develop. Rates of individual ESL language development are influenced by multiple internal and external factors, such as learning style, cognitive style, motivation, personality, educational background, and L1 background
2. Social language competence in English is different than academic language competence necessary to achieve academically across content areas. The development of social competence in ESL can take from 2 to 3 years. In contrast, the development of academic competence in ESL can take from 5 to 7 years. The development of academic competence in ESL takes more developmental time because it requires learners to increase their developmental skills and reach higher stages. Thus, it is important to maintain and continue developing L1 for stimulating developmental growth and academic achievement in ESL learners
3. Every language varies across multiple external or sociocultural factors including: person, topic, purpose, situation, and group differences. All these sociocultural factors vary in relation to social class and ethnicity (e.g., dialects, vernaculars), and academic and social domains. All language varieties have distinctive structural and functional characteristics

Socioemotional Development

1. External family, community, and school conditions linked to affective and emotional variables (i.e., mental health of parents, quality of parent–child relationship, expectations, attitudes, values and belief systems, etc.) influence language-minority and majority students' learning and academic achievement

The Role of Teachers

1. Teachers of at-risk students need to create classroom environments that nurture learning through caring and collaborative relations. The focus of instruction should be on developing a sense of belonging to a learning community so that *all* students, language-minority and language-majority, develop intrinsic motivation and participate actively in all learning activities
2. Teachers need to become caring, committed, and emphatic mentors and sociocultural mediators for helping ESL, and mainstream, low SES children to bridge their minority home cultural environments and their mainstream school cultural experiences
3. Teachers need to nurture ESL children for developing rapport or a friendship relationship that offers mutual trust and respect for cultural and linguistic diversity, and idiosyncratic differences
4. *All* students, language-minority and language-majority, need to be helped by teachers acting as mediators to understand why, when, and how factual knowledge and abstract learning principles (or conceptual frameworks) can be transferred or transformed, and can become relevant to other knowledge and problem domains

In sum, these three major philosophical and theoretical principles integrate best educational practices derived from two modules of knowledge: (1) mainstream contemporary research in cognitive and developmental psychology and cognitive science, delineated by the National Research Council (1999a, 1999b), and (2) research in ESL and bilingual education that delineates educational practices for meeting diverse students' needs. These major principles emphasize an integration approach that interfaces developmental areas across cognitive, language and literacy, and socioemotional domains. As discussed in the section below, these three major philosophical and theoretical principles have important pedagogical implications for improving learning and teaching processes in at-risk, ESL, and mainstream children.

PEDAGOGICAL PRINCIPLES FOR DEVELOPMENT AND ACADEMIC ACHIEVEMENT IN ESL STUDENTS

In the second subsection below, we present five derived pedagogical principles from the formerly discussed three core philosophical and theoretical principles. These five pedagogical principles follow recommendations for educational practice derived from research made by the National Research Council (1999a, 1999b). These five pedagogical principles are presented across cognitive, language and literacy, and socioemotional developmental areas. See Table 5.2 for a list of the five pedagogical principles.

Development of Higher-Level Cognitive Strategies

Cognitive Development

1. Students need to be stimulated to develop conceptual competence (i.e., understanding of knowledge structures) in factual knowledge (i.e., topic and content knowledge). All children need to develop a deep foundation of factual knowledge and a strong conceptual knowledge framework for transforming information into abstract meaningful knowledge and principles that can be transferred to other knowledge and problem-solving domains. Abstract or conceptual knowledge refers to the students' ability to represent or construct learning principles (or conceptual frameworks) and transform them into higher level learning strategies (i.e., critical thinking and cognitive, metacognitive, and metalinguistic skills) that can be applied to multiple academic content and real-world problem and situations

2. All students, language-minority and mainstream, need to be stimulated "to learn how to learn," "learn how to think," and "learn how to think about language" through the use of cognitive, metacognitive, and metalinguistic strategies. It is considered important to stimulate ESL students to generate new concepts, so that not only assimilation of concepts is achieved, but also accommodation of concepts occurs for the generation of new knowledge. The focus of instruction is on concept development through inquiry-based learning such as active and discovery learning, learner-centered classrooms, and collaborative problem-solving activities that lead to flexibility of thinking and creativity

Language and Literacy Development

1. Two complementary processes occur in language learning in bilingual students, the instantiation of a concept already constructed in one language to the other (resulting in assimilation learning processes and positive transference of learning), and the construction of a new concept for representing unique sociocultural symbolic meanings of one of the languages (resulting in accommodation learning processes). In the first case, when transference across languages is appropriate, then the L1 proficiency contributes to L2 acquisition. For instance, the general understanding of structures and functions of L1 can be transferred implicitly by ESL learners, especially in reference to academic literacy skills (similar to abstract conceptual frameworks, or general principles for thinking and learning, such as metacognitive strategies). In the second case, when one language has unique culturally loaded concepts, then ESL learners need to form new sociocultural concepts resulting in new knowledge for achieving higher levels of cognitive strategies (e.g., metalinguistic awareness) and development

TABLE 5.2 Five Pedagogical Principles on Development and Academic Achievement in ESL and Mainstream, Low SES Students

GENERAL PRINCIPLES	SPECIFIC PRINCIPLES*
1. DEVELOPMENT OF HIGHER-LEVEL COGNITIVE STRATEGIES	
Cognitive Development	• All students need to develop conceptual competence (i.e., principles that can be transformed into higher level learning strategies and critical-thinking skills) and be able to apply it to factual knowledge gained in multiple academic content and real-world problem situations. • All students need to develop concepts through inquiry-based learning (i.e., active and discovery learning, learner-centered classrooms, and collaborative problem-solving activities)
Language and literacy development	• Two complementary processes occur in L1 and L2 learning: assimilation (i.e., positive transference of concepts) and accommodation (i.e., formation of new sociocultural concepts in L2) • L1 and L2 learning processes can result in higher level cognitive processes such as abstract and metacognitive skills
Socioemotional development	• Developing metacognitive skills provides insight into self-regulation and independent thinking and learning processes • L1 is a conceptual tool for learning and representing sociocultural, affective, and emotional processes (i.e., cultural and bicultural identity)
2. CONNECTION TO PRIOR SOCIOCULTURAL KNOWLEDGE	
Cognitive Development	• Indissoluble connection between language and cognition, both influenced by sociocultural processes. • Central role of prior knowledge in learner-centered classrooms, such as culturally and socially loaded preconceptions
Language and literacy development	• L1 and L2 is a cultural process in which children need to acquire sociocultural competence and new cultural knowledge • Language is used by schools to socialize children to be literate and use reading and writing as a major tool for learning
Socioemotional development	• L1 and L2 learners need to develop positive attitudes toward additive bilingualism and biculturalism. • Cultural beliefs about the nature of intelligence is related to ESL students' academic achievement

(continued)

TABLE 5.2 Continued

GENERAL PRINCIPLES	SPECIFIC PRINCIPLES

3. CONNECTION TO REAL-WORLD EXPERIENCES

GENERAL PRINCIPLES	SPECIFIC PRINCIPLES
Cognitive Development	• Use of a community-centered approach and collaboration and cooperation with peers as pedagogical strategies to develop knowledge and topic competence • Conceptual competence and topic knowledge can be stimulated by applying concepts to real-life problems
Language and literacy development	• Use of real-world socio-cultural references for L1 and L2 learners to enhance their semantic development and academic knowledge, and pragmatic and social communication skills.
Socioemotional development	• Language is a tool for communication and socialization, processes through which children learn from role models and cultural mediators

4. THEMATIC CURRICULUMS

GENERAL PRINCIPLES	SPECIFIC PRINCIPLES
Cognitive Development	• Thematic curriculums can stimulate students to develop deep conceptual competence and factual knowledge, and use multiple thinking skills and strategies across content areas, and problem and knowledge domains • Thematic curriculums can be used as topics to stimulate cognitive and metacognitive skills

5. INTERACTION OF COGNITIVE, CULTURAL, AND SOCIOCULTURAL DEVELOPMENTAL PROCESSES AND ACADEMIC ACHIEVEMENT

GENERAL PRINCIPLES	SPECIFIC PRINCIPLES
	• Goal of ESL instruction is to increase academic achievement Rhetoric or academic competence is necessary for developing conceptual and topic knowledge in specific content areas • Language is a learning tool to transmit cultural and social frameworks of conceptual and topic knowledge Language is a socialization tool to initiate children in cultural thinking styles, cultural affective and spiritual styles, and verbal and nonverbal cultural styles of social interaction • Bilingual developmental programs have an epistemological cognitive orientation in which L1 and L2 learning is considered an active process of concept formation

* Adapted and expanded for the case of ESL students from documents developed by the National Research Council (1999a, 1999b).

2. Language provides preschool children the ability to move from perceptual to concrete, and to abstract and metacognitive and metalinguistic levels of thinking. That is, through internal symbolic thinking, children can detach from immediate time and space, and manipulate and transform reality into nonverbal and verbal mental symbols in unique ways through problem solving, concept formation, active learning, creativity, and flexibility of thinking. For instance, through language, children can engage in intra-personal thinking via verbal thoughts; or interpersonal thinking via group brainstorming, instructional conversations, dialogue, and inquiry-based learning, and so forth. When young children can learn two languages simultaneously, the presence of two sociocultural symbolic systems enhances their cognitive, language and literacy, and socioemotional development. Bilingualism, then, results in higher level cognitive processes such as metalinguistic awareness (for further discussion of this topic see Gonzalez & Schallert, 1999).

3. Bilingualism is an individual and societal asset because it can stimulate higher level cognitive and metacognitive and metalinguistic skills and strategies, provided that an additive bilingual environment is supporting the learner. Bilingualism benefits the individual and the nation, and schools need to promote the development of multiple languages

Socioemotional Development

1. All students, language-minority and majority, need to develop greater insight into their own thinking and learning processes (i.e., metacognition) for becoming independent thinkers with self-regulation

2. It is important to continue developing the students' native or minority language because it is a conceptual tool for learning and for representing sociocultural, affective, and emotional processes. Cultural identity needs to be developed in both L1 and L2 and in both cultures because it mediates other important socioemotional and sociocultural developmental processes (i.e., self-concept, self-esteem, attitudes, belief and value systems, and motivation for learning) that significantly influence learning and academic achievement

Connection to Prior Sociocultural Knowledge

Cognitive Development

1. Language and cognitive development are indissoluble, culturally loaded processes. Language provides sociocultural conventions that can be used as symbolic tools (semantic development or academic language) for communicating nonverbal and verbal thoughts, concepts, ideas, and meaning

2. Prior knowledge has a central role in learning processes in all children. Classrooms need to be learner centered in which teachers consider students' preconceptions (i.e., existing misunderstandings and misconceptions about specific real-world, topic and content or subject-matter knowledge) influencing learning, which are culturally loaded as they were learned within social environments

Language and Literacy Development

1. Language learning is a cultural learning process for both monolingual and bilingual children. That is, children acquire linguistic, patterns and structures that vary across cultures and reflect differences in values, norms, and beliefs about social roles and relationships. Then, to develop L1 and L2 proficiency is also to acquire sociocultural competence and new cultural knowledge
2. At the school culture, language is used to socialize children to be "literate" through a cultural and social orientation towards using reading and writing as major tools for learning

Socioemotional Development

1. Bilingual education programs provide developmental enrichment that can benefit minority and majority students. All learners should develop attitudes of additive bilingualism and biculturalism, and ESL students need to maintain and develop their L1 and culture and learn a L2 and cultural competence. Bilingual education programs provide equal educational opportunity by providing meaningful education in L1 and culturally appropriate education across the curriculum areas
2. Language use at home and at school is related to the degree of acculturation and ethnic, cultural, and social identity present among parents, siblings, and other extended family members (e.g., grandparents, aunts and uncles, cousins, etc.). That is the rationale explaining why language proficiency levels in minority students are connected with identity and affective factors such as self-concept and self-esteem
3. There is a powerful effect of language-minority and majority students' cultural beliefs on their academic achievement such as the nature of intelligence (i.e., whether luck, aptitude, or effort make a difference on school performance). In order to increase students' intrinsic motivation and academic performance, teachers need to socialize students to understand that intelligence is connected to effort, multiple trials and practice, and spending time and energy in improving skills and abilities, and acquiring new knowledge

Connection to Real-World Experiences

Cognitive Development

1. Classroom environments need to have a community-centered approach with connection to the language-minority and majority students' real-world experiences, and the use of collaboration and cooperation with peers to develop knowledge and topic competence
2. All students can develop conceptual competence and topic knowledge through applying concepts to multiple examples of real-life problems, across content areas, relating prior and new knowledge; and engaging in multiple cognitive , metacognitive, and metalinguistic processes (i.e., comparison, evaluation, categorization, using feedback, elaboration, etc.)

Language and Literacy Development

1. Language acquisition occurs through meaningful and significant use and interaction within a "natural" sociocultural environment. Through the use of real-world experiences, L1 and L2 learners can have access to sociocultural references to develop verbal and nonverbal symbolic representations (semantic development or academic language), and pragmatic and social communication skills

Socioemotional Development

1. Language is used in real-world experiences as a tool for communication and learning from social interactions with role models and cultural mediators (i.e., parents, caretakers, and teachers). Therefore, language is a tool for socialization of emotional and affective development in children

Thematic Curriculums

Cognitive Development

1. Deep conceptual competence and factual knowledge can be stimulated in all students, by concentrating in fewer topics throughout the school year(s) across content areas. By presenting a thematic curriculum, students can use multiple thinking skills and strategies for applications and transformations to other problem and knowledge domains
2. Content areas or subject matter need to be used by teachers of all students as topics to think about, talk about, write about in collaboration with peers; and as stimuli to develop cognitive and metacognitive skills

Interaction of Cognitive, Cultural, and Social Developmental Processes and Academic Achievement

1. The goal of ESL instruction is to function effectively in English and through English while learning challenging academic content and, ultimately, to increase academic achievement
2. All students need to gain "rhetoric" competence (cognitive academic language proficiency skills—CALPS) so that they have the discourse needed to understand and communicate about conceptual and topic knowledge in specific content areas
3. Learning is a social process that uses language and other cultural representational symbolic systems to transmit cultural and social frameworks resulting in learning conceptual and topic knowledge. Then, social and cultural variables affect the quality of learning among minority students (i.e., the L1 and L2 thinking, socioemotional, and learning processes in bilinguals is qualitatively different than monolinguals)

4. Language learning is used as a socialization tool that involves learning how to think in culturally appropriate manners by transmitting implicitly cultural values, cultural styles of thinking, religious and spiritual cultural styles, nonverbal styles of social interaction, and patterns of sociocultural uses of language
5. The bilingual developmental education model proposed has an epistemological cognitive orientation that considers learning as an active process in which concepts are constructed through cognitive, affective, and sociocultural symbols that are represented verbally in L1 and L2 and nonverbally in first and second cultures

Thus, in this second subsection emphasis has been given to the integration of pedagogical applications of research-based knowledge derived from contemporary mainstream studies in cognitive and developmental psychology and cognitive science (National Research Council, 19991,1999b), and ESL and bilingual education. In the section below a closer look at the educational implications of *ESL Standards* will be discussed.

THREE ASPECTS OF L1 AND L2 COMPETENCE DERIVED FROM NATIONAL STANDARDS FOR TEACHING ENGLISH AS A L2 (TESOL)

This third subsection presents the TESOL (1997) *ESL Standards* in relation to three aspects of L1 and L2 competence necessary for ESL students to meet federal- and state-mandated mainstream academic achievement standards. The discussion of these *ESL Standards* is approached from a socioconstructivistic perspective, the selected philosophical and theoretical position endorsed in this book.

In 1997, with the publication of the *ESL Standards for Pre-K–12 Students*, the Teachers of English to Speakers of Other Languages (TESOL) national professional association and their state affiliates, and other collaborative organizations (including the National Association for Bilingual Education [NABE], were responding to the high-stakes standards initiative and the school reform and school restructuring movement.

The *ESL Standards* provide guidelines that can be used by state departments of education and local school districts to develop best educational practices to meet the needs of language-minority students. The *ESL Standards* establish goals and descriptors, progress indicators, and best classroom strategies across grade levels The *ESL Standards* take into consideration other national standards, such as the English language arts and foreign language standards. Even though there are commonalities between the *ESL* and other standards, the former acknowledges the particular needs of ESL students, including: (1) the central role of language in learning content; and (2) the cultural, linguistic, and developmental factors affecting learning and instructional processes, such as exposure to limited formal schooling.

Figure 5.1 presents the three general English language competence areas. Table 5.3 presents the interconnection among the three core philosophical and theoretical principles, the five pedagogical principles, and the three ESL competence areas.

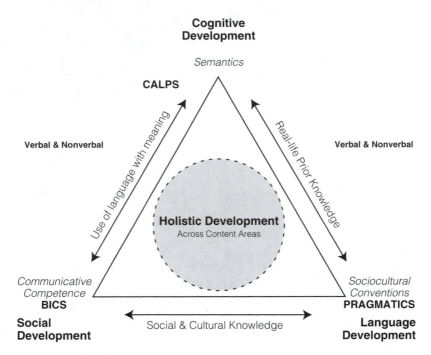

FIGURE 5.1   Four Integrative Components of First- and Second-Language Processes and Academic Achievement from a Holistic Developmental Perspective

Using the *ESL Standards* (TESOL, 1997) document as a springboard, and other research-based knowledge in the bilingual/ESL education area, we will interpret and discuss three broad and interconnected goals for developing English language competence in language-minority students:

1. To use English to communicate and interact in social settings for personal expression and enjoyment, while maintaining ESL students' social competence in their native language. This language ability has been called Bilingual Interpersonal Communication Skills (BICS) in the literature of bilingual/ESL education by Cummins (1991)

2. To use ESL to learn and achieve academic competence across content areas at grade level, following mainstream competence standards. Students need to be able to use English for interacting in the classroom with teachers and peers while engaging in academic activities. Students need to be able to use English as a learning tool to encode, process, construct, and express factual and conceptual knowledge across

TABLE 5.3 Relationships among Three Core Philosophical and Theoretical Principles and Five Pedagogical Principles for Development and Academic Achievement, and Three ESL Language Competence Areas

Three Core Philosophical and Theoretical Principles	Five Pedagogical Principles for Development and Academic Achievement	Three Interconnected ESL Language Competence Areas**
1. *In reference to children's learning:* • A holistic developmental perspective for learning across cognitive, linguistic, and sociocultural developmental and academic areas *In reference to teachers' approach to instruction:* • A holistic developmental perspective in teachers who can respond to children's individual psychological and sociocultural differences (i.e., ethnic, linguistic, cultural, and SES backgrounds)	**1.** Development of higher-level cognitive strategies • Cognitive development • Language and literacy development • Socioemotional development **2.** Connection to prior sociocultural knowledge • Cognitive development • Language and literacy development • Socioemotional development	**1.** Bilingual Interpersonal Communicative Skills **BICS** **2.** Cognitive Academic Language Proficiency Skills **CALPS**

(continued)

TABLE 5.3 Continued

2. Interaction of internal and external factors in L1 and L2 learning; and cognitive, literacy, and sociocultural developmental areas and academic achievement content areas

3. Role of teachers as sociocultural mediators for learning, and committed advocates and mentors for linking school and family environments

3. Connection to real-world experiences
   - Cognitive development
   - Language and literacy development
   - Socioemotional development

4. Thematic curriculums
   - Cognitive development

5. Interaction of cognitive, cultural, and socioemotional developmental processes and academic achievement

3. Sociolinguistic and sociocultural competence

   PRAGMATICS

Source: Adapted and expanded for the case of ESL students from documents developed by the National Research Council (1999a, 1999b)
* Based on TESOL *ESL Standards* (TESOL, 1997)

content areas. Students also need to use English as an abstract symbolic tool for engaging in critical thinking, problemsolving, active learning, and high-level cognitive, metacognitive, and metalinguistic thinking strategies. This ability has been called in the literature of bilingual/ESL education as Cognitive Academic Language Proficiency Skills (CALPS, Cummins, 1991)

3. To use English in socially and culturally appropriate ways by developing sociolinguistic and sociocultural competence. That is, the development of linguistic cultural competence or pragmatics. Language learning is embedded in learning social and cultural competence in order to understand contextual uses of language (according to variety, genre, register, audience, purpose, and setting), nonverbal communication or paralinguistic representations (e.g., gestures, physical proximity to people, eye-to-eye contact, etc.), and appropriate learning strategies

Next we extend the discussion of these three English language competence skills and their interaction: (1) BICS; (2) CALPS (in relation to pre-literacy and literacy abilities); (3) pragmatics or sociolinguistic and sociocultural competence; and (4) interaction of BICS, CALPS, and pragmatic competence areas.

Bilingual Interpersonal Communication Skills (BICS)

This ability refers to the acquisition of communicative competence in order to achieve some social functions. According to Shafer, Staab, and Smith (1983) children use language to fulfill some social functions, including to: (1) assert and maintain social needs and relations (i.e., make a demand, criticize; and assert identities, opinions, and observations); (2) inform (i.e., talk about events, make comparisons and generalizations, request information, and communicate past or present events); (3) project into novel situations (i.e., make-believe roles in their symbolic play; and experience vicariously through other person's perceptions, observations, thoughts, and feelings); (4) control the self and others (i.e., monitor self in actions), and (5) direct attention, memory, and thinking as a learning tool (i.e., apply strategies for language or content learning, use language as a cognitive or heuristic tool to discover information, think about causal relations, predict events, make inferences).

It is important to note that different cultures use diverse social communication styles and norms. For instance, the amount of nonverbal expressiveness or gestures and movement of the hands and body, proximity between speakers, and eye-to-eye contact varies dramatically across users of different languages. Other expressions of affective and emotional variables also differ widely across cultures, such as turn-taking between speakers, tone and pitch of voice, fluency or speed of talk, rhythm, volume of voice, and so on. For instance, native-Spanish speakers tend to speak very quickly and tend to interrupt each other while in a conversation as the negotiation of turn-taking requires intervening in the other speakers' utterances and completing or following their thoughts, it is certainly a cultural "art" that nonnative speakers find difficult to master.

Cognitive Academic Language Proficiency Skills (CALPS)

This ability refers to the use of conceptual knowledge as a tool for learning across content areas. That is, competence in CALPS helps ESL students to acquire new verbal (or semantic) and nonverbal concepts through the use of prior knowledge (i.e., assimilation) and the formation of new concepts (i.e., accommodation). Preliteracy and literacy skills emerge when ESL students achieve oral language maturity, and conceptual competence or CALPS. Conceptual competence refers to the ability to: (1) use verbal and nonverbal representations to encode, store, and transform ideas, abstractions, generalizations, and categorizations; and (2) express verbal and nonverbal representations in the form of cognitive, metacognitive, and metalinguistic processes and learning behaviors (e.g., identifying attributes, events, and similarities, for making comparisons and groupings). Below a more specific discussion of prereading and prewriting abilities will be presented; with emphasis on the interaction of language and cognitive processes, such as oral language and cognitive academic language competence, and the effects of literacy development on academic achievement across content areas.

Prereading abilities.   As explained above in relation to CALPS, ESL learners need to achieve maturation in oral language proficiency as a prerequisite for developing preliteracy skills, which result from the interaction of cognitive and language development within a print rich social environment. Preliteracy skills for reading processes include: constructs about print, ability to discriminate letters, phonemic awareness, acquisition of phoneme-grapheme knowledge, and reading comprehension.

According to Piper (1998), there are five processes of reading used by young children: (1) automatization of lexical access (for recognizing letters and words without conscious effort), (2) memory strategies, (3) use of prior knowledge, (4) self-monitoring of reading comprehension (i.e., checking for understanding of paragraphs or specific words as they read a story), and (5) adaptation of strategies to the demands of specific tasks (e.g., narrative versus dialogue texts, stories read in different languages). It is important to highlight that reading comprehension precedes and is much more important than the ability to decode printed matter. Reading comprehension involves the child's ability to create text meaning by using cognitive, metacognitive, and metalinguistic strategies (e.g., use of elaboration and categorization for connecting prior knowledge to new text, such as the use of scripts of fairy tales to understand a story, use of daily real-life experiences).

Prewriting abilities.   The development of writing skills is a much more complicated process than learning how to read. Storytelling helps children as a strategy to learn how to write, because when children dictate stories (they have heard or they create based on their prior sociocultural experiences) to an adult they make the conceptual connection between scripts as a recording method of oral conceptual language. Then, children use real-life sociocultural experiences represented in reading and writing activities as a learning and discovery process (Piper, 1998). Children can then understand conceptually the process of writing by applying analysis and synthesis strategies for: (1) linking details with whole sentences, paragraphs, and ultimately to the whole text in a meaningful manner; and (2) making connections between scripts and their prior knowledge about real-life sociocultural experiences.

The process of making conceptual connections between semantic or abstract verbal representations (i.e., signs such as graphemes, phonemes, and words) to actual meaning construction through writing is the result of a complex developmental process. As explained below and illustrated in Figures 5.2 and 5.3, there are three representational levels that are acquired in a developmental sequence: (1) from perceptual experiences with nonverbal concrete objects that expose young children to tridimensional models encountered in real-life experiences; (2) to symbolic experiences with nonverbal or graphic two-dimensional models, such as pictures, photos, rebus symbols, art, and imagery; and (3) to verbal signs or unidimensional models that represent sounds in a printed format such as making connections between phonemes, graphemes, and words (i.e., defined as phonemic awareness).

Therefore, authentic language and authentic tasks, that represent the daily-life experiences of children, leading to meaningful social interactions with peers and the teacher, need to be used as learning and teaching strategies for developing preliteracy skills. All subject areas need to be integrated into a holistic curriculum that uses genuine language for stimulating literacy skills, development across areas (i.e., linguistic, cognitive, and socioemotional), and subject matter across content areas (i.e., language arts, mathematics, social science, and social studies).

Some implications for ESL children are that language stimulation at school should be presented as a natural learning process that requires children to be exposed to social learning opportunities that respect their cultural identity, and home and community experiences. Language learning should be a nurturing process that involves the collaborative partnership of educators, administrators, parents, and the whole community.

In sum, the socioconstructivistic position endorsed in this book considers that preliteracy and literacy skills involve the interaction of language and cognitive processes (verbal or semantic and nonverbal, such as attention, perception, memory, and conceptual thinking) with literacy and academic content learning within a social and cultural environment.

Pragmatic Development

Pragmatic development refers to the use of language for communication purposes in social and real-life situations. It involves the use of cultural and prior social knowledge, and results in the development of sociolinguistic and sociocultural competence. An example of pragmatic competence is the ability to use sociocultural conventions for meeting specific purposes (e.g., use of active or passive voice to connote suggestions or orders, identification of a specific language to use to communicate particular content to a selected person, as in the case of bilingual individuals). Therefore, language provides membership to a community by learning the social rules of language

Index Learning:

Children develop conceptual understanding of objects, situations, and events by actually building experiences through contact with real-world and daily sociocultural activities. Constructions represent tridimensional objects that are not present.
E.g., using blocks to build a house

Symbolic Learning:

Figural representation of two-dimensional objects through images, such as pictures, photographs, and graphs.
E.g., drawing, sketching, or finger painting to create dimensions.

Imitation: actions that represent experiences while the model is present (i.e., direct imitation) or absent (i.e., deferred imitation)
E.g., pantomime-imitating mom washing the dishes.

Make-believe, fantasy, or sociodramatic play: taking roles and pretending to be someone or something other than themselves in the absence of the real action or model.

High Order/Signs Learning

Onomatopoeia: use of unidimensional abstractions, such as sounds, to represent objects, events and situations.
E.g., sounds of birds, dogs, ambulance and other means to advance their development and learning linguistically.

Graphemes: use of letters to represent objects, actions, and experiences.
E.g., rhyming with words, phonemic awareness of beginning and ending sounds in words.

Pragmatics: use of punctuation marks to signal ending of sentence (e.g., period) and intonation (e.g., question marks).

FIGURE 5.2   Definitions and Examples of the Three Representational Levels of Instructional Activities

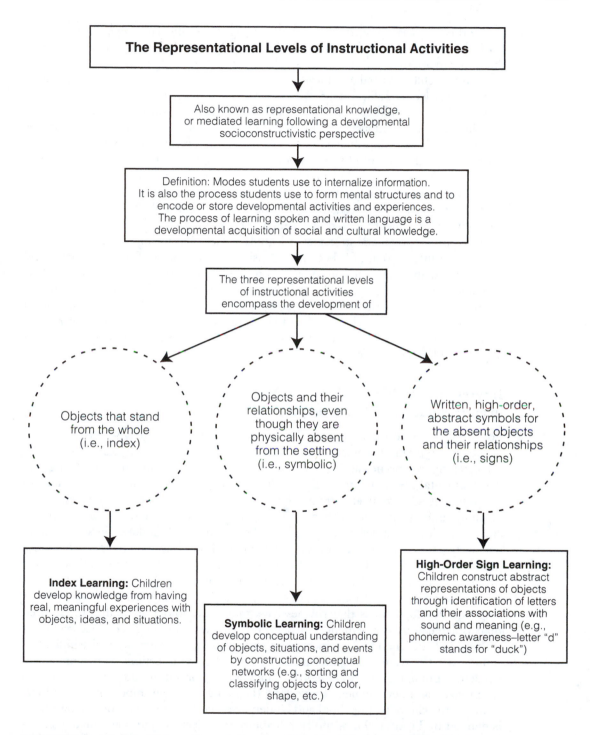

FIGURE 5.3   Model of Three Representational Levels of Instructional Activities

use within a social context. Thus, by learning a specific language, speakers also learn the rules of effective communication for a large variety of purposes and in many different situations.

Young children need to achieve a balance between conceptual and language development in order to be able to express their content knowledge via conversational competence. That is, children need to learn pragmatics (involving terminology and sociolinguistic conventions) so that they can express meaning (achieved via semantic or cognitive academic competence). Then, pragmatic and semantic development are interconnected, as children need to learn both how to form verbal concepts and also how to communicate them in sociocultural appropriate manners through the use of language.

Children learn pragmatics or conversational competence in natural contexts such as school and home. Schooling provides the sociocultural context to learn pragmatics in order to meet the cognitive demands of learning tasks. For instance, children learn important pragmatic strategies at school such as: (1) learning to take the listener's perspective into account; (2) becoming sensitive to relevance of topic, content, and useful information; (3) learning to make conversational repairs, such as monitor their oral and written language; (4) learning how to express their thoughts, opinions, suggestions, and requests in a socially acceptable manner; and (5) becoming socialized to different styles of speech according to cultural factors and contexts (e.g., academic versus social language, jargon and style of a specific content area, gender-based linguistic differences, accents, dialects, etc.).

Interaction of BICS, CALPS, and Pragmatics in an Holistic L1 and L2 Competence

For fulfilling educational and methodological purposes, language competence or proficiency typically is compartmentalized into four language abilities: (1) speaking, (2) listening comprehension, (3) reading, and (4) writing; and into five language developmental areas: (1) pronunciation or phonological development, (2) vocabulary development, (3) syntax and grammar development, (4) semantics or understanding meaning underlying linguistic forms, and (5) pragmatics or developing sociolinguistic and sociocultural competence. The bilingual developmental model endorses a holistic perspective for L1 and L2 acquisition, in which the three basic components of language proficiency (i.e., BICS, CALPS, and pragmatics) interface into one multidimensional language competence skill (see Figure 5.1 for an illustration).

An example of the interaction of social, cognitive, and pragmatic competence for language development is that rhymes have more psychological validity to children than isolated words or sentences that do not rhyme. Phonological processes occur within a holistic L1 and L2 competence as children learning rhymes acquire individual sounds and the syllable structure in words by making connections to meanings and concepts. Phonological awareness becomes an important preliteracy skill that is emphasized as a developmental milestone (i.e., considered an important educational standard to achieve by preschool and kindergarten children). Phonological awareness is defined by Piper (1998) as the child's ability to reflect on and manipulate components of spoken words, which becomes a metalinguistic ability. To think about the similarities and differences between L1 and L2 in bilinguals, see example of metalinguistic ability in children provided in the next section.

EXAMPLES OF METALINGUISTIC ABILITY IN BILINGUAL CHILDREN

A case of metalinguistic ability is exemplified by bilingual children's realization of rhyming similarities in linguistic forms in their two languages, which connote different meanings. In the context of a bilingual preschool, young children were having their snack and enjoying ham sandwiches. Suddenly, one of the youngsters made the observation that they were eating ham, which was *jamon* in Spanish, which rhymed with the word *jabon* (soap) in Spanish. So, this bilingual preschooler made the interesting observation that they were eating *jamon* (ham), but not *jabon* (soap) sandwiches. All the other children found this observation hilarious, and celebrated and repeatedly enjoyed the humor discovered by their classmate through metalinguistic awareness processes in action in real-life sociocultural situations. These little children were literally enjoying the advantages of their bilingualism: the discovery of humor through metalinguistic processes such as phonemic awareness.

Another example of a metalinguistic awareness process is for bilingual children to do translations for monolingual classmates; typically, this happens naturally as the need arises in their school environments. For example, I once observed a monolingual Spanish-speaking kindergartner about to leave her classroom and her monolingual English teacher trying to stop her. A bilingual English/Spanish classmate voluntarily intervened and said to the little girl: "*Te quedas aqui*" (You stay here) and it worked! This is also a good example of another metalinguistic skill of bilingual children: They are able to choose in what language they want and need to speak depending on the register and social or cultural situation.

Semantic development, the development of concepts through language, or the development of verbal concepts is also connected with cultural representations of a particular language. Cultural representations influence language representations, which become semantic concepts, such as cultural and linguistic categories and labels for colors. An example of a semantic process is semantic memory, in which children can recall episodic and sequential events such as their experience of going to a restaurant or to visit the zoo or library on their field trips.

In sum, the third subsection endorses the socioconstructivistic perspective that L1 and L2 competence is a holistic ability that is based on conceptual, sociocultural, and socioemotional processes. Bilingual children are exposed to two cultural and linguistic representational systems that result in qualitative differences in their semantic and preliteracy and literacy development, when compared to monolingual children. It is important to understand that oral social competence (BICS) is the basis for academic competence that is in turn interconnected with cognitive, metacognitive, and metalinguistic skills (CALPS). When ESL children are exposed to additive bilingual school environments, they can show the advantages of bilingualism in their cognitive, metacognitive, and metalinguistic skills in both L1 and L2.

BILINGUAL DEVELOPMENTAL CURRICULUM

The second major section presents the actual bilingual developmental curriculum that applies the core philosophical and theoretical principles, the derived pedagogical principles, and the ESL Standards and L1 and L2 competencies (discussed in the first section) into goals and objectives, and instructional strategies for preschool ESL and mainstream children. A set of sample instructional activities and lesson plans, implementing the pedagogical principles, are presented in the companion Web site for the book. The curriculum presented has been pilot tested and is in the process of program evaluation by the first author of the book (for more information please see our Webpage at www.uc.edu/bpdc).

The bilingual developmental curriculum includes three major subsections:

1. Goals and objectives
2. Three representational levels of instructional activities:
   a. Perceptual
   b. Symbolic
   c. Semantic
3. Instructional strategies using a parallel format to the five pedagogical principles (reviewed in the first section of the chapter), which are:
   a. Development of higher level cognitive strategies
   b. Connection to prior sociocultural knowledge
   c. Connection to real-world experiences
   d. Thematic curriculums
   e. Interaction of cognitive, cultural, and socioemotional developmental processes and academic achievement

Goals and Objectives for the Bilingual Developmental Curriculum

The essential goals and objectives of a bilingual developmental program, as highlighted by CREDE (2002), include:

1. Content core (or subject matter) academic instruction and literacy (or preliteracy) instruction is provided to all students (language-minority and mainstream) in L1 and L2
2. Programs integrate language-minority and mainstream students for academic instruction
3. All students develop high levels of social (BICS) and academic (CALPS) language proficiency in their L1 and L2 through an additive bilingual and developmental classroom environment that uses L1 and L2 as methods of instruction
4. All students develop academic achievement at or above grade level across subject areas (following the same high-stake standards for mainstream students and the same core academic curriculum) as they develop L1 and L2 BICS and CALPS

5. All students develop positive attitudes and behaviors toward both languages and cultures
6. Characteristics of effective schools are present, such as qualified teachers who act as sociocultural mediators, committed advocates, and mentors, and who can increase children's learning and collaboration between home and school

See Figure 5.4. for a representation of the goals and objectives.

Three Representational Levels of Instructional Activities

Three different representational levels of instructional activities (see Figures 5.2 and 5.3) are used in the bilingual developmental curriculum:

1. Perceptual or index (i.e., concrete tridimensional models such as make-believe—plastic food and animals—and real-world objects), which are nonverbal
2. Symbolic (i.e., graphic symbols that offer two-dimensional models—pictorial images or rebus, pictures), which are nonverbal
3. Semantic or abstract (i.e., use of signs that offer unidimensional models such as graphemes, phonemes, words in oral or written form), which are verbal

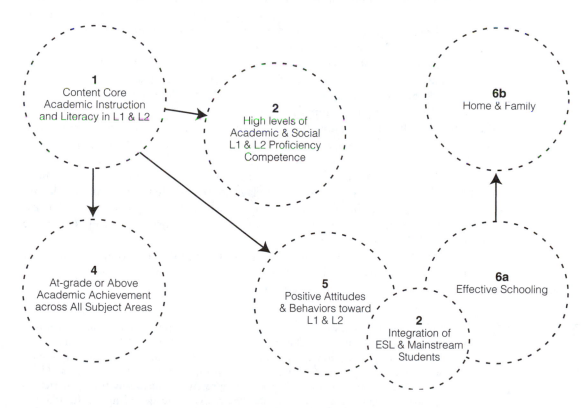

FIGURE 5.4   Goals and Objectives of the Bilingual Educational Curriculum

As presented in a previous book (see Gonzalez et al., 1997), the first instructional level, the perceptual or index level, provides ESL learners with meaningful learning experiences with real-life or make-believe objects (in tridimensional representations) and social and cultural situations. For instance, a visit to the zoo can expose ESL students to real-world experiences with animals. Then, in the classroom, plastic animals can be used for engaging in symbolic play to represent real-world experiences and build new sociocultural knowledge.

The second instructional level, the symbolic level, provides ESL students with two-dimensional symbols to represent real-world objects, experiences, ideas, and sociocultural situations. For instance, three apples can be represented using three blocks or a pie-shape graph representing three pieces. These two-dimension representational forms use flat-surface media such as paper, easels, watercolors, and finger paint, for ESL students to engage in drawing, painting, sketching, and creating figurative or nonverbal aids to concept formation.

The third level of semantic or abstract learning requires students to make a link between the real-life experience with an object, idea, or situation with the sound or print. For instance, the development of phonemic awareness requires ESL students to acquire the ability to pair up real-world sounds with cultural conventions such as onomatopoeic sounds and language, to recognize words that rhyme, and to identify the first or ending sounds or graphemes of words. An illustration of phonemic awareness is to have ESL students engage in using onomatopoeic sounds to represent objects, experiences, ideas, and sociocultural situations. For instance, ESL learners can engage in conceptual representation of sounds of animals or means of transportation, by imitating sociocultural conventions of their L1 and L2. It is interesting to note that some onomatopoeic sounds are represented differently by languages. For example, in Spanish chicks are perceived to say "*pio, pio, pio,*" dogs say "*gua, gua,*" and roosters say "*kikirikiki.*" In contrast, other animals make common sounds, but they are represented differently according to the phonetic systems of both languages (i.e., *meow* in English and *miao* in Spanish for cats, and *mooo* in English and *muuu* in Spanish for cows). Another way to represent semantic or abstract learning may be by using make-believe, fantasy, sociodramatic play, and drama. By using stories from books as a unidimensional model to act out and take roles to engage in make-believe and pretend playing activities (e.g., playing shopping at the supermarket, pretending to be a waitress in a pizzeria restaurant), ESL students can internalize abstract concepts that are communicated via print.

In order for ESL students to achieve at the highest developmental level of semantic learning, instructional activities need to represent this complexity. As well articulated by Gonzalez and collaborators (1997),

> The representation of knowledge of signs in the form of writing and recognizing words in print [phonemic awareness ability] is *not* the beginning and ending of classroom instruction, diagnosis, or prescription. If the classroom does not provide index- and symbol-level experiences prior to sign-level teaching, how can we expect our CLD [Culturally and Linguistically Diverse] students to recognize and represent automatically their experiences through spoken and written words in either their native language or English? (p. 153)

These three representational levels of instructional activities are presented in the instructional strategies discussed in the next section.

Instructional Strategies

Based on an integration of guidelines provided by Gonzalez and coauthors (1997) Ovando, Collier, and Combs (2003); and CREDE (2002), the instructional strategies endorsed by the bilingual developmental curriculum include: (1) stimulation of higher level cognitive strategies; (2) connection to prior sociocultural knowledge; (3) connection to real-world experiences; (4) thematic curriculums; and (5) interaction of cognitive, linguistic, and sociocultural processes and academic achievement. These five instructional strategies are discussed below in light of research-based mainstream and ESL literature. See Figure 5.5 for a representation of the instructional strategies.

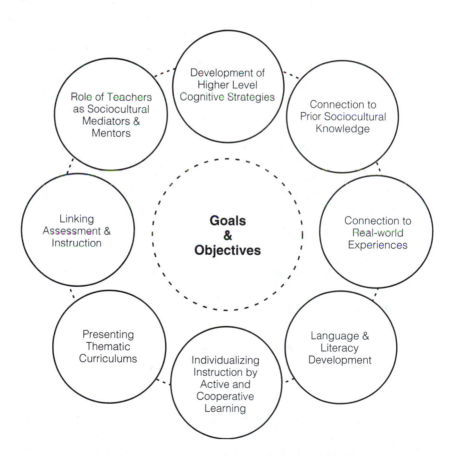

FIGURE 5.5   Implementation of the Bilingual Education Curriculum's Goals and Objectives through Eight Instructional Strategies

Development of higher level cognitive strategies. The focus of instruction is on stimulating ESL students to develop abstract conceptual knowledge that can be transformed and applied to multiple instances of problem-solving situations in real-life settings and across academic content areas (National Research Council, 1999a, 1999b). The emphasis is on gaining general principles of learning and thinking that can abstract and generalize conceptual frameworks for ESL students to apply cognitive, metacognitive, and metalinguistic strategies.

An illustration of a metacognitive strategy is the use of analogical reasoning, or syllogistic and other more abstract forms of verbal logic and reasoning. In turn, an illustration of analogical reasoning is the ability to transpose knowledge across different content domains, such as a 4-year-old making a comparison between his body sounds and musical instruments, by saying "My stomach makes noises like a piano." Another illustration of analogical reasoning is to interact with peers through collaborative problem-solving activities that can help learners to broaden self-centered perspectives into flexible thinking processes. For instance, ESL learners engaged in learning how water converts into ice, can depart from their own real-life experiences with rain and snow, make hypothesis and predictions, engage in the actual experience of manipulating different elements, and discover what happened and why; and finally, learn the language expressions necessary to articulate their thoughts.

Specific instructional strategies that can be used in classroom settings are explained below:

1. To use instructional activities and lessons with high-cognitive complexity for stimulating higher level thinking skills and strategies (i.e., abstract conceptual knowledge and topic knowledge, cognitive and metacognitive, metalinguistic learning strategies, critical-thinking skills, problem-solving abilities, etc.)
2. To offer instructional opportunities for ESL students to do applications and transformations of conceptual knowledge in-school and out-of-school contexts, through problem-solving activities and using creativity and flexibility of thinking. Teachers can help students develop adaptive expertise for using metacognitive strategies for how to think (metacognition), how to think with language (metalinguistic awareness), and how to learn (metalearning) when facing daily-life problem-solving situations
3. To emphasize the formation of new concepts through discovery and exploration and the stimulation of assimilation and accommodation learning processes. Inquiry-based learning using active learning, discovery of concepts, and higher level critical-thinking skills (i.e., metacognitive/metalinguistic strategies) needs to be modeled by teachers in relation to specific content areas because thinking and learning strategies are not generic
4. To use meaningful instructional conversations for modeling cognitive, metacognitive, and metalinguistic strategies for learning and thinking at higher levels (e.g., articulating observations and making deductions and elaborations)
5. To develop awareness in ESL students of their characteristics as learners (i.e., learning styles, interests, strengths and weaknesses) so that they can learn how to use appropriate metacognitive, cognitive, and affective strategies for enhancing the learning process

Connection to prior sociocultural knowledge.   Active, inquiry-based classrooms use students' prior and cultural knowledge to create meaningful learning (National Research Council, 1999a, 1999b). When language-minority students do not share the same cultural knowledge, teachers need to create learning opportunities in the classroom for building life experiences that anchor the formation of new cultural knowledge. The bilingual developmental curriculum stimulates L1 and L2 development through meaningful social and authentic text that represents the actual reality of students at home and at school. See the example provided here of using this instructional strategy with ESL students. For instance, language-minority preschool children in the Midwest, who are listening to a story about *What Happens in the Fall?* need to develop new cultural experiences with the American concepts of pumpkins, scarecrows, leaves changing colors and falling from trees, squirrels piling up nuts and acorns, and so on. When teachers just read this book, language-minority children just listen to strings of words with empty meanings. But when teachers bring out leaves of multiple colors and sizes and ask students to count the leaves, sort them by color and size, and then demonstrate the spatial concept of "up and down" by dropping the leaves; language-minority children engage in the activity and build meaningful life experiences that can anchor their newly formed cultural concepts.

Another instructional strategy for connecting learning to prior knowledge is to use L1 and L2 as methods of instruction within a bilingual developmental curriculum, resulting in a spiral curriculum that can represent languages by teacher, by subject area, or by time scheduled. By using both L1 and L2 as symbolic tools for learning content and concepts, ESL students can transfer their prior verbal and nonverbal sociocultural knowledge to learning new content, resulting in faster ESL learning and higher levels of academic achievement.

Specific instructional strategies for stimulating ESL learners to make connections between prior sociocultural knowledge and new concepts across content areas is discussed below:

1. To select developmentally appropriate and linguistically and culturally authentic instructional materials and teaching strategies so that instruction and the curriculum can be adapted to the ESL students' sociocultural and linguistic prior knowledge
2. To build on the prior sociocultural knowledge-base that ESL students are familiar with in home and community environments (including their L1 and cultural values). To value home language and cultural experiences (e.g., dialect and values) as a way of affirming language-minority students' identity and motivating students to learn
3. Connection to prior sociocultural knowledge can also be accomplished by using home or native languages for instruction, within a bilingual environment where English is taught as a second language. It is recommended that both languages of instruction be kept separate, by representing languages by teacher or by content area or time scheduled. For instance, separation of languages by the same teacher according to content area, or by different teachers across time allocation (e.g., subject areas could be shared by both languages during different days of the week)
4. To use both languages as methods of instruction by presenting parallel and complementary instructional activities for stimulating the same developmental objectives

and educational standards. Lessons should never be repeated back as translations (this practice encourages the presentation of authentic cultural material)

5. To use an appropriate percentage of instructional time in each language according to the needs of the students (e.g., for non-English speakers instruction should probably emphasize more the children's first and only language at the beginning of the school years)

6. To use interactive dialogue or instructional conversations as an individual and group strategy for recalling lived experiences by the student (e.g., real-life daily events such as eating lunch at the school cafeteria and recalling the menu) and providing verbal descriptions and explanations of the sequence of events. Community and sociocultural contexts are ideal authentic experiences for linking oral language and literacy development in ESL learners

7. To use Sheltered Instruction, that is, the integration of language and content instruction, in which teachers use strategies that adapt to English language learners (e.g., using nonverbal materials such as manipulative materials and pictures, speaking slowly and clearly, using repeated patterns of language, building on prior knowledge)

8. High-quality teaching can help students increase their intrinsic motivation for learning, such as instructional activities that are varied, engaging, socially relevant for real-life ("authentic" and project oriented), and involve cooperative and collaborative learning

9. To stimulate the formation of positive attitudes, high motivation, high self-expectations, and high self-esteem toward learning both languages and cultures through instructional activities and teachers as role models. Students are encouraged to develop positive attitudes toward speaking both languages, and a high motivational level for using both languages for learning

10. To individualize instruction, as part of a learner-centered instruction that takes into account prior knowledge, in order to set developmental prerequisites needed for accomplishing tasks for maximizing success and minimizing failure in the educational process

11. To individualize instruction to represent multiple and diverse students' learning needs including their learning pace; strengths and weaknesses across cognitive, linguistic, affective, and social developmental areas; and their learning styles (visual, auditory, kinesthetic, etc.). Individualization of instruction can be accomplished by teachers offering choices in the classroom environment such as alternative activities, various teaching and learning strategies, and a variety of assignments

12. To involve parents in the educational process by teachers engaging in home visits for better understanding ESL students' educational needs

13. To develop classroom environments in which the role of teachers is to act as mentors, advocates, role models, and social mediators for fostering caring and collaborative, nurturing and motivating learning communities

Connection to real-world experiences.   High-quality bilingual and ESL programs, such as the bilingual developmental model, encourage connection to real-world experiences by emphasizing active learning. Student-centered learning allows children to actively develop conceptual knowledge through discovery and dynamic interaction with meaningful instructional materials representing different content areas and objectives. Students engage in inquiry-based learning by constructing new meanings and concepts, creating original uses of language and information, and engaging in authentic communication and dialogue with peers and teachers.

According to Gonzalez and colleagues (1997), active learning requires that ESL "students must interact or come in contact with their environments in some fashion . . . [and] . . . must be provided . . . [with opportunities for] . . . emphasis on process and concrete object manipulation" (p. 158). Thus, for young ESL learners, the availability of multiple objects that they can touch, smell, see, and manipulate to sort, seriate, order, and use for symbolic play and problem-solving activities generates opportunities for developing conceptual mental abilities. For example, for ESL students to discover why *autumn* is also called *fall*, they need to manipulate actual leaves of different colors, shapes, and sizes and understand what happens when they drop them into a table or pail of water. Young ESL students can discover by doing that the season *fall* is named after so many leaves that "fall" from trees by engaging in collaborative learning with peers through instructional conversation activities that require higher level thinking and problem-solving processes such as probing, trial and error, deduction, prediction, elaboration, and the use of prior knowledge. Example of developing connections to real-world experiences.

Another example of curricular activities that stimulate L1 and L2 development through exposing children to authentic sociocultural experiences is to provide concrete "anchors" for developing concepts. Most every primary-level class starts with a group time for describing the weather, and identifying the date and month. When young children are asked to repeat strings of words, even within the context of a song, language becomes empty of meaning and most young children disengage from learning weather concepts because they are presented without concrete experiential anchors. Instead, when preschoolers are provided with manipulative materials for developing connections to real-life experiences, such as creating lived experiences in the classrooms, and they can attach language to these experiences; motivation for learning increases dramatically among young ESL students. A good source of manipulative anchors may be representations of clouds in the form of cotton balls falling from the sky that preschoolers need to catch in a basket within the context of small groups. Then, with the help of a teacher as a mediator, children can engage in counting, adding, and subtracting quantities in relation to how many clouds other groups were able to gather. The actual prior real-life experience of "catching clouds" provides young children the opportunity to build connections between prior and new knowledge across content areas, and to develop conceptual understanding of the abstract concept of "cloudiness," having had the opportunity to develop meaning for a previously empty label. Now, coming back to the singing about how the weather is today, young children can experience that words in the song are meaningful, because they have now developed prior conceptual knowledge through exposure to real-life social and cultural experiences. Young children now become engaged, happy singers, who are actively learning the meaning of language. You can tell by their happy faces and their body language!

Another instructional strategy for emphasizing the connection of school with real-world experiences is to use *cooperative learning*. It is one of the best instructional strategies for helping ESL student acquire conceptual knowledge, increase their academic achievement and also their English language proficiency. Within the context of the bilingual developmental program, peers can use cooperative learning for modeling learning and thinking strategies, and for acting as mentors and mediators or social resources for each other. Both mainstream and ESL students can act as resources for each other because there are both native-speakers of one of the languages used as a method of instruction. Thus, the bilingual developmental classroom is transformed into an enrichment educational program for both groups of students, the mainstream monolingual English group and the ESL group.

Through the use of cooperative learning strategies, teachers can use the help of peer groups to increase conceptual learning, integrating prior knowledge to subject and topic learning, and ultimately to increase academic achievement. The participation in teams also helps students to improve emotional and affective developmental aspects, such as self-esteem and self-concept, identity; and social skills such as group identity, trust, mutual respect, mutual support, and a sense of synergy. Roles of group members should be rotated so that every student becomes responsible for different tasks and actively engages in all aspects of the learning tasks. For instance, some roles suggested by Ovando and colleagues (2003) for group members are: quiet captains, timekeepers, cheerleaders, presenters, recorders, reflectors, and bilingual facilitators.

The diversity in students' ethnic and cultural background, language proficiency levels, achievement levels, learning styles, personalities, developmental strengths and weaknesses can increase the team group productivity, and can enhance the utility of cooperative learning as a successful teaching strategy. Groups should be formed based on heterogeneous characteristics of students, and should be rotated to maximize exposure to a diverse array of peer characteristics. Always, team or group work should avoid tracking of students by level of academic achievement or language proficiency backgrounds. In fact, it is beneficial for ESL students to be exposed to students achieving at higher levels, in both academics and language proficiency. By experiencing exposure to a diverse background of peers, students can improve their attitudes toward mainstream and minority groups and improve their communicative and cultural competence.

Specific instructional strategies for stimulating ESL students to make connections between real-world experiences and academic content learned are discussed below:

1. To create learner-centered classroom environments that stimulate active, discovery, and inquiry-based learning
2. To use cooperative learning for developing experiential knowledge and building linguistic and cultural competence in ESL learners
3. To build concrete "anchors" or authentic sociocultural experiences for stimulating higher levels of learning (from perceptual to symbolic to semantic) across content areas

Thematic curriculums. Thematic and topical presentation of instructional material can be used to connect cultural and social prior knowledge and real-life, daily experiences with academic content and topical subject matter. Themes need to represent the cultural background of students and also serve as vehicles to introduce them to mainstream school and American culture. In this way the curriculum can help ESL students to develop cultural adaptation and a bicultural identity, resulting in higher academic achievement. *Offering choices* is one way of adapting the thematic curriculum to the unique interest, developmental needs, and linguistic and cultural characteristics of ESL students. Offering choices in the classroom environment such as "alternate activities, alternate channels of learning, and alternate assignments . . . presents real learning opportunities for decision-making, social participation, and successes" (Gonzalez et al., 1997, p. 160). By allowing students to make learning choices, teachers foster their motivation, self-esteem, and self-concept as they become independent thinkers who experience affective and cognitive involvement in their success in task completion. Teachers also can encourage ESL students' personal initiative in making choices, follow-through on a decision with persistence in task completion, and better understanding of their potentials as learners.

Another way to individualize instruction is through the use of *thematic interdisciplinary instruction*, because, by using themes that connect to students' cultural prior knowledge, teachers can create classroom environments that motivate students to engage in the learning activity. Thematic instruction creates a meaningful context for exploring multiple content areas to stimulate cognitive development and academic achievement. Themes can develop intrinsic motivation for students to become actively engaged in learning, thinking, and application of concepts to their social and cultural reality. Themes can use art and language as symbolic representational tools for learning and thinking, and media through which students can use their senses, perception, memory, and stored conceptual knowledge to learn new content areas (such as literacy skills, math, social studies, and science).

Specific instructional strategies for using thematic curriculums for stimulating learning in ESL students are discussed below:

1. To use thematic curriculums for integrating content areas (i.e., language arts, mathematics, science, and social studies) and for exposing students to repetition of concepts throughout the academic year, with the use of a variety of instructional activities and materials
2. To allow overlearning through extended periods of practice for the assimilation of new content. The presence of a thematic curriculum will allow for continuity of topics and concepts stimulated across content areas. The use of "mass experiences" or continuous and different experiences, as a strategy for extending concepts across content areas, and learning situations and applications
3. To link assessment and instruction by using alternative assessments such as narrative and structured observations and portfolios, for the planning of teaching activities and the development of instructional materials

Interaction of cognitive, cultural, and socioemotional developmental processes and academic achievement.   Several instructional strategies that interface cognitive, cultural, and socioemotional developmental processes were recommended by Gonzalez and collaborators (1997) for increasing social and academic language in ESL learners, including: storytelling, story reading, and interactive dialogue and instructional conversations based on experiences.

Storytelling.   Storytelling can help ESL young children to make the connection between prior knowledge and real-life experiences and new content learned. Young children can be helped by teachers to develop a script out of real-life experiences within their home, family, and community environments; and even to re-create such experiences in the classrooms thorough nonverbal and verbal behaviors.

By talking about lived experiences at home, and then re-creating them in the classroom through symbolic play, young children can be stimulated by their teachers for developing their L1 and L2 oral skills, conceptual development, and affective processes. For instance, young children can transform lived experiences and symbolic play into scripts or verbal narrations (i.e., the creation of a story that narrates personal experiences) for developing their identity, and social development such as learning from vicarious experiences (other classmates' experiences). Besides symbolic play, ESL students can also benefit from using other nonverbal manipulative stimuli for facilitating the verbal expression and re-creating of their lived experiences, such as puppets, a flannel board, and other props such as costumes and concrete representations of objects and other referents (e.g., plastic food, dolls, a store, a purse, etc.).

Example of using scripts and storytelling in thematic curriculums.   Teachers can use such natural "scripts" acted out by young children in their symbolic play for building on these nonverbal behaviors and engaging in the creation of stories of verbal *scripts*. For instance, three preschool Hispanic girls are engaging very eagerly in the "house" symbolic play area in their classroom. They are very actively gathering some "food" for preparing dinner. One is washing "the vegetables" in the sink, while the other is cutting the "vegetables," and yet the third girl is setting up the table. Once they finished preparing dinner, they sit together at the table and use their napkins and utensils for "eating" their food. Immediately after they are done with their food, they again cooperate in sharing the household duties: one little girls picks up the dishes from the table and gets busy washing them in the sink, another little girl goes off to "do the laundry" and very carefully folds clothes. The third little girl "hears" the babies crying, and runs to attend to their needs. As an observer of this pretend household scenario, it is obvious to me that the three little girls are reliving daily life experiences, and that they come from pretty organized family environments. Their play is very organized and unfolds in a natural collaboration that is unspoken, they just engage in unison in complementary activities: Their unspoken script is enacting common daily life-experiences that follow a natural sequence or script.

Story reading.   Reading stories in L1 or L2 can be used by teachers as opportunities for making connections across content areas through the use of a thematic curriculum. Books can be a very good way to emphasize themes across content areas, and to provide opportunities for generalizing concepts and learning "the rhetoric" to talk about lived experiences at home and in the classrooms. Reading stories can be used by teachers for making connections between prior sociocultural knowledge and the language necessary to express such knowledge in the form of text. Young children need to develop preliteracy skills, such as awareness of the connection between print and meaning, and real-life experiences and verbal representations. Young children need to understand the usefulness of books, and literacy skills in general, as a tool for fulfilling many daily life needs, such as reading a recipe, reading a map for finding the location of an unknown place, and reading a note, invitation, or ad. The classroom can become a real-life setting for understanding the symbolic nature of reading and its social functions. Together the teacher and children can follow a recipe, by reading through the sequence of steps involved in the preparation of cookies, and experiencing together the value of literacy. In the same manner, a map can be drawn by children for understanding the location of any real space (e.g., the playground, the supermarket, the mailbox down the street, etc.) in relation to their classroom. Any of these real-life experiences can generate concrete anchors for children to understand conceptually the symbolic function of language, through using print for conveying social and culturally valued meanings.

Interactive dialogue and instructional conversations.   Dialogue and conversations can provide children with the opportunity to learn from their teachers how to think and how to learn. Together, teachers and children can engage in inquiry-based activities that use cognitive and metacognitive strategies, such as brainstorming, elaboration, the use of trial and error for problem solving, and the use of language as a vehicle for thinking aloud and asking explanatory questions (what, how, when, and why). In this way, teachers can serve as role models for ESL children to learn how to use language as an internal mental tool for thinking, by modeling critical thinking strategies such as analysis, synthesis, elaboration, comparison, imagery, transformation, abstraction, generalization, deduction, etc. Teachers acting as models for inquiry-based learning promote an active and learner-centered classroom environment. This teaching approach promotes intrinsic motivation for learning in students, stimulates creativity and flexibility of thinking, conceptual understanding, and in general creates the ideal environment for stimulating independent problem solvers. This teaching approach also helps ESL students to focus on conceptual learning across content areas, and to use L1 and L2 as symbolic tools for learning, that positively stimulate their cognitive academic language competence (CALPS) in English at a faster rate.

The result is a focus on the process for learning, rather than on the product, and on conceptual learning and the development of higher level critical-thinking skills rather than on memorization of information. The development of critical-thinking skills will provide ESL students with the mental abilities for learning topic and content knowledge at a faster rate because they have developed the mental tools necessary for transforming topic knowledge into general conceptual principles and networks. For instance, numbers are no longer isolated pieces of information that need to be memorized in a string of words through a song. Instead, numbers become concepts attached to prior experiences and conceptual knowledge that provides the ability to engage in one-to-one correspondence when using counting for solving a real-life problem. That is, helping the teacher and classmates to follow a recipe, by "reading" first how many eggs are needed for making cookies, and then by breaking the exact number of eggs that the recipe calls for: 6! No less and no more.

In sum, teachers are facilitators, mentors, role models, or social mediators who engage in cooperative discovery with students and mode learning and critical-thinking strategies. Students and teachers interact through meaningful instructional dialogue using both their L1 and L2. As recommended by Ovando and coauthors (2003), students share with teachers the responsibility for learning and integrating real-life experiences, prior and cultural knowledge, and new content learned in school. A prototype for instructional activities and model lesson plans are provided in the companion Web site for the book.

SUMMARY AND CONCLUSIONS

The most important ideas that Chapter 5 has presented in relation to best instructional practices for ESL students, derived from contemporary research, refers to presenting developmentally adequate curriculums and instructional strategies and activities that accommodate to individual and linguistic and cultural diverse characteristics of learners. This developmentally adequate curriculum, which individualizes instruction, is based on a socioconstructivistic philosophical and theoretical orientation that uses inquiry-based, active and discovery learning, and problem-solving activities for stimulating conceptual development.

The most important goal of a developmental socioconstructivistic curriculum is to stimulate ESL children to transform topic knowledge and content knowledge across content areas into general conceptual principles and networks. For instance, numbers can become concepts attached to prior experiences and conceptual knowledge when children do a one-to-one correspondence between cupcakes and dolls can help to solve a real-life problem. General conceptual principles include cognitive processes necessary for developing higher level critical-thinking skills (including cognitive, metacognitive, and metalinguistic strategies). Among the most important cognitive strategies for conceptual learning are the use of prior knowledge and sociocultural experiences. Instructional activities need to represent three levels of conceptual understanding in young children, which go from perceptual to symbolic to abstract or semantic. For instance preliteracy and literacy development involves a progression from nonverbal concrete experiences with real-life objects to symbolic, nonverbal representations (such as pictures and graphs), and ultimately to abstract representations using languages (such as graphemes, words, and meaning). *ESL Standards* also highlights the integration of cognitive and language processes in literacy development and academic achievement, such as the integration of social and academic language with prior sociolinguistic and sociocultural competence. Thus, the development of literacy and biliteracy requires ESL children to develop conceptual connections between real-life experiences, verbal representations, and meaning and ultimately print.

In sum, development across cognitive, linguistic, and socioemotional domains, and academic achievement across content areas can be enhanced by providing an enriched socioconstructivistic curriculum that stimulates children to form concepts and responds to the individual and cultural and linguistic needs of ESL children. The language and literacy competence of ESL children can be stimulated by using both L1 and L2 as methods of instruction, and linking prior sociocultural knowledge and experiences to new content and topic knowledge acquired in school.

REVIEW QUESTIONS

1. How does knowledge of a bilingual developmental perspective help ESL teachers to develop social and moral responsibility? Explain what kind of professional development activities can help teachers to develop advocacy, commitment, empathy, and rapport when serving ESL students at-risk of underachievement.

2. Use the saying "There is nothing more practical than a good theory" to explain how the instructional effectiveness of an ESL teacher can increase by knowing the most important philosophical, theoretical, and pedagogical principles recommended by the bilingual developmental model? Discuss how the philosophical, theoretical, and pedagogical principles of the bilingual developmental model are interconnected to instructional strategies that can increase the academic achievement of ESL students?

3. Discuss at least three specific ways in which ESL teachers can use research trends (derived from cognitive and developmental psychology and cognitive science, and bilingual education and ESL areas) to improve the instructional quality in their classrooms. Is it important for ESL teachers to be knowledgeable about research trends? How can research knowledge help ESL teachers to increase the academic achievement of ESL students?

4. Why is it important for ESL teachers to be knowledgeable about the standards created by professional organizations? Explain your views in relation to the *ESL Standards* developed by the Teaching English as a Second Language (TESOL, 1997). How can knowledge of the TESOL *Standards* can help ESL teachers in their educational practice? Explain some rationales.

5. Why is it important for ESL teachers to develop a personal and professional position about their philosophical and theoretical principles? How can ESL teachers use educational principles of the socioconstructivistic and ethnic educator perspectives to increase the academic achievement of ESL students? How are educational principles connected to pedagogical strategies used by ESL teachers?

CRITICAL THINKING QUESTIONS

1. Think about how teachers model for ESL students social and cultural styles of learning and thinking. Think of examples of particular verbal and nonverbal teachers' behaviors that transmit cultural values and styles to ESL students (e.g., particular ways of talking, gestures, classroom rules, dress codes, etc.).

2. Reflect about your personal position in relation to the educational principles discussed. Placed special attention on the educational principle that endorses an integration approach that interfaces developmental areas across cognitive, language and literacy, and socioemotional domains. What is your opinion about this particular educational principle? Do you feel that the application of this educational principle can help you improve ESL students' academic achievement? Explain the rationale for your position. Share your position with classmates

and learn from how teachers' views can have similarities and differences.

3. Reflect about your personal position and opinion about the ESL competence areas. How are these concepts helpful for you to understand the complexity of L2 learning among ESL students, and their relationship with their academic achievement? Can you think of an example observed that illustrates the interconnection among the three ESL competence areas (BICS, CALPS, and pragmatics) for the case of an ESL student?

4. Are the goals and objectives of the bilingual developmental curriculum applicable to the ESL and mainstream students that you teach? What adaptations would you propose for the goals and objectives to match the developmental, individual, and cultural and linguistic characteristics of the ESL and mainstream students that you serve?

5. What is your preferred instructional ESL strategy, why do you think it would work best for your ESL students? What other instructional ESL strategies might work for improving learning processes and increasing academic achievement among ESL students? Using as models the examples for strategies provided in Chapter 5, develop your own example of your preferred instructional strategy.

ACTIVITIES

1. Brainstorm about educational applications that ESL teachers can do of a holistic developmental instructional approach that uses L1 and L2 as methods of instruction for increasing ESL students achievement' across subject areas. Share with a classmate your ideas and present some examples of the educational applications selected.

2. Study Table 5.2, listing five pedagogical principles across cognitive, language and literacy, and socioemotional developmental areas. According to your preference, rank-order the level of applicability in an ESL classroom of these five pedagogical principles (from 5—highly applicable, to 1—low degree of applicability). Think of an example of an instructional strategy that uses your preferred pedagogical principle for the case of ESL students. Share your example with a classmate and explain to him or her the reason why you think this selected principle would work for ESL students.

3. Read carefully the two examples of metalinguistic ability in bilingual children presented in Chapter 5. Interview the parents or teachers of a bilingual child: First, explain to them in simple words what metalinguistic ability is and why it is common among children exposed to two languages, and then ask them to think of some examples of metalinguistic ability in their children. Bring examples to class and share with classmates, and compare differences and similarities that may be found across examples of children of different ages.

4. Study carefully Figure 5.1, presenting the three general English language competence areas, and Table 5.3, presenting the interconnection among the three core philosophical and theoretical principles, the five pedagogical principles, and the three ESL competence areas. Develop a rationale for how ESL teachers can use pedagogical principles for increasing any selected competence area (e.g., CALPS, BICS) in ESL students. Then, develop a rationale for how understanding the philosophical and theoretical principles can help ESL teachers to increase their understanding of ESL competence areas. Finally, use the developed rationales for informing a colleague of the potential usefulness of philosophical, theoretical, and pedagogical principles to increase ESL competence among students. Is their position about the potential usefulness of these principles similar to or different than yours?

GLOSSARY

instructional strategies The application of specific educational materials, and procedures to teach students specific content. Best instructional strategies are based on research trends and apply recommendations that are proved to improve students' learning. Most effective instructional strategies offer teachers some decision-making power as professionals that takes into consideration individual differences, cultural and linguistic diversity, developmental factors, variation due to characteristics of content or subject area, and, in general, differences introduced by setting and students' characteristics (e.g., level of socioeconomic status, educational level of parents, literacy level at household, language spoken at home, level of cultural adaptation of the family, etc.).

pedagogical principles These are the recommendations for general guidelines about how to teach students in order to increase their learning and academic achievement. Pedagogical principles are derived from research-based trends, and represent an intermediate level that stands between philosophy, theory, and instructional strategies. These general principles or guidelines support and are later translated into specific instructional strategies such as materials and procedures.

philosophical principles These are general assumptions about the nature of learning and teaching processes. Philosophies are based on personal experiences about how an individual can learn better and how a teacher can help students to learn more effectively.

social and moral responsibility Teachers are not only doing a job, but are professionals who are charged by schools, as a social institution, to socialize their students into a specific school culture represented through content and objectives and standards built into a curriculum. Thus teachers as professionals are charged by society with social and moral responsibilities: to instill in their students a particular set of cultural content representing cultural knowledge, and values and beliefs. The degree of academic achievement of students in relation to a particular school culture and curriculum becomes the responsibility of the teacher and the school system, also called "teacher or school effectiveness." Thus, the teacher and the entire school system is responsible for the academic achievement of their students' and for the social and educational outcomes of their students' performance within the school institution and in the general society.

theoretical principles These are patterns derived from research studies' results that provide some information or evidence about what specific learning processes take place in students, and how teachers can use instruction more effectively. A theory is based on research data, showing patterns or trends of commonalties across the results of bodies of research studies. A model is a set of hypotheses that have not been proved yet in light of research data. A model requires revision through a set of evaluation studies that will provide research-based evidence for building a theory once bodies of research are accumulated.

REFERENCES

Center for Research on Education, Diversity, and Excellence (CREDE). (2002). A practical guide to understanding and implementing two-way immersion programs. *Talking Leaves, 6*(2), Summer, 1, & 9–10.

Cole, M. (1996). *Cultural psychology: A once and future discipline*. Cambridge, MA: Harvard University Press.

Cummins, J. (1991). Interdependence of L1 and L2 proficiency in bilingual children. In E. Bialystock (Ed.),

Language processing in bilingual children (pp. 70–89). Cambridge: Cambridge University Press.

Gonzalez, V. (2001). The role of socioeconomic and sociocultural factors in language-minority children's development: An ecological research view. *Bilingual Research Journal, 25*(1, 2), 1–30.

Gonzalez, V., Brusca-Vega, R., & Yawkey, T. (1997). *Assessment and instruction of culturally and linguistically diverse students with or at-risk of learning problems: From research to practice.* Needham Heights, MA: Allyn and Bacon.

Gonzalez, V., & Schallert, D. L. (1999). An integrative analysis of the cognitive development of bilingual and bicultural children and adults. In V. Gonzalez (Ed.), *Language and cognitive development in L2 learning: Educational implications for children and adults* (pp. 19–55). Needham Heights, MA: Allyn and Bacon.

Hatano, G., & Inagaki, K. (1986). Two courses of expertise. In H. Stevenson, H. Azuma, & K. Hakuta (Eds.), *Child development and education in Japan,* (pp. 89–122). Freedman: New York.

National Research Council. (1999a). *How people learn.* Washington, DC: National Academy Press.

National Research Council .(1999b). *Improving student learning.* Washington, DC: National Academy Press.

Ovando, C. J., Collier, V. P., & Combs, M. C. (2003). *Bilingunal and ESLClass rooms: Teaching in multicultural contexts* (3rd ed.). Boston: McGraw Hill.

Piper, T. (1998). *Language and learning: The home and school years.* Upper Saddle River, NJ: Prentice Hall.

Resnick, L. B., & Kloper, L. E. (1989). Toward the thinking curriculum: Current cognitive research. *Yearbook of the Association for Supervision and Curriculum Development.* Alexandria, VA: Association for Supervision and Curriculum Development.

Shafer, R. E., Staab, C., & Smith, K. (1983). Language functions and school success. Glenview, IL: Scott, Foresman & Co.

Stroup, A. L., & Robins, L. N. (1972). Elementary school predictors of high school dropouts among black males. *Sociology of Education, 45*(2), 212–222.

TESOL. (1997). *ESL standards for pre-k–12 students.* Washington, DC: TESOL.

INCREASING ACADEMIC ACHIEVEMENT AND LANGUAGE ACQUISITION FOR ENGLISH LANGUAGE LEARNERS ACROSS GRADE LEVELS

LEARNING OBJECTIVES

1. Understand the applications of best ESL educational models and effective teaching strategies for content areas
2. Recognize models and content area lessons used across grade and proficiency levels using national standards and benchmarks
3. Identify assessment practices with research-based instructional practices across developmental areas for ELLs
4. Understand the application of research into model programs and protocols on language and standards-based content instruction

PREVIEW QUESTIONS

1. What are the reasons for ESL and content area teachers to work together?
2. Have you ever tried to learn a second language? If so, how difficult/easy did you find the process of learning a second language?
3. Which are the main myths and misconceptions about learning and teaching a second language? Discuss ways to dispel those myths.
4. How can the instructional conversation contribute to the learning process?
5. In what ways do you think that cooperative learning strategies can be used effectively in classrooms with ELLs? Describe the benefits.
6. How can you use the SIOP in planning and delivering your lessons to teach ELLs? What will your focus be?

Chapter 6 focuses on applications of best ESL methods and classroom teaching strategies for content areas at the middle and high school levels. It applies the descriptions and discussions on curriculum standards, theoretical models, educational approaches, and teaching strategies addressed in Chapters 2, 3, and 4.

The first major section introduces *all* teachers, whether they are in bilingual, ESL, or mainstream classrooms, to a number of important concepts and effective research-based applications in: (1) language and content teaching methodology and strategies, and (2) instructional models and lesson plans that have been successful in classrooms across the United States. Chapter 6 has the goal of making all teachers aware that ELLs may be able to participate in content courses with grade-level objectives as the teachers deliver modified instruction to make information comprehensible to them. Chapter 6 also encourages educators who are attempting to meet the linguistic and academic needs of ELLs to reflect on the constraints and opportunities they face when teaching ELLs and to consider these concepts and strategies as feasible avenues of instruction, lesson planning, and assessment of academic achievement and language proficiency. Chapter 6 uses the information presented in Chapters 2, 3, and 4 and describes specific lesson plans with professional development models to embed recent research-based strategies in teaching modules and lessons.

The second major section encourages educators to realize that there is no quick fix to teach ELLs because language and academic development take time and are complex processes that they need to become familiar with and be prepared for in order to succeed. By dispelling myths and misconceptions about second language (L2) learning, educators will understand the process of L2 acquisition. By becoming familiar with their students' educational needs, they will be able to apply, revise, and implement the models, lesson plans, training modules, and problem-solving scenarios from this chapter to help ELLs develop language and academic proficiency and to succeed in school. By implementing national standards for language and academic achievement, teachers can use this chapter as a resource from which to draw.

The position or perspective of Chapter 6 and this entire book is one of pluralism. Our intention is to assist educators develop their own lessons and modules using the information presented in the chapters of this book on effective models, methods, and strategies to teach ELLs. Therefore, Chapter 6 is connected to the second theme of the book because it (1) applies the **background knowledge** presented in several chapters of the book in specific lessons; (2) addresses myths and misconceptions about ELLs' education; and, (3) promotes reflection among teachers to improve on their craft. Chapter 6 aims to provide an understanding of the teaching-learning process and focuses both on students who need to succeed academically and teachers who need to excel.

ESL AND CONTENT AREA TEACHERS WORKING TOGETHER

Help, somebody! I have three students in my classroom who do not speak English. What should I do?

—Junior High School Teacher

Does this cry sound familiar? If you happen to be a mainstream, English teacher in your school, your answer would be a resounding affirmation. Mainstream teachers are confronted with groups of students who are very diverse both ethnically and linguistically. No longer do mainstream teachers in our public schools face a homogeneous class of learners who are at the appropriate level of English mastery for their age and grade. This is because: (1) the large majority of English language learners (ELLs) attend mainstream classrooms, and (2) ESL and bilingual teachers are no longer able to contain within their classrooms the growing numbers of new ELL arrivals to the school community. Now the mainstream classroom teacher needs to teach both content and language to the ELLs.

The idea that ESL and bilingual education should be totally compartmentalized areas of the curriculum is somehow prevalent among educators in the mainstream program. It is common for staff developers and trainers in schools with large numbers of ELLs who have offered workshops in second language (L2) teaching techniques to mainstream teachers to hear the comment from a number of participants that such activity is not applicable to them because they do not teach English—they teach *in* English. Nevertheless, the arrival of the 2001 No Child Left Behind Act has raised the stakes for *all* children, including ELLs, as most states need to restructure their accountability measures. As discussed in Chapter 2, this legislation aims at eliminating the educational and achievement gaps between disadvantaged children and their peers. Schools are now responsible for improving the academic performance of all students with real consequences for school systems failing to make progress.

Thus, the issue confronting schools at present is teacher quality and ways to offer all teachers the preparation they need to help students succeed in a school reform context that affects positive changes in the instructional practices in all classrooms. ESL and content area teachers do have many things in common. Figure 6.1. illustrates one approach to integrate ESL content teaching techniques and quality teaching.

ESL teachers assist students to use English to communicate in social settings. There is also room in ESL classrooms to use other languages for instruction. Content area teachers assist students in acquiring specific subject or content knowledge. They use English for instruction. There is room for an integrated approach for teachers of ELLs that:

1. Assists students to use English to achieve academically in all content areas.
2. Promotes classroom interactions, and cooperative learning communities.
3. Uses English to obtain, process, construct, and provide subject matter in spoken and written form.
4. Uses appropriate learning strategies to construct and apply academic language.
5. Provides cognitively challenging activities.
6. Connects school to students' lives.
7. Uses joint productive or cooperative learning activities
8. Uses **realia**, or real-life objects and artifacts.

What is language proficiency? Language proficiency may be defined as the ability to use a language effectively and appropriately throughout the range of social, personal, school, and work situations required for daily living in a given society. We

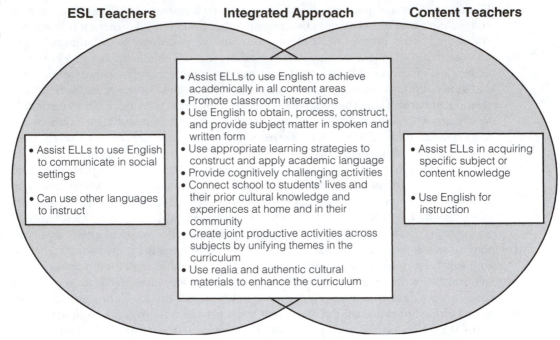

ESL Teachers   **Integrated Approach**   **Content Teachers**

- Assist ELLs to use English to achieve academically in all content areas
- Promote classroom interactions
- Use English to obtain, process, construct, and provide subject matter in spoken and written form
- Use appropriate learning strategies to construct and apply academic language
- Provide cognitively challenging activities
- Connect school to students' lives and their prior cultural knowledge and experiences at home and in their community
- Create joint productive activities across subjects by unifying themes in the curriculum
- Use realia and authentic cultural materials to enhance the curriculum

- Assist ELLs to use English to communicate in social settings
- Can use other languages to instruct

- Assist ELLs in acquiring specific subject or content knowledge
- Use English for instruction

FIGURE 6.1   An Integrated Approach for ESL and Content Teachers

want our students to become competent in the four language processes: listening, speaking, reading, and writing (Peregoy & Boyle, 2001). A teacher of ELLs may be responsible for English language development, subject-matter teaching, or both (Peregoy & Boyle, 2001). Subject areas such as science and mathematics contain unique terminology that are often difficult for students to acquire quickly.

Standards for Teaching of ELLs

The standards for teaching have been described in Chapter 2. The teaching standards posted by national professional organizations guide teachers to improve academic achievement. A brief summary of the national standards follows:

1. The Teachers of English to Speakers of Other Languages (TESOL) organization has set forth three goals and three sets of standards (TESOL, 1997). ELLs need to become proficient in English, to communicate in social settings, to have unrestricted access to grade-appropriate instruction in challenging academic subjects, and, ultimately, to live rich and productive lives in socially and culturally appropriate ways.
2. The National Science Education Standards (NSES) has set forth goals based on "hands-on" experimentation and learner-generated questions, investigation,

hypotheses, and models. NSES outline what students need to know, and be able to understand to become scientifically literate at different grade levels (National Research Council of the National Committee on Science Education Standards and Assessment, 1994).

3. The National Council of Teachers of Mathematics (NCTM) has issued standards calling for mathematics classrooms where problem solving, concept development, and the construction of learner-generated solutions are given more importance than memorizing procedures (Romberg & Wilson, 1995). NCTM (1989) calls for opportunities for students to understand mathematics and its applications by viewing the same phenomena from various mathematical perspectives.

4. The Center for Research on Education Diversity and Excellence (**CREDE**) has set forth five standards for effective pedagogy to provide teachers with tools to enact best teaching practices (Dalton, 1998). They are: **joint productive activity,** in which teachers and students produce together; students or students and teacher work together for a common product or goal; *language development*, which encompasses the development of language and literacy across the curriculum fostered best through meaningful use and purposeful conversation between teachers and students; *contextualization*, when the teacher finds connections between the students' reality and the curriculum and uses students' knowledge and skills as a foundation for new knowledge; *academically challenging activity* that encourages students toward cognitive complexity; and, dialogue or the **instructional conversation** (IC) promoted by questioning and sharing ideas and knowledge (Quiñones Feliciano de Benítez, 2001).

These four sets of standards focus on down-to-earth opportunities and experiences by engaging students in significant and authentic schooling. They have the potential to engage all students critically in a kind of learning that enables them to recognize themselves, name their experiences, and learn how to change existing conditions, for themselves as well as for others in their communities. Table 6.1 compares and relates the characteristics of the four sets of standards for instruction using five common variables—collaboration, communication, contextualization, cognitive demand, and dialogic thinking.

DISPELLING MYTHS ABOUT L2 LEARNING

Learning a L2 is no easy task (Cummins & Fillmore, 2000; McLaughlin, 1992). All teachers of ELLs need to understand that L2 learning is a long, hard, and complex process. Unfortunately, there are a number of myths and misconceptions about how ELLs learn English, their L2. These issues include the ease and rapidity with which children learn a L2, the optimal age at which to begin L2 instruction, the importance of the extent of exposure to the L2, the relationship between oral communication skills and academic language skills, and cultural and individual differences in L2 learning styles. This section connects with the second book theme and to Chapter 11, which

TABLE 6.1 A Comparison of Language and Content-Area Standards

CREDE STANDARDS FOR EFFECTIVE PEDAGOGY	NATIONAL SCIENCE EDUCATION STANDARDS	NATIONAL COUNCIL OF TEACHERS OF MATHEMATICS	TESOL STANDARDS
JOINT PRODUCTIVE ACTIVITY • Students and teacher working together • Students assist one another • Students develop a product	**COLLABORATION** • Group of students analyzing and synthesizing data to defend conclusions • Public communication of students' ideas and work with classmates	**COLLABORATION** • Groups of students creating and using representations to organize, record, and communicate mathematical ideas	**COLLABORATION** • Language learning through students' collaboration and meaningful activities.
LANGUAGE DEVELOPMENT • Language developed in a meaningful context • Oral and written language development through questioning, restating, and modeling	**COMMUNICATION** • Communicating science explanations • Understanding scientific concepts and developing abilities of inquiry	**COMMUNICATION** • Select, apply, and translate among mathematical representations to solve problems • Use representations to model and interpret physical, social, and mathematical phenomena	**COMMUNICATION** • Language learning through meaningful and significant use • The importance of developing oral, reading, and writing skills
CONTEXTUALIZATION • Students' knowledge as a foundation for new knowledge • Connecting school to students' lives	**CONTEXTUALIZATION** • Process skills in context • Activities that investigate and analyze scientific questions • Use of multiple process skills such as manipulation, cognitive, and procedural	**CONTEXTUALIZATION** • Using various representations of objects to be able to recognize common mathematical structures across different contexts	**CONTEXTUALIZATION** • The role of students' native languages in their English language and general academic development • Cultural, social, and cognitive processes in language and academic development

CHALLENGING ACTIVITY

- Cognitively challenging instruction
- Focus on thinking and analysis of appropriate levels of tasks

INSTRUCTIONAL CONVERSATION

- Dialogue, questioning, sharing ideas and knowledge
- Assistance dialogue to develop thinking and problem solving, to express ideas orally and in writing

COGNITIVE DEMAND

- Activities that investigate and analyze science questions
- Doing more investigations in order to develop understanding, ability, values of inquiry and knowledge of science content
- Investigation over extended periods of time

DIALOGIC THINKING

- Communicating science explanations and sharing ideas and work with other classmates

COGNITIVE DEMAND

- Create and interpret models of more complex phenomena, drawn from a wider range of contexts, by identifying essential features of a situation and by findings representations that capture mathematical relationships among those features

DIALOGIC THINKING

- Promoting dialogue and interaction among teacher–students, and students–students to share ideas about mathematical problems

COGNITIVE DEMAND

- The use of scaffolding to move students from challenging activities to more complex activities that require the use of more complex vocabulary

DIALOGIC THINKING

- The importance of language as communication
- Promoting active participation of students during classroom discussion, and dialogue among them

address myths commonly held by preservice and in-service educators about the effect that having an ESL background can have on Pre-K–Grade 12 students' learning, development, and academic achievement.

The following five myths are clarified with research and educational implications in the area of L2 acquisition:

Myth 1: Children learn L2s quickly and easily
Myth 2: The younger the learner, the more skilled in learning a L2
Myth 3: The more time students spend in a L2 context, the quicker they learn the language
Myth 4: Children have learned a L2 once they can speak it
Myth 5: All children learn a L2 in the same way

Myth 1: Children Learn L2s Quickly and Easily

One frequently hears that children can learn a L2 faster than adults; that immigrant children translate for their parents who have not learned English; and that young learners speak without a foreign accent, whereas this is impossible for adult learners. Research has demonstrated that L2 learning is very complex and a painstaking learning process for children and adults; some research has demonstrated that adolescents and adults can perform better than young children under controlled conditions (e.g., Asher & Garcia, 1969; Snow & Hoefnagel-Hohle, 1978). One exception is in the area of pronunciation. We also need not apply the same criteria of language proficiency to both the child and the adult. The requirements to communicate as a child are quite different from the requirements to communicate as an adult. The child's constructions are usually shorter and simpler, and vocabulary is relatively small when compared with what is necessary for adults to speak at the same level of competence in a L2 as they do in their first language. The child does not have to learn as much as an adult to achieve competence in communicating. Consequently, there is the illusion that the child learns more quickly than the adult, whereas when controlled research is conducted, in both formal and informal learning situations, results typically indicate that adult (and adolescent) learners perform better than young children (Krashen, Long, & Scarcella, 1979).

Myth 1: Implications for educators and programs for ELLs

- Do not expect miraculous results from young ELLs in your classroom. At the very least, expect that learning a L2 is as difficult for young ELLs as it is for adolescents and adults. In fact, it may be more difficult, as young children do not have access to the memory techniques and other strategies that more experienced learners can use in acquiring vocabulary and in learning the grammatical rules of the L2.
- Do not assume that young ELLs have fewer inhibitions or are less embarrassed than adults when they make mistakes in their L2. If anything, children are likely

to be shyer and more embarrassed before their peers than are more mature adults. Consider that young ELLs from some cultural backgrounds are extremely anxious when singled out and called on to perform in English as they are in the process of learning it. Do not assume that, because children supposedly learn the L2 quickly, such discomfort will quickly pass.

Myth 2: The Younger the Learner, the More Skilled in Learning a L2

What is the best time to start L2 learning? Certainly, the optimal way is to begin at birth and learn two languages simultaneously. According to brain development and neuroplasticity studies, children who are exposed to two languages early in life do extremely well in reaching full mastery in two languages (Genesee, 2000). Even children who begin as late as 9 years old are likely to become fully bilingual (Holowka, Brosseau-Lapré, & Petitto, 2002). Children who are exposed to two languages do very well in each language (ibid, 2002). They also read better because learning two language massages the child's phonological analysis and capacity. In fact, these children are learn to read without some of the difficulties that a monolingual child has—their phonological analysis is richer.

Pronunciation is one aspect of L2 learning in which the younger-is-better hypothesis may have validity. A number of studies have found that the younger one begins to learn a L2, the more native-like the accent one develops in that language (Dulay, Burt, & Krashen, 1982). This may be because pronunciation involves motor patterns that have been fossilized in the first language and are difficult to alter after a certain age because of the nature of the neurophysiologic mechanisms involved. It may also be that we do not understand very well how to teach phonology in a L2. Some research, however, suggests that younger children do not necessarily have an advantage over older children because of their cognitive and experiential limitations when compared to older children.

Myth 2: Implications for educators and programs for ELLs

- Do not conclude that early exposure to a L2 is in some way detrimental to a young ELL. All ELLs, regardless of their age, need to be exposed to their second language as early as possible in their programs. An early start for ELLs allows for a long sequence of instruction leading to potential language and academic proficiency. Allow ELLs to view L2 learning and the insights they acquire into a second culture as normal and integral parts of schooling. Early exposure to English is needed in U.S. classrooms to meet federal and state mandates for ELLs to master English as quickly as possible, while at the same time learning subject-matter content. The implication for educators is let's *not* hold back in exposing a young student to two languages until there is a cognitive base; holding the child back is not in his or her best interest or biology.
- Do not expect miracles of young ELLs. The research suggests that older students will show quicker gains, though younger children may have an advantage in pronunciation. Certainly, beginning language instruction in Grades K–1 gives ELLs more exposure to the language than beginning in Grades 5 or 6.

Myth 3: The More Time Students Spend in a L2 context, the Quicker They Learn the Language

Research evidence indicates that in bilingual program classes, where there is exposure to the home language and to English, ELLs have been found to acquire English language skills equivalent to those acquired by children who have been in English-only programs (Cummins, 1996; Ovando, Collier, & Combs, 2003). Researchers caution against withdrawing the support of the home language too soon. There is a great deal of evidence that, whereas oral communication skills in a L2 may be acquired within two or three years, it may take up to four to six years to acquire the level of proficiency for understanding the language in its instructional uses (Collier, 1995; Thomas & Collier, 2003).

ELLs do not have it easy when they have to learn English to communicate and to succeed in school. Each and every one varies in the way they learn their L2. It would help greatly if they already read in their L1 and know the content areas in L1 because several skills can transfer easily from one language to the other. They do this particularly at the beginning stages of proficiency: they lean on their L1 knowledge to analyze patterns in English. They rely less on this transfer as they become proficient and comfortable in English, their second language (Genesee, 2000). Motivation to learn English is important, as is bringing together ELLs and their English-speaking peers or advanced ELLs to give them plenty of access and make English learning possible (Ovando, Collier, & Combs, 2003).

Both social, conversational, everyday, playground English and academic, school English are demanding tasks. Social language is a dimension of language proficiency, for example, when teachers and students use a lot of contextual, nonverbal clues, hands-on activities, face-to-face conversations, and written feedback on an e-mail message. When ELLs use English to talk to their friends, in play, in conversation, they may begin to talk in a few months. However, ELLs, whether they are children, adolescents, or adults, may take 2 or more years to develop their vocabulary, grammar, phonology, semantics, and pragmatics.

Academic and social English is just one language; they are not separate languages. Academic English is an extension of social English. But it is more complex than social English; it is for schooling across all content areas. It is more demanding with very few contextual clues to comprehension. ELLs will be learning academic English throughout their schooling. All students—English speakers and ELLs—learn the deeper and higher levels of academic proficiency in English. It takes ELLs 4+ years to learn academic English.

Myth 3: Implications for educators and programs for ELLs

- Where possible, give ELLs the support of their home or first language (L1). Using ELLs' L1 in the classroom enables them to avoid falling behind in school work, and it also provides a mutually reinforcing bond between the home and the school. In fact, the home language acts as a bridge for ELLs, enabling them to participate more effectively in school activities while they are learning English.

- Two-way bilingual programs have been shown to benefit from extended intensive exposure to minority (ELLs' L1) and majority (English-speaking) languages and students learn language and academics using both languages. The research clearly shows that two-way programs are not detrimental to learning content material in that language, as long as the home language continues to develop and is supported (Lindholm-Leary, 2001; Calderón & Minaya-Rowe, 2003).

Myth 4: Children Have Learned a L2 Once They Can Speak It

Educators often assume that once ELLs can converse comfortably in English, they are in full control of the language. In fact, it is like a linguistic facade, whereby ELLs appear to be fluent in English oral skills but have not mastered the more complex and cognitively demanding aspects of the language as in literacy skills (Cummins, 1984). There is much more involved in learning a L2 than learning how to speak it; a student needs to achieve proficiency in the more abstract academic language needed to engage in content area demands, such as reading, academic vocabulary, and grammar. Such demanding activities require the student to separate language from the context of actual experience and to learn to deal with abstract meanings.

It takes longer to become fully proficient when ELLs are not literate in their L1; when they are literate, they maintain grade-level norms in L1 and reach grade-level norms in English (Carlo, et al., in press). Literate ELLs will learn how to read in English quicker. Research tells that when ELLs are fully literate in their L1, they will transfer their literacy skills in Spanish to read in English (National Reading Panel, 2000). Once you can read, you can read; once you are educated, you are educated. For example, some skills ELLs transfer from Spanish, their L1, to English reading are: phonological awareness, word recognition, vocabulary, comprehension strategies, reading practice, print awareness, alphabetic awareness, and orthographic awareness (August & Hakuta, 1997; Christian & Genessee, 2001). When an ELL is literate in Spanish, that student will be able to develop literacy in English quicker than an ELL who is not.

Myth 4: Implications for educators and programs for ELLs

- Do not exit ELLs with English oral conversational and social proficiency from programs in which they have the support of their L1 or if they are provided with language transition support services. Exiting ELLs who are not ready, without their academic language in place, to the all-English classroom may be harmful to their academic success.
- Do not use only oral language assessment instruments to assess whether the ELL is ready to be exited into an all-English classroom. Instead, batteries of assessments representing higher order thinking skills shared by both L1 and L2 are needed that encompass alternative assessments and multiple evaluations. Chapters 7 and 8 of this book delve deeper into assessment issues.
- Consider that an ELL may be having problems in reading and writing that are not apparent in his or her oral abilities. Many problems that ELLs have in reading

and writing at the middle school and high school levels stem from limitations in academic vocabulary and syntactic knowledge in the L2 (August, 2003). Even ELLs who are skilled orally can have these gaps.

Myth 5: All Students Learn a L2 in the Same Way

Not all students learn the L2 in the same way or at the same rate. Yet this seems to be the assumption underlying a great deal of practice. There are at least four issues to address here:

1. Mainstream American families and the families of many ELLs have different ways of talking (Heath, 1983). Mainstream children are accustomed to an analytic style, in which the truth of specific arguments is deduced from general propositions. Many children from minority groups are accustomed to an inductive style of talking, in which fundamental assumptions must be inferred from a series of concrete statements.
2. American schools emphasize the language functions and styles of talk that predominate in mainstream families. Language is used to communicate meaning, to convey information, to control social behavior, and to solve problems. In the upper grades, especially, the style of talk is analytic and deductive. Students are rewarded for clear and logical thinking. It is no wonder that ELLs who come to school accustomed to using language in a manner that is very different from what is expected in school experience tension and frustration.
3. There are also social class differences. In literate, technologically advanced societies, middle-class parents teach their children through language. Instructions are given verbally from a very early age. This contrasts to the experience of immigrant children from less technologically advanced and sometimes nonurbanized societies. Traditionally, teaching in these cultural contexts is carried out primarily through nonverbal means (Heath, 1983). Technical skills, such as cooking, driving a car, or building a house, are learned through observation, supervised participation, and self-initiated repetition. There is none of the information testing through questions that characterizes the teaching-learning process in urban and suburban middle-class homes.
4. Some ELLs are more accustomed to learning from peers than from adults. From their earliest years, they grow up with older siblings or cousins and their extended family. They learned to be quiet in the presence of adults and have little experience in interacting with them. When they enter school, they are more likely to pay attention to what their peers are doing than to what the teacher is saying. At this point, the other children are more important to them than adults.
5. There are also temperamental and personality differences in how ELLs react to school and develop learning styles. Some children are outgoing, talkative, and sociable and learn the L2 quickly because they want to be like their English-speaking peers. They do not worry about mistakes, but use limited resources to generate input from native speakers. Other children are shy, laconic, and quiet. They learn

by listening and by attending to what is happening and being said around them. They say little, for fear of making a mistake. Nonetheless, research shows that both types of learners can be successful L2 learners. In classrooms where group work is stressed, the socially active child is more likely to be successful; in the traditional, teacher-oriented classroom, children who are "active listeners" have been found to be more successful than highly sociable children (Wong Fillmore, 1991).

Myth 5: Implications for educators and programs for ELLs

- Be aware of culture and individual differences in learners' styles. Consider the cognitive and social norms that ELLs bring with them that might differ from those that govern the mainstream all-English classroom.
- Modify your expectations of the ELL's ability and your response to him or her. Consider that some ELLs may be less able to make the functional adaptation to the interpersonal setting of the mainstream school culture; behaviors such as paying attention and persisting at tasks are valued. Be aware of such cultural differences because the ELL's lack of attentiveness and lack of persistence can influence your expectations and the way you interact with these students.
- Use a variety of instructional activities—small group work, cooperative learning, peer tutoring, individualized instruction strategies that take the ELLs' diversity of experience into account. Become familiar with current innovations and practice such as untracking and mixed-age grouping. They are the direct result of teachers adapting their teaching to the challenges posed by ELLs.
- Become familiar with the ELL's experiences at home and with his or her home culture, values, patterns of language use, and interpersonal style. ELLs are likely to be more responsive if you are sensitive to their culture and its behavioral patterns. This means going beyond such cognitive activities as history lessons, slide shows of life in Puerto Rico, Mexico, Cambodia, or the like. Such cognitive activities, while important, do not reach children effectively. Affirm the values of ELLs' home culture and try to develop a positive emotional attitude toward their background.

CROSS-CUTTING METHODS

Three methods have been consistently linked to quality instruction in all settings; they are particularly important when used in classrooms with ELLs: The **instructional conversation** and cooperative learning as tools for language and content development, and teachers learning communities as the overarching method to improve the teaching-learning process and teacher communication (Calderón, August, & Minaya-Rowe, 2004). A brief description follows.

The Instructional Conversation (IC)

The IC is one of the five standards for effective pedagogy in multicultural settings (Tharp, Estrada, Dalton, & Yamauchi, 2000). It promotes learning by weaving together prior knowledge, experiences, and new concepts (Tharp & Yamauchi, 1994). All of the standards interacted when nested in an IC:

- The teacher can implement an IC in the classroom to select a theme and activate background knowledge while eliciting students' contributions and reasoning.
- The teacher can provide direct teaching when needed.
- The conversational elements promote teacher responsiveness to students and fewer "known-answer" questions.
- Interactive discourse and general participation occurs in a challenging but non-threatening environment.
- The elements promote higher cognitive abilities such as: analysis, reflection, and critical thinking.

In the IC, the teacher listens carefully, makes guesses about intended meaning, and adjusts responses to assist students' efforts. The IC provides opportunities for the development of the languages of instruction and subject matter. Table 6.2 describes the 10 instructional and conversational elements of ICs when enacted in the classroom (Quiñones Feliciano de Benítez, 2001).

The IC is based on assumptions that are fundamentally different from those of traditional lessons. In traditional classrooms, teaching is through the recitation scripts, in which the teacher repeatedly assigns and assesses. The IC is an important tool for classrooms to be transformed into communities of learners through dialogic teaching, and when teachers reduce the distance between themselves and their students by constructing lessons from common understanding of each others' experience and ideas and make teaching a warm, interpersonal and collaborative activity.

A teacher who uses the IC—just as parents use it in natural teaching—assume that the student has something to say beyond the known answers in his or her head. The teacher listens carefully, makes guesses about the intended meaning, and adjusts responses to assist the student's efforts and engages in conversation. Such conversation reveals the knowledge, skills, and values and the culture of the students, enabling the teacher to contextualize teaching to fit the learner's experience base.

The IC promotes a balanced participation; teacher talk occurs less than student talk by promoting an activity setting that requires student participation with the provision of a topic focus (Dalton, 1998). The conversational aspects of the IC provide the hook that facilitates the connection of formal schooled knowledge to practice knowledge, providing opportunities for responsive. General participation, including self-selected turns, is a must if the IC is to promote the academic development of all participants and a balanced participation as illustrated in Table 6.3.

Evidently, the IC is based on the notion that higher cognitive activities are developed on the basis of interaction with more competent others (Tharp et al., 2000). As opposed to traditional teacher-centered schooling, the IC is a dialogue between teacher and learner that promotes higher understanding by weaving prior knowledge and experiences together with new materials (Dalton & Sison, 1995).

TABLE 6.2   The Instructional and Conversational Elements of the IC

Instructional Elements

1. *Thematic focus.* The teacher selects a theme or idea to serve as a starting point to focus the discussion and has a general plan for how the theme will unfold, including how to "chunk" the text to permit optimal exploration of the theme

2. *Activation and use of background and relevant schemata.* The teacher either "hooks into" or provides students with pertinent background knowledge and relevant schemata necessary for understanding a text. Background knowledge and schemata are then woven into the discussion that follows

3. *Direct teaching.* When necessary, the teacher provides direct teaching of a skill or concept

4. *Promotion of more complex language and expression.* The teacher elicits more extended student contributions by using a variety of elicitation techniques; for example
   - Invitations to expand—"Tell me more about . . . "
   - Questions—"What do you mean by . . . "
   - Restatements—"In other words, . . . "
   - Pauses

5. *Promotion of bases for statements of positions.* The teacher promotes students' use of text, pictures, and reasoning to support an argument or position. Without overwhelming students, the teacher probes for the bases of students' statements:
   - "How do you know?"
   - "What makes you think that . . . ?"
   - "Show us where it says . . . "

Conversational Elements

6. *Few known-answer questions.* Much of the discussion centers on questions and answers for which there might be more than one correct answer

7. *Responsiveness to student contributions.* Besides having an initial plan and maintaining the focus and coherence of the discussion, the teacher is also responsive to students' statements and the opportunities they provide

8. *Connected discourse.* The discussion is characterized by multiple, interactive, connected turns; succeeding utterances build on and extend previous ones

9. *A challenging, but nonthreatening atmosphere.* The teacher creates a **"zone of proximal development"** in which a challenging atmosphere is balanced by a positive affective climate. The teacher is more collaborator than evaluator and creates an atmosphere that challenges students and allows them to negotiate and construct the meaning of the text

10. *General participation, including self-selected turns.* The teacher encourages general participation among students; she or he does not hold exclusive rights to determine who talks, and students are encouraged to volunteer or otherwise influence the selection of speaking turns

TABLE 6.3   Balanced Participation in an IC

TEACHER TALK	STUDENT TALK
• Occurs less than total student talk	• Occurs more than teacher talk
• Sets up opportunities for student talk	• Is every student's product
• Has a topic to scaffold the discussion	• Addresses the topic
• Is responsive to student talk and caffolds the discussion when needed	• Uses own preferred style
	• Conarration, simultaneous
• Models proper forms of the language	• Uses proper forms in response
• Elicits students' language through probes about reasoning and feeling	• Uses content lexicon and concepts in response to model

Cooperative Learning

Learning content and a second language can best be facilitated by quality interaction. Cooperative learning is an instructional strategy that facilitates a social and linguistically interactive classroom environment (Calderón, 1991). Cooperative learning structures draw from the individual knowledge and talents of learners to facilitate team building, communication building, content mastery, and other interactive skills (Kagan, 1992; Slavin, 1990). There is an interdependence established among the students in each group as they strive for the achievement of group or individual objectives (Johnson, Johnson, & Smith, 1991). ELLs tend to benefit from the interaction in cooperative learning, increased contact and rich linguistic experiences (Calderón & Carreón, 1994; Hertz-Lazarowitz & Calderón, 1994). The five elements of cooperative learning are:

1. Positive interdependence—a sense of working together for a common goal
2. Individual accountability—every team member is in charge of their own and their teammates learning and makes an active contribution to the group
3. Abundant face-to-face interaction—students explain, argue, elaborate, and link current material with what they already know
4. Sufficient communication skills—explicit teaching of appropriate leadership, trust, and conflict resolution skills
5. Team reflection and debriefing—assessing what they have learned, how well they are working together, and how they might do better as a team

We learn something when we have an opportunity to discuss it with a peer. Cooperative learning strategies are most important for ELLs. They provide opportunities for students to practice the new language in safe contexts. Cooperative learning is basic to the development and use of communicative skills and social interaction skills (Calderón & Minaya-Rowe, 2003). Table 6.4. lists the norms and protocols used in successful cooperative learning strategies.

TABLE 6.4   Social Norms and Cooperative Protocols

• Everyone contributes ideas	• Respect others
• Everyone has a specific task (not role)	• Be positive
• Everyone learns from one another	• Accept opinions
• Everyone works with an open mind	• Contribute to the discussions
	• Help others
	• Accept help
	• Stay on task
	• Accept responsibility

Source: Calderón, August, and Minaya-Rowe (2004).

There is an array of cooperative learning strategies that can be used with ELLs at all levels of language proficiency and academic development. A brief sample follows.

Numbered heads together.   In this cooperative learning strategy, groups of four students first select their team name and each team member is assigned a number (1, 2, 3, or 4). Teams listen to the question, put their heads together for 2 minutes, and come up with the answer. Everyone in the group must know the answer and be prepared to answer the question. The teacher then randomly picks a number and a team name. One student from that team answers for the group. Then the teacher selects another question, and after two minutes another number and team is called. A variation of the activity is to call a number and have all the team representatives with the number stand, with each student giving a different point of view.

Roundtable.   Students sit in a circle and clear their table/desks. Only one paper and a pencil are used. Each student writes an answer and passes the paper to the right. Everyone must write an answer. Invented spelling is acceptable. They continue this process (usually for two minutes) until the teacher calls time out. The roundtable strategy can be used for

- Writing the names of the states, presidents, months of the year
- Brainstorming adjectives to describe a particular character
- Writing words that come to mind when students hear a word such as *democracy*, knowing that this is a key word in an upcoming chapter

In-house jigsaw.   Each of four students in a team is responsible for reading one part of a chapter or story or problem. Each teaches the others the information. Each prepares 1 or 2 test questions. In this way, the **jigsaw** puzzle parts become a whole. The jigsaw can be used for

- Answering lists of questions
- Putting together a team project
- Mastering mathematical or scientific processes

Sheltered English Instruction

Chapter 4 has examined in detail the concept of **sheltered English instruction (SEI)** as an approach for teaching content to ELLs in strategic ways that make the subject-matter concepts comprehensible while promoting the students' English language development (Echevarria, Vogt, & Short, 2000). SEI provides ELLs with a medium to develop their academic and linguistic skills in English (Shaw, Echevarria, & Short, 1999; Short, 1999). SEI is also defined as

- The concept of comprehensible subject-matter teaching (math, science, social studies, etc.) with English, the L2, as the medium of instruction
- SEI differs from what native English speakers receive in the regular all-English program (subject-matter instruction in English) in that SEI is aimed at providing both language (listening, speaking, reading, and writing) and academic instruction to ELLs

SEI is more than just quality instruction or good teaching. It is a model of classroom instruction where:

- Language and content objectives are systematically woven into each lesson
- The subject curriculum or academic content (social studies, science, math) is modified instruction in English
- ELLs' academic language proficiency must be developed consistently and regularly as part of their lessons
- Language proficiency aims at language development in listening, speaking, reading, and writing skills
- Instruction is **scaffolded** by beginning at a level that encourages ELL success and provides support to move them to a higher level of understanding and accomplishment
- Cultural background of the students is integrated into the lesson planning

Overview of Sheltered English Instruction

Table 6.5 summarizes the implications of SEI in classrooms with ELLs. It is followed by a brief explanation of SEI characteristics.

   1. *Language goals are aimed at academic English proficiency.* These goals include reading, writing, speaking, or listening. For example, by the end of a science lesson an ELL is expected to write about how electricity flows through a circuit. On the other hand, academic goals are the district content goals for all students. From the example here the academic goal would be understanding what a circuit is and how it works. In a SEI lesson, teachers are expected to write both types of goals in simple form for the students to see at the beginning of the lesson. The teacher should be aware of the ELLs' characteristics that exist in their classroom and should decide if the ELLs' levels are intermediate, limited, or no English. Chapter 4 describes the stages of language proficiency. The ELL's

TABLE 6.5   Overview of Sheltered English Instruction

Language goals	:	Academic English Proficiency
Academic goals	:	District goals for all students
ELL characteristics	:	Intermediate, limited, no English
Grades served	:	All grades
Entry grades	:	Any grade
Teachers involved	:	Mainstream, Bilingual, ESL, Language Transition Support Services (LTSS)
Language of instruction	:	In English with adaptations, visuals, realia, and the Sheltered Instruction Observation Protocol (SIOP)

Source: Genesee (1999)

level of proficiency is important to know when deciding on the language goals, the types of activities prepared, and how the students are assessed.

2. *SEI serves all grade levels.* SEI teaching can be done at any grade with ELLs at various English language proficiencies in the classroom. ELLs can enter school at any grade level. SEI is for all teachers. Mainstream, bilingual, ESL, and Language Transition Support Services teachers are all expected to help ELLs succeed. SEI uses English as the language of instruction. ELLs of various language proficiencies can be served with SEI by adapting the English spoken with visuals, realia, and the SIOP model of instruction, which will be discussed later.

3. *SEI is not watering down the curriculum for ELLs.* Curriculum should be just as demanding as in any other mainstream class. This chapter provides suggestions on how to achieve curriculum goals while still reaching ELLs' language and academic development. The uses of SEI techniques have for the most part been inconsistent from class to class, discipline to discipline, school to school, and district to district. By incorporating SEI into every mainstream classroom, ELLs will have the consistency and stability necessary for their success.

4. *Ways to plan SEI.* Standards for instruction were discussed above. They involve what to teach in the language objectives. These objectives include listening, speaking, reading, and writing in English. Teachers already include these items in their lesson plans at all grade levels and in all subject areas. Students need to be able to listen, speak, read, and write in English in order to be successful. Table 6.6 provides guidance in order to plan for SEI.

5. *SEI involves the methodology of teaching.* SEI does not involve anything new to teaching. Preparation is a key; the teacher must have clear content and language objectives. If you enter the classroom without first preparing your lessons, you become an ineffective teacher. Part of lesson preparation includes building on the background information of the students. Consider past learning and student experiences linked to new concepts and vocabulary. This makes the content more interesting to learn. **Comprehensible input** may be a new term to many teachers but it is not a new

TABLE 6.6   SEI Planning

ESL STANDARDS (WHAT TO TEACH)	HOW TO TEACH SEI (METHODOLOGY)	CONTENT AREA STANDARDS (WHAT TO TEACH)
Listening in English	Preparation	Standard
Speaking in English	Building Background	Benchmark
Reading in English	Comprehensible Input	
Writing in English	Strategies	
	Interaction	
	Practice/Application	
	Lesson Delivery	
	Review/Assessment	

Source: Echevarria, Vogt, and Short (2000).

concept. Making content and academic tasks comprehensible and clear involves increasing the clarity of what you say by using visuals, realia, and hands-on activities. For example, you could hold up a model of a cell when you start teaching about it or you could hold up two fingers whenever you say the number two. All teachers have a grab bag of strategies for how they present their material. It could be anything from creating a catchy rhyme to remember important information to playing a game to review for a test. Consider learning strategies, questioning techniques, and scaffolding instructions. Learning also involves interaction. This interaction can be between the teacher and students, between students and students, and between the students and the material. Teachers know that if they want their students to learn the material they must practice and apply it. Hands-on activities are crucial in the classroom with ELLs. Lesson delivery is also important. It involves the level of student participation and quality of work. If the lesson is dull and boring then the students will be uninterested but if the teacher is interested personally in the topic she or he will deliver the lesson in a manner that will catch the students' attention. Finally, to be sure that the students learned the material, the teacher must review and then assess how much they learned. Regular feedback and monitoring are important SEI components. The only difference in the assessment of ELLs is that you must make sure that the assessment is reliable. For example, you do not want to base an ELL's knowledge on an essay test. This will not accurately portray their knowledge because they have not mastered the academic English skills to write an essay successfully (Echevarria et al., 2000).

   6. *SEI is based on content area standards.* Every state has its own standards and benchmarks that teachers are required to meet. The No Child Left Behind Act mandates that all students must have access to the mainstream content standards and benchmarks. ELLs cannot be denied quality standards-based instruction just because their language proficiency is not level with the rest of the students (Hernández Ferrier, 2003).

   7. *Characteristics of SEI.* The following characteristics are self-explanatory; they are not new but are friendly reminders of quality teaching and L2 development considerations for instruction.

- Slower speech
- Shorter, simpler sentences
- Clear enunciation
- Avoidance of idiomatic expressions
- Use of body language, gestures, and movement
- Use of visuals and manipulatives in the classroom
- Use of music and other audio materials
- Teachers speak only in English, but allow ELLs to use first language in class
- Frequent checks for understanding
- Student-centered lessons
- Clarification and restatement of ELLs' responses

The Sheltered Instruction Observation Protocol (SIOP)

The **SIOP** proposed by Echevarria, Vogt, and Short (2000) is an instrument that determines elements of SEI methodology present in the planning and delivery of a lesson. The SIOP provides teachers of ELLs with training and a framework to develop the academic and linguistic demands in their L2 (Shaw, Echevarria, & Short, 1999; Short, 1999). The SIOP provides concrete examples of the features of SEI to enhance and expand teachers' instructional practice.

The SIOP Lesson Planning Guide's thirty items grouped into three main sections—Preparation, Instruction, and Review/Assessment—are used to develop lessons and templates, and to enhance instructional practices.

- The Preparation items are used to determine the language and content objectives, the use of supplementary materials, and the relevance of the activities in our lessons
- The Instruction items are incorporated in the lessons to build background, provide comprehensible input, encourage interaction, use strategies, and deliver the SI lesson
- The Review/Assessment section is used to review the key vocabulary and content concepts, assess student learning, and provide feedback to students on their output

Table 6.7 summarizes the SIOP components.

All the components of the SIOP are a part of good teaching practices. The SIOP Model gives teachers an outline to use as a guide while lesson planning to be sure that none of these important components are left out in a classroom with ELLs. This is important because ELLs have a more difficult time filling in the gaps than mainstream native-English speakers. There are a few things that should be mentioned once more to adjust instruction for ELLs.

1. *Never assume ELLs do not have prior knowledge.* No matter where they come from or what they have experienced, ELLs have something in their prior knowledge that

TABLE 6.7   Summary of SIOP Components

PREPARATION	INSTRUCTION	REVIEW/ASSESSMENT
• Lesson planning • Language and content objectives • Use of supplementary materials • Meaningful activities	• Building background • Comprehensible input • Strategies • Interaction • Practice/application	• Review of key vocabulary and content concepts • Assess student learning • Feedback to students

could relate to the topic you are teaching. Prior knowledge is an important place to start in a lesson because it allows ELLs to add details to the things that they already know. It also gives them confidence because they feel that they know something and are able to contribute to the lesson. If you can access this prior knowledge in ELLs then you make them one-step closer to understanding what you are trying to teach. Use a **KWL (Know-Want to know-Learned)** chart. Every time you start a new topic of study at any grade level or level of language proficiency. Write the topic at the top of the table and have the students fill out what they already know about the topic and what they want to know. For those ELLs who are too young to write or whose language proficiency level is as beginner, they can draw pictures in place of words. You could have students complete these charts individually or in small groups. Once the charts are filled out, you compile the ideas of each individual student or group into one big class chart so that all students feel they have contributed to the topic of study. After you have completed the study of the topic, you have the students return to the chart and list the things that they have learned. It is a helpful way to conclude the lesson because it keeps the students focused on the task at hand and it allows them and you to see how much they have learned over the course of the lesson. An illustration of a KWL chart is presented in Table 6.8.

2. *Manipulatives are also a part of prior knowledge.* You could tell the students something and they have no idea what you said because they lack the vocabulary to

TABLE 6.8   KWL Chart

K	W	L
What I *K*now about _____?	What I *W*ant to learn about _____?	What I *L*earned about _____?

comprehend it but when you add manipulatives to your inquiry about a student's prior knowledge you are able to access much more. Manipulatives are items that the students can touch and move around. For example, an ELL may have no idea what the word *telephone* means but if you hold up a telephone while you ask them about it, the manipulative accesses prior knowledge that the word itself was unable to access. There are many forms of manipulatives that can be used in all subject levels including patterns, pictures, and blocks of various sizes, shapes, and colors.

3. *Increase the comprehensible input of your lesson by being careful of the English vocabulary you use.* Be aware of words that have multiple meanings. Your ELLs may be aware of one of the meanings of a word you use in class but may not have heard it in the context that you are using. This will activate the incorrect prior knowledge, leading them away from what you are trying to teach them. For example, you may be trying to teach a lesson on measuring the volume of liquids but the word *volume* may make the ELL think about the loudness of their stereo. It is important to address words that may have multiple meanings in order to keep the students focused on the meaning you want them to study. Be sure to avoid idiomatic expressions in your explanations. These are culture specific and tend to be very confusing to ELLs because they interpret them literally. For example, "you drive me up the wall" is an idiomatic expression that would be difficult for an ELL to understand. We use idioms daily as we speak. If you use them in the classroom, a disadvantage is created for the ELLs. Incorporate adjusted speech into your mainstream classroom to make your lessons more comprehensible to ELLs. Slow down your rate of speech to give the ELLs a chance to distinguish between individual words. Native speakers of a language speak it very quickly, making it difficult for nonnative speakers to comprehend. Slowing the rate of speech in the classroom is a simple thing we can do to help ELLs. Slower rate also refers to response time. It is important to give ELLs a longer wait-time for them to respond to questions because it takes them longer to process the question. Use the total physical response (TPR), that is, have the students link their learning to movements of the body. TPR can take place across grade levels; for example, a song like "The Hokie-Pokie" involves TPR. Finally, keep your speech in the active voice instead of the passive voice. Passive voice is difficult to understand and is generally not learned until advanced English grammar. Keep the passive voice out of your speech and it will be easier for your ELLs to comprehend what you are saying (Echevarria & Graves, 1998). Table 6.9 illustrates the problem via a classroom scenario.

4. *How you explain a task is extremely important.* Many times ELLs get lost at the beginning of a task because they did not understand your directions. Many ELLs need directions listed in a step-by-step format in both written and oral forms. Using a systematic and short form for presenting directions is important because students get lost in lengthy explanations written in paragraph form. Providing the directions in written form gives the students something to refer back to after the explanation is over. An oral explanation of the directions helps the students comprehend what is being asked, especially if there are written words that they do not recognize. Elicit students to repeat the directions after you have finished explaining them. Choose a student who has difficulty understanding directions to explain them back to you and the class. If she

TABLE 6.9   Where Is Your Homework?

FIRST DAY

Mr. Taylor: Open your text to page 19. For homework, I want you to read the explanation at the top of the page and complete all the odd problems.

NEXT DAY

Mr. Taylor to Jajaira (an ELL):   Where is your homework?

Jajaira: I didn't know which problems to do.

Mr. Taylor: Why not? Everyone else did their work and you were volunteering answers in class. I know you can do the work. Why aren't you trying harder to get your homework in?

Jajaira: I didn't know which problems to do.

Mr. Taylor: Why not? Everyone else did their work. Did you write the assignment down?

Jajaira: Yes, here it is. I didn't know what "odd" means. I mean, I know it means strange, but all the problems looked OK to me.

Mr. Taylor: Maybe you just have to listen carefully.

or he is successful, you know the majority of the students understand your directions. Students can also help to clarify directions by substituting words that are more common in their own vocabulary.

5. *Use a variety of techniques.* The types of techniques you use determine the success or lack of success in your classroom. Use a variety of techniques because not everyone learns in the same manner. There are visual, verbal, and manipulative learners. Consequently, your techniques need to include visual aids, manipulatives, demonstrations, gestures, body language, and modeling. **Modeling** is particularly important. For example, when you ask the students to complete an experiment using tools that may not be familiar to them, first model or demonstrate how to use these tools to complete the experiment and there will be a higher rate of success in that experiment.

6. *SIOP Strategies.* An example of general SIOP strategies to be used in Grades 4, 5, 6 include:

- Comprehensible Input: content/language
- Prior Knowledge: KWL, manipulatives (i.e., patterns, blocks)
- Speech: slower; total physical response; words/pictures/realia
- Explanation of Tasks: step-by-step written/oral directions—List (1, 2, 3, etc.), elicit students to repeat directions
- Techniques: visual aids, manipulatives, demonstrations, gestures, body language, modeling

7. *Rubrics.* The SIOP Model goes into detail about things a teacher must consider while preparing lessons that will include ELLs. It has abbreviated and extended SIOP scoring rubrics. You can use this rubric to score your own lesson plans to see if there are any areas in which you could improve for making your lessons more comprehensible for your students who are ELLs. The items included in this rubric not only help ELLs succeed in an SEI lesson, but they are good practices to use for all students. The key is to use them consistently.

Language Objectives

All SEI and SIOP lesson plans need to include techniques that support ELLs' language development. Inform your students of the language objectives for the class. Your language objectives need to include the following tasks.

- Developing students' vocabulary
- Reading comprehension skills practice or the writing process (brainstorm, outline, draft, revise, edit, and complete a text)
- Functional language use (how to request information, justify opinions, provide detailed explanations, etc.)
- Higher order thinking skills (articulating predictions or hypotheses, stating conclusions, summarizing information, and making comparisons)
- Grammar points (capitalization, and language structure)

Examples of ways to integrate language (SEI) and content objectives using content and language strategies are presented in Tables 6.10 and 6.11.

TABLE 6.10   Middle School Math and SEI Strategies

MATH STRATEGIES	SEI MATH LESSON: GRAPHS AND APPLICATIONS
• Interpreting graphs and charts • Using geometry • Using estimation • Building number sense	*Content Objectives:* ELLs will: 1. Make a graph for plotting coordinate points 2. Copy sets of ordered pairs and directions onto their graph paper 3. Graph coordinate points and follow the directions in order to draw a geometrical design
READING STRATEGIES • Understanding sequences • Developing an interpretation • Finding word meaning in context • Comparing and contrasting	*Language Objectives:* ELLs will be able to: 1. Articulate what vertical and horizontal lines are 2. Identify the names of these lines as the y-axis and the x-axis respectively 3. Identify where the origin is on the graph and understand the "origin" as meaning the "beginning" 4. Explain how to plot a coordinate point given an ordered pair 5. Describe how coordinate points are important in real life situations

TABLE 6.11   Fourth- and Fifth-Grade Reading and Science/Social Studies SEI Strategies

READING COMPREHENSION STRANDS

- Forming an initial understanding
- Understanding sequences
- Developing an interpretation
- Demonstrating a critical stance
- Finding word meaning in context
- Comparing and contrasting
- Composing and revising

SEI SOCIAL STUDIES AND SCIENCE LESSON: HOW WE RESPOND TO NATURAL DISASTERS

Content Objectives: ELLs will:

Social Studies:

1. Make a map showing where major floods and hurricanes happen
2. Create a public service poster to help people prepare for a disaster

Science:

1. Illustrate the formation of a hurricane
2. Identify two reasons why rivers flood

Language Objectives: ELLs will be able to:

- Participate orally in a KWL exercise on natural disasters
- Read aloud and silently sections of a news article
- Use new words in the context of a disaster and how people struggle to rebuild
- Read for information using photos, captions, and maps to understand the article
- Use grammatical forms orally and in writing, such as adverbs of comparison: stronger, highest, calmer, greatest, less, more
- Identify compound words such as *mudslide, earthquake, firefighters*
- Sum up information from the article
- Express personal ideas and/or feelings about natural disasters

SEI AND SIOP LESSON PLANS AND MODULES

A First-Grade Sheltered Mathematics Lesson: Months-of-the-Year Pictograph

Content Objectives.

1. Students will be able to construct a group unit pictograph using prior knowledge
2. Students will use, with the support of the teacher or facilitator, the quantitative data obtained from the previous night's homework assignment sheet containing the different birth dates of their family members

Language Objectives.

1. Students will be able to express their own birth date, write it, and recognize it on a calendar in the correct month, as well as the birth dates of their family members
2. Students will be able to orally express, write, and recognize the names of the months in order by using the *Subject + Copula + Predicate:* My mother's birthday is in _____ (month)._____ (month) is month number _____. My brother's birthday is in _____. _____ is month number _____.

Vocabulary used: January, February, March, April, May, June, July, August, September, October, November, December, Graph, Pictograph, vertical line, horizontal line, title/name.

Materials Needed for "Months-of-the-Year Pictograph".   Wall calendar poster, birthday cake laminated cards, transparency of a year calendar, tape, construction poster paper, chart paper, list of students' birth dates, completed homework assignment sheet containing list of dates of the different family members' birthdays (mother, father, grandmother, brother, sister, aunt, uncle, etc.), laminated figures, birthday story books, birthday cake stickers, sentence strips, copies of year calendar for each student

Procedure.   Cooperative learning groups to meet individual needs. Distribute three poster papers to each group. Ask the students to look at their homework sheet and, while you read the different months, have them raise their hands when they hear the month of a family member called. Give the student a laminated figure of a parent or relative as it fits the situation. Consider color coding the laminated figures according to monthly gemstone colors. After reading all the months and handing out the different laminated figures to the students, encourage the students to construct their own work group pictograph with the birth dates represented by the figures. This activity can be done either on a wall, blackboard, or by taping the three poster papers together and having the students work on the floor to place their coded laminated figures.

Review and Assessment.

-   Comprehensive review of key vocabulary: Attention to the pronunciation and meaning of lesson vocabulary, repetition and reinforcing of words at the beginning, in the middle, and again at the end of the lesson
-   Comprehensive review of key content concepts: Attention to content vocabulary related to content objectives in **cooperative learning** groups with opportunities for correcting errors and for clarifying misunderstandings
-   Feedback to student: Scaffolding students' learning by clarifying, discussing, and correcting responses; encouraging support within groups
-   Assessment of student comprehension and learning of all lesson objectives: Group/individual response that could be readily assessed, throughout the lesson, informal, authentic, multidimensional, directly linked to content and language objectives

A Third-Grade Sheltered Mathematics and Science Lesson: Pulse Rates: How Does Exercise Affect Pulse Rate?

Content Objectives.   Using an activity related to heart rate during rest and exercise, students will:

1. Record information on data tables
2. Draw a graph of their findings
3. Subtract pulse rates to find differences
4. Draw conclusions about the work of the heart system in response to different levels of activity

Language Objectives.

1. Use key vocabulary in oral, written, and reading activities
2. Formulate questions to elicit information patterns:
   - What is (your, his, her) resting heart (pulse) rate?
   - What is (your, his, her) heart rate at exercise? Which is higher? How much higher?
   - Which is lower? How much lower?
   - What is (your, his, her) heart rate at recovery?
   - How much lower is your recovery rate than your exercise rate?
3. Use language patterns to provide information:
   - My (his, her) _____ (pulse/heart) rate is _____.
4. Give commands: Give . . . Take . . . Write . . .
5. Use comparative degree to contrast: Higher . . . Lower . . .

Vocabulary Used.

> *Stethoscope:* An instrument used for listening to sounds produced within the body
> *Throbbing:* To beat rapidly; a pound. To vibrate rhythmically; pulsate
> *Pulse:* The rhythmical throbbing of arteries produced by the regular contractions of the heart
> *Data:* Information organized for analysis or used to make decisions
> *Graph:* A diagram that exhibits a relationship between two sets of numbers

Materials Needed.   Notebooks, stethoscope (from the school nurse or the Health education department), stopwatch (options: classroom clock with seconds, or teacher's wristwatch), body outline with/without pulse points, graph paper, data table, heart shapes (to build the graph with the student scores), KWL chart, word wall (to introduce key vocabulary words)

Procedure.   As an introduction you may want to begin with the questions: "What kinds of things does your doctor do when you go for a checkup? What is the doctor doing when she or he uses a stethoscope?" (Use the picture of the child being examined by the doctor.)

Activity #1.   Students begin by listening to their heart using the stethoscope (or placing their ear on a classmate chest—girl to girl, boy to boy). Students will write about what they hear in their notebooks. Guide them to record statements that indicate a rhythm or pattern to the heartbeats.

1. Have students place their hands on their chest to find the area where the heartbeat is strongest. This is where they will place the bell of the stethoscope or place their ear on someone else's chest
2. Students will record information in their notebook
3. Students will try to find the pulse in their arm, wrist, temples, or neck and indicate them on the body outline. Some pulse points are already identified for you *To take a pulse:* Use your index (pointer) finger and your middle finger. Gently place your finger on the pulse point and press lightly. You should feel a throbbing against your finger. Do not use your thumb as it has an artery in it, and you may feel your own pulse instead of the one you are trying to feel.
4. Have students enter what they learned and what they would like to learn on a KWL chart (What you already know, what you want to know, and what you will learn)

Activity #2.   Students will take their pulse by counting the number of beats they feel in 1 minute (You may want to count for 30 seconds and then add the same amount of heart pulse to complete the minute.) while resting, exercising, and recovering. You will use the stopwatch to time the whole class. Each trial will be recorded on the data table. Using the information recorded in the data table, teacher and students will record all the data at a graph.
Suggestion for the class graph:

- Use blue color for resting heart rate
- Use red for heart rate at exercise
- Use yellow for heart rate at recovery (5 minutes after exercise)

Review and Assessment

- Students will compare with others to see if they notice any trends or if they can account for differences on the class graph. Have students write a conclusion about what they learned from their graphs
- Have students predict, on the basis of their experiences, what will happen to their respiration when they exercise. Students should write a paragraph justifying their prediction
- Provide time for students to update their KWL charts. When they do this, encourage them to share their insights and information with others in the groups. Check to see that students have made the connection between exercise and increase in pulse rate

■ Have students select an item from the L column of their KWL chart related to heart rate. Have them write short multiple-choice questions based on the items. Students challenge each other to answer the questions

Individual Student Data Table

Name _____

Activity: Pulse Rate

	REST	EXERCISE	RECOVERY (5 MINUTES AFTER EXERCISE)
Trial 1			
Trial 2 (optional)			

Graph for Heart/Pulse Rate at Rest, Exercise, and Recovery (to be enlarged for class purposes)

160			
150			
140			
130			
120			
110			
100			
90			
80			
70			
60			
50			

Rest   Exercise   Recovery (5 minutes after exercise)

A High School Sheltered Health and Science Lesson: The Environment Is a Factor That Affects Your Total Health

Content Objective. Students will develop awareness on how the neighborhood a person lives in may affect his or her life (total health) in a positive or a negative way.

■ To learn how the environment plays a role in our personal health
■ To increase awareness of how our behavior to make healthier choices can improve the quality of our life

Language Objectives.

- Students will read the lesson instructions presented on the activity sheet
- List (write) the elements presented in their picture
- Discuss and explain how each element affects the environment (critical thinking, writing, and oral skills)
- Evaluate how their personal behavior may affect the environment he or she lives in (analysis and writing skills)
- Draw conclusions about what information was learned with the activity. Write one or two complete sentences

Concepts/Vocabulary: *environment, neighborhood, elements,* and *affects* and all the neighborhood picture "elements" drawn by the students

Materials Needed.   Drawing paper, pencil, coloring pencils, rulers

Procedure.   Students will fill out a KWL Chart. Review what they know about environment; discuss what they want to know about it; and what they will learn with this project. Class is divided in small cooperative teams (groups of 4 or 5). Teams are assigned to a "healthy neighborhood" or an "unhealthy neighborhood." Teams are to list as many elements as they can think of which make that neighborhood a healthy or an unhealthy environment (no less than five elements is suggested). Draw and color a neighborhood using the elements of the list—as other ideas flow they may be added to the picture. Prepare to do a presentation for the entire class explaining the elements in your assigned project and how these elements impact their health. Each individual student in the group must present an element.

Review and Assessment:.   Class will compare and contrast the different elements pointed out by the groups as positives or negatives. Activities for cooperative groups to give ideas on how a community involvement activity, a team may help improve the quality of a selected unhealthy neighborhood. Students are to draw an evaluation form (a rubric) to grade each others' efforts in this project. Students are to evaluate their own personal behavior, which may affect their neighborhood in a negative way and suggest what they can do to change that behavior to a positive one. Tell in 3 to 5 or more written sentences what they have learned with this project.

SUMMARY AND CONCLUSIONS: EFFECTIVE LANGUAGE AND CONTENT TEACHING FOR ELLS

The chapter delves deeper into effective teaching in ESL and content area classrooms across grade levels and stages of second language proficiency. Chapter 6 applies the curriculum standards, theoretical models, educational approaches, and teaching strategies addressed in Chapters 2, 3, and 4 and provides illustrations with instructional models and lesson plans and strategy descriptions.

The first major section discusses the complementary roles of ESL and content area teachers to teach ELLs with a focus on middle-and high school levels. It also examines existing myths and misconceptions about learning a second language and about the challenges of schooling ELLs. Chapter 6 has the goal of making all teachers aware that ELLs may be able to participate in content courses with grade-level objectives as the teachers deliver modified instruction to make information comprehensible to them. The academic success of ELLs and all students depends on teachers' knowledge and applications of effective teaching in the classroom to meet their language and academic needs.

The second major section encourages educators to apply cross-cutting methods in their craft. By using the instructional conversations, cooperative learning strategies and the SIOP model, lesson plans, problem-solving scenarios, teachers can become aware of the latest research on language acquisition, research-based methods for teaching ELLs, and effective pedagogy. With this knowledge, all teachers can become aware and empowered to help their ELLs: They will tend to measure ELLs' academic performance by the research-based standards and will raise their expectations of ELLs as gifted students who are capable of learning using two languages. With this information, core subject teachers can incorporate language skills into their curricula; they will be able to integrate and do two things in one way without making instruction for ELLs a time-consuming task. They can also accomplish successful teaching using these strategies with the selected curricula and within the time frame stipulated by their district or school. *All* teachers need to provide their students, including the ELLs in their classrooms, with the better of two worlds—English skills—while at the same time increasing the knowledge base of their students in their respective academic disciplines. This chapter can become a useful tool to accomplish this important goal in our U.S. educational reality.

REVIEW QUESTIONS

1. How would you compare the roles of the mainstream, ESL, and, if applicable, bilingual teachers? Is there a middle ground for cooperation, integration of content and language, application of methods and strategies for second-language development?

2. Discuss with your peers Table 6.2. and the 5 variables used for cross-standards comparisons. Examine and relate to your content area of expertise or TESOL expertise. How realistic and applicable for curriculum planning and schooling structures is this comparison? How would you use it? How would you improve it to fit your classroom/school reality?

3. Identify and examine a myth about language development and review its educational implications for ELLs. Design a module to train a partially trained audience: Describe the myth in simple terms and list educational recommendations.

4. What are the main components of the instructional conversation? Do you agree with the idea of "balanced" participation in the classroom? How can teacher talk and student talk coexist in the classroom?

5. What cooperative learning strategies are you familiar with? In your opinion, how do these strategies help any students? How

beneficial are they for classrooms that have ELLs? List your reasons.

6. What are the main components of the SIOP? Examine each of them and identify the sheltered strategies you are familiar with. Do you foresee that teachers will use the protocol in its entirety? How would you use the protocol in planning and delivering your lessons to ELLs?

CRITICAL THINKING QUESTIONS

1. Think of two reasons why teachers at all levels of instruction need to work together (e.g., planning lessons, using similar teaching strategies). Use Table 6.2: modify it to meet your needs and come up with a model for collaboration.

2. Visit a classroom and use the five variables from the comparisons as a template; identify each as you observe a content and/or language lesson. Describe your observations; give examples of each variable being practiced. Interview the teacher briefly: How does she or he label these variables? Do they have a different name? Why does he or she use them?

3. Design a graph, a table, or a summary to explain to a partially trained audience how the other four standards for effective pedagogy—joint productive activity, language and literacy development, challenging activities/complex thinking, contextualization—can be embodied in this important standard.

4. Develop a language and content objective for a lesson of your choice; consider grade level, content area, and ELLs' language development. Relate to the district's standards and benchmarks.

ACTIVITIES

1. Review the myths discussed in the chapter and reflect on those you did not know existed. What other questions, concerns, or misconceptions do you know of and would like to address? Talk to your peers about some of the misunderstandings that they may have and how this chapter can clarify some of their questions.

2. Examine the 10 components of the IC and provide examples of how they would become instructional recommendations in your school or program. Devise a plan of implementation for a partially trained audience; include examples for your content area peers. Are there any IC components that need to be prioritized? If so, which ones would go first? Which ones next?

3. Design a strategy to reinforce a topic of a particular lesson, including all the four language skills if possible. Write detailed directions for students to follow. Explain your strategy to peers in simple terms.

4. Examine a standards-based curriculum in a content area of your choice and grade level. Determine the language level of the ELLs. How would you strengthen the curriculum with the SIOP protocol? Provide an explanation/rationale for your decision.

5. Develop a lesson plan for developing ELLs' listening, speaking, reading, and writing English skills with the subject area of your choice. Select the grade level and language development stage of your ELLs. Demonstrate the lesson to your peers.

GLOSSARY

background knowledge Students' prior knowledge and experience with the topic (Tharp et al., 2000).

cognitive guided instruction Assumes that learning is an active mental process on the part of the student, which the teacher facilitates (Padron & Waxman, 1999).

communicative competence Often used instead of language proficiency to emphasize the idea that proficient language use extends beyond grammatical forms to include language (Richard-Amato, 1996).

comprehensible input Making adjustments to speech so that the message to the student is understandable using gestures, body language, realia, and slow, clear speech. (Echevarria, Vogt, & Short, 2000). Comprehensible input functions as well as social conventions of language to achieve communication (Krashen, 1989).

cooperative learning Allows students to take active roles in working and interacting together and the teacher assumes a role of facilitator (Calderón, 1991).

CREDE The Center for Research on Education, Diversity and Excellence is in charge of the research that supports the five standards for effective pedagogy.

culturally responsive instruction Instruction that promotes racial, ethnic, and linguistic harmony and equality as differences to be celebrated as an asset to the school community (Padron & Waxman 1999).

instructional conversation (IC) The IC is one of the five standards for effective pedagogy. It is the practice that allows students to engage in meaningful communication about the task at hand with each other and their teacher (Tharp, 1999; Tharp & Gallimore, 1988).

input hypothesis ($i + 1$) The $i + 1$ concept supports comprehensible teaching. It explains that a student understands language that is slightly above or beyond his or her current level of competence because of contextual clues or adapted use of language by the teacher and peers (Krashen, 1989).

jigsaw A cooperative learning activity that requires all students to take responsibility for one another's learning (Calderón, 1991).

joint productive activity One of the five standards for effective pedagogy. It refers to teamwork between teacher and students and among students themselves reaching toward a common end or product (Tharp et al., 2000).

KWL (Know-Want to Know-Learned). A worksheet with a 3-column chart to illustrate a continuum of learning. The first column is label "K" or "Know", (students would list everything they "know" about a topic), the second column "W" or "Want to know" (students would ask questions about what they want to learn about a topic), the third column is labeled "L" or "Learned" (students would complete this column after learning about a topic). The last column can also provide feedback to the teacher about the students' comprehension. The first two columns are usually generated through a whole class discussion facilitated by the teacher.

modeling Demonstrating proper use of language providing students with comprehensible input (Peregoy & Boyle, 2001).

realia Real-life objects and artifacts used to supplement teaching; it can provide effective visual scaffolds for ELLs (Schifini, 2000).

scaffolding Teacher support for learning and student performance of tasks through instruction, modeling, questioning, feedback, and graphic organizers. These supports are gradually withdrawn, thus transferring more and more autonomy to the student. Scaffolding activities provide support for learning that can be removed as learners are able to demonstrate strategic behaviors in their own learning activities (Echevarria, Vogt, & Short, 2000).

Sheltered English Instruction (SEI)   A concept of lesson planning and teaching that systematically weaves both language and content objectives through modified instruction in English without diluting the grade-level curriculum (Short, 1999). Teachers provide substantial amounts of support and assistance in the earliest stages of teaching a new concept or strategy, and then decrease the amount of support as the learner acquires experience through multiple practice opportunities (Echevarria, et al., 2000).

SIOP (Sheltered Instruction Observation Protocol)   The SIOP is a model of sheltered instruction that integrates content and language curriculum to be used with English learners (Echevarria, et al., 2000).

zone of proximal development (ZPD)   The ZPD is the distance between actual performance level of a student and that higher performance this student may be able to achieve as he or she works with his or her peers through the stimuli of cooperative learning and the use of language in a variety of forms to accomplish a task (Vygotsky, 1986).

REFERENCES

August, D. (2003, October). *Helping English language learners meet high literacy standards: Key issues and promising practices.* Keynote address delivered at the Waterbury Public Schools' First Annual Conference on Effective Strategies for Teaching Reading and Language Through Content to Diverse Students, Waterbury, CT.

August, D., & Hakuta, K. (Eds.). (1997). *Improving schooling for language-minority children: A research agenda.* Washington, DC: National Academy Press.

Asher, J., & Garcia, R. (1969). The optimal age to learn a foreign language. *Modern Language Journal, 53,* 334–341.

Calderón, M. E. (1991). The benefits of cooperative learning for Hispanic students. *Texas Researcher Journal, 2,* 39–57.

Calderón, M., August, D., & Minaya-Rowe, L. (2004). *ExC-ELL. Expediting comprehension for English-language learners. Training manual.* El Paso, TX: CRESPAR.

Calderón, M. E., & Minaya-Rowe, L. (2003). *Designing and implementing two-way bilingual programs. A step-by step guide for administrators, teachers and parents.* Thousand Oaks, CA: Corwin Press.

Calderón, M. E., & Carreón, A. (1994). Educators and students use cooperative learning to become biliterate and bilingual. *Cooperative Learning, 14*(3), 6–9.

Carlo, M. S., August, D., McLaughlin, B., Snow, C. E., et al. (in press). Closing the gap: Addressing the vocabulary needs of English language learners in bilingual and mainstream classrooms. *Reading Research Quarterly.*

Christian, D., & Genesee, F. (Eds.). (2001). *Bilingual education.* Alexandria, VA: TESOL.

Collier, V. P. (1995). *Promoting academic success for ESL students: Understanding second language acquisition for school.* Elizabeth: New Jersey Teachers of English to Speakers of Other Languages-Bilingual Educators.

Cummins, J. (1984). *Bilingualism and special education: Issues in assessment and pedagogy.* Clevedon, England: Multilingual Matters.

Cummins, J. (1996). *Negotiating identities: Education for empowerment in a diverse society.* Ontario: California Association for Bilingual Education.

Cummins, J., & Fillmore, L. W. (2000). *Language and education: What every teacher (and administrator) needs to know.* (Casette Recording No. NABE00-FS10A). Dallas, TX: CopyCats.

Dalton, S. S. (1998). *Pedagogy matters: Standards for effective teaching practice.* Santa Cruz, CA: Center for Research on Education, Diversity and Excellence.

Dalton, S., & Sison, J. (1995). *Enacting instructional conversations with Spanish-speaking students in middle and school mathematics.* Santa Cruz, CA:

National Center for Research on Cultural Diversity and Second Language Learning.

Dulay, H., Burt, M., & Krashen, S. (1982). *Language two.* New York: Oxford University Press.

Echevarria, J., Vogt, M. E., & Short, D. J. (2000). *Making content comprehensible for English language learners: The SIOP model.* Needham Heights, MA: Allyn & Bacon.

Echevarria, J., & Graves, A. (1998). *Sheltered content instruction: Teaching English-language learners with diverse abilities.* Boston, MA: Allyn and Bacon.

Genesee, F. (2000). *Brain research: Implications for second language learning.* Retrieved September 29, 2004 from the World Wide Web: www.cal.org/resources/digest/0012brain.html

Genesee, F. (1999). *Program alternatives for linguistically diverse students.* Santa Cruz, CA: Center for Research in Education, Diversity, & Excellence.

Heath, S. B. (1983). *Ways with words: Language, life, and work in communities and classrooms.* Cambridge: Cambridge University Press.

Hernández Ferrier, M. (2003, October). *No Child Left Behind, a new era in education—Providing hope for all children.* Keynote address delivered at the Waterbury Public Schools' First Annual Conference on Effective Strategies for Teaching Reading and Language Through Content to Diverse Students, Waterbury, CT.

Hertz-Lazarowitz, R., & Calderón, M. (1994). Facilitating teachers' power through collaboration: Implementing cooperative learning in elementary schools. In S. Sharan (Ed.), *Handbook of cooperative learning methods* (pp. 300–317). New York: Praeger.

Holowka, S., Brosseau-Lapré, F., & Petitto, L. A. (2002). Semantic and conceptual knowledge underlying bilingual babies' first signs and words. *Language Learning, 52,* 205–262.

Johnson, D. W., Johnson, R. T., & Smith, K. A. (1991). *Active learning: Cooperation in the college classroom.* Edina, MN: Interaction.

Kagan, S. (1992). *Cooperative learning.* San Juan Capistrano, CA: Kagan Cooperative Learning.

Krashen, S. D. (1989). We acquire vocabulary and spelling by reading: Additional evidence for the Input Hypothesis. *Modern Language Journal 73,* 440–464.

Krashen, S. D., Long, M., & Scarcella, R. (1979). Age, rate, and eventual attainment in second language acquisition. *TESOL Quarterly 13,* 573–582.

Lindholm-Leary, K. J. (2001). *Dual language education.* Clevedon, England: Multilingual Matters.

McLaughlin, B. (1992). *Myths and misconceptions about second language learning: What every teacher needs to unlearn.* Santa Cruz, CA: National Center for Research on Cultural Diversity and Second Language Learning.

National Reading Panel. (2000). *Teaching children to read: An evidence-based assessment of the scientific research literature on reading and its implications for reading instruction.* Washington, DC: National Institute of Child Health and Human Development.

National Research Council of the National Committee on Science Education Standards and Assessment. (1994). *National science education standards.* Washington, DC: Author.

Ovando, C. J., Collier, V. P., & Combs, M. C. (2003). *Bilingual and ESL classrooms. Teaching in multicultural contexts* (3rd ed.). Boston: McGraw Hill.

Padrón, Y. N., & Waxman, H. C. (1999). Classroom observations of the Five Standards for Effective Teaching in urban classrooms with ELLs. *Teaching and Change, 7,* 79–100.

Peregoy, S. F., & Boyle, O. F. (2001). *Reading, writing, and learning in ESL* (3rd ed.). New York: Longman.

Quiñones Feliciano de Benítez, A. B. (2001). *Training teachers of English language learners through instructional conversations: A metalogue.* Unpublished dissertation. Storrs: University of Connecticut Press.

Richard-Amato, P. A. (1996). *Making it happen: Interaction in the second language classroom.* White Plains, NY: Longman.

Romberg, T., & Wilson, L. (1995). Issues related to the development of an authentic assessment system for school mathematics. In T. Romberg (Ed.), *Reforming in school mathematics and authentic assessment* (pp. 1–18). Albany: State University of New York Press.

Shaw, J. M., Echevarria, J., & Short, D. J. (1999, April). *Sheltered instruction: Bridging diverse cultures for academic success.* Paper presented at the annual meeting of the American Educational Research Association, Montreal.

Schifini, A. (2000). *Second language learning at its best: The stages of language acquisition.* Carmel, CA: Hampton Brown.

Short, D. J. (1999). Integrating language and content for effective sheltered instruction programs. In C. Faltis & P. Wolfe (Eds.), *So much to say: Adolescents, bilingualism, and ESL in secondary schools* (pp. 105–137). New York: Teachers College Press.

Slavin, R. E. (1990). *Cooperative learning: Theory, research, and practice.* Englewood Cliffs, NJ: Prentice Hall.

Snow, C., & Hoefuagel-Hohle, M. (1978). Age difference in second language acquisition. In E. Hatch (Ed.), *Second language acquisition* (pp. 333–344). Rowley, MA: Newbury House.

Teachers of English to Speakers of Other Languages (TESOL). (1997). *ESL standards for pre-K–12 students.* Alexandria, VA: Author.

Tharp, R. G. (1999). *Proofs and evidence: Effectiveness of the five standards for effective teaching.* Santa Cruz, CA: Center for Research in Education, Diversity, & Excellence.

Tharp, R. G., Estrada, P., Dalton, S. S., & Yamauchi, L. A. (2000). *Teaching transformed: Achieving excellence, fairness, inclusion, and harmony.* Boulder, CO: Westview.

Tharp, R. G., & Yamauchi, L. A. (1994). *Effective instructional conversations in Native American classrooms* (Educational Practice Report No. 10). Santa Cruz, CA: National Center for Research on Cultural Diversity and Second Language Learning.

Tharp, R. G., & Gallimore, R. (1988). *Rousing minds to life: Teaching, learning, and schooling in social context.* New York: Cambridge University Press.

Thomas, W. P., & Collier, V. P. (2003). The multiple benefits of dual language. *Educational Leadership, 61*(2), 61–64.

Vygotsky, L. S. (1986). *Thought and language.* Cambridge, MA: MIT Press.

Wong Fillmore, L. (1991). Second language learning in children: A model of language learning in social context. In E. Bialystok (Ed.), *Language processing in bilingual children* (pp. 49–69). New York: Cambridge University Press.

ASSESSING LEARNING AND ACADEMIC ACHIEVEMENT IN ESL STUDENTS FOR INSTRUCTIONAL AND ACCOUNTABILITY PURPOSES

LEARNING OBJECTIVES

1. Understand core terminology and definitions of the psychometric paradigm, and assessment standards

2. Apply assessment recommendations derived from socioconstructivistic theory of development and learning

3. Apply principles, strategies, and standards of the alternative assessment model proposed

4. The reader will develop an attitude of commitment, advocacy, and empathy when serving ESL students

PREVIEW QUESTIONS

1. How are psychometric and alternative assessment model principles represented in standards developed by major professional organizations?

2. What are most important principles and assessment strategies of the psychometric and alternative assessment models?

3. How can ESL teachers apply recommendations derived from socioconstructivistic theory for the assessment of ESL students' learning?

4. Why is it important for ESL teachers to develop an attitude of commitment, advocacy, and empathy when serving ESL students?

Chapter 7 centers on the topic of how ESL and *all* teachers can conduct assessments of learning, development, and academic achievement in ESL classrooms, and do so in a systematic, valid, and reliable manner that fulfills both instructional and accountability purposes of the *Standards* movement. This objective is achieved by integrating research-based knowledge with best educational practices for ESL students in two areas, represented in Chapter 7 in two sections:

1. A contemporary view of the psychometric paradigm with its derived terminology and application of principles, centered on issues of validity and reliability, and **standards** given by professional organizations (e.g., American Educational Research Association [AERA], American Psychological Association [APA], & National Council on Measurement in Education [NCME], 1999) as criteria or guidelines of best practices for educational and psychological testing. This section emphasizes the need to provide lines of validity and reliability evidence for the specific uses and characteristics of the ESL student population for both standardized and alternative measures. That is, lines of validity and reliability evidence supported by data-based research in relation to: (a) the development or construction and validation of the instruments; and (b) most important, the knowledge level and personality factors (i.e., attitudes, values, beliefs, personal cultural and linguistic backgrounds, philosophical and theoretical schools of thought endorsed, etc.) introduced by evaluators when making interpretations and inferences leading to assessment, evaluation, and diagnostic decisions.

2. A proposed alternative assessment model that is based on an ethnic educator philosophy (the latter term first presented by the authors in Gonzalez, Brusca-Vega, & Yawkey, 1997) and an Ecological perspective, with its derived applications, including: (a) developmental stages of first-and-second-language learning (L1 and L2); (b) principles of alternative assessment that elaborate on standards provided by AERA, APA, and NCME (1999) based on best research-based practices for ESL students; (c) instructional and accountability purposes of assessment centered on how ESL teachers can implement classroom-based assessments; and (d) the implementation of a portfolio assessment system that is illustrated through vignettes in the companion Web site, www.ablongman.com/gonzalez1e.

In Chapter 7, we provide access for educators to the theoretical and educationally applied understanding of how to implement research-based knowledge, principles, and standards to link assessment to instruction (i.e., instructional purpose) and program evaluation (i.e., accountability purpose). Readers will be provided with plenty of examples of how to relate assessment and instruction back to principles and best practice recommended by research-based knowledge and national standards. Much like Chapter 5, the objective of Chapter 7 connects to the first theme of this book: to infuse an ethnic educator philosophy in order for school personnel to develop cultural awareness of the powerful effect of their attitudes and assessment and instructional practices on ESL and majority, low SES students' development and academic achievement. Together, all chapters of this book advocate the same ethnic educator philosophical and theoretical approach for ESL teachers to establish a smooth connection between instruction and assessment when serving ESL students in their classrooms. Through building understanding of philosophical and theoretical principles, and actual assessment principles and standards, we will try to persuade educators serving ESL and mainstream students at-risk of underachievement to:

1. Assume social and moral responsibility
2. Develop advocacy, commitment, empathy, and rapport
3. Adopt an ethnic educator philosophical approach and an ecological theoretical and educationally applied perspective

Finally, conclusions and theoretical and educationally applied implications close Chapter 7, with recommendations for classroom teachers of ESL students for the successful implementation of linking assessment to instructional strategies and practices.

A CONTEMPORARY VIEW OF THE PSYCHOMETRIC ASSESSMENT MODEL

Very few psychometrically sound assessment instruments are now available for ESL learners. Most standardized tests, even the ones created for ESL learners, have major methodological flaws. One major problem with standardized tests is that the measure of linguistic, cognitive, and learning variables are confounded with cultural, linguistic, and socioeconomic status (SES) differences, making diagnosis very difficult if evaluators solely rely on these assessment tools. More specifically, standardized tests confound normal ESL learning stages with developmental delays, and genuine handicapping conditions and disabilities (such as learning disabilities, speech handicaps, language disorders, and mental retardation). This methodological problem will be discussed more extensively in relation to the *Standards*. This problem results in the overrepresentation of ESL students in special education programs at the national level, already identified since the early 1980s. In the ESL population, most children are at-risk of developmental delays because of the negative impact of dysfunctional or negative external sociocultural and socioeconomic (SES) status conditions (e.g., parental educational level—connected to level of literacy in L1 and English; occupation and income of parents; level of social and cultural adaptation of parents; access to mainstream social benefits, such as health care, retirement, etc.; family and community—neighborhood quality of life; mental health of parents; etc.). For further discussion of this topic from an ecological perspective, see Gonzalez (2001).

The best tools for documenting program evaluation for meeting accountability purposes are still alternative assessments that can document teachers' effectiveness on students' progress in academic achievement and development. In addition to meeting the accountability purpose, alternative assessments can also meet instructional purposes. However, alternative or authentic assessments also need to be constructed and validated following strict psychometric principles and procedures. For instance, developmental scales and portfolios, including observational scales and teachers' rating scales as examples of classroom- and performance-based assessments also need to follow strict psychometric principles centered on validity and reliability. The alternative assessment system presented in the second section builds a multimedia portfolio that encompasses a teachers' rating scale and an observation scale that are constructed and used by classroom teachers following strict psychometric principles and procedures. Batteries of assessments also can include some standardized tests, but these should be used cautiously within a developmental and ecological frame work that complements them with alternative assessments (that are valid and reliable) across periods of time, developmental areas (i.e., a holistic assessment of physical, cognitive, linguistic, and socioemotional areas), content areas (i.e., encompassing language arts, literacy, mathematics, social science, and science), evaluators (i.e., including educators, parents, and support school personnel—school psychologists, social workers, physicians, etc.), and contexts (i.e., representing the family and school settings). Thus, psychometric principles, centered on validity and reliability constructs and other issues related to standards become key theoretical and research-based knowledge that ESL teachers need to master. The three subsections below bring for readers an in-depth discussion of how to apply knowledge of validity, reliability, and *Standards* into best classroom-based assessments for meeting instructional and accountability purposes.

VALIDITY CONSTRUCT: DIFFERENT LINES OF VALIDITY EVIDENCE SUPPORTING A SPECIFIC USE AND POPULATION

The most significant challenge in assessing ESL students is to understand how they develop their L1 and L2 as thinking and learning tools for enriching their cognitive, social, and emotional development, and for assimilating academic content. By increasing our knowledge base of how ESL children think, develop, and learn we can also increase different lines of **validity** evidence such as construct validity of assessment instruments (both authentic and standardized), which will also result in better internal validity (i.e., content or curriculum validity) and external validity (i.e., concurrent and predictive) and reliability. By improving curriculum validity we can also increase the link between assessment and instruction. By collecting accurate records of progress in learning, development, and academic achievement, we can also build systematic records for accountability and program evaluation (resulting also in improved curriculum and criterion-based validity). By properly training evaluators, including independent evaluators and classroom teachers, we can improve **reliability** (i.e., degree of agreement between raters), and also validity (all types of both internal and external validity).

Another important difficulty in social sciences, such as education, is to assess abstract constructs such as learning, development, and academic achievement. These abstractions or "constructs" are translated into "operational definitions" that transform abstractions such as mental processes into observable behaviors or characteristics in the form of performances and products that can be measured through test items. However, connections between constructs and behaviors are based on inferences and interpretations of the observations that connect the characteristics represented in test items into concepts or abstractions. Thus, it is important that the concepts or abstractions

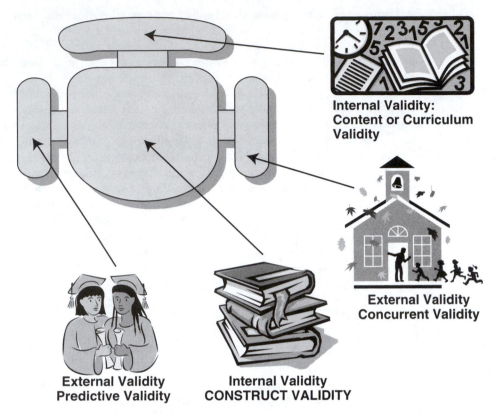

**Internal Validity:
Content or Curriculum
Validity**

**External Validity
Concurrent Validity**

**External Validity
Predictive Validity**

**Internal Validity
CONSTRUCT VALIDITY**

**FIGURE 7.1   Holistic View of Different Lines of Validity Evidence Centered on
Construct Validity**

supporting constructs be based on data-driven research that provides lines of validity evidence that supports experimentally the inferences and interpretations made based on students' test scores and response patterns. See Figure 7.1 for a representation of a holistic view of different lines of validity evidence.

An important evolution in the field of psychometrics has been moving from the traditional types of validity (i.e., external and internal with its subtypes of construct, content or curriculum, predictive, concurrent, etc.) to the more contemporary conceptualization of validity as "different lines of evidence, all in service of providing information relevant to a specific intended interpretation of test scores" (AERA, APA, & NCME, 1999). The emphasis of this modern conceptualization of validity is on establishing construct validity as "many lines of evidence [that] can contribute to an understanding of the construct meaning of test scores" (p. 5). Validity in modern terms refers to a "unitary concept," which is centered on construct validity and it encompasses internal and external validity within a holistic perspective thus, validity is "the degree to which all the accumulated evidence supports the intended interpretation of test scores for the proposed purpose" (p. 11). See Figure 7.2 for a graphical representation of the validity construct as a unitary concept of internal and external validity within a holistic perspective.

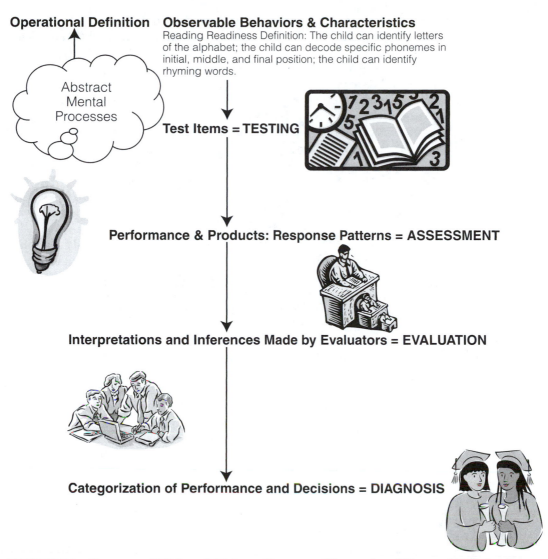

Operational Definition   **Observable Behaviors & Characteristics**
Reading Readiness Definition: The child can identify letters of the alphabet; the child can decode specific phonemes in initial, middle, and final position; the child can identify rhyming words.

Abstract Mental Processes

Test Items = TESTING

Performance & Products: Response Patterns = ASSESSMENT

Interpretations and Inferences Made by Evaluators = EVALUATION

Categorization of Performance and Decisions = DIAGNOSIS

FIGURE 7.2   Construct Validity: A Unitary Concept of Internal and External Validity from a Holistic Perspective

Thus validity "refers to the degree to which evidence and theory support the interpretations of test scores entailed by proposed uses of tests" (AERA, APA, & NCME, 1999, p. 9). Research-based evidence needs to be accumulated to support a proposed use of a test, through many lines of evidence for each specific intended interpretation of scores for a particular population. That is, tests are not validated in a vacuum, or, in general, independent of context of use and population; but must be supported by research-based evidence to provide a sound scientific basis for demonstrating a "rationale for the relevance of the interpretation to the proposed use" (p. 9).

The conceptual framework, supported by scientific evidence, demonstrates how constructs are different and relate to other constructs, resulting in specific "knowledge, skills, abilities, processes, or characteristics to be assessed" (p. 9).

In addition, a central idea is that "the validity of test score interpretations may be limited by construct-irrelevant components or construct underrepresentation" (ibid, p. 9). That is, when the use of a test results in unintended consequences, such as misdiagnosis over-representing ESL children in special education categories or in limited English proficient categories, the test lacks construct validity either because: (1) it is sensitive to characteristics not intended to be measured, or (2) the test fails to represent the construct to be assessed (in the form of behavioral manifestations that are not represented or mapped into test items). It is very important for educators to understand that the specific "conceptual framework points to the kinds of evidence that might be collected to evaluate the proposed interpretation in light of the purposes of testing" (AERA, APA, & NCME, 1999, p. 9).

Then, validation process can include evidence of how judges record and evaluate data and "analyses of its appropriateness of these processes to the intended interpretation or construct definition" (p. 13). Thus, the process of construction and validation of tests entails the development of "scientifically sound validity arguments to support the intended interpretation of test scores and their relevance to the proposed use" (p. 9).

According to the *Standards* document (AERA, APA, & NCME, 1999, pp. 11–17), there are six different procedures to demonstrate validity evidence when constructing and/or validating a test (see Figure 7.3), including:

1. Evidence based on *test content by experts* who analyze parts of the test, such as test items or tasks, for judging how well they represent various aspects of its content that differ systematically in relation to the construct and behaviors it supposedly measures, and to the inferences made in relation to its use and population. Evidence relates to potential sources of irrelevant difficulty or easiness to the content of a test

---

1. Evidence based on *test content* by experts

---

2. Evidence based on *response processes* by experts

---

3. Evidence based on *internal structure of a test*

---

4. Evidence based on *relations to other variables external to the test*

---

5. Evidence based of the *relation of test scores to a relevant criterion,* either in a predictive or concurrent manner

---

6. Evidence based on *educational and social consequences of testing,* both *intended* and *unintended*

FIGURE 7.3   Six Different Procedures Demonstrating Validity Evidence When Constructing and/or Validating an Assessment Instrument

that bring in construct underrepresentation or construct-irrelevant components with unfair advantages or disadvantages to particular subgroups of examinees.

2. Evidence based on *response processes* by experts conducting analysis of individual responses and strategies to test items, and between the test and other variables. By having experts analyze the response processes of actual examinees, valuable evidence about the actual meaning of interpretations and inferences made out of test responses can be obtained. In addition, the analysis of processes is also done in relation to observers or judges evaluating the examinee's performances or products. The analysis is focused on judging the degree of consistency of evaluators' application of relevant criteria and resulting interpretations of performances or behaviors. Thus, as stated in the *Standards* document, "validation may include empirical studies of how observers or judges record and evaluate data along with analyses of the appropriateness of these processes to the intended interpretation or construct definition" (AERA, APA, & NCME, 1999, p. 13). Gonzalez, Bauerle, Black, and Felix-Holt (1999) conducted a study of the effect of evaluators' prior knowledge, cultural and linguistic backgrounds, and attitudes on ESL students' diagnosis with educational assessments. This study demonstrated with evidence the tremendous effect of evaluators' processes on their interpretations and inferences made out of batteries of educational assessments.

3. Evidence based on *internal structure of a test* can provide an indication of the relationship among test items and test components, the construct measured, and the behaviors, performances, and products based on which inferences and interpretations are made. A test can measure a single dimension of behavior, or multiple components that are homogeneous but also distinct from each other. Patterns of response for particular or groups of items need to be identified, especially in relation to groups of examinees.

4. Evidence based on *relations to other variables external to the test*, such as relation to other tests measuring the same construct, different constructs, or related constructs. These relationships should be consistent with expectations based on the underlying construct that the test measures. Convergent evidence is provided by tests expected to measure the same construct (e.g., two tests of reading readiness), and "discriminant" evidence is provided by test measuring different constructs (e.g., a test of reading readiness and a test of English language proficiency). This empirical evidence is provided by correlations.

5. Evidence of the *relation of test scores to a relevant criterion*, either in a predictive or concurrent manner. The degree of accuracy of predictive (for long-term implications such as future performance for placement or admission purposes) or concurrent tests (for short-term implications such as instructional decisions) may be different. In addition, the criterion may have different meanings for different uses and populations, so it is important to analyze the inferences and interpretations of test performance for specific purposes.

6. Evidence based on *consequences of testing*, both intended and unintended: educational placement, instructional, grouping in ability levels, grade passing or retention, and all other social and educational short- and long-term consequences. For instance, placement of ESL children into special education classes are among the

most serious consequences of testing, because they are long-term and may carry some construct underrepresentation or construct-irrelevant components for that particular use and population.

The integration of various lines of validity evidence therefore requires expert judgment on the part of informed educators who have received high-quality professional development on assessment issues. The validation process includes professional judgment to examine relevant literature on theory and data-based research conducted, and to collect and analyze local evidence within the actual contexts of use that can support interpretation of the test use for a particular population. Test developers have the responsibility of presenting rationales for each recommended interpretation and use of test scores, supported by evidence and theory. However, test users are liable for judging the quality of the validity evidence provided by test developers and publishers and its relevance to local educational uses and populations. This is a very important issue for ESL educators: to assume responsibility for accurate assessment. Educators must understand that "no test is valid for all purposes or in all situations" (Gonzalez et al., 1999, p. 18). Ultimately, it is the professional ESL educator who needs to take a leadership role in guiding local education agencies in engaging *local validation processes*, in light of relevant literature, professional judgment, and collection of different lines of validity evidence for the specific use and population. It is important to understand that test users share responsibility of test validity with test developers and publishers. As well stated in the *Standards* (1999), "the test user is ultimately responsible for evaluating the evidence in the particular setting in which the test is to be used" (p. 11), especially when the use for which the test was developed is different than the use that the test is given for by an evaluator. Research findings reported in published studies can inform ESL educators of relevant conceptual frameworks and validity evidence for the appropriateness of context of use and population of a specific test. Research studies relevant to the test use and population that are published in academic and applied outlets during the last 5 years need to be consulted. Good sources include academic journals, books, and critiques and evaluations of tests, which appear in databases (such as ERIC and PSYLIT) and the Buros Mental Yearbook (see the Companion Web site for links).

RELIABILITY CONSTRUCT: NECESSARY BUT NOT SUFFICIENT CONDITION FOR VALIDITY

Reliability is defined as the consistency or stability of measurement of a behavior or underlying construct across repeated testing sessions and across evaluators (AERA, APA, & NCME, 1999). However, a person's true score is just an abstraction because in real-life settings individuals will always exhibit some degree of variation in their performance in a test, and always there will be some subjectivity involved in evaluators who are administering, scoring, and interpreting test performances. Whenever testing occurs, even in the most appropriate conditions, there always will be some degree of error of measurement, which can be random or systematic, and may affect groups or individuals. Some external factors may affect the degree of test reliability, such as evaluators' subjectivity or testing conditions.

In addition, some internal factors may also affect the degree of test reliability, such as individual factors of an examinees' motivation, interest, attention span, physical health, tiredness, and so on. However, some changes in performance are not the result of error of measurement, but of maturational or developmental changes, or just an intervention or learning process that occurred between measures (i.e., comparison of first and second testing for reliability purposes). As a rule of thumb, especially for young children, measures are *not* comparable after 6 months intervals because of developmental factors. Furthermore, different forms of a test should be used to avoid transfer of learning effect that invalidates comparability of measures between testing sessions for reliability purposes. Thus, internal and/or external factors may reduce the extent to which test scores and its uses and interpretations can be generalized within a given confidence level.

According to the *Standards* document (1999, pp. 27–31), reliability is estimated by three broad procedures, by administering:

1. Parallel forms of a test on separate sessions (i.e., alternate form coefficients)
2. Same instrument on separate occasions (i.e., leading to test-retest or stability coefficients)
3. Same instrument analyzed based on individual items or subsets of the items within a single administration (i.e., leading to internal consistency coefficients)

In order to get high reliability values it is recommended that data be collected for the specific use and population of interest at the local level, because a nationally represented sample reported by a test publisher may differ widely from that obtained for a more homogeneous sample. It is important to understand that also for reliability, as indicated above for validity, error of measurement can be introduced by the test itself as well as by the evaluator. This error of measurement affects not only standardized test, but also alternative assessments, such as observations and portfolios. As well stated by the *Standards* (1999),

> Measurements derived from observations of behavior or evaluations of products are especially sensitive to a variety of error factors. These include evaluator biases and idiosyncrasies, scoring subjectivity, and intra-examinee factors that cause variation from one performance or product to another. (p. 29)

It is also important to highlight that a test can be reliable but not valid. That is, measurement can generate consistent scores or results, but that the measurement shows reliability does *not* mean that we are measuring appropriately or validly the characteristic or behavior (and underlying construct) that we want to measure. Thus, validity is a necessary, but not sufficient, condition for reliability.

Standards

In 1999, AERA, APA, and NCME published the *Standards for Educational and Psychological Testing*. The *Standards* document is the result of a joint effort of a Management Committee representing these three sponsoring organizations in collaboration with a large number of other sponsoring organizations from scientific, professional, trade, and advocacy groups. The 1999 version of the *Standards* was produced with extensive feedback provided by individuals representing a large number of sponsoring organizations that participated in revision efforts encompassing three rounds of comments and written feedback. The purpose of the *Standards* is to "promote the sound and ethical use of tests and to provide a basis for evaluating the quality of testing practice" (1999, AERA, APA, & NCME, p. 1), and "to provide criteria for the evaluation of tests, testing practices, and the effects of test use" (p. 2).

The *Standards* document recognized that the most important contribution of psychological and educational research has been the development of assessment instruments, which if well developed can help individuals and social institutions, and the society at large, develop and achieve their educational goals. However, educational and psychological assessment instruments need to have extensive data-driven evidence supporting its accuracy or validity for both the test construction and validation processes for a particular purpose or use and population. Deviations from uses supported by validity evidence can create improper uses of tests that can become very harmful to individual test takers, institutions, and the society at large, and ultimately become an obstacle for a more equitable access to education and employment.

Discussion of *Standards*.   The specific *Standards* for ESL students discussed below will review the conditions or context under which a given standard is relevant for the proper use of assessments supported by validity evidence, proper training of evaluators, and decision making in relation to policy and instructional issues.

> **Standard 1.** Testing practice should be designed to reduce threats to the reliability and validity of test score inferences that may arise from *language differences*. For all test takers, tests that use language are in part measures of their language skills. This issue is even more important for ESL students when tests are in English, or constructed for English-speaking populations and then translated to their native language.
>
> **Standard 2.** When credible research evidence reports that test scores differ in meaning across subgroups of linguistically diverse test takers, then, to the extent feasible, test developers should collect for *each linguistic subgroup* studied the same form of validity evidence collected for the examinee population as a whole. Several variations may be present in relation to appropriateness of test content, internal structure of test responses, relation of test scores to other external variables, or other response processes used by examiners. Consequently, if ESL students are not represented in the validation or standardization sample, then norms are not valid and reliable for its use with that particular population.
>
> **Standard 3.** When testing an examinee proficient in two or more languages for which the test is available, the examinee's *relative language proficiencies* should be determined. The test generally should be administered in the test taker's more proficient language, unless proficiency in the less proficient language is part of the assessment. If an examinee is not proficient in the language of assessment, then construct-irrelevant components are introduced in the assessment process.

Standard 4. *Linguistic modifications* recommended by test publishers, as well as the rationales for the modification, should be described in detail in the test manual. Typically, unless noted otherwise in the test manual, deviations from standardized administration procedures mean that the norms cannot be applied to the interpretation of test scores. Clinical administrations of standardized tests, also known as testing-the-limits techniques, are useful for instructional purposes but interpretation of individual performance cannot be done anymore in relation to standardized test scores or "norms" (i.e., defined above as *relative standards*).

Standard 5. When there is credible evidence of score comparability across regular and modified tests or administrations, no flag should be attached to a score. When such evidence is lacking, specific information about the nature of the modification should be provided, if permitted by law, to assist test users to interpret and act properly on test scores. This standard is related to the previous one, as federal and state policies mandate test modifications for ESL students, who are still in the process of acquiring English, who need to be provided with dictionaries, oral instructions in their native language, and so forth. Yet, altering standardized administration procedures may introduce error of measurement and invalidates norms. Therefore, knowledgeable educators need to use their professional judgment to find validity evidence, in the form of previous data-based research studies, and develop local norms in order to decide on the appropriateness of a specific test use and its educational implications for ESL students.

Standard 6. When a test is recommended for use with linguistically diverse test takers, test developers and publishers should provide the information necessary for appropriate test use and interpretation. Even though publishers are required to provide validity and reliability information in test manuals, data-based lines of evidence may not be referenced due to scarcity of representation of language-minority students in norm samples, and the large number of diverse cultural and linguistic groups in the United States. Therefore, educators have the responsibility to conduct local studies of the appropriateness of use of a particular test for the specific ESL students' groups that are present in their region.

Standard 7. When a test is translated from one language to another, the methods used in establishing the adequacy of the translation should be described, and empirical and logical evidence should be provided for score reliability and the validity of the translated test's score inferences for the uses intended in the linguistic groups to be tested. It is important to understand that there is wide diversity of dialectal variation even within the same language group of Spanish-speaking students. That is to say that Puerto Rican, Mexican American, and several groups represented in Central American (i.e., Dominican Republic, Panama, Nicaragua, Guatemala, Costa Rica) and South American regions (e.g., Andes countries—Ecuador, Colombia, Venezuela, Peru, Chile, and Bolivia; Argentina, Paraguay, and Uruguay) have sociohistorical factors affecting their communicative use of the Spanish language. Even though individuals from these countries use the same academic language, their social communicative use of Spanish varies widely in vocabulary use, syntax and grammar structures, and semantic and sociolinguistic conventions.

Standard 8. When multiple language versions of a test are intended to be comparable, test developers should report evidence of test comparability. Tests that have been translated to different languages, or adapted for different dialects, should have parallel norms, uses, and interpretations and inferences based on examinees' test performance.

Standard 9. Inferences about a test taker's general language proficiency should be based on tests that measure a range of language features, and should not be based on a single linguistic skill. Language proficiency is a complex or multidimensional construct and cannot be measured by single trait or discrete-point tests. For instance, a test of vocabulary ability cannot be considered as representative of an ESL student's English language proficiency level. In addition, it is important to understand that a bilingual individual may have different language proficiency levels across a variety of language functions (i.e., social and academic across content areas) and language skills (i.e., listening comprehension, reading and writing, and oral skills). As well stated by the *Standards* document, "Measures of competency in all relevant English language skills (e.g., communicative competence, literacy, grammar, pronunciation, and comprehension) are likely to be most valuable in the school context" (1999, p. 94). Then, a bilingual individual may not present a continuous degree of language proficiency level, but variations in relation to types and degrees of bilingualism, and language dominance, and a variety of individual differences (i.e., degree of familiarity with test-taking situations and skills developed, literacy levels in L1 and L2, cognitive skills and aptitudes, motivational and attitudinal factors, etc.).

Standard 10. When an interpreter is used in testing, the interpreter should be fluent in both the language of the test and the examinee's native language, should have expertise in translating, and should have a basic understanding of the assessment process. This is a very important standard because most school districts are using interpreters for accommodating tests to the needs of ESL students. Interpreters functioning as evaluators, or helping evaluators, should be knowledgeable of administration and interpretation procedures, constructs measured, and lines of validity in relation to uses of tests and populations tested. The ideal situation is to have a trained bilingual examiner so that no significant threats are introduced to the validity of inferences based on test results.

Discussion of Issues Related to the *Standards*

Differentiating among testing, assessment, evaluation, and diagnosis. An important point made by the *Standards* is to differentiate between *testing* and *assessment*. Testing is defined as the use of "an evaluative device or procedure in which a sample of an examinee's behavior in a specified domain is obtained and subsequently evaluated and scored using a standardized process" (AERA, APA, & NCME, 1999, p. 3). Assessment comprises a broader term, "commonly referring to a process that integrates test information with information from other sources" (p. 3), such as a battery of assessments comprised of educational and family history, neurological evaluations, and other alternative assessments (i.e., teachers ratings, portfolios, parents' surveys and interviews, observations, etc.).

Moreover, it is our position that testing and assessment are the first two steps in the process, followed by *evaluation* and *diagnosis* (see Figure 7.2). Then, we propose the existence of a four-layered process that includes (from more superficial to more complex): testing, assessment, evaluation, and diagnosis. We define *evaluation* as the analysis of the underlying abilities and skills assessed in order for the evaluator to be able to make interpretations of students' test scores and performances. Then, evaluation involves a knowledgeable examiner who can analyze student's responses and patterns of responses and transform them into meaningful educational applications, such as strengths and weaknesses in relation to developmental patterns and individual and group characteristics. Evaluation has as a purpose to provide instructional or curriculum validity for linking information gained on assessment processes to instruction. However, evaluators need to be knowledgeable about the link between content represented in test items and subtests and the underlying constructs measured, which required theoretical prior knowledge on abilities and skills assessed (e.g., how ESL students learn L1 and L2 language and what cognitive and academic language skills are transferred from L1 to L2 across content areas) as well as on psychometrics (e.g., process of test construction and validation, basic concepts such as validity and reliability). Thus, *evaluation* stresses the importance of *training* among evaluators because it is through their personality and knowledge levels that they will analyze and derive interpretations and inferences from students' test scores as evidenced by behaviors, performances, and/or products.

Finally, *diagnosis* is a decision-making process in which the evaluator engages in synthesis of information gained through the analytic process of evaluating students' individual performances or profiles. Then, diagnosis emphasizes synthesis, and evaluation focuses on analysis. When doing a diagnosis, evaluators engage in categorization of analyzed strengths and weaknesses, and individual and group characteristics, into a conclusive or holistic picture of the student's development, learning, and related educational decisions as they connect to criterion-referenced instruments or standards used as benchmarks (i.e., placement, learning and teaching accommodations or treatments, and potential and expressed ability).

For the case of ESL students, diagnosis also involves making a difference between normal L2 learning situations and genuine learning difficulties, disabilities, and handicapping conditions. Since the early 1970s and the early 1980s, educators have raised the flag for the overrepresentation of ESL students in special education categories, such as learning disabilities, language disorders, speech handicaps, and mental retardation (i.e., Mercer, 1973, for the case of mental retardation, and Ortiz and Yates, 1983, for the case of learning disabled). Thus, *differential diagnosis* is an "art" that evaluators need to master by developing expertise in theory, research evidence, and psychometrics, and most important, an *attitude of advocacy and commitment* for representing the best educational interest of ESL students and their families. Evaluators who act as committed advocates for ESL students can recommend language development and enrichment educational programs to develop the ESL students' potential for learning before any final mislabeling or misdiagnosis is reached prematurely. High-quality language development and enrichment educational programs for ESL students, with a sustained record of research evidence are rare, but do exist. Among the most recognized ones are one-way and two-way bilingual educational programs (for a summary record of research evidence collected during the last 2 decades, see Collier & Thomas, 2004, and Chapter 5 in this book).

Three situations of differential diagnosis of ESL students.   Some guidelines that we can provide educators for attempting to conduct an accurate differential diagnosis between normal L2 learning situations and genuine learning difficulties and handicapping conditions include three situations that compare language learning and cognitive processes (see Table 7.1). The first situation of resilient ESL students is the easiest and most clear-cut diagnosis: students are fluent in both L1 and L2, or are fluent in at least L1 even though L2 is still at low proficiency levels. This language maturation is accompanied by cognitive processes that are developing at normal or above-normal levels for chronological age.

The second situation of at-risk ESL students involves limited proficiency in both L1 and L2, but they still show a normal nonverbal cognitive development when examined with valid and reliable instruments and by knowledgeable and committed evaluators. These students are at-risk of experiencing learning difficulties if placed in a language remedial program that understimulates their potential and results in developmental delays, and even developmental regression. This is the case, for instance, for Kindergarten Hispanic students whose dominant language is Spanish, but who come

TABLE 7.1.   Three Situations of Differential Diagnosis between Normal L1 and L2 Learning Processes and Genuine Learning Disabilities and Handicapping Conditions

SITUATION	COGNITIVE PROCESSES	L1 AND L2 PROCESSES
Resilient ESL students	Normal or above normal	Fluent L1 & L2 Fluent L1 and low L2
ESL students at-risk due to external factors (e.g., poverty, schooling, low socioeconomic factors, etc.)	Developmental delays due to external factors Normal nonverbal cognitive development No disabilities No handicapping conditions	Limited L1 & L2 in certain areas
Genuine special education cases (possible disabilities and/or possible handicapping conditions)	Below normal verbal and nonverbal cognitive development with possible Mental Retardation Normal or above normal verbal and nonverbal cognitive development with possible speech or language impairment or specific learning disability (with some areas of weakness, e.g., attention, perceptions, memory, mental representations or images).	Limited L1 & L2 across areas (flat profile) Limited L1 & L2 in certain areas ("peaks and valleys" profile)

from low literacy families, and who show some social language proficiency but not much academic language proficiency in either Spanish and/or English. If these at-risk students are misplaced in regular English classrooms, they will show developmental delays due to external inappropriate educational conditions, and not because of genuine internal handicapping conditions or disabilities (e.g., learning disabilities or mental retardation).

The third situation of genuine special education ESL students represents the presence of genuine learning difficulties or disabilities or handicapping conditions. That is, students are also limited in L1 and L2 (just like the second situation), but in addition do show particular profiles of verbal and nonverbal cognitive development as measured by accurate measures and committed evaluators.

Table 7.1 shows three possible scenarios of genuine disabilities or handicapping conditions. The first scenario is *mental retardation*, with a below-normal cognitive ability, typically demonstrated by a "flat" profile in both cognitive and language processes. The Individuals with Disabilities Education Act (IDEA) defines mental retardation as "significant sub-average general intellectual functioning existing concurrently with deficits in adaptive behavior and manifested during the developmental period, which adversely affects a child's educational performance" (Gonzalez, et al., 1997, p. 23). The second scenario presents the case of *speech* or *language impairments*, defined by IDEA as "a communication disorder such as stuttering, impaired articulation, a language impairment, or a voice impairment, that adversely affects a child's educational performance" (p. 24). The second case is illustrated by above-normal or normal cognitive processes, and limited L1 and L2 processes only in certain areas, such as oral language in reference to pronunciation, phonological development, and auditory discrimination. The third scenario refers to *specific learning disabilities* that are illustrated by overall or general normal or above-normal cognitive processes, with some areas of weaknesses referring to memory, perception, or attention skills (what is referred to as a "peaks and valleys" profile). Language processes are limited for L1 and L2 only across certain areas that relate to attention, perception, and memory cognitive processes. Specific learning disabilities are defined by IDEA as:

> A disorder in one or more of the basic psychological processes involved in understanding or using language, spoken or written, which may manifest itself as an imperfect ability to listen, think, speak, read, write, spell, or do mathematical calculations. The term includes such conditions as perceptual disabilities, brain injury, brain dysfunction, dyslexia, and developmental aphasia. The term does not apply to children who have learning problems that are primarily the result of visual, hearing, or motor handicaps, of mental retardation, or emotional disturbance or of environmental, cultural, or economic disadvantage. (p. 24)

It is important to emphasize that for demonstrating the presence of genuine handicapping conditions or disabilities both verbal and nonverbal cognitive assessments that take into consideration cultural and linguistic differences have been used. In addition, a battery of standardized and authentic assessments needs to be collected, which involves multiple evaluators across contexts and across developmental and academic achievement or content areas. Multiple samples of behaviors across school and home contexts will bring ecological validity to the differential diagnosis. The Multimedia Portfolio presented in the last section of this chapter, and also in the form of vignettes in the companion Web site, illustrates an educational application to the case of ESL young students that has ecological validity.

Differences between tests and scales or inventories.   It is interesting also to note that the *test* and *scale or inventory* labels also carry conceptual differences. A "test: is an instrument on which responses are evaluated for their correctness or quality" . . . [whereas] . . . "scales or inventories are measures of attitudes, interests, and dispositions" (AERA, APA, NCME, 1999, p. 3) that can also be standardized, such as tests. Both tests and scales or inventories have a number of variable dimensions: (1) the mode in which the materials are presented (such as paper and pencil or computerized tests), (2) the degree of standardization of testing materials (multiple choice or true false selection from a menu, or the production of an open-ended response), and (3) the degree of similarity with natural context in which the behavior measured occurs (simulation or a particular setting). Standardization of tests just means the development of a process or methodology by which "test-taker responses to test materials are evaluated and scored" (p. 3). Standardized scores can only be used when administration, scoring, and interpretation conditions match the use and population for which the test was originally constructed and validated.

Definition of *absolute and relative standards*.   It is also important to define a **standard** as the interpretation of test scores in an absolute manner. "Absolute interpretations relate the status of an individual or group to defined standards. These *absolute standards* may originate in empirical data for one or more populations or be based on authoritative judgment" (AERA, APA, & NCME, 1999, p. 29). The *Standards* developed by AERA, APA, and NCME (1999) impose authoritative judgment on best practices to comply with when using educational and psychological testing. In addition, federal and state mandates impose on educators a set of relative standards, that is, "the standing on an individual or group within a reference population" (p. 29).

Role of evaluators' training on validity.   Evaluators also need to be properly trained to use assessment instruments because their personality becomes the most important tool for assessment, ultimately affecting the validity of the administration, scoring, and interpretation of tests scores and diagnostic and placement or other instructional decisions (for further discussion see Gonzalez et al., 1999). As well stated in the *Standards* document (AERA, APA, & NCME, 1999), "test developers and those selecting and interpreting tests need adequate knowledge of psychometric principles such as validity and reliability" (p. 2). Furthermore, evaluating and using the *Standards* "involves professional judgment that is based on knowledge of behavioral science, psychometrics, and the community standards in which the professional field to which the test applies" (p. 4). That is, ESL educators need to apply their "research and experiential evidence regarding feasibility of meeting the standard" for the particular use and population for which they select a test (p. 4).

By having sets of criteria or standards, we can advocate that those involved in policy debate and educational practice and decision-making processes must be fully informed. That is the rationale for using this chapter for informing ESL teachers and all teachers about the existence of the *Standards* document and its meaning and application in the assessment of ESL students. Thus, both the proper use of the tests and the high-quality professional development of evaluators, including knowledge of standards and criteria, are major points for implementing valid and reliable educational and psychological assessments.

Alternative Assessment Model

Developmental stages of L1 and L2 learning.   The alternative assessment model that we endorse recognizes the need for educators of ESL students to understand some principles of L1 and L2 learning and development. We also argue that educators of ESL students need to understand the interface of language development with cognitive and socioemotional development. We present a brief discussion of language developmental stages in ESL students, which also take into account related cognitive and socioemotional development.

Some researchers (McLaughlin, Blanchard, & Osanai, 1995; Saville-Troike, 1987; Tabors & Snow, 1993) have conducted data-based studies that provide some guidelines for the sequential stage-like developmental progression of L1 and L2 acquisition in young children. Of course, this developmental sequence of L1 and L2 acquisition is also subject to internal and external factors affecting its variation, such as degree of exposure, high or low opportunity or high or low extrinsic and/or intrinsic motivation for using the languages, quality of instructional experience, home environments and family structure factors, individual differences, level of socioeconomic status, and so forth (see Gonzalez, 2001, for an in-depth discussion of these factors).

There are four sequential developmental stages for L1 and L2 learning that have been identified in the literature (McLaughlin, Blanchard, & Osanai, 1995; Saville-Troike, 1987; Tabors & Snow, 1993; see Figure 7. 4), encompassing:

1. **Silent period or L1 stage.** The first stage refers to the use of the home language in different social settings. At first, ESL children have the choice of either continuing to speak the only language they are proficient in—their home language—or to remain silent. Many children choose the former alternative for a period of time, but there are others who choose the latter silent way. Both groups

1. Silent Period or L1 Stage

2. Nonverbal Stage

3. Telegraphic and Formulaic Speech Stage

4. Productive Language Use Stage

FIGURE 7.4   Four Sequential Developmental Stages for L1 and L2 Learning

of ESL children will eventually experience frustration, with the second alternative becoming most children's choice after a period of time

2. **Nonverbal stage.** The second stage appears after both groups of children described above remain silent surrounded by an environment that represents a different language and culture. Depending on individual differences and quality of environments this period can last for a short or long period of time. Even though ESL children may not actively be using verbal language for communication, they do still use nonverbal modes of communication, such as pragmatics and paralinguistic strategies (i.e., pointing; gestures; body language—nodding, proximity, movement of eyes; etc.). During this period ESL children may seem passive, but in reality they are active listeners, trying to decode the meaning conveyed by the L2 based on external clues (i.e., contextual nonverbal information), and paying attention to new sounds and formulaic speech that they try to repeat

3. **Telegraphic and formulaic speech stage.** This third stage ends the nonverbal period, and starts when ESL children become active speakers of the L2. Children begin talking by using content words, without function words or morphological markers. Most of these words function as "chunks" of language that have *meaning function*, such as memorized strings of words or routine phrases. Children have stored these "chunks" that surrounding adults and peers have used and attempt to repeat them when similar social contexts of communication appear for them. It is important to highlight that social agents act as role models for socializing the ESL children to use the L2 language in appropriate and meaningful social communication contexts

4. **Productive language use stage.** This fourth stage is marked by the appearance of new utterances that have been constructed by the child, following newly acquired syntactic and morphological knowledge. Many times these "unheard chunks" of language overgeneralize syntactic and grammatical rules, such as conjugating an irregular verb following a regular pattern (e.g., *I goed* for *I went*)

Moreover, developmental stages of L2 acquisition are flexible and vary in dynamic ways, as children transition between periods and maintain some features of the previous stage(s) as they make progress. Flexibility of developmental progress translates into multiple forms, such as progress in spurs, at a slow pace, or in peaks and valleys; depending on individual differences (i.e., maturational factors, motivational levels, degree of aptitude, attitudinal factors, and so forth). It is important for educators to remember that different children will respond in idiosyncratic ways to the same educational strategies and methodologies. Depending on their individual differences, and their unique strengths and weaknesses across linguistic, cognitive, and socioemotional developmental areas (e.g., auditory discrimination of sounds, phonemic awareness, auditory and visual memory skills, attention span, shyness or extroversion, degree of assertiveness, etc.) ESL children will present a variation of the language developmental stages described here. Finally, ESL educators have an important responsibility in L2 learning, because they become the central role models for ESL children to identify with them, internalize their linguistic and sociocultural models, and become speakers of the L2 and develop a bicultural identity. Thus, L1 and L2 language learning processes occur within a sociocultural environment, either in the classroom or home setting, and involve the interface of linguistic, cognitive, and socioemotional developmental skills in ESL students.

Principles of alternative assessment.   As said throughout this chapter, alternative assessment needs also to abide to the same psychometric principles or standards that assure objectivity in the evaluation process. The appropriate use of standards results in valid and reliable alternative assessments and diagnosis. Some of the specific principles applicable to alternative assessments need to be even more rigorous than for the case of standardized tests. As already discussed, the most important tool for assessment is the evaluator's personality, including their knowledge levels of how to administer and interpret examinees' performance based on research evidence, their attitudes and value systems, and their cultural and linguistic backgrounds. In fact, evaluators can introduce even more biases when using alternative measures than when using standardized tests. However, if evaluators are trained properly for using alternative assessments in a valid and reliable manner and become committed advocates, alternative assessments have many advantages, including:

1. *Individualization,* such as conducting clinical testing (adaptation of administration to individual characteristics) and applying "testing the limits" techniques (for further discussion see Gonzalez, Castellano, Bauerle, & Duran, 1996)
2. Interpretation of *process,* such as understanding the developmental stages involved in learning L1 and L2 and its interface with cognitive and socioemotional development, and measuring potential for learning (and not only the amount of learned information—a product-based approach of standardized tests)
3. Application of interpretation and diagnostic results to *instruction,* resulting in transformation of analysis of developmental processes into best pedagogy: strategies and methodology and materials for instruction

Thus, it is the job of evaluators to adapt administration procedures and to interpret and transform ESL students' performance in alternative assessments into *instructional purposes:* (1) an analysis of skills and abilities, and strengths and weaknesses (i.e., assessment stage); and (2) a synthesis process for linking assessment to instruction and making informed pedagogical decisions (i.e., evaluation and diagnosis stages).

Based on a thorough compilation of a number of documents (i.e., Gonzalez, Bauerle, and Felix-Holt, 1996; National Education Goals Panel, 1998; McLaughlin, Blanchard, and Yawkey, 1995; Regional Educational Laboratory at SERVE, 2003), we have selected five recommended assessment principles that should be followed when designing and using assessment instruments for ESL students and all students, which are discussed below and listed in Table 7.2.

First Assessment Principle.   **Assessments need to be developmentally and culturally appropriate in order to avoid biases and discriminatory practices when administering and interpreting evaluation results.** Assessment of young children is

TABLE 7.2   Five Recommended Principles for the Design and Use of Assessment Instruments for ESL and *All* Students

First Assessment Principle

Assessments need to be developmentally and culturally appropriate in order to avoid biases and discriminatory practices when administering and interpreting evaluation results

Second Assessment Principle

Developmental differences in bilingual children in comparison to monolingual counterparts

Third Assessment Principle

Need for evaluators to undergo an intense and systematic process of professional development

Fourth Assessment Principle

Need to conduct assessments across developmental and learning contexts, involving the participation of multiple evaluators

Fifth Assessment Principle

Assessments across contexts should also include a variety of measures

---

difficult because most measures use language as a vehicle for evaluation of skills and abilities across developmental areas. As highlighted by the National Education Goals Panel (NEGP, 1998), and as discussed above in relation to Standards (AERA, APA, & NCME, 1999), it is important to recognize that "to some extent all assessments are measures of language ... [and that] assessment results are easily confounded by language proficiency" (NEGP, p. 6). This panel recognized that the latter scenario is especially relevant "for children who come from home backgrounds with limited exposure to English, for whom the assessment would essentially be an assessment of their English proficiency" (p. 6). Because young children (either monolingual or bilingual) are not yet proficient in the use of language in any form (i.e., oral or literacy skills), their assessment is challenging and the situation can become a worst-case scenario for ESL students. Moreover, the Regional Educational Laboratory at SERVE (2003) recommended that

> all assessment instruments must be able to accommodate the linguistic needs of children in major language groups... [and] will be available in English and Spanish and, for other languages, the school will attempt to identify an interpreter to assist with the screening. (pp. 20–21)

In light of this methodological challenge, Gonzalez and collaborators (1996) recommended the use of verbal and nonverbal assessment procedures for young ESL students. Nonverbal assessment measures can provide developmentally appropriate tools for young ESL students to express their progress in cognitive development and academic achievement, as well as their potential for learning. Nonverbal methods of assessment also provide familiar contexts for ESL children to demonstrate their abilities. Furthermore, by offering alternatives to paper-and-pencil tests, ESL students can represent and express their knowledge through concrete behaviors, rather than by engaging in abstract language forms such as talking or writing (NEGP, 1998). Another difficulty of assessing ESL and all students during their early childhood years (i.e., from birth through 8 years of age) is that their development across areas (i.e., linguistic, cognitive, and socioemotional) has a very fast pace. This fact presents a difficulty for evaluation because measures need to be taken at least every 6 months to keep up with the fast growth rate, or even better in a longitudinal manner to map out rapid change and developmental progress.

Moreover, the Regional Educational Laboratory at SERVE (2003), highlights that the assessment of young children involves developmental factors such as their dynamic growth patterns, resulting in learning rates that are different between the early childhood years (i.e., infancy through 8 years of age) and the older students. They stated, "young children learn best by listening, observing, questioning, and experimenting, and they . . . represent their knowledge by showing or talking . . . " (p. 6). In addition, other characteristics of young children's learning make its assessment challenging, their "learning is highly integrated and extremely episodic, so tests given at one point in time and focusing in one content area (e.g., mathematics or literacy) are not adequate proxies for the full scope and depth of the knowledge young children possess" (p. 6). Furthermore, formal measures may not represent accurately young children's learning because they "are often inexperienced in adapting to new situations" (p. 6). Finally, because of the strong effect of prior knowledge and learning experiences encountered in their external social and cultural environments (i.e., primarily school and home) on young children's rate of development, it is recommended that educators "cannot assume that measures of past learning are evidence of what might be learned" (p. 6). Especially for the case of economically disadvantaged ESL students, their particular potential for learning might be exponentially higher than their actual degree of development and academic achievement.

Furthermore, the Regional Educational Laboratory at SERVE (2003) recommended as a developmental principle that "school readiness is the match between the condition of young children as they enter school and the capacity of schools to educate all children" (p. 20). That is, the concept of readiness becomes a dual process: not only the child's intrinsic "developmental readiness," but, most important, the school's readiness to adapt to the child's needs. Then, school readiness is an interactive construct, "focusing on the fit between children's characteristics upon entry and the characteristics and resources of the schools receiving the children" (p. 61). For the case of ESL students, the challenge becomes "how to measure school readiness to receive children whose first language is not English" (p. 61). Then, an ecological assessment perspective for readiness takes into consideration the interaction between the child's developmental readiness and the school readiness. That is the rationale for developmentally appropriate assessment practices to also be based on an ecological perspective that takes into account the interaction of external and internal factors on development and learning processes. When identifying children at-risk of learning difficulties, or with potential developmental delays, a battery of multiple assessments across learning contexts (i.e., home and school), representing multiple evaluators (i.e., most important, parents and teachers), across multiple developmental areas (i.e., physical, cognitive, linguistic, social, and emotional), and over a period of time should be implemented.

Thus, given all these challenges, standardized and alternative assessments need to be examined for their scientific (or psychometric properties, such as validity and reliability), and their developmental, and cultural and linguistic appropriateness (Regional Educational Laboratory at SERVE, 2003). That is, it is imperative for educators, administrators, and policy makers to become aware of the complexity of this challenge: to collect wide-scale assessments for instructional and accountability purposes. This is the first and most important step toward the development of an appropriate assessment system or program.

Second Assessment Principle.   **Developmental differences in bilingual children in comparison to monolingual counterparts.** It is necessary to assess ESL students in both L1 and L2, not only in terms of language proficiency levels but also in relation to skills and abilities across content areas. As recommended by the National Education Goals Panel (1998), "for children with more than one language, primary language assessments should be used to ensure that language difference is not mistaken for disability" (p. 16). For instance, bilingual children use *code mixing* (i.e., use of two languages within the same utterance or sentence) and *code switching* (i.e., use of two languages sequentially, after a unit of speech has been completed—one complete sentence in L1 followed by another complete sentence in L2) as a normal L2 practice modeled by their sociocultural context of development, such as parents, siblings, and peers.

In addition, L2 development is a *dynamic and complex process* (as already discussed), which results from the influence of multidimensional internal and external factors. In relation to this guideline, Gonzalez and collaborators (1996) recommended individualizing assessment for increasing validity in the assessment of development and academic achievement in ESL students. That is, alternative assessments provide the possibility for adapting measures to reflect the unique characteristics and needs of ESL students. For instance, in the early stages of reading readiness, ESL students may show strong visual memory skills for internalizing quickly new sight-words, but have weak auditory discrimination for sounds and phonemic awareness. A classroom-based assessment measure that can capture both the strengths and weaknesses of how ESL students develop, show learning potential, and *do* learn and *do* show progress is an important record to keep in the child's permanent file, and thus show the importance of individualizing assessment.

Third Assessment Principle.   **Need for evaluators to undergo an intense and systematic process of professional development.** This training involves several areas, including learning "the use of narrative reporting, observations of language development, and sampling the child's language abilities . . . what developmentally appropriate outcomes can be expected based on research in first and second language learning . . . [and] . . . the variety of ways in which children develop a second language" (McLaughlin et al., 1995, p. 6). The National Education Goals Panel

(1998) recommended that, "To use assessment information effectively, caregivers and teachers must have enough knowledge about child development and cultural variations to be able to understand the meaning of a child's response and to locate it on a developmental continuum" (p. 11). They also highlighted the importance for policy makers and school administrators to support professional development for both understanding development and for teachers to systematically document students' progress through standardized and alternative assessments. Specific skills that teachers should develop include: a clear understanding of what typical development looks like for children in the process of learning English, normal variation, departure from mainstream benchmarks related to cultural and linguistic differences, and differential diagnosis between the normal L2 learning process and potential genuine handicapping conditions or disabilities, understanding the difference between developmental delays and disabilities, etc. In the section on standards we highlighted the importance of evaluators' knowledge levels in relation to four layers (from more superficial to more complex): testing, assessment, evaluation, and diagnosis.

Classroom teachers who are collecting evaluations need to be provided with specific training on assessment principles and the use of targeted observations and teachers' ratings. This training should focus on methodology and techniques for collecting, analyzing or coding, and interpreting data. Teachers should be provided with technical and administration manuals, samples of data collected, a training CD-ROM or other materials, supervised practice, and mentors who provide individualized feedback on training sessions and in the field. Teachers need to be provided with practice at every level of the implementation process when using alternative assessments such as observation and rating scales.

Moreover, educators acting as evaluators within classroom-based assessment models can also introduce biases in assessment because the most important tool for assessment is not the tests themselves, but the evaluators' personality traits (see Gonzalez et al., 1999, for further discussion of this topic). Gonzalez and collaborators found in a data-based research study that the levels of prior knowledge of L2 language learners' development, cultural and linguistic backgrounds, and attitudinal and belief systems toward L2 learners of in-service teachers and school psychologists affected their diagnostic decisions in ESL students. It is important to highlight that the myth of blaming tests for inaccurate assessments of ESL students needs to stop, as well as the search for the panacea (see Gonzalez et al., 1997, for a more extensive discussion of this topic). Instead, educators need to realize that their personality is the most important tool for assuring objectivity or validity and reliability in assessment, and for avoiding biases and discrimination of ESL students. By becoming knowledgeable in assessment and L2 developmental principles, educators can successfully collect systematic records of performance for linking assessment to instruction through classroom-based assessments. Ultimately, by showing accurate proof or evidence of developmental and appropriate progress in L2 learning, educators of ESL students become mentors, committed advocates, and empowering role models.

Furthermore, The Regional Educational Laboratory at SERVE (2003), recommended that assessment measures used for the purpose of improving learning and program evaluation should be administered by classroom teachers because they are familiar with students and they need to implement performance-based information into educational applications. With adequate professional development at both the pre-service and in-service levels, classroom teachers can become knowledgeable about how to translate the diversity of their students' assessment performance into: (1) meaningful instructional strategies, methodologies, and materials; and (2) reports for parents, school administrators, and policy makers at the federal, state, regional, and local levels. However, classroom teachers need to be appropriately trained to be able to use assessment instruments accurately and not to introduce biases, and teachers also need to be knowledgeable in order to select valid and reliable measures for the specific use and population in order to have adequate levels of validity and reliability (i.e., psychometric accuracy or precision that controls error of measurement to an adequate level). The bottom line is that precision can be controlled by obtaining large samples with measures with a lower accuracy, or with a smaller sample with highly accurate measures. However, biases in teachers that introduce unacceptable errors of measurement, due to lack of training, cannot be controlled by sample size or high precision of instruments.

Fourth Assessment Principle.   **Need to conduct assessments across developmental and learning contexts, involving the participation of multiple evaluators.** That is, McLaughlin and colleagues (1995) recommended that assessment processes should include the participation of teachers, other school personnel (e.g., social worker, school psychologist, reading specialist, special education teacher, etc.), and family and community members as necessary (e.g., parents, grandparents, extended relatives, parent advocate, etc.). In fact, standards recommended by AERA, APA, and NCME (1999) also endorse the use of assessment teams and multiple contexts of assessment for ESL students. Gonzalez and colleagues (1996) also recommended the use of L1 and L2 as methods of evaluation, and as a way to examine learning and development across linguistic contexts. Dual-language assessments need to be conducted by different informants (across the school and home contexts), who represent the language use of the ESL students across sociocultural communities. In addition, Gonzalez and colleagues recommended the use of code-mixing and code-switching, which should also be considered a form of dual-language assessment.

The Regional Educational Laboratory (2003) recommended that parents and other family members be included as informants in the assessment process, with surveys and checklists as appropriate tools for collecting information about their home environment and perspectives. An ecological assessment perspective, endorsed in this book, needs to capitalize on parents' feedback and the inclusion of home environmental factors and parental perspectives and perceptions of their ESL children's development that bring important cultural and linguistic factors (see Gonzalez & Riojas-Clark, 1999, for a discussion of this issue in relation to the identification of gifted ESL students). That is, "non-child dimensions of readiness, including assessments of schools' readiness for children and communities' support for young children and their families" (Regional Educational Laboratory, 2003, p. 9) need to be collected within an ecological assessment perspective.

Fifth Assessment Principle.   **Assessments across contexts should also include a variety of measures.** This principle is related to the previously discussed assessment principles. Gonzalez and colleagues (1996) enforced this recommendation, stating that there is a need for multiple and complementary measures that form a battery of assessments across developmental areas (i.e., linguistic, cognitive, and socioemotional) and content areas of instruction (i.e., language arts, math, science, and social studies). In addition, batteries of assessments also need to take an ecological perspective and include both external and internal factors influencing development and learning. Therefore, according to the National Education Goals Panel (1998) two different types of measures should be used: (1) *social indicators* for assessing the adequacy of external factors such as living and social conditions and adequacy of services provided by the home environment, neighborhood, and community; and (2) *direct* and *indirect measures* of children's behaviors by multiple evaluators across contexts, with direct measures accounting for samples of behaviors, and indirect measures referring to evaluators' perceptions or ratings of past behaviors observed. One single or discrete-point assessment (i.e., only in oral vocabulary, such as the Peabody Picture Vocabulary Test) has no meaning or validity in isolation, it has to be interpreted within the context provided by a complete battery of assessments. Moreover, this battery of assessments needs to be collected across contexts and multiple informants (as referred by the previous assessment guidelines).

Thus, as stated throughout these five recommended principles for the assessment of ESL students and all students, ESL teachers need also to be knowledgeable about how to conduct alternative assessments in an accurate manner in order to link assessment and instruction. ESL teachers need to undergo professional development in order to gain an understanding of how to use their personalities as a tool for implementing best alternative assessments and pedagogical strategies and methodologies.

ESL teachers need to act as mentors and advocates of diverse students by participating in the alternative assessment process in multiple ways:

1. As *team players* in the assessment process, by learning how to keep systematic records of progress that are valid and reliable
2. As *active record keepers*, by documenting learning potential and strengths through the analysis of performance in ESL students' behavioral processes and products
3. As *performance-based assessment experts* by interpreting and transforming the analysis of evaluated behaviors into pedagogical strategies, methodologies, and materials that meet the individual and culturally and linguistically diverse needs of their ESL and all students
4. As *cultural brokers* or *mediators* who can serve as role models for their mainstream colleagues in how to communicate and advocate for their ESL students and their culturally and linguistically diverse families

INSTRUCTIONAL AND ACCOUNTABILITY PURPOSES OF ASSESSMENT

The National Education Goals Panel called attention to the misuse of assessment instruments by stating that " . . . the instruments developed for one purpose or even one age group of children have been misapplied to other groups" (1998, p. 4). It is important to highlight that standardized or alternative measures are constructed and validated for a specific purpose of assessment and norms are created for a specific population (in relation to a variety of demographic characteristics such as age, geographic location, ethnicity, level of socioeconomic status, including the level of education of parents and other family structure factors).

Following criteria established by the National Education Goals Panel (1998) and the Regional Educational Laboratory at SERVE (2003), there are two broad purposes or uses of assessment:

1. Instructional, which encompasses linking *assessment* to instruction by documenting support for learning (i.e., teacher effectiveness reflected in students' progress and improvement of instruction), and for special and diverse educational students' needs (i.e., individualization of instruction and adaptation of pedagogy to cultural and linguistic diversity)
2. Accountability, which includes *program evaluation* and monitoring trends or benchmarks (i.e., milestones); and high-stakes accountability based on federal, state, and professional organization standards (i.e., based on policy and demographics for meeting criteria for securing federal and state funding)

It is important to highlight that different terminology is applied to different purposes of assessment. The term *assessment* is related to instructional purposes of learning, and is typically connected to classroom-based or alternative measures, such as ongoing observational assessments that are more appropriate for young children (i.e., higher ecological or curriculum validity). For meeting accountability purposes geared toward program evaluation and teachers' effectiveness based on students' progress, a more comprehensive battery of assessments (or an assessment system) is needed, based on high-quality alternative assessments and standardized tests, which measures both external and internal factors over a period of time. For instance, for the case of ESL students, if the purpose of assessment is to help teachers make informed instructional decisions, then a longitudinal record of alternative assessments of L1 and L2 development would be most appropriate. However, if the assessment purpose is to make comparisons across school buildings and school districts at the state, regional, or even national levels, then it would be better to assess degree of language proficiency at the beginning of the school year (i.e., pre-test) and again measure progress quarterly, or at the end of the school year (post-test) with a standardized measured by independent evaluators. Here, highly precise measures, with validity and reliability for the population and purpose of assessment, would have to be used by highly trained evaluators. In order to be cost effective, a sample of children could be assessed and assigned randomly to some assessment items; a procedure called matrix sampling (Regional Educational Laboratory at SERVE, 2003). This procedure also categorizes children's developmental progress at specific points along a continua of readiness or proficiency or competency. These categories represent established criteria or norms or standards for meeting selected state- and federal-level educational goals and objectives.

Even though highly trained teachers can collect valid observational data and teachers' ratings, "their self-interest in evaluation of their own programs creates an apparent conflict of interest for them as data collectors" (Regional Educational

Laboratory at SERVE, 2003, p. 38). However, teachers also have an advantage over independent evaluators, they have access to a much wider sample for children's behaviors and products over an extended period of time. In relation to this conflict of interest, a better approach for assessing young ESL children might be to complement teachers' ratings and observations in the classroom with independent evaluators' observations and ratings with one-on-one developmental scales and standardized tests (ibid). These recommendations support the principles of assessment highlighting the need to use a battery of assessments across time, contexts, evaluators, and developmental areas (as discussed in the previous section).

It is important to understand that the quality of assessment and testing is both connected to the validity and reliability of instruments as applicable to the population and purpose, as well as to the training of the evaluators (as discussed in the section above on principles of assessment). Valid and reliable assessment systems are "systematic inquiry methods that enable us to improve the accuracy of our descriptions . . . [and] to correct biases of our natural sense-making efforts and extend the reach of the observations that any individual can make" (Regional Educational Laboratory at SERVE, 2003, pp. 25–26). Assessment systems are in fact the result of theory building and heuristic research, because assessment systems can provide "data to enhance knowledge by developing classification systems or testing theories" (ibid, p. 27). Therefore, it is important for ESL and all teachers to understand that classroom-based assessment needs to be based on the systematic use of alternative assessments that are valid and reliable for the use and population, and, more important, that classroom-based assessment conducted by teachers is a form of research inquiry that we call *action research*, the systematic collection of samples of behaviors through some form of systematic and valid and reliable observational records.

Interestingly, the Regional Educational Laboratory at SERVE (2003) suggested addressing actual assessment issues and challenges through empirical research. They pinpoint that "it might be fruitful to have a special study looking at how scores from measures to support instruction might 'map' onto those from direct assessments" (p. 60). This kind of research studies can shed some light on educational solutions for issues such as the appropriateness of aggregation of alternative and standardized data collected by classroom teachers and other independent evaluators, across natural situations in the classrooms and one-to-one evaluations. That is, an empirical study of the issue of aggregation of evaluation data collected for different purposes: for instructional purposes by teachers and for accountability purposes by evaluators.

The first purpose supports the idea that "assessment and teaching are inseparable processes" (National Education Goals Panel, 1998, p. 9) and that "content of classroom assessments must be closely aligned with what children are learning" (p. 11) or should show curriculum or content validity. As recommended by the National Education Goals Panel (NEGP) (1998), the most important reason for conducting assessments is to support children's learning and development, to help them learn, and therefore should be a natural part of instructional activities. In addition, the first purpose refers to the evaluation of children with suspected special education needs, whose ability to learn must be evaluated over time by providing focused learning opportunities interactively with assessment, and by using curriculum-aligned assessment tasks (p. 11).

The second purpose of assessment, program evaluation, helps to document the quality of program delivery and "to determine whether programs are effective in achieving intended outcomes . . . [and] . . . hold programs 'accountable' and hold states 'accountable' for the adequacy of social conditions and services to young children" (p. 24). Program evaluations typically present both *aggregated* (analyzed by group) and *disaggregated data* (analyzed separatedly by categories based on demographic and other relevant educational categories). Program evaluations give feedback to the system, especially to policymakers, the school administrators and school boards and other decision makers, social service providers, parents, and the general public (p. 24).

In addition, the second purpose provides mandated standards for school districts to comply with national and international, and state and regional comparisons of academic achievement of all students across developmental and academic achievement areas. The outcome of the wide-scale assessment to collect aggregated and disaggregated data and the data comparison with federal and state high-stakes standards has important effects on: (1) funding received by school districts from federal and state educational agencies; and (2) teachers' evaluations and their resulting liability on students' developmental and academic achievement progress, and ultimately on teachers' salaries and benefits.

Moreover, state-level assessment systems are being developed presently, and establish screenings or assessment programs or criteria and recommendations (Regional Educational Laboratory at SERVE, 2003). Wide-scale assessment brings a number of technical or psychometric challenges, especially for the case of ESL young children. As explained in this section, assessment measures are created for two broad purposes, and measures used for instructional purposes cannot be used to meet accountability purposes, and vice versa. As well stated by the Regional Educational Laboratory at SERVE (2003), wide-scale assessment on the progress of developmental and academic achievement of all students has brought a number of challenges and "concerns about the purpose of the assessments, the nature of the assessment processes, and the implications of how the data are being used" (p. 1).

There are broadly four categories of challenging issues for states to develop assessment systems and programs: design, instrumentation, implementation, and data utilization (Regional Educational Laboratory at SERVE, 2003). Some examples of these challenging issues that policymakers and administrators of school districts, and ultimately educators and evaluators need to resolve, are:

> Why are assessments being conducted, and are states clear on the purpose of such assessment? Do they distinguish between, for example, assessment to improve instruction and assessment to make high-stakes decisions about children or programs? How can assessment data be collected on a wide scale in a manner that is technically sound and beneficial for both the children and the stakeholders interested in using the results? And how are the data being used? Is the use matching the original intentions, or are the instruments designed for one purpose being used for another? (p. 1)

With the high-stakes assessment movement, during the late 1990s a new era started the increase of formal assessment for younger students, with test results being used for making important educational decisions that may have long-term and even lifetime impact. Some of these high-stakes decisions include "tracking youngsters into high and low ability groups, (mis)labeling or retaining them, or using test results to sort children into or out of kindergarten and preschools" (National Education Goal Panel, 1998, p. 4). According to the National Education Goal Panel, the result of such inadequate high-stakes decisions include labels of *not ready* for learning or *too immature* for *large proportions of youngsters* (often boys and non-English speakers) (p. 4).

Thus, understanding psychometric principles such as the constructs of validity and reliability empowers ESL educators to advocate for the appropriate use of standardized and alternative assessments. The most important psychometric principle is that tests are *not* validated in general terms, for all purposes and populations, but instead *for a specific purpose of assessment* (e.g., identifying gifted students, evaluating academic achievement in mathematics, selecting students with specific talents, or predicting performance in a future placement). As well stated by the National Education Goals Panel (1998), assessments should be "tailored to a specific purpose and should be reliable, valid, and fair for that purpose" (p. 5). They emphasize "misuse" and "abuses" of testing, specifically for the case of young children, due to evaluators' and administrators' lack of knowledge regarding the limitations of the assessment's purpose for which a test is created and validated or for which norms are created. It is the responsibility of users of assessments to verify whether specific tests match the characteristics of their population and their own purpose for assessment. It is also important to understand that assessments are created following certain criteria or standards, and theories or constructs that are the product of cultural and social contexts; and therefore are *not* culture-free or universal but always culturally and linguistically embedded or loaded.

CLASSROOM-BASED ASSESSMENT

Because this L2 book is geared toward ESL educators as a main audience, for the purpose of professional development in teachers, we will expand in this section on the instructional purposes of assessment. The objective is to provide useful information for teachers to be able to implement alternative assessments in their classrooms for improving the learning progress and academic achievement of ESL students and all students. Classroom-based assessments can be used by ESL teachers as tools for linking assessment to instruction (i.e., instructional purpose) and program evaluation (i.e., accountability purpose). For both purposes, classroom-based assessments need to be used by ESL teachers as systematic records of students' progress in learning, development, and academic achievement. Systematic records are based on the establishment of criteria or standards. That is, criteria or standards are operational defined performances in terms of behaviors and products that are identified based on a set of developmental benchmarks or objectives, also called criteria or standards.

These educational or learning objectives or goals are set on the basis of expected developmental outcomes following criteria or standards defined by federal and state agencies, and/or professional organizations (i.e., for the case of ESL students, we abide by the Teachers of English to Speakers of Other Languages [TESOL]; see Chapters 4, 5, and 6 for an extended discussion). As well stated by the National Education Goal Panel (1998), "Pressed by demands for greater accountability and enhanced educational performance, states are developing standards for school-age children and are creating new criteria and approaches for assessing the achievement of challenging academic goals" (p. 5). These federal, state, and professional organization standards set minimum performances by grade level that need to be achieved across content areas as evidence or records of meeting standards, which are used as accountability systems for program evaluation and teachers' effectiveness. However, accountability systems are based on assessment systems or programs that need to comply with basic psychometric standards assuring validity and reliability (see section on assessment principles).

Using alternative assessments is the best strategy to accomplish the first broad purposes of assessment: (1) to inform instruction, by helping ESL students to reach higher academic achievement levels. The second purpose of assessment needs to be accomplished by documenting program evaluation and teachers' effectiveness for meeting accountability purposes through both alternative and standardized assessments (see section on purposes of assessment). The recommended alternative assessment strategies to meet these two assessment purposes are narrative and structured obser- vations and portfolio assessments. These two alternative assessment strategies offer natural and nonintrusive methods of documenting *baseline* (or *formative*) and *progress data* (or *summative* measures) about the individual and group performance of students in relation to demographic and educational factors (aggregated and disaggregated data) in relation to teachers' ratings, standards, and developmentally appropriate rubrics.

As already discussed in relation to the principles of assessment, continuous eval- uation of progress is key for using alternative assessment feedback to introduce indi- vidualization of instruction in teaching and learning strategies and curriculum development, and for implementing lesson plans. With ESL learners, it is important to record learning and developmental progress, as the normal process of ESL learning can coincide with learning and developmental delays in immigrant and low-income students at-risk of underachievement (see section under Standards on the differential diagnosis of ESL students). As recommended previously by Gonzalez and collabora- tors (1997), to record summative evaluations at successive established intervals (like, for instance, quarters) can help teachers document and demonstrate developmental growth and potential for learning through qualitative descriptions and evaluations of significant changes (i.e., showing the achievement of milestones and benchmarks) in learning processes and products. As we have discussed in this chapter, alternative assessments provide:

1. Explicit links to instruction via descriptive, qualitative, and educationally applied feedback (i.e., in the form of analysis of thinking and learning processes, strengths and weaknesses, individual needs and interests)
2. A direct or authentic way of evaluating students' behaviors in their natural learning environments: the real classroom setting

Thus, by using individual data of alternative assessments, educators can meet the first purpose of assessment (i.e., to link assessment to instruction), and by using group data, educators can meet the second purpose of assessment (i.e., to validly and reliably collect wide-scale accountability data of students' progress in development and academic achievement, and a systematic record of program evaluation and teachers' effectiveness).

AN ALTERNATIVE ASSESSMENT SYSTEM FOR INSTRUCTIONAL AND ACCOUNTABILITY PURPOSES: DESCRIPTION OF THE VIGNETTES

A portfolio assessment can provide an authentic, valid, and reliable assessment battery for measuring cognitive and L1 and L2 learning, and sociolinguistic development, and academic achievement across content areas (i.e., language arts, mathematics, science, and social science) in bilingual preschool children (i.e., 3 to 5 years of age). This portfolio system can encompass an observation scale of cognitive, L1 and L2, and sociolinguistic development, and a teachers' rating scale of children's achievement and developmental processes and products. These alternative measures need to be constructed on sound developmental theory for bilingual young children; and represent developmental state, federal, and national Teaching English to Speakers of Other Languages (TESOL) professional standards for academic achievement. This portfolio system needs to be constructed for the instructional purpose of linking assessment and instruction, and for informing teachers about ESL students' progress across developmental areas (i.e., cognitive, linguistic, and socioemotional) and content areas (i.e., language arts, literacy, math, social studies, and science). This portfolio assessment system can also be used for accountability purposes, in conjunction with other alternative and standardized assessments across contexts (i.e., home and school) and across evaluators (adding independent examiners).

More specifically, the portfolio assessment system is a performance-based assessment that shows a record of products and behaviors, which are analyzed as learning and developmental processes. Samples of products and behaviors are collected in a systematic and longitudinal manner in relation to standards across developmental (i.e., cognitive, linguistic, and socioemotional) and content areas (i.e., language arts, literacy, math, social studies, and science). *Absolute standards* established by AERA, APA, and NCME (1999) and *relative standards* established by federal and state regulations and professional organizations (TESOL, 1997) are used. Absolute standards provide authoritative judgment of psychometric properties that accurate measures should align to in order to establish validity and reliability. Relative standards provide benchmarks that individuals should meet in relation to comparative groups and subgroups, such as grade level and minimum performances required for complying with a set of instructional objectives. Logical analysis of the criteria or standards, the behavior-based and product-based tasks, using theory, conceptual analysis based on previous research, and analysis and implementation of the absolute and relative standards document the extent to which the portfolio assessment system complies with validity and reliability properties.

The portfolio assessment can include a teacher's rating scale and an observation scale of behavior-based and product-based samples over the course of an academic year, collected at three points in time: end of fall quarter, end of winter quarter, and end of spring quarter. Teachers' ratings can be completed for the Spanish and English performance of preschoolers across selected standards for developmental areas and content areas that respond to both absolute and relative standards. Spanish ratings can be completed quarterly by the Spanish teacher, and English ratings can be completed quarterly by the English teacher, both working as partners within a two-way bilingual educational program. Observation scales can be constructed based on socioconstructivistic theory that establishes construct validity and reliability. For both measures, absolute standards can be used for providing several lines of evidence that supported construct validity for the use and population, as well as training for the teachers working as evaluators for assuring systematic application of criteria leading to reliable judgments of children's performances in the form of interpretations and inferences (following psychometric recommendations from AERA, APA, & NCME, 1999). In addition, for both measures, relative standards can be used for assuring that children's performance was comparable to benchmarks set by federal, state, and professional organizations (namely, Ohio Pre-K and K standards, and TESOL standards established for ESL students; both responding to federal mandates).

The entries for the teachers' ratings of products-based performance can represent samples of performance (i.e., products) in relation to standards or benchmarks. It is important to highlight that products collected need to represent classroom performance as part of the curriculum activities that responded to the standards judged. Judgments need to represent both progress of children's performance in relation to absolute and relative standards, and therefore fulfill instructional purposes of assessments. That is, there needs to be a link between assessment and instruction, leading to curriculum or content validity of measures. Judgments also represent teachers' effectiveness and therefore are measures of accountability fulfilling program evaluation needs.

The portfolio assessment system is proposed as an alternative assessment methodology that fulfills three purposes of assessment: (1) a student–teacher mode of evaluation, representing a record of instructional purpose of assessment, allowing teachers to link assessment to instruction; (2) a classroom-based assessment system that can be used for program evaluation, in conjunction with other alternative and standardized assessments across contexts (i.e., home and school) and across evaluators (by adding independent examiners); and (3) a systematic assessment system showing validity and reliability that can be used for accountability purposes based on standards. A portfolio assessment system needs to be constructed and pilot tested through case studies, and needs to undergo the process of validation.

SUMMARY AND CONCLUSIONS

Summary and conclusions and theoretical and educationally applied implications close Chapter 7, with emphasis on recommendations for ESL educators and all classroom teachers for the successful implementation of linking assessment to instruction, and for local and state education agencies to fulfill the accountability purpose of assessment.

This chapter has presented an ecological perspective to assessment and instruction through the central idea of "school readiness" (as opposed to the traditional concept of children's readiness for learning). School readiness is defined in Chapter 7 as the school capacity to educate properly children from an ESL background. The ecological perspective conceptualizes school readiness as the result of the interaction between internal and external factors. That is, school readiness results from the interaction between the child's developmental readiness and the school's readiness.

Chapter 7 has established the basic principles and standards for assessment, including psychometric constructs (i.e., validity and reliability) based on a contemporary view of the psychometric assessment model. The central idea presented in Chapter 7 in relation to assessment principles and standards is that standardized and alternative assessments need to be examined for their scientific (or psychometric properties, such as validity and reliability) and their developmental, and cultural and linguistic appropriateness. Two basic purposes of assessment were discussed widely in Chapter 7: instructional and accountability purposes. The instructional purpose of assessment was defined as classroom- or teacher-based assessments that link assessment to instruction, which consist of systematic, valid, and reliable alternative assessments that are clustered as a system (i.e., portfolios). In this way, an alternative assessment system also becomes a valid and reliable methodology for collecting samples and records of performance or process and products, and, as such, a case of action research in the classroom. The accountability purpose of assessment was defined as a battery of valid and reliable alternative and standardized assessments collected by different evaluators (i.e., classroom teachers and independent examiners, and parents), across contexts (i.e., school and home settings), across developmental and content areas, and across time (i.e., longitudinal data that includes a pre-test and several posttests, with at least a quarterly evaluation). The accountability purpose involves program evaluation in relation to high-stakes benchmarks or criteria of minimum performance by grade level established by federal and state standards.

Chapter 7 has also presented an alternative assessment model that takes into consideration developmental stages of L1 and L2 acquisition, principles of alternative assessment, and instructional and accountability purposes of assessment. Chapter 7 also reinforces the first theme of the book by infusing an ethnic educator perspective. We make an appeal to ESL teachers and all educators to dispel the myth of blaming tests as the causes for the inaccurate assessment of ESL students, as well as to stop the search for the panacea. Instead, ESL and all educators need to realize that their personality is the most important tool for assuring objectivity or validity and reliability in assessment, and for avoiding biases and discrimination for ESL students. It is important to understand that assessments are created following certain standards or criteria, and that theories and constructs are the product of cultural and social contexts. Therefore, assessment instruments are *not* culture-free or universal, but always are culturally and linguistically embedded or loaded.

In sum, an ecologically valid and reliable assessment system uses authentic classroom contexts for selecting records of samples of genuine behaviors or performances—process and products in L1 and L2 across developmental and content areas. This assessment model includes a battery of alternative and standardized assessments and a team of trained evaluators who can make appropriate decisions about valid uses of instruments for appropriate populations, and who can make valid interpretations and inferences about ESL students' performance. Appropriately trained evaluators accommodate for individual and developmental differences, respect cultural and linguistic diversity, and are knowledgeable about theoretical and psychometric principles. Most important, appropriately trained evaluators can use systematically valid and reliable classroom-based assessments to control for their subjectivity and biases introduced by the most important tool for assessment: their own personalities including their cultural and linguistic backgrounds, the philosophies and theories that they endorse, and, ultimately, their level of commitment and advocacy for ESL students. Thus, we have recommended strongly that federal and state and local education agencies, and ESL and all educators stop the search for the panacea, or culture-free and linguistic-universal instruments, and instead adopt an ecological assessment perspective that involves the interaction between school readiness and developmental readiness among ESL students. School readiness for assessment means to get ESL and all educators, and assessment team members, "ready" in theoretical and psychometric principles of assessment for ESL students by providing them with high-quality professional development for fulfilling instructional purposes for assessment, and for local education agencies to adapt mandated high-stakes standards to the uses and populations they are serving for fulfilling accountability purposes.

REVIEW QUESTIONS

1. What are the most important classroom applications of the principles of validity and reliability and core terminology and definitions of the traditional or psychometric paradigm? How can the principles and standards of assessment help ESL teachers to improve their assessment practices in the classroom?

2. In your opinion, which are the three most important assessment principles derived from the socioconstructivistic theory of development and learning? Why do you think that the application of these principles can improve your classroom assessment practices with ESL students?

3. How are the central principles and assessment strategies of the alternative assessment model similar to or different than the traditional psychometric paradigm? How are the assessment standards recommended by most important professional organizations related to assessment principles and strategies recommended by the alternative assessment model and the traditional psychometric paradigm?

4. What kind of professional development activities can help ESL teachers to develop an attitude of commitment, advocacy, and empathy, based on an ethnic educator philosophy, when serving ESL students? How can ESL teachers benefit from "assuming moral and social responsibility" for the successful education of their ESL students?

CRITICAL THINKING QUESTIONS

1. Study Figure 7.1, which shows the relationship between different lines of validity evidence, in relation to the explanation provided in the text. Explain the concept of a holistic view of validity that centers on construct validity. Why is construct validity

evidence necessary for the presence of other kinds of internal and external validity? What is the relevance for the educational applications of this concept of construct validity for the assessment of ESL students? Is it important for ESL teachers to become knowledgeable of the validity and reliability principles?

2. Study Figure 7.2, which illustrates the unitary concept of internal and external validity and the relationship between testing, assessment, evaluation, and diagnosis. Then, read carefully the descriptions provided in the text. Explain how abstract mental processes, such as learning, can be measured. How can educators make a link between abstractions and observable behaviors and characteristics through the use of operational definitions? How is testing different from assessment? How can ESL teachers use assessment and evaluation to describe and interpret the performance of ESL students in a more valid and reliable manner? How is assessment and evaluation more useful than testing for ESL teachers? How can diagnosis become a useful educational decision-making process for ESL teachers?

3. Study Figure 7.3, which lists six different procedures demonstrating validity evidence when constructing and/or validating an assessment instrument; and read carefully the descriptions provided in the text. Explain how expert judges can provide evidence for validating test content and response processes, can ESL teachers use this procedure when developing a set of test questions—either essay or multiple choice. Provide an example of how evidence based on the internal structure of a test can help improve the validity of a test? What can be considered a relevant criterion for academic achievement for a specific content area of your choice? Provide an example of educational and social consequences of testing for ESL students (i.e., think of cases of misdiagnosis and misplacement in special education).

4. Study Figure 7.4, which provides a sequence of four developmental stages for L1 and L2 learning; and read carefully the descriptions provided in the text. Are these four sequential stages coincident with your experience and observations of ESL students? Provide an example of your observations and explain how the stages may be applicable as explanations for the ESL students' L1 and L2 learning processes? How is knowledge of research useful for ESL teachers to better understand the L1 and L2 process in ESL students?

ACTIVITIES

1. Study Table 7.1, which describes three situations of differential diagnosis between normal L1 and L2 learning processes and genuine learning disabilities and handicapping conditions; and read carefully the descriptions provided in the text. How is the first situation of diagnosing resilient ESL students different than the case of diagnosing at-risk ESL students? Provide an example of your observations and explain how the first and second situation of differential diagnosis may be similar and different? What are the specific characteristics of the third situation of genuine special education cases, and how is it different than the other two differential diagnosis situations? Are these descriptions of three differential diagnosis situations useful for ESL teachers? Explain your views on its educational applications.

2. Study Table 7.2, which describes five recommended principles for the design and use of assessment instruments for ESL students; and read carefully the descriptions provided in the text. What is the principle that seems more useful for the classroom assessment

of your ESL students? Rank-order to five recommendations in terms of their usefulness, from 5 (the most useful), to 1 (the least useful). Provide an example of your observations and explain why the selected recommendation is the most useful for the more accurate assessment of your ESL students? Why is it important to assess ESL students differently than monolingual mainstream students? Why should assessments of ESL students be conducted across contexts by multiple evaluators? What are the specific areas in which ESL teachers need training for improving their understanding of the assessment of ESL students? What specific professional development activities would you recommend?

GLOSSARY

reliability   Reliability refers to the degree of agreement between sources of evidence, such as between evaluators or raters and pieces of evidence (e.g., scores on different tests, scores on the same test in different occasions, etc.). By properly training evaluators, including independent evaluators and classroom teachers, we can improve reliability and validity (all types of both internal and external validity). There cannot be reliability without validity.

standards   They are criteria or guidelines of best practices for educational and psychological testing. Standards are given by professional organizations (e.g., American Educational Research Association [AERA], American Psychological Association [APA], & National Council on Measurement in Education [NCME], 1999), and also as recommendations derived from research (e.g., National Research Council, 1999a, 1999b).

validity   The accuracy with which a student's performance can be measured or tested. It is based on supporting criterion or evidence collected for demonstrating two traditional types of validity: (1) internal validity (i.e., content or curriculum validity) and external validity (i.e., concurrent and predictive).

    An important evolution in the field of psychometrics has been the move from the traditional types of validity (i.e., external and internal with its subtypes of construct, content or curriculum, predictive, concurrent, etc.) to the more contemporary conceptualization of validity as "different lines of evidence, all in service of providing information relevant to a specific intended interpretation of test scores" (AERA, APA, & NCME, 1999, p. 9). The emphasis of this modern conceptualization of validity is on establishing construct validity as "many lines of evidence [that] can contribute to an understanding of the construct meaning of test scores" (p. 5). *Validity* in modern terms refers to a unitary concept, which is centered on construct validity, which encompasses internal and external validity within a holistic perspective. Validity is "the degree to which all the accumulated evidence supports the intended interpretation of test scores for the proposed purpose" (p. 11). See Figure 7.2 for a graphical representation of the validity construct as a unitary concept of internal and external validity within a holistic perspective.

    By improving curriculum validity we can also increase the link between assessment and instruction. By collecting accurate records of progress in learning, development, and academic achievement, we can also build systematic records for accountability and program evaluation (resulting also in improved curriculum and criterion-based validity).

REFERENCES

American Educational Research Association (AERA), American Psychological Association (APA), and National Council on Measurement in Education (NCME). (1999). *Standards for educational and psychological testing.* Washington, DC: AERA.

Collier, V. P., & Thomas, W. P. (2004). The astounding effectiveness of dual language education for all. *NABE Journal of Research and Practice (NJRP), 3*(1), pp. 1–20 (available at njrp.tamu.edu/2004.htm).

Gonzalez, V. (2001). The role of socioeconomic and sociocultural factors in language-minority children's development: An ecological research view. *Bilingual Research Journal, 25*(1, 2), 1–30.

Gonzalez. V., Bauerle, P., Black, W., & Felix-Holt, M. (1999). Influence of evaluators' beliefs and personal backgrounds on their diagnostic and placement decisions. In V. Gonzalez. (Ed.), *Language and cognitive development in second language learning: Educational implications for children and adults* (pp. 269–297). Needham Heights, MA: Allyn and Bacon.

Gonzalez. V., Bauerle, P., & Felix-Holt, M. (1996). Theoretical and practical implications of assessing cognitive and language development in bilingual children with qualitative methods. *Bilingual Research Journal, 20*(1), 93–131.

Gonzalez, V., Brusca-Vega, R., & Yawkey, T. (1997). *Assessment and instruction of culturally and linguistically diverse students with or at-risk of learning problems: From research to practice.* Needham Heights, MA: Allyn and Bacon.

Gonzalez, V., Castellano, J., Bauerle, P., & Duran, R. (1996). Testing the limits in the assessment of LEP students: Research on the perceptions and applications of practitioners. *Bilingual Research Journal, 20*(3 & 4), 433–463.

Gonzalez, V., & Riojas-Clark, E. (1999). Folkloric and historical views of giftedness in language-minority children. In V. Gonzalez (Ed.), *Language and cognitive development in second language learning: Educational implications for children and adults* (pp. 1–18). Needham Heights, MA: Allyn and Bacon.

McLaughlin, B., Blanchard, A. G., & Osanai, Y. (1995). Assessing language development in bilingual preschool children. *National Clearinghouse for Bilingual Education (NCBE) Program Information Guide Series, 22,* Summer, 1–19.

Mercer, J. R. (1973). *Labeling the mentally retarded.* Los Angeles: University of California Press.

National Education Goals Panel (1998). *Principles and recommendations for early childhood assessments.* Washington, DC: U.S. Government Printing Office. www.negp.gov

National Research Council. (1999a). *How people learn.* Washington, DC: National Academy Press.

National Research Council. (1999b). *Improving student learning.* Washington, DC: National Academy Press.

Ortiz, A. A., & Yates, J. R. (1983). Incidence of exceptionality among Hispanics: Implications for manpower planning. *NABE Journal, 7*(3), 41–53.

Regional Educational Laboratory at SERVE. (2003). *Assessing the state of state assessments: Perspectives on assessing young children.* SERVE: University of North Carolina at Greensboro.

Saville-Troike, M. (1987). Bilingual discourse: The negotiation of meaning without a common code. *Linguistics, 25,* 81–106.

Tabors, P. O., & Snow, C. E. (1993). Language skills that relate to literacy development. In B. Spodek & O. Saracho (Eds.), *Yearbook in Early Childhood Education, 4.* New York: Teachers College Press.

INTEGRATING TECHNOLOGY FOR ASSESSING AND INSTRUCTING ESL STUDENTS

LEARNING OBJECTIVES

1. Recognize the applications of computer technologies and their integration for language and content skill development in the ESL classroom

2. Understand the implications of constructivism in technology used across grade, curriculum, and proficiency levels using national standards and benchmarks

3. Examine the role of content standards and interdisciplinary field for technology application in the classrooms

4. Recognize the parameters among student assessment, technology facilitation and instruction

PREVIEW QUESTIONS

1. List three reasons for technology use in ESL and content classrooms.

2. How does constructivism contribute to our understanding of technology used for student success? Design a graphic organizer to illustrate your thinking.

3. How can standards and technology be best integrated in the curriculum? Discuss ways to use this integration to also develop L2 proficiency.

4. Provide examples of technology implementation at a grade level of your choice. Name and describe two of them.

5. How important is technology in student assessment? How important are technology and teacher quality in assessment of ELLs?

Chapter 8 focuses on a conceptual framework and implementation model for integrating educational technology for providing quality instruction and assessment to ESL students.

It includes practical applications of educational technology in the daily class-room setting and action research environment for teachers of ELLs to use them in the classroom to support their teaching. It also includes ways for teachers to become familiar and involved in the use of technology as an instructional tool and to keep abreast of developments through communities of teachers learning and working together toward this goal. By integrating educational technology with best practices in ESL education, teachers can use instructional technologies as a tool for enhancing the learning potential and learning outcome in ELLs.

The first major section examines the constructivist use of technology with instruction and assessment, how technology can be used to assess and instruct students and teachers to construct meaning in their classrooms. It also examines the need to foster a technology culture in the classroom—whether they be bilingual, ESL, or mainstream. It also provides ideas for teachers to become familiar with the use of technology in the classroom. It also underscores the fact that technology use in the classroom provides access to linguistic and cultural materials. Chapter 8 has the goal of making all teachers aware that technology can be part of their everyday teaching; technology advances provide opportunities for two-way communication. It also provides teachers with the opportunity to give feedback to their students' products.

The second major section introduces educators to online educational projects and content area standards; this section examines the factors to be considered when implementing technology in the classroom. It also recommends the most efficient and economical ways to proceed. When implementing national and state standards for language and academic achievement with technology advances, teachers can use this chapter as a resource from which to draw. The chapter also presents a medley of activities, lesson plans, formats, and how to teach them as part of language and content area development. The position or perspective of Chapter 8 and this entire book is one of pluralism. Our intention is to assist educators develop their own lessons and modules using the information presented in the chapters of this book on effective models, methods, and strategies to teach ELLs. Therefore, Chapter 8 is connected to the second theme of the book because it (1) applies the background knowledge presented in several chapters into specific lessons; (2) addresses technology and assessment issues for classroom implementation; and, (3) promotes reflection among teachers to improve on their craft. Chapter 8 aims to provide an understanding of technology in the teaching–learning process and focuses on both students who need to succeed academically and teachers who need to excel.

THE NEED FOR TECHNOLOGY
IN THE CLASSROOM

Technology is everywhere: in our homes, at our work sites, and in our cars. Even with this daily exposure, there are still many people who fear technology. If we as educators can overcome our fear and develop some proficiency in new, computer-related skills, we may discover that it is easier to use technology than we think. Once we acquire a level of comfort with and basic skills in using new technology, we can integrate a great number of technological tools and teaching aids into our classrooms.

As new technology becomes more widely used in the classroom, it is no longer enough for teachers to simply know how to use computers for the purposes of word-processing. Standards developed by the National Council for Accreditation of Teacher Education (NCATE) require that teachers be prepared to integrate technology into their instruction (Wong, 1998). This requirement is further reflected in the job market. Specifically, applicants to teaching positions at various grade levels are asked to demonstrate experience in the use of instructional technology.

Recent studies on technology and instruction indicate that teachers and students can work together in a variety of settings of specific educational projects or tasks that require problem-solving skills, reasoning, and reflection (Norman, 1998). Technology use in the classroom represents a shift from traditional approaches to learning and teaching to one that combines objectivist and constructivist philosophical components that allow students to construct knowledge and collaborate with classmates in and outside of the classroom while working as part of a team (Conway, 1997). The knowledge that students actively construct with peers is based on personal experiences, mental structures, and belief systems that enable them to interpret external reality and events.

TECHNOLOGY FROM THE POINT OF VIEW OF CONSTRUCTIVISM

According to constructivism, students tend to learn most effectively when they are actively engaged in their education. The more students participate in the lesson, the better they will perform; they benefit of learning by doing; and they learn through increased interaction and independent time for learning. The more opportunities provided for students to participate and be involved in the learning process, the better they ought to achieve in school. Technology integration can be used in the classroom to promote student involvement in their learning. By using technology, students can create products to achieve the benefits of the constructivist learning theories (Healey & Klinghammer, 2002).

There are two major types of constructivism, cognitive and social, that can extrapolate with the use of technology in the classroom.

- *Cognitive constructivism* refers to the student-centered aspects. Students are not passive recipients of learning; they construct their own knowledge from information received.
- *Social constructivism* refers to student assistance. More advanced students help other students understand ideas or concepts beyond their baseline level of understanding (Vygotsky, 1986).

In a constructivist environment, the student is the center of the learning process, the one who constructs knowledge and meaning, linking incoming or new knowledge and information to existing knowledge. The teacher provides or facilitates the environment for relevant learning by creating whole, authentic, inherently interesting activities and by setting up multiple representations of reality and actual experience for students, thus enabling them to construct their own knowledge. Typical activities for such an environment are investigation, discussion, collaboration, and negotiation.

Technology can be used to create such environments and facilitate the activities within them. By thinking of technology as a valuable tool in a constructivist learning environment, we can use the power and potential of technology not only to teach technical skills but also to help ELLs create knowledge. Using technology in education is a broad topic but we can be inspired to try more activities of our own design or taken from the Internet.

THE ROLE OF TECHNOLOGY IN INSTRUCTION AND ASSESSMENT

As new technologies permeate our communities, they are also becoming more and more of a factor in today's classrooms. The promise of technology in education is significant. Technology offers the potential of individualized instruction and assessment for every student as students become actively engaged in and responsible for their own learning. The capability to develop every student into a lifelong student is now even more achievable with developments in technology. Technology beckons educators with more opportunities for learning and increases in student achievement (Jonassen, 1995).

In fact, many see technology as the new dynamic in the traditional student–teacher relationship (National Education Association, 2001). However, the most important influence in student learning and achievement is still teacher quality. The true challenge of effectively integrating technology in education is human rather than technological. While technology advances hold the promise of improved learning instruction, technology-focused professional development for teachers is critical if technology is truly to be used to promote learning in all students (Moursund, 1999).

Most schools offer teachers different levels of support, but the ones that stand apart belong to districts that have long-term commitments to professional development as a major component of effective technology implementation. One-shot trainings and workshops are not effective. A comprehensive, well-thought-out professional development plan that moves educators along the continuum from novice to integrator over time, regardless of their starting position, demonstrates investment, commitment, and thoroughness on the part of the district. As teachers develop their core technology skills, they need ongoing support through a professional development environment that is consistently interwoven with hands-on use of technology to reinforce their efforts and learning (World Wide Web Consortium, 2001).

Teachers need information, training, and assistance to ensure that new technology tools benefit student learning. Effective technology professional development should include:

- Providing teachers with access to technology tools and time to learn how to integrate them in their teaching

- Participation in online and in-person learning communities in which educators share expertise
- Ongoing technology support at the school site

FOSTERING A TECHNOLOGY CULTURE IN THE CLASSROOM

A successful, comprehensive professional development program is based on a long-term plan and vision that fosters a district technology culture (Cunningham, 2003). Effective implementation begins with a clear definition of what the learning goals are, including specific logistical and tactical strategies for implementing technology in the classroom (Rockman, Walker, & Chessler, 2000). The districts in which technology has transformed teaching and instruction are districts in which the administrative leadership is committed to the use of technology to enhance learning for all students.

Professional development programs focus on changing teaching methods and making teachers facilitators and mentors in the learning process using a multidimensional approach, rather than the more traditional, one-dimensional methods of instruction relying on just textbooks and teachers. Well-planned, sustained professional development for effective technology implementation requires systems change at the most fundamental levels in a district or school. Professional development is the key component to fostering the technology culture, because educators are needed to apply and integrate technology with the curriculum, and engage students in different learning projects aligned with their learning goals (Hanson-Smith, 2000; Kern, 1995).

Effective professional development programs utilize modeling and peer-coaching methods to help teachers integrate technology and become coaches and facilitators of learning with technology as the tool. Again, collaboration requires time during the day and the week to share ideas and experiences, successes and challenges. Schools can consider having an early-release practice for students on a weekday. During this time, teachers can attend district and/or building workshops offered by technology specialists. The training/workshop curriculum can come from a variety of sources, including materials from out-of-district conferences and technology vendor training materials. Well-thought-out training and materials from technology vendors can be woven into the professional development program, but the district needs to assume ownership for follow-up and implementation (North Central Region Educational Laboratory, 1996).

Teams of teachers can be in charge of reviewing software and Web sites, creating curriculum resources, scanning text into a digital format, and developing tutorials. In addition, technology specialists can work closely with teachers and teams who are developing special projects that include language and content area for all students, including ELLs. All areas of the curriculum are supported, and every building downloads the resources onto school computers for same-day use. Materials include supports for balanced literacy, digital textbooks, writing supports, modified tests, study guides, and integrated language arts and math activities (Warschauer, 1997).

HOW TEACHERS MAY BECOME FAMILIAR WITH AND INTEGRATE TECHNOLOGY WITH ESL INSTRUCTION

These are considerations to reach more teachers to use and apply technology in their classrooms (Bray, 2003).

- Show teachers how technology can improve their students' learning; and provide opportunities for teachers to learn, plan, practice, experiment, reflect and share the use of technology
- Review content standards so teachers can make sure the topic meets what they are supposed to be teaching
- Model several lessons with student examples, including some simple lessons so teachers are not discouraged or afraid to jump in
- Show teachers how to find rich, relevant and appropriate resources
- Provide templates, support materials, and a mentor or coach
- Team an early adopter with a teacher new to technology so the excitement rubs off
- Give teachers lots of hands-on time to practice, plan, and reflect on what they learned
- Feed them and provide incentives such as prizes and stipends
- Provide "talk time" so teachers can share what they learn

TECHNOLOGY IN THE CLASSROOM

When effectively integrated into the curriculum, technology tools can extend learning in powerful ways. The Internet and multimedia can provide students and teachers with a number of benefits as both attend to the standards-based curriculum (Hanson-Smith, 2000). These include:

- Access to up-to-date, primary source material
- Ways to collaborate with students, teachers, and experts around the world
- Opportunities for expressing understanding via images, sound, and text

The integration of technology into classroom with ELLs can be both technically and pedagogically challenging for teachers (Sotillo, 2002). Some school districts require technology integration into the curriculum and allocate a considerable budget to ensure that classes are scheduled and taught by the regular classroom teacher. Some teachers must embrace technological change without necessarily having had prior experience with it themselves. As a consequence, there can be a danger of using technology as an add-on rather than as an integrated part of the curriculum (Marlowe & Page, 1998).

Many electronic tools—e-mail, e-journals, chat rooms, and virtual classrooms—offer ELLs and their teachers opportunities to construct meaning. These tools offer the following benefits

- Provide real-life L2 language experiences with opportunities to communicate with a real audience for a real purpose, not just with the teacher (Dixon-Krauss, 1996)
- Expose ELLs to other means of communication through the use of Internet elements, such as Web sites, hyperlinks, animations, and other visual data (Snyder, 1999)
- Introduce ELLs to new forms of literacy on the Web from which they learn to visually analyze multimedia components (e.g., text, animation, video displays, and audio recording) (Kress, 1997; Sutherland-Smith, 2002)

TECHNOLOGY PROVIDES ACCESS TO LINGUISTIC AND CULTURAL MATERIALS

Technology has the potential to provide access and exposure to engaging, authentic, and comprehensible curriculum materials in the L2. It can be a great resource for teachers of ELLs. The following three areas proposed by Salaberry (2001) for foreign language education can also help enhance instruction to meet the specific needs of ELLs.

1. *Enhancing efficiency through digital multimedia technologies.* Digital multimedia technologies are used to make access to learning materials in an efficient manner because (a) multimedia (visual, audio, and text) presentations can create strong memory links and (b) digital technology allows instant and accurate playbacks, which helps the student to access specific segments (Shea, 2000).

2. *Enhancing authenticity using video and the Internet.* Video materials can bring language and context-rich curriculum materials to the ELL; the Internet enables the student to access a wealth of information in English, their L2, that can reflect current cultural changes more effectively than printed sources (Hanson-Smith, 1999).

3. *Enhancing comprehensibility through student control and multimedia annotations.* Comprehensible input is necessary for language learning but useful learning materials must also contain enough unfamiliar materials (Krashen, Candin, & Terrell, 1996). For language students, especially beginning and intermediate ones, authentic materials are often beyond their language proficiency and may become incomprehensible without help. To enhance comprehensibility of spoken materials, full caption, keyword caption, or slowing down the speech rate have been found to be effective (Shea, 2000). For reading materials, glossing or multimedia annotations have been effective means to enhance comprehension (Al-Seghayer, 2001).

PROVIDING OPPORTUNITIES
FOR COMMUNICATION

Technology can also help ELLs to engage in authentic communication in the L2 as it is an essential condition for successful language learning. Technology can be used in many different ways to create opportunities for language students to communicate in the L2 (Hanson-Smith, 1999). Efforts to promote interaction: with the computer and through the computer with remote audiences are briefly described.

1. *Interactions with the computer.* Communicative interactions can occur in either written or spoken language or a combination of both. At the simplest level, a computer program can generate utterances either orally or in writing that require the student to respond by selecting an answer with a mouse click or providing simple written responses (Hanson-Smith, 1999). The ELL also can carry on near-natural conversations with a computer program around preselected and programmed topics (Wachowicz & Scott, 1999). The student can also give either written or spoken commands to a computer program in a simulation and safe environment. The computer program would then perform the command (Holland, Kaplan, & Sabol, 1999).

2. *Interactions with remote audiences through the computer.* Computer-mediated communication and teleconferencing technologies have created authentic communication opportunities for students since the 1980s. The uses of technologies, such as electronic mail, bulletin boards, and chat rooms can also be beneficial as they bring the much needed audience to the student with an effective participation, leading to more oral and written output in the L2 (Salaberry, 2001).

ASSESSING AND PROVIDING FEEDBACK

The capacity for computers to provide instant and individualized feedback has long been recognized by all educators, including second language educators. Whereas early applications tended to follow the behaviorist tradition by simply assessing the student's performance and providing simplistic feedback in a correct-or-wrong fashion, more recent applications are much more contextualized and pedagogically sound (Salaberry, 2001).

1. *Computer-based grammar checkers and spell checkers* are potentially powerful ways to provide feedback about students' written output (Jacobs & Rodgers, 1999). Although immediate, the feedback provided by current grammar checkers is not always accurate, because of its inability to perform semantic analysis and process deep-level structures.

2. *Automatic speech recognition technology* holds the potential to provide valuable feedback. Pronunciation is a fundamental element of language learning but to provide feedback that can be easily accessible and useful is difficult. Automatic speech recognition technology can assist the teacher in providing feedback to the student's pronunciation and in modeling, not only by repeating the student's pronunciation and explaining how the sound should be produced, but by supplying visual feedback, template-based, and model-based input. A computer program can analyze a student's utterance and display the features visually, perhaps with a comparison to that of a native speaker. A computer program can also display the position and movements of the tongue when a student produces an utterance, and then compare it to that of a native speaker. Furthermore, computer programs can compare student pronunciation of individual words or sentences to prerecorded templates. Pronunciation can also be evaluated against pronunciation models. In this approach, student pronunciation is not limited to preselected words because the model is a generalization of a template.

3. *Tracking and analyzing student errors and behaviors* is another approach language educators can experiment with so as to provide more helpful feedback of word-level errors (e.g., vocabulary and conjugation errors) or sentence-level errors (e.g., word order errors). Computer programs can store student responses, which then can be analyzed by the teacher and the computer.

The following examples illustrate computer technology used to create environments that facilitate the teaching activities within them. Technology is a valuable tool to help students create knowledge. These technology-integrated projects can be implemented in the classroom by bilingual, ESL, or mainstream teachers with ELLs in their classrooms.

ONLINE EDUCATIONAL PROJECTS AND CONTENT AREA STANDARDS

Factors to Consider When Choosing Online Projects

In the classroom, we can teach multiple standards with online educational projects by using an integrated curriculum while encouraging peer collaboration with the use of real-world situations. With so many online projects, it would be complex to choose the right one. There are at least 10 factors that need to be considered when choosing an online project (Shaw, 2004): cost, the content area focus (science, social studies, literature, mathematics, etc.), interweaving of other curriculums, standards (national/state education standards), quality of project, amount of time required, degree of collaboration, personal benefits, other benefits, and number of participants.

1. *Cost.* There are many free, excellent online educational projects. Space Day and Listening to the Walls Talk are online projects that have a lot of good things that are applicable to the classroom. There are also some excellent projects that do cost money (e.g., JASON).

2. *The content area focus.* What we plan to teach will determine our main curriculum content focus. We need to decide which academic area we are going to focus on: Mathematics? Science? Social Studies? Language Arts? Art? Music? For the most part, it is best to focus on a single subject.

3. *Interweaving of other curriculums.* We also need to decide how we are going to connect other curriculums to the project. Students often do not understand the interconnectivity of subjects taught independently. However, there is always the question of: "Did the students learn the content?" We have to know beforehand that this content meets the educational standards. When creating an online project, we begin by realizing that implementing national and state standards into our project is easy and an effective way to teach. They need to understand mathematics, but then, they also need to see how it will be used in their real world. They need to understand how to write a 5-paragraph essay, but they also need to know that the essay is a viable form of communication that easily allows others to see the results of research. There are projects that focus on one subject but they can easily include and interweave other subjects. For example, "Listening to the Walls Talk" (www.millennium.scps.k12.fl.us/walls.html) is a project whose main focus is social studies. The goal of this project is to teach students basic geographic and research skills. A secondary, but possibly more important, goal of this project is to record the history of houses and neighborhoods around the world.

4. *Standards (national/state education standards).* Standards are at the core of teaching and learning. We can choose ready-made projects and check to see if they follow the mandated standards. When we create a project, we need to choose which standards we want to teach before we begin. We know that there is no better way to teach any curriculum concept than by having students participate in authentic hands-on, project-based learning and using **authentic assessments.** We can have an interdisciplinary array of curricula represented. Students can practice mathematics, science, language arts, social studies, and fine arts skills, all in one project. Education World lists several national and education organizations that have taken on the challenge of creating educational standards or guidelines to be used on a national level, including the following:

National Council of Teachers of Mathematics (www.nctm.org)
National Council of Teachers of English (www.ncte.org)
National Geographic Society (www.nationalgeographic.org)
National Council on Economic Education (www.ncee.net)
National Council for the Social Studies (www.ncss.org)
Center for Civic Education (www.civiced.org/index.html)
Consortium of National Arts Education Associations (http://artsedge.kennedy center.org/professional_resources/standards/nat_standards_main.html)
National Center for History in the Schools (www.sscnet.ucla.edu/nchs/)
International Society for Technology in Education, or ISTE (http://cnets.iste.org/index.html)
National Academies of Science (www.nas.edu/)
For state standards, we want to visit Education World (www.education-world.com/standards/state/index.shtml).

5. *Quality of project.* There are a number of free, quality projects with ready-made lessons, quizzes, and activities. For example, ENO, or Environment Online, is a global Web school for environmental awareness. It studies four environmental themes (dimensions of sustainable development) within a school year (social, natural, cultural environment, and a sustainable way of living) on a weekly basis. The ENO Program (http://eno.joensuu.fi/) is a strong and active network of schools. Up and running since 2000 and administrated by the city of Joensuu, Finland, it is supported by the National Board of Education and European Commission.

6. *Amount of time required.* With all the requirements facing us in the classroom, it is hard to find time to incorporate projects, to fully read through a project, check it out against our standards, and see if it is compatible with what we are teaching. However, a project can become a group effort (e.g., a project that includes the ESL teacher and the content area teacher selecting the right project, working together during planning time, making sure that the project can be accomplished during the intended class period, etc.). There are rewards to giving up some time to read through a project. Often there will be ready-made and useable lessons, alignment with standards, and even ready-made assessment tools.

7. *Degree of collaboration.* Collaboration is good and fun for the students. Students work together in joint productive activities, especially in an academically challenging effort. Students can do research with others in another state, country, or continent. Imagine the benefits of seeing students in Connecticut coming up with some information while their partners in Ohio or Germany come up with different (but still correct) information. This gives the students the chance to see how much information is out there, and how people can have different ideas about the same project.

A collaborative project actually takes more time than working individually. But we have to be able to constantly steer the students into academic exchanges, and keep them focused. But, the extra effort is almost always worth it, for the students come away with more than new friends; they learn future work and social skills. Collaboration teaches students how to cooperate and be part of a team.

8. *Personal benefits.* Liking the topic makes it personally more fun to come in, day after day, and teach. If we are teaching something we like, we spend more time learning about it. It could be teaching about historic preservation, and talking about preservation, restoration, and adaptive re use. If we like it, it is going to work with one of our projects. And we infuse so much personal enthusiasm into the project that the students become interested and are willing to do it. We can also look for projects that incorporate content areas and technology as it help the state test scores.

9. *Other benefits.* We need to let our principal/administrators know that we are using the content area standards with our technology projects (e.g., mathematics with technology). There are some projects that offer awards or even prizes. This is a good incentive for the students—a certificate, a letter of commendation—can motivate students to continue striving.

10. *Number of participants.* An important criterion for online project selection is whether your entire class can participate—that they are not designed for small groups. All students—English speakers and ELLs—need to have the opportunity to participate. We can never choose just our best and brightest students to do projects, because it is not always the "star students" who do the best. We cannot select English speakers to do projects and not include ELLs. Often, the ELLs can outshine English speakers. We need to take advantage of technology and online projects because they have the potential to level the playing field for all students. It would be totally unfair to deny opportunity to some students while giving those who usually get the best of everything the extra opportunities.

Online Learning Model in the Elementary Classroom

The integration of an online learning environment with a traditional elementary school classroom ideally would combine all benefits of both modes of teaching. The traditional face-to-face elementary classroom imparts the social contact that children need to guide their learning whereas the online, or Web-based, learning environment offers flexibility and opportunities not possible in a traditional classroom. To create a learning environment using both modes to enhance the learning experiences of the students would provide the greatest benefit.

This dual mode, or blended learning environment, although increasingly common in higher education and even some high schools, has not been readily embraced at the elementary (K–5) school level. However, it is feasible at the elementary level.

1. Start by setting up an online extension of the classroom using Think.com. This environment already has everything needed to set up an online class, and saves many hours of work. With Think.com we can quickly make learning objects using templates, store them, edit them, and publish them. It is password protected so only the students in a particular class are able to see what is happening on the page

2. The site has several activities each week. One can be a list of links to Internet sites related to the students' classroom studies for that week. There are always at least four different links that extend what is being covered in the subject areas.

3. After exploring the links, students vote on their favorite and the teacher shows them which site won in the voting.

4. Another weekly activity is the student of the week. Each week this student is in the "hot seat." The other students will ask them questions such as "What is your favorite movie?" or "Where was your favorite vacation?" and the student of the week would answer the questions asynchronously. A question in a discussion thread related to the current mathematics, science, social studies unit is also a regular feature

5. Supplement the regular features with various activities that fit with a particular topic that week, and an ongoing history, geography, or science unit. The units

have weekly assignments and are downloadable forms posted for the students to access when they are ready to work on the project. Overall, there are three different types of activities: the weekly regulars, the timely surprises that fit with a topic of study, and the content area unit

6. Set up the activities for each week so that the students can either do them quickly or with deeper thought, depending on their own interest in the topic and the amount of time available to them that week. As the school year goes along, the students become more willing to disclose areas of difficulty in math, science, social studies during the discussion periods. In all areas the discussion and questions seem to become more thoughtful as the students become more comfortable with the site

DEVELOPING A WEB SITE TO TEACH SCIENTIFIC COLLABORATION IN THE MIDDLE SCHOOL

Often when a scientist, engineer, or medical practitioner makes a discovery, develops a new procedure, or invents a new device, he or she writes a paper explaining what he or she has done. This paper is usually published in a scientific journal or, increasingly today, over the Internet. One reason for publishing these discoveries or new procedures is to give peers the opportunity to see if the discovery or procedure is reproducible. If an experiment, discovery, or new procedure is reproducible then it is considered valid (Calhoun, 2004).

Middle school science teachers have the challenge to try to develop in their students an understanding of this important process. Thanks to the **computer technology** and transportation revolutions, scientists from many different countries and cultures work together on a variety of projects collaboratively. The successful scientific collaborations require tolerance of others and the ability to interact in diverse settings. This is also a concept that all students need to understand and to appreciate.

When a science classroom is blessed with both a lab for conducting experiments, and enough Internet-connected computers for every two students, then it is possible to do a series of Web-based activities that teach the importance of scientific reproducibility, peer review, and the acceptance of different opinions.

Cyberlab

Cyberlab, a Web site developed and maintained by Calhoun (2004), is designed to introduce students to the science protocol of peer review and research reproducibility. The Cyberlab site contains a narrative project assignment. Each project begins with a problem-solving scenario, followed by a detailed list of requirements for carrying out the project and making a final report. There are links to needed real data, as well as links to supplementary study material. The Web site includes search engines to facilitate more in-depth investigations.

Cyberlab Narratives Are Multicultural.   Students live in an era of increasing racial and ethnic diversity. The ranks of students who need extra help learning English have burgeoned in recent decades. Almost 4 million public school children—nearly 1 in 12—received special assistance to learn English in 2001–2002, according to the U.S. Department of Education (National Center for Education Statistics [NCES], 2002). In a 1998 *Children Now* poll, over three-fourths of children reported having a best friend of a different race. While diversity is easily seen in many children's lives, the question is: Should they not also see it portrayed when it comes to scientific collaboration? Young people get clear messages about racial, ethnic, language, and class divisions and their own identity through the characters they see on television and other media. The Internet is a visual medium that goes beyond television in that it is interactive. The use of the Cyberlab Web page and other Web pages can raise the awareness of students to the linguistic and cultural diversity, gender integration, and **multicultural** nature of scientific collaboration.

Project assignments range widely: there is one to verify the reproducibility of a middle school student's procedure for making a plastic-like substance from milk; another to analyze a genetic karyotype to diagnosis Down's syndrome; and a third to investigate data concerning the discovery of a new element by British high school students. When a project is completed, students use e-mail to distribute their results to other participating classes in the school.

Setting Up a Cyberlab Type Web Page.   It is easy to develop and publish a Web page similar to Cyberlab without the need to learn complicated computer programming codes. The software to create web pages is generically known as "Web page authoring tools." Three of the best and the easiest to use are *Microsoft FrontPage 2000, Dreamweaver,* and *Netscape Composer.* Also, many word processors can convert documents into Web pages.

After the Web page is developed, it can be published or uploaded to one of the many free Web providers, which is especially helpful given tight school budgets. Many of these Web providers offer free Web space, e-mail service, and provide simple online Web page-making tools. Three companies that will publish Web pages for free are *Tripod, Homestead,* and *20megsFree.* Cyberlab is hosted on Homestead.com and 20megs-free.com. Also, commercial online services (America Online, MSN, etc.) make it possible for members to publish Web pages for free as well.

Why Develop a Web Page Like Cyberlab?   The following are some reasons for developing one's own Web site.

- You can control the content of the site
- Because the site is on the Internet, families are able to work with their children on the activities at home, and by doing so become exposed to the multicultural narratives
- The site also can contain a dedicated e-mail address so students and their teachers from other schools can make comments and suggestions. For example, the class

can receive e-mail from students, teachers, and interested people from around the world
- Other subjects besides science can be covered using the Cyberlab approach

CLASSROOM COMPUTER INTEGRATION AT THE HIGH SCHOOL LEVEL

Most students—ELLs and all—are perhaps more computer-technology literate than the majority of teachers instructing them everyday. Some even know how to use Excel and PowerPoint. Many high school students have probably already taken a computer literacy course and a word-processing class in high school. However, most students do not practice these important skills in class. Our job is to reintegrate into our classes the technology to which they have already been exposed. With two computers in one classroom, integrating them into the class is not difficult (Gildersleeve, 2004).

The following are some adjustments to be made to a traditional teacher's pen-and-paper-driven curriculum.

1. Give out extra points to students in your classes for doing the selected course assignments using Microsoft Word. For science and social studies presentations, give a complete letter-grade bump for any student who does his or her presentation using PowerPoint.

2. Integrate technology into the Physical Education (P.E.) curriculum. For example, when one of the P.E. activities is a softball unit, include two games against the high school in X City. The student who is excused from softball would be the score-keeper, and one of her or his tasks is to keep batting averages of the players in both games using Excel.

SELECTED EXAMPLES OF TECHNOLOGY PROJECTS

A Science-Technology Integrated Project

This project can be part of a science unit. It involves computer skills and instruction. Technology is the means to completion, not the focus, of the project (Reinhardt & Isbell, 2002).

Theme: Recycling

Goals:
1. Students will gain a greater awareness of garbage volume and recycling efforts in the community
2. Students will express their awareness through a variety of media.
3. Students will construct a survey and make a video.

Grade Level (s): Upper elementary, middle, and high school
Language Proficiency Levels: Intermediate and advanced English language proficiency levels with ELLs and mainstream English-speaking students

Technology needed:
1. Online discussion bulletin board and chat room accessed through the class/school/district homepage, if available
2. Word processing and spreadsheet/graphing software
3. Video camcorders
4. Video editing software

Specific **computer software** *needed:*
- Apple iMovie 1.0
- Excel 4.90
- WebBoard 4.0
- Word 98

Language Focus: Speaking, writing, language form, pronunciation, intonation, and vocabulary skills as needed

Student Assessment: Students are assessed on the basis of
- Their participation in group tasks
- Satisfactory completion of each stage of the project
- The overall quality of the final products, report and the video

Activities:

Landfill and/or Recycling Center Visit.

1. In the first part of the project, the class visits a local incinerator, landfill, and/or recycling center. Students videotape and write notes about their impressions
2. Back in the classroom, students reflect and answer questions such as: What was something new you learned about recycling? Students use WebBoard TM (1999), an online discussion bulletin board
3. Students later use these responses and notes to write the commentary for the video portion of the project.

Survey.

1. Students first log onto an online class chat session using WebBoard to brainstorm questions to ask in the survey about recycling
2. Students e-mail the teacher the questions they feel should be included in the survey and the questions are compiled into a single class survey
3. Pairs of students are responsible for asking individual students, teachers, administrators, staff, and the school community to respond to the survey. Each pair has to videotape themselves administering the survey to one respondent

4. The class tabulates the results. Each student is responsible for writing a report about one of the survey questions. The student chooses two subgroups and compares the average response for each group based on age, gender, nationality, or combinations

5. The reports include an introduction with basic survey description, the findings with two paragraphs (one for the whole group and another for the subgroup comparison), a graph generated with Microsoft® ExcelTM (Version 4.90, 1977), and a conclusion.

6. During class, students type the reports using Microsoft® Word 98 Macintosh® Edition (1997)

7. When needed, the instructor provides vocabulary and language accuracy

Video Production.

1. Students integrate the information from the visit to the local incinerator, landfill, and/or recycling center and their survey findings into a documentary format. They also include footage from the visit and the taped interviews of survey respondents.

2. This is usually the most time- and labor-intensive portion of the project. The class first decides on the overall structure of the documentary. Groups of students then choose one section of the video to design and develop.

3. The various roles that students share include: director, scriptwriter, reporter, storyboard author, cameraperson, and keyboardist.

4. Groups use Apple® iMovieTM (Version 1.0, 1999) software to import the footage into the computer; edit it by cropping and rearranging clips. They also enhance their product with titles, transitions, imported still images, voice-overs, and music.

5. Language instruction focuses on pronunciation and accuracy of the scripts.

6. The video is presented to the school at a monthly school meeting or as decided.

A Social Studies-Technology Integrated Project

This project can be part of a geography unit (Jun, 2002). It involves computer skills and instruction. Technology is the means to completion, not the focus, of the project.

Theme: A Trip to Puerto Rico
Goal: Students will produce an itinerary and a budget for a trip to Puerto Rico

Objectives:
1. Students will create a one-week virtual touring itinerary of Puerto Rico
2. Students will make airplane, hotel, and car rental reservations
3. Students will locate places to eat
4. Students will plan interesting sights to visit and things to do

Grade Level (s): Middle and high school
Language Proficiency Levels: Intermediate and advanced English language proficiency levels with ELLs and mainstream English-speaking students

Language Focus: Speaking, writing, language form, pronunciation, intonation, and vocabulary skills as needed. Students' presentations—involving reporting, discussing, writing, and commenting—are opportunities for students to enhance their oral and written communication skills in their second language

Student assessment: Students are assessed on the basis of
- Their participation in the group project. The teacher establishes rubrics at the beginning of the project so that students know what is expected of them.
- Satisfactory completion of each stage of the project
- The overall quality of the itinerary

Activities:

Selecting Places to Visit.

1. The teacher demonstrates how to use search engines (e.g., Google, Yahoo!) to locate Web sites for students who are unfamiliar with the Internet. Groups of two or three students search Web sites for information about Puerto Rico. The teacher either provides students with a list of sites or allows them to explore the Internet. Some popular travel Web sites are:
- www.travelocity.com
- www.puertorico.com
- www.travel.yahoo.com
- www.greatbuildings.com

2. The groups negotiate one to three cities they want to visit in Puerto Rico. The teacher selects one member of the group to be the group leader and report to the class where his or her group would like to go in Puerto Rico and why.

3. The entire class discusses the group suggestions and agrees on the places they would like most to visit during the week-long trip.

Creating Task Assignments.

1. The class creates a list of tasks to prepare for the trip (e.g., making airplane, hotel, and car/bus rental reservations; finding places to visit; locating places to eat; planning activities).
2. The teacher prepares writing guidelines for the task assignments (e.g., the Places to Visit or Touring Group will search different places in the island, visiting museums and theme attractions). The writing should include a brief introduction and information about museum's hours of operation, admissions costs, and how to get there. The group leaders type the groups' descriptions on the computer.
3. The groups will include a list of expenses to use later for the budget (e.g., the Finding Places to Eat Group lists the names and locations of the chosen restaurants,

menus, and costs). If price information is not available on the Web sites, the group needs to calculate approximate costs based on ratings given to the restaurants by the reviews if available. Other means to obtain this information include: group members' personal dining and travel experiences, or faxing to the restaurants and hotels using contact numbers listed on the Web sites. This activity will give students practice in requesting information as a means to prepare a more accurate budget.

4. The groups exchange their descriptions and budgets electronically by e-mail for comment.

Writing the Itinerary.

1. The students discuss the feedback via e-mail exchanged among groups and select the final content of the one-week itinerary. The teacher provides the class with published travel guides to use as model for planning the itinerary. Such guidebooks are available from Puerto Rico Tourism Office.

2. Each group writes the activities and budget for one touring day in the itinerary and the group leaders types the text on the computer. The teacher is a resource, answering questions and ensuring that everyone is contributing to the group assignment.

3. The group leaders send the drafts via e-mail to the other groups for feedback.

4. Each group discusses the feedback received from the other groups and revises their texts. They may have up to 3 drafts. The revision also includes grammar corrections and content clarification. The groups may also appoint a class editor-in-chief who will compile via e-mail each group's 1-day itinerary into a final 7-day itinerary.

5. The students print the class itinerary.

A Computer-Mediated Class Memory Book.

This project can become an annual yearbook for those ELLs whose families may not be able to afford to purchase the school-produced book and are unable to join in the fun of getting their books signed by their classmates (Conrad & Conrad, 2002). For the most part, few ELLs have computers in their homes. This project is important for the entire class but for ELLs it may have the following additional benefits

- Helps build self-esteem in students who may be left out of candid school photos
- Enhances student creativity and computer literacy
- Promotes a feeling of belonging to the larger school community
- Encourages English usage in meaningful ways

Theme: A Memory Book
Goal: Students will produce a class memory book using special memories and sharing them with friends.

Objectives:
1. Students will use the English language they are learning to produce their memory books
2. Students will write photo captions in English
3. Students will edit their photos using the computer graphics program
4. Students will negotiate their language and technology difficulties with peers

Grade Level(s): Middle school
Language Proficiency Levels: Beginning and intermediate English language proficiency levels
Language Focus: Speaking, writing, language form, pronunciation, intonation and vocabulary skills as needed. Students' negotiation of meaning using their developing English or their first language helps them to learn English as a natural by-product of a meaningful task or activity (Lee, 2000; Nunan, 1999).

Student assessment: Students are assessed the basis of
- Their participation in the memory book project. The teacher establishes rubrics at the beginning of the project so that students know what is expected of them.
- Satisfactory participation in the project throughout the school year
- The overall quality of the individual memory book

Technology needed:
- A digital camera, or a disposable 35mm camera (photo departments can develop the 35mm film on a floppy disk or CD)
- 3 1/2" floppy disk or CD for each student and one more disk or CD for the entire class
- Any computer with a floppy drive, word-processing software, graphics application, e.g. Microsoft® Paint [Windows 95; 1981–1996] and about 25 MB (megabytes) of hard-disk storage space

Activities:
1. The teacher introduces the entire process to produce the memory book to the class. She or he shows memory-book models from previous classes, families, personal, and so on.
2. Students become familiar with how to use the digital camera.
3. The teacher explains proper picture-taking etiquette and clarifies class and school rules about when and how pictures can be taken.
4. The teacher facilitates schedules in and outside of class to take photos during the school year of friends, classmates, teachers, and school staff in various situations.
5. The teacher shows students how to transfer their photos from the disks to the computer, view and modify them, and place them on a page with subtitles.

6. The teacher facilitates a simple and clear list of steps involved in transferring the photos, using computer software programs and features to modify them in various ways (e.g., rotating, reducing, cropping, adding caption and text), and saving final modifications.
7. Students work periodically throughout the school year on two pages each time for their final memory book. When computers are limited, students work in pairs, deciding together which pictures to use.
8. Students spend several days at the end of the year to finalize a 5- to 8-page memory book on the computer and to print and staple together the final product.
9. The teacher assists students to design creative covers and bindings using thread, ribbon, cloth, paint, and other art supplies and materials.
10. The teacher distributes the memory book on school yearbook day.
11. Students read, sign, and enjoy their memory books.

ASSESSMENT ISSUES

Chapter 7 delves deeper into the issue of assessment. Two themes have dominated public discourse on education in the United States for the last two decades.

1. The need for public schools to demonstrate more accountability to the communities they serve and to the organizations that fund them
2. Ways in which schools should accommodate the rapid growth of ELLs and ways of addressing the persistent educational underachievement of many ELLs

States have responded to these themes in different ways. Some states have increased the use of standardized tests once a year while others have attempted to use **authentic assessment** venues on a continuous basis throughout the school year (Darling-Hammond, 2001). Large-scale assessments, like all assessments, are designed for a specific purpose. Those used in most states today are designed to rank-order schools and students for the purpose of accountability. However, assessments designed for ranking generally are not good instruments for helping teachers improve their instruction or modify their approach to individual students (Guskey, 2000; 2003). The following three reasons illustrate the problem of one-shot deal, large-scale assessments:

1. Students take them at the end of the school year, when most instructional activities are near completion
2. Teachers and schools do not receive the results until two or three months later, by which time, their students probably have moved to other teachers
3. The results that schools and teachers receive usually lack the level of detail needed to target specific improvements (Kifer, 2001)

An issue of inequity and **assessment bias** is present when ELLs are assessed too soon in their academic English development. Research has demonstrated that it takes at least 5 years to develop the academic language skills in English (Collier & Thomas,

2001; Thomas & Collier, 2003). By testing ELLs using standardized tests before they are ready, educators are doing a disservice these students and underestimating ELLs potentials. There are, for example, two major flaws in the 2001 No Child Left Behind (NCLB) federal legislation that need to be corrected if ELLs are to be served with equity:

1. Educators are required to compare the performance of this year's students with that of last year's students instead of following the progress of the same students over time. Because one class and one school can change dramatically from year to year, the cross-sectional comparison mandated by NCLB does not measure students' actual progress.

2. The NCLB legislation does not address the issue of how long it takes for ELLs to close their achievement gap with native English speakers. States' policymakers have converged on the politically expedient 3-year or 30-month limit for instructional support in bilingual or ESL programs, and educators are engaging in wishful thinking when they assume that minimally achieving former ELLs will continue to close the achievement gap—that is, gain faster than native English speakers do—after they leave their special support program and enter the mainstream program. As stated earlier, research continues to prove that ELLs need 5 to 6 years to achieve full parity with average native English speakers, not only in English language proficiency but also in the mastery of the high standards content curriculum

Assessment and Teaching

Assessment is closely related to instruction and indispensable in professional development. For instance, authentic assessment is possible only in the context of teaching and learning processes that are student centered. The teacher's role is to facilitate and moderate the instruction. This role is in contrast to teacher-centered instruction where students are passive recipients of a transmission behaviorist, cemetery-style model (Tharp, 2000). Teachers need

- Ongoing professional development and support
- Opportunities to collaborate with other teachers when trying out new assessments
- Learning communities to share ways to refine the assessments for effective instruction

The teacher is an integral partner in the assessment process and has the responsibility to continue assessing student progress and growth across the standards-based curriculum and **benchmarks**, oral language development, reading, writing, and the content areas. In a bilingual or two-way bilingual program, the curricular areas taught in the L1 must be assessed in L1 and the themes or subject areas taught through L2 must be assessed in L2.

SUMMARY AND CONCLUSIONS: EFFECTIVE TECHNOLOGY INSTRUCTION FOR ELLS

The chapter examines the role of technology in ESL and content area classrooms across grade levels and stages of second language proficiency. It poses the need to implement technology advances in the classrooms and links them to quality teaching and content area standards, constructivist model and educational approaches and teaching strategies addressed in Chapters 2, 3, 4, and 6, and provides illustrations with instructional models and lesson plans embedded in technology.

The first major section discusses the benefits of technology and frames it within the constructivist approach (cognitive and social) of this book to help students and teachers to construct meaning in their classrooms. It underscores the role of the students who are not passive recipients of learning and who are able to construct their own knowledge from information received. Chapter 8 has the goal of making all teachers aware that ELLs may benefit by the infusion of technology in ESL and content courses. It also suggests ways for teachers to provide the technology environment for relevant learning by creating whole, authentic, inherently interesting activities.

The second major section encourages educators to apply technology in their classrooms and that technology is up to par with recent effective teaching methods. By using technology in their everyday teaching, teachers can become aware that technology also facilitates student assessment and that both assessment and instruction are closely related. For instance, teachers can follow their own authentic assessment techniques in the context of technology and learning processes that are student-centered. By understanding the constructivist perspective, teachers can perform their role as facilitators and moderators of instruction. By focusing on the content area standards, teachers will use the technology activities and incorporate them in their daily instructional activities to meet ELLs' needs.

With this knowledge of technology and its uses in the classroom, all teachers can become aware and empowered to help their ELLs: they will tend to measure ELLs' academic performance by the research-based standards; and raise their expectations of ELLs as gifted students who are capable of learning content and language(s). With this information, core subject teachers can incorporate technology and language skills into their curricula. They also can accomplish successful teaching using these strategies with the selected curricula and within the time frame stipulated by their district or school.

REVIEW QUESTIONS

1. How would you describe the need for technology in the classroom? What would a school or classroom you are familiar with need in order to implement technology? In your opinion, what are the main factors to infuse technology?

2. Discuss with your peers how you would use technology for instruction and assessment. Select a grade level and explain with examples the linkages of the three. Design a chart/graphic organizer to illustrate your points.

3. Design a minimodule for a partially trained audience on uses of the computer, Internet, Web pages, and so forth. Present it to peers for their feedback.

4. How beneficial is technology for ELLs? Would they improve their writing if they use it? Please explain. How about content area?

5. What technology are you familiar with? In your opinion, how do these programs help you in your craft? List your responses.

CRITICAL THINKING QUESTIONS

1. Think of two reasons why teachers at all levels of instruction need to transform their classrooms into technology-rich environments—e.g., using EXCELL, Web pages, PowerPoint as important strategies to develop language and academics.

2. Go online and use some of the Web sites listed in the chapter to find the information; identify two descriptors of these roles. As much as possible, link them to the education of ELLs. Make a PowerPoint presentation with your findings.

3. Do you communicate with someone you do not know personally? If so, how comfortable do you feel without face-to-face communication? What have you learned about this person's culture and language?

4. Develop a rubric that includes assessing language and content through technology. Relate this to the district's standards and benchmarks.

ACTIVITIES

1. Review the medley of technology applications with content standards instruction. What other activities or programs are you familiar with? Survey your peers about some of the activities they know. Prepare a list of their contributions and yours.

2. Select one activity and prepare to teach it to peers; practice and time the activity. Ask for peers' feedback on ways to infuse technology in the classroom. Write a paragraph-long position statement.

3. Design a technology strategy to reinforce a topic of a particular lesson. As much as possible, include the standard(s) you are using and the language skills you want to reinforce. Write your strategy in detail with directions for ELLs to follow. Explain your strategy to peers in simple terms.

4. Assess the needs of a classroom/school of your choice. Interview the teacher and find out how much she or he knows about how to use technology in her or his classroom. Compare the classroom with other classrooms in terms of technology equipment and use, and make recommendations about first steps to be taken.

5. What areas, courses, subjects, and themes are the easiest to implement with technology? Select a grade level and develop a lesson plan for developing ELLs' listening, speaking, reading, and writing English skills with the subject area of your choice. Select the grade level and language development stage of your ELLs. Demonstrate the lesson to your peers.

GLOSSARY

assessment   The orderly process of gathering, analyzing, interpreting, and reporting student performance data, ideally from multiple sources over a period of time.

assessment bias   Bias that occurs when the linguistic and cultural background of diverse students is not considered.

authentic assessment   Assessments that are linked to the instruction delivered in the classrooms and to real-world activities.

benchmarks   Models or examples of student work used to demonstrate various levels on a scoring rubric.

computer technology   The application of science to computers and software.

computer software   Programs, symbolic language, essential to the operation of computers.

multiculturalism   The capacity to negotiate effectively within two or more different cultural systems.

multicultural   An idea or concept based on democratic values and beliefs. It seeks to affirm cultural pluralism within culturally diverse societies and interdependent worlds. It incorporates the ideas of democratic challenges and opportunities for school achievement regardless of race, ethnic background, gender, or socioeconomic status.

USEFUL WEB SITES

1. The Knowledge Loom Guidebook
   http:// knowledgeloom.org/guidebook

2. Voices from the Field: Almost the Real World
   www.alliance.brown.edu/pubs/voices/

3. Recycling Research Project
   www.personal.psu.edu/jsr199/mic/fall00/sci151/

4. Instant Web's Online Computing Dictionary
   www.InstantWeb.com/d/dictionary

5. NetMeeting Software
   www.microsoft.com/windows/netmeeting/

6. Search Engines
   http://lib.berkeley.edu/TeachingLib/Guides/Internet/SearchEngines.html

7. International Society for Technology in Education
   www.iste.com

8. Power To Learn
   www.powertolearn.com

REFERENCES

Al-Seghayer, K. (2001). The effect of multimedia annotation modes on L2 vocabulary acquisition: A comparative study. *Language Learning and Technology, 5*(1), 202–232.

Apple iMovie 1.0 [Computer software]. (1999). Cupertino, CA: Apple Computer.

Bray, B. (2003). Learn by doing: A hands-on approach to help teachers use technology. Retrieved December 15, 2003, from the World Wide Web: www.techlearning.com/db_area/archives/WCE/archives/primarbb.html

Calhoun, M. (2004). Cyberlab: An ally for teaching scientific collaboration. Retrieved October 2, 2004, from the World Wide Web: www.techlearning.com/db_area/archives/WCE/archives/primarbb.html

Collier, V., & Thomas, W. (2001, February). *California dreamin': The real effect of Proposition 227 on test scores.* Feature speech presented at the National Association for Bilingual Education conference, Phoenix, AZ.

Conrad, K. B., & Conrad, T. R. (2002). Creating an ESL computer-mediated class memory book. *TESOL Journal, 11*(3), 47–48.

Conway, J. (1997). *Educational technology's effect on models of instruction.* Retrieved November 20, 2003, from the World Wide Web: copland.udel.edu/~jconway/EDST666.htm

Cunningham, J. (2003). Between technology and teacher effectiveness: Professional development. Retrieved December 13, 2003, from the World Wide Web: www.techlearning.com/db_area/archives/WCE/archives/primarbb.html

Darling-Hammond, L. (2001, April 11). *Educational research and educational reform: Drawing the connections between research, policy, and practice.* Invited address presented at the annual meeting of the American Educational Research Association, Seattle, WA.

Dixon-Krauss, L. (1996). *Vygotsky in the classroom: Mediated literacy instruction and assessment.* New York: Longman.

Excel (Version 4.90) [Computer software]. (1997). Redmond, WA: Microsoft Corporation.

Gildersleeve, M. (2004) Classroom computer integration at the high school level.

Retrieved October 2, 2004, from the World Wide Web: www.techlearning.com/db_area/archives/WCE/archives/primarbb.html

Guskey, T. R. (2000). *Evaluating professional development.* Thousand Oaks, CA: Corwin.

Guskey, T. R. (2003). How classroom assessments improve learning. *Educational Leadership, 60*(5), 6–11.

Hanson-Smith, E. (1999). Classroom practice: Using multimedia for input and interaction in CALL environments. In E. Hanson-Smith (Ed.), *CALL environments: Research, practice, and critical issues* (pp. 189–215). Alexandria, VA: TESOL.

Hanson-Smith, E. (Ed.). (2000). Technology-enhanced learning environments. Alexandria, VA: TESOL.

Healey, D. D., & Klinghammer, S. J. (2002). Constructing meaning with computers. *TESOL Journal 11*(3), 3.

Holland, V. M., Kaplan, J. D., & Sabol, M. A. (1999). Preliminary tests of language learning in a speech-interactive graphics micro world. *CALICO Journal, 16*(3), 339–359.

Jonassen, D. H. (1995). *Supporting communities of learners with technology: A vision for integrating technology with learning in schools.* Retrieved October 16, 2003, from the World Wide Web: www.itd. depaul.edu/website/pages/TrainingEvents/ CourseMaterials/jonassen.asp

Jun, W. (2002). A trip to Tahiti. *TESOL Journal, 11*(3), 45–46.

Kern, R. G. (1995). Restructuring classroom interaction with networked computers: Effects on quality and characteristics of language production. *Modern Language Journal, 79*(4), 457–476.

Kifer, E. (2001). *Large-scale assessment: Dimensions, dilemmas, and policies.* Thousand Oaks, CA: Corwin.

Krashen, S. D., Candin, C. N., & Terrell, T. D. (1996). *The natural approach: Language acquisition in the classroom.* New York: Simon & Schuster International Group.

Kress, G. (1997). Visual and verbal modes of representation in electronically mediated communication: The potential of new forms of text. In I. Snyder (Ed.), *Page to screen: Taking literacy into the electronic era* (pp. 53–79). Sydney, Australia: Allen & Unwin.

Lee, J. F. (2000). *Tasks and communicating in language classrooms.* Boston: McGraw-Hill.

Marlowe, B. A., & Page, M. L. (1998). *Creating and sustaining the constructivist classroom.* Thousand Oaks, CA: Corwin.

Moursund, D. (1999). *Project-based learning using information technology.* Retrieved November 8, 2003, from the World Wide Web: darkwing.uoregon.edu/~moursund/PBL%20Book%201999/index.htm

National Center for Education Statistics. (2002). *Public elementary/secondary school universe survey 2001–2002 and local education agency universe survey 2001–2002.* Washington, DC: U.S. Department of Education.

National Education Association. (2001). The wireless revolution. *NEA Today, 19*(6), 8–9.

Norman, S. (1998). *EPSS: A constructivist learning environment?* [Slideshow]. Retrieved October 28, 2003 from the University of West Florida Web site: http://scholar.coe.uwf.edu/students/snorman/webpages/

North Central Regional Educational Laboratory. (1996). *Constructivist teaching and learning models.* Retrieved November 21, 2003, from the World Wide Web: www.ncerl.org/sdrs/areas/issues/envrnmnt/drugfree/sa3const.htm

Nunan, D. H. (1999). *Second language teaching and learning.* Boston: Heinle & Heinle.

Reinhardt, J., & Isbell, K. (2002). The recycling research documentary: A technology-integrated project. *TESOL Journal, 11*(3), 41–42.

Rockman, S., Walker, L., & Chessler, M. (2000). *A more complete picture: Laptop use and impact in the context of changing home and school access.* Retrieved December 18, 2003, from the World Wide Web: www.Microsoft.com/education/ download/aal/

Salaberry, M. R. (2001). The use of technology for second language learning and teaching: A retrospective. *Modern Language Journal, 85*(1), 39–56.

Shea, P. (2000). Leveling the playing field: A study of captioned interactive video for second language learning. *Journal of Educational Computing Research, 22*(3), 243–263.

Shaw, R. (2004). *Implementing the standards into projects.* Retrieved October 2, 2004, from the World Wide Web: www.techlearning.com/db_area/ archives/WCE/archives/primarbb.html

Sotillo, S. M. (2002). Constructivist and collaborative learning in a wireless environment. *TESOL Journal, 11*(3), 16–20.

Sutherland-Smith, W. (2002). Weaving the literacy web: Changes in reading from page to screen. *The Reading Teacher, 55*(7), 2–9.

Snyder, I. (1999). Digital literacies: Renegotiating the visual and the verbal in communication. *Prospect, 14*(3), 13–23.

Thomas, W. P., & Collier, V. P. (2003). The multiple benefits of dual language. *Educational Leadership, 61*(2), 61–64.

Vygotsky, L. S. (1986). *Thought and language.* Cambridge, MA: MIT Press.

Wachowicz, K. A., & Scott, B. (1999). Software that listens: It's not a question of whether, it's a question of how. *CALICO Journal, 16*(3), 253–276.

Warschauer, M. (1997). Computer-mediated collaborative learning: Theory and practice. *Modern Language Learning, 81*(4), 470–481.

WebBoard (Version 4.0) [Computer software]. (1999). Carlsbad, CA: ChatSpace.

Wong, S. (1998, August/September). TESOL joins NCATE. *TESOL Matters, 8*(4), 1.

World Wide Web Consortium. (2001). *Web accessibility initiative.* Retrieved December 3, 2003, from the World Wide Web: www.w3.org/WAI/

CONCLUSIONS: A DIALOGUE ABOUT MYTHS HELD BY EDUCATORS AND RECOMMENDATIONS FOR BETTER EDUCATIONAL PRACTICES FOR ESL STUDENTS

LEARNING OBJECTIVES

1. Readers will develop a personal connection to the sociohistorical presence of ESL immigrants in public schools in the United States
2. Readers will understand the importance of providing high-quality instruction and assessment for ESL learners
3. Readers will become committed advocates for better serving ESL students and their families

PREVIEW QUESTIONS

1. Think about some similarities and differences between ESL immigrants during the Ellis Island years and today's Hispanic and Asian ESL students. Develop a personal position about the "myth of rapid assimilation of earlier ESL immigrants," as described by the TESOL quote presented on page 330.
2. Do you know of any case of a family whose ancestors came through Ellis Island to the United States? Was that your family, the family of a friend or a classmate? Develop a personal connection to this immigration story that can help you understand the sociohistorical presence of ESL immigrants in public schools in the United States.
3. How important is it for ESL students to receive high-quality instruction? How can external educational environments affect the development and learning of low-income ESL students?

4. How important is it for the professional development of ESL and all teachers to learn the importance of becoming committed advocates for better serving their ESL students and their families?

5. How commonly held are the ten myths presented in this chapter by ESL and all teachers? What information can be presented to ESL and all teachers to dispel these myths and develop instead accurate knowledge?

Chapter 9 provides closure for the book in the form of a dialogue among coauthors centered on myths commonly held by educators, and some recommendations for better educational practices with ESL students in relation to the first and second themes of the book referring to educators: (1) developing a personal connection to the socio-historical presence of English-as-a-second-language (ESL) immigrants in the U.S. public schools, and (2) becoming committed advocates for better serving ESL students. In relation to these two themes, the dialogue among coauthors will be centered on myths, related to controversial issues and dilemmas, commonly held by preservice and in-service educators when serving ESL students and their families. The main idea underlying these myths is how internal (i.e., developmental and psychological characteristics) and external factors (i.e., school and family environments) interact to make ESL students resilient or at-risk of underachievement.

The book, throughout its chapters, has presented evidence and examples of how high-quality teaching can make a difference for dispelling these myths about ESL learners. The companion Web site also presents abundant information centered on the fist and second themes of the book, and can be used by readers as a major instructional and learning resource.

The need to dispel myths commonly held by educators has also been mentioned by the *ESL Standards for Pre-K–12 Students*, the Teachers of English to Speakers of Other Languages (TESOL), published in 1997. According to TESOL *Standards*, there is a need to dispel the myth that

> In earlier times immigrant children learned English rapidly and assimilated into American life . . . [in fact] . . . Many immigrant students during the early part of this century did not learn English quickly or well. Many dropped out of school to work in jobs that did not require the kinds of academic achievement and communication skills that substantive employment opportunities require today. (1997, p. 3)

In addition, there is another commonly held myth among U.S. educators that only ESL teachers are responsible for language-minority students' academic achievement and progress toward meeting high-stakes standards. According to the *ESL Standards* from TESOL (1997), *all* education personnel need to share responsibility and engage in collaborative teaching for the education of ESL students. All educators need professional development to

> expand their knowledge base . . . [toward] . . . the understanding of similarities and differences in first and second language (L2) acquisition, the role of native language in

L2 and content learning, instructional methods and strategies that facilitate both English language and content learning, instructional practices that accommodate individual differences and learning styles, the interrelation between culture, cognition, and academic achievement; alternative approaches to assessment, and the importance of community-school linkages in education. (p. 4)

ESL Standards also promote the idea that "native-English-speaking students, teachers, administrators, and school staff should learn about the world and its languages from ESL students, their families, and their communities" (p. 5).

The four most important myths, and related issues, discussed in Chapter 9 include:

1. Understanding and differentiating between external and internal factors affecting development and learning in ESL students. The need for educators to fully understand that low socioeconomic (SES) factors and cultural and linguistic differences (all external factors) can have on intelligence, development, and learning (internal or psychological factors, including first-and-second-language—L1 and L2—learning); and that may result in low SES children needing extra developmental time and individualized, high-quality, ESL and/or bilingual instruction.

2. Understanding similarities and differences between monolingual students' learning and developmental needs, and ESL students' idiosyncratic educational needs. For instance, developmental time needed for L1 and L2 learning among ESL students (i.e., readiness for reading and writing, difference between social and academic English language proficiency, the role of L1 in English as a L2 and content learning) resulting in most effective ESL and bilingual education pedagogical strategies (i.e., instructional practices that accommodate need for establishing rapport or socioemotional bonding between students and educators, individual differences and learning styles, and cultural and linguistic diversity).

3. Understanding the need for linking assessment to instruction, through performance-based or classroom-based evaluations, for separating cultural and linguistic diversity from genuine learning difficulties. A battery of alternative assessments across contexts and evaluators needs to be used by an interdisciplinary team of professionals for measuring academic achievement and development in ESL students. This assessment battery needs to evaluate both the individual child and the social learning and developmental contexts in the school and family settings.

4. Understanding the need for *all* educators, not only ESL teachers, to reach out to minority parents to become collaborative partners, mentors, and committed advocates with educators in the successful schooling process of ESL students.

See Table 9.1 for a list and definitions of all four myths and related issues discussed in Chapter 9.

TABLE 9.1   Four Most Important Myths, and Related Issues

FIRST MYTH: UNDERSTANDING AND DIFFERENTIATING BETWEEN EXTERNAL AND INTERNAL FACTORS AFFECTING DEVELOPMENT AND LEARNING IN ESL STUDENTS

Definition. This myth refers to the need for educators to fully understand that low socioeconomic (SES) factors and cultural and linguistic differences (all *external factors*) can have on intelligence, development, and learning (internal or psychological factors, including first- and second-language—L1 and L2—learning); and that may result in low SES children needing extra developmental time and individualized, high-quality, ESL and/or bilingual instruction

Myth 1:
"Having a L1 Other Than English Puts Students At-Risk of Underachievement"

SECOND MYTH: UNDERSTANDING SIMILARITIES AND DIFFERENCES BETWEEN MONOLINGUAL STUDENTS' LEARNING AND DEVELOPMENTAL NEEDS

Definition. This myth refers to individual differences and diversity existing within minority groups. For instance, developmental time needed for L1 and L2 learning among ESL students (i.e., readiness for reading and writing, difference between social and academic English language proficiency, the role of L1 in English as a L2 and content learning) resulting in most effective ESL and bilingual education pedagogical strategies (i.e., instructional practices that accommodate need for establishing rapport or socioemotional bonding between students and educators, individual differences and learning styles, and cultural and linguistic diversity)

Myth 2:
"Stimulating Learning in ESL Students Requires Only Providing a Cognitive-Academic Experience and Immersion into Mainstream English-Only Classrooms"

Myth 3:
"Concentrate on Academics, No Need for Nurturing the 'Whole' Learner, Including Social, Emotional/Affective Development"

Myth 4:
"When Learning ESL, the L1 and L2 Should Be Kept Separate within Home and School Environments"

Myth 5:
"Facility of Young Children for Acquiring a L2"

Myth 6:
"L2 Learning Is Parallel to L1 Learning: Search for 'Panaceas' and Simplistic Theories and Practices"

THIRD MYTH: NEED TO LINK ASSESSMENT TO INSTRUCTION FOR UNDERSTANDING DIVERSITY AS SEPARATE FROM LEARNING PROBLEMS

Definition. This myth refers to understanding the need for linking assessment to instruction, through performance-based or classroom-based evaluations, for separating cultural and linguistic diversity from genuine learning difficulties. A battery of alternative assessments across contexts and evaluators needs to be used by an interdisciplinary team of professionals for measuring academic achievement and development in ESL students. This assessment battery needs to evaluate both the individual child and the social learning and developmental contexts in the school and family settings

Myth 7:
"Fix the Difficult-to-Teach ESL Students in Special Education Settings"

Myth 8:
"Exposing LEP Students to a Monolingual Regular English Curriculum Helps Them Learn English Faster"

Myth 9:
"Mainstream Academic English Is the Only Acceptable Standard"

FOURTH MYTH: ROLE OF TEACHERS AS CULTURAL MEDIATORS AND COMMITTED ADVOCATES FOR ESL STUDENTS AND THEIR FAMILIES

Definition. This myth refers to understanding the need for *all* educators, not only the ESL teachers, to reach out to minority parents to become collaborative partners, mentors, and committed advocates with educators in the successful schooling process of ESL students

Myth 10:
"Role of Teachers as Cultural Mediators and Committed Advocates for ESL Students and Their Families"

FIRST MYTH: UNDERSTANDING AND DIFFERENTIATING BETWEEN EXTERNAL AND INTERNAL FACTORS AFFECTING DEVELOPMENT AND LEARNING IN ESL STUDENTS

Myth: *"Having a L1 Other Than English Puts Students At-Risk of Underachievement"*

Dr. Gonzalez: Bilingualism per se does not put children at risk, but SES factors associated with poverty highly present in language-minority groups, such as Hispanics, does place ESL children at-risk of underachievement and developmental delays. The problem arises when the same developmental standards and achievement expectations are applied to both mainstream, middle-class monolingual English and bilingual (or ESL, or monolingual other than English), economically disadvantaged children. The developmental principle underlying is that *"one plus one monolingual does NOT equal a bilingual."* That is, bilingual and ESL children do not develop at the same rate as monolingual and mainstream children, especially when there is also a compound effect of socioeconomic factors (e.g., primarily income level and educational level of parents). Young ESL children do not need to be identified as delayed or with learning problems since very early, but if they are at-risk of learning difficulties they need to be exposed since preschool years to a high-quality bilingual or ESL educational program. Educators need to adopt a "wait-and-see" approach, giving the benefit of the doubt to the child, while observing his or her potential for learning across time and providing high-quality and appropriate bilingual or ESL education.

Developmental time needed sometimes is extensive, but should at least encompass 6 months to 1 year, for conducting a performance-based assessment of progress in learning, and potential for learning, in a longitudinal manner. Educators also need to take into account that academic language proficiency takes from 5 to 8 years, and is a dynamic and individual learning process that is highly influenced by external educational factors. That is, educators need to provide developmental time and different kinds of learning opportunities for young ESL children to acquire concepts and content across time. ESL students need extra and high-quality conceptual stimulation in both their L1 and L2, because they are learning double the amount of vocabulary, grammatical and syntactic rules, and cultural concepts than monolingual children. Educators need to focus on what children *can do*, their strengths as observed in their L1 and native culture, and also on gains made while high-quality educational opportunities have been provided for developing their potential. Systematic records of performance-based assessment linked to instruction need to be collected across developmental (i.e., cognitive, language, and socioemotional) and content (i.e., language arts, mathematics, social studies, and science) areas.

Dr. Yawkey: "Having a L1 other than English puts students at-risk of underachievement" is constantly heard in the field from practitioners and in the "ivy towers" from well-meaning colleagues. Having taught ESL graduate courses for many years to in-service teachers and worked in academe for over 30 years, I have heard this stated by many. However, as Dr. Gonzalez has pointed out in the previous paragraphs and repeatedly at NABE and TESOL presentations, this "fact" is a myth, misconception, and misinformation.

The sources for this myth may, in part, rest in simple observations of bilinguals speaking English and simple comparisons between bilinguals and monolinguals in conversation (for details see Heath, 1983; Rogoff, 1990). Briefly, Heath, from a cultural anthropological perspective, notes that it is easy to distinguish different ways of "talk" between monolingual English speakers and bilinguals. Whether communicating information or using language in problem solving, differences emerge and comparisons are made. In similar fashion, Rogoff said that in non-Western, less urbanized societies, much of the teaching is done through modeling to the child, observing, modeling again and then prompting by the adult. In Western, more urbanized and middle-class societies, teaching is simply a predominance of verbal and print languages. And, comparisons are made and misconceptions may arise over the misinformation that the L2 puts children at risk of underachieving. This is another example of what Dr. Gonzalez notes as, "applying same developmental standards and achievement expectations to monolingual English and bilingual speakers."

These misconceptions become confounded and highly confusing when SES factors are put into the equation of L1 plus L2. Coming from low social and economic classes, many of our bilinguals require "time" . . . time for cultural adjustment, time for initial adaptation to society, time for developing self-confidence in a new and different culture, time for learning, and so forth. Can we, as ESL teachers, give our bilinguals and *all* children the necessary time? However, this extra time requires the development and use of high-quality school programs, of different and varied instructional or classroom teaching strategies, and adaptations made richly and routinely with bilinguals and *all* children, to connect with appropriate and meaningful learning and understandings. As ESL teachers, we need to become aware of this misconception and "work its alternative," to reduce misunderstanding and misdiagnosing our bilingual and *all* students showing similar patterns.

Dr. Minaya-Rowe: I agree with Dr. Gonzalez and Dr. Yawkey that the L1 does not put language-minority students at-risk of underachievement. It is a myth and a misconception that needs to be dispelled. One way to address this issue is in terms of whether ESL students are learning English and achieving in academics in order to provide them with a quality education.

Despite a growing influx of immigrants to the United States from non-English-speaking countries, the large majority of immigrants are learning English and learning it well. U.S. Census data show that among foreign-born residents, nearly three-quarters of those 5 years of age or older spoke English "well" or "very well" in both 1979 and 1989 (U.S. Bureau of Census, 1997). This is rather extraordinary considering that the numbers of new immigrants to the United States increased by almost 75 percent in this 10-year period.

Furthermore, immigrant students are often doing as well as native-born, native English-speaking students (Rong & Preissle, 1998). Students who are still limited in English have, as might be expected, higher dropout rates than native-English speakers, whether they come from families of high or low income. But foreign-born students who are fluent in English have the same lower dropout rates than English-only students.

Dr. Gonzalez points out that often "the same developmental standards and achievement expectations are applied to both mainstream, middle-class monolingual and bilingual (or ESL or monolingual other than English), economically disadvantaged children." The 2001 No Child Left Behind federal legislation aims to close the achievement gap by measuring adequate yearly progress on test scores. In response to this legislation, education reforms have raised the bar to close the achievement gap for ESL students and other groups while increasing all students' mastery of state education standards. *All* students in the United States must finish school and participate in the economic and social world of the new century. Thomas and Collier (2003) pose that two-way or dual-language programs can be the response to attending to all students since these programs offer grade-level and accelerated instruction in two languages to both language-minority and majority students. Two-way programs are additive; they add or reinforce a new language at no cost of the students' L1. *All* students benefit from quality, meaningful, challenging and accelerated instruction. *All* students in two-way programs benefit from the same and without being remedial or compensatory in nature. The two-way program offers full proficiency and mastery of the curriculum in two languages. Both groups receive accelerated instructional benefits from their other language peers and from the instructor's/teacher's use of cooperative learning group strategies to capitalize on this effect. Learning together increases student interest and motivation to learn (Calderón & Minaya-Rowe, 2003).

Thus, our point is that high-quality instruction leading ESL students to become proficient in English can help close the achievement gap between foreign- or U.S.-born ESL and mainstream students. The fact of having an ESL status is mediated by poverty and quality of educational programs that develop school parental involvement through partnerships between home and school (and family structure factors, such as cultural values and level of cultural adaptation; for further discussion see Gonzalez, 2001). Poverty places children at risk of underachievement, but high-quality educational programs over an adequate developmental time can become powerful mediators for increasing achievement up to federally mandated standards. Finally, and most important, high-quality teaching can only take place when ESL and *all* teachers are supported by professional development in best educational practices for serving diverse and *all* students.

SECOND MYTH: UNDERSTANDING SIMILARITIES AND DIFFERENCES BETWEEN MONOLINGUAL STUDENTS' LEARNING AND DEVELOPMENTAL NEEDS

Myth: *"Stimulating Learning in ESL Students Requires Only Providing a Cognitive-Academic Experience and Immersion into Mainstream English-Only Classrooms"*

Dr. Gonzalez: I believe learning takes place in a meaningful nurturing classroom or home environment in which educators and parents are able to establish a trusting, friendship relationship with the child, or a *rapport*. The most important teaching strategy for better serving ESL student is to develop a social and affective bonding between teachers and children, a friendship and vote of confidence in each other, mutual respect and understanding of cultural backgrounds. Learning can only take place if adults can establish a personal connection with the child, and stimulate positively emotional and affective learning mechanisms such as identification and internalization of role models, imitation, self-concept, self-esteem, and cultural identity. Moreover, educators need to generate emotional or social bridges between home and school by creating an integrated curriculum and a school environment that resembles students' real-life experiences of language in their natural home environment. Teachers need to develop a positive and accepting classroom environment that offers praise, encouragement, and especially reassurance; and not only acceptance but also celebration of minority linguistic and cultural identities of students. This classroom environment should nurture ESL students' social and emotional development, as well as stimulate them to learn and develop their whole developmental potential. That is, this safe classroom environment should encourage ESL students to negotiate meaning with teachers and peers, to interact with L2 learning models, and to learn their L2 in a natural and nurturing setting.

Dr. Yawkey: Within ESL perspectives, it is now common knowledge that there are two types or levels of language proficiency. These levels are: BICS and CALPS. Briefly, BICS stands for Basic Interpersonal Communication Skills and CALPS represents, Cognitive Academic Language Proficiency Skills. BICS are more of the social language used in and outside of classroom settings, such as, "What is your name? How are you doing? What do you think about all this cold (or hot or rainy) weather we have been having?" and so forth. We need BICS for everyday communication and conversation. Indeed, BICS is the language of everyday conversing and communicating.

As we know, BICS takes 1 to 3 years to acquire. However, the myth that stimulating learning requires providing a cognitive-academic experience in classrooms focuses on CALPS not BICS. Briefly, CALPS is school-and subject-matter oriented. In classroom settings, CALPS is the language required in content subject areas of mathematics, literacy, social studies, and "all" other content areas. It is the language of homework . . . of schoolwork . . . of content teacher talk. Common understandings of CALPS say that the English language learner (ELL) requires 7 to 10 years to acquire and use English meaningfully. So, a far more global picture is to view the ESL student on a dimension of social to more academic English language. Developing language systems along these dimensions take time and in addition teachers' skills. For teacher skill, Dr. Lilly Wong Fillmore's terms most appropriately describe this type of teacher as one who continually stretches and pushes the student to the next levels of English language usage.

This "stretching and pushing" the ELL student to the next levels of English is seen in the teacher's use of language learning strategies. These language learning strategies are communication and mental processes used by ESL students to function and learn a L2. Some examples of these language learner strategies include: using (1) linguistic knowledge of L1 to learn L2s; (2) making intelligent guesses about words, their meanings, and how to pronounce them; and (3) learning how to move conversation along and keep it moving (e.g., production techniques). In this regard, Nunan (1991) noted that "good" language learners are more apt to reflect on and describe how they learn language and use these reflections in their language learning. In addition, the results of comparing more effective with less effective language learners show far greater uses of language learning strategies (Chamot & O'Malley, 1990).

So, this myth ignores the bases of good English language learning such as: using the native speaker's knowledge of his native language, doing some good old-fashioned guessing about word meanings, using mnemonics such as rhymes and rhythms as cognitive and language organizers. Said differently, stimulating learning in ESL students is more than cognitive-academic language and immersion into *Main Street–English only* classrooms. Stimulating learning in ESL students requires immersing them into ESL or bilingual classrooms.

Dr. Minaya-Rowe: I strongly agree with Dr. Gonzalez and Dr. Yawkey that ESL students require more than just an academic and cognitive experience. ESL students definitely do not need to be immersed into English-only classrooms. I would like to add that teachers play an important role as they can enrich the linguistic context for their students using communication clues like pictures, gestures, and intonation. Teachers can also draw on students' interests and background knowledge. Background knowledge needs to be accessed because students can easily use BICS to communicate their ideas. Once their thoughts have been brought to the surface of their brain, teachers can scaffold them into a lesson that brings them to a higher level of CALP. All teachers should try to increase their student's level of communicative competence. This is not just the job of the ESL teacher. Speech is more comprehensible when combined with actions and the language is context embedded. The students have control and can ask for repetition and clarification. Group work also provides opportunities for both social and academic language development (Peregoy & Boyle, 2001). Cooperative groups are useful for L2 acquisition for many reasons. Students have the opportunity for interaction with more advanced ELLs or with native-speaking peers who make good language models. When organizing group work it is more important to have quality opportunities for interaction than to worry about the formal or informal structure of the group. Create a relaxed atmosphere to promote a low-anxiety environment. If the class consists of students knowing the same native language encourage the use of groups for practicing L2. On the other hand, L2 becomes the common language in multilingual classes. An ideal group would include both native or advanced English speakers and newcomers.

Whenever possible create heterogeneous groups including gender, ethnicity, language proficiency, personality, and academic achievement. Assign roles to each member of the group including recorder, observer, timekeeper, encourager, and reporter. Build positive interdependence by assigning each member a part so that the finished product cannot be achieved without all the individuals participating and assure the quality of the final product depends on the quality of each individual. This myth lacks substance. It does not attend to important developments in English language development that include types of language taught, meaning-based approaches, students' prior knowledge, heterogeneous groupings, and standards-based goals for instruction.

Thus, we strongly support that educators using high-quality teaching practices can provide meaningful pedagogy, much needed developmental time, and meaningful academic and social interactions for improving achievement and development in ESL learners.

Myth: *"Concentrate on Academics, No Need for Nurturing the "Whole" Learner, Including Social, Emotional/Affective Development"*

Dr. Gonzalez: Depending on the social and cultural distance between the ESL children and the target language and culture, they may experience *culture shock* and *language shock*. Due to my background in educational and clinical psychology, I strongly believe in the powerful influence of emotional and affective factors such as individual differences, temperament and personality characteristics, attitudes, values, and beliefs. That is the reason why it is important for educators to endorse transculturation models in order to help ESL children adapt to a new culture and language, while maintaining their L1 and cultural heritage, resulting in bicultural identities. In contrast, assimilation models infuse transitioning children to monolingualism in English and monoculturalism in the mainstream American culture. There are some constructs in the L2 literature supporting the transculturalism approach to the education of ESL students. For instance, the affective filter hypothesis developed by Krashen centers on the idea that affective and emotional factors influence cultural adaptation and L2 learning in ESL students. More specifically, this hypothesis refers to the learner's needs, interests, motivation, attitudes, and emotional states affecting their L2 learning process.

Dr. Yawkey: Focusing totally on academic and ignoring social, emotional, and affective factors of the "whole" learner implies that English language learning generalizes to all developmental areas. Relatedly, some might even say that focusing exclusively on English language learning makes learning quicker or faster in other subject areas. Of course, and however related, both are misconceptions. English language successes are not solely attributed to cognitive or academic focus. Rather, successes in learning English and *all* other languages depend on academic, social, emotional, and affective factors that of course interact and intertwine between and within these major factors. A corollary to this myth is that teachers much wait and wait until students learn English before teaching them content subjects such as social studies, or mathematics and so forth. In reality, it is really not necessary to wait and wait for signs of English language emergence or patterned English language learning prior to teaching ELLs subject matter areas.

ESL and regular classroom teachers can teach content area subjects through the medium of sheltered English subjects and also through nonnative languages using learner strategy training techniques. Similar to teaching *all* students across the grades, we as teachers cannot ignore social, emotional, and affective growth areas in favor of emphasizing solely academic areas. This emphasis does not produce faster English language development because our meaningful learning stresses "multi-growth" areas and not solely "unigrowth" with a cognitive or academic focus.

Dr. Minaya-Rowe: I endorse Dr. Gonzalez's and Dr. Yawkey's positions. I would like to add that if education of ELLs, that is, theories of L2 learning or teaching methods, is only based on cognitive considerations, we would be omitting the most fundamental side of human behavior (Brown, 2001). For example, the affective domain has a central role in L2 development. Central to the affective domain are attitudes, motivation, and level of anxiety. These concepts are strongly influenced by acculturation and personality factors.

Attitudes that are determined by what ELLs have experienced and by the people with whom they identify (e.g., peers, parents, teachers) influence the way ELLs see the world and their place in it. Motivation is also a strong force in determining how proficient ELLs will become, whether they want to integrate with the majority group, whether they want to succeed economically in the mainstream society.

Anxious students can have difficulty in learning the L2. Teachers of ELLs need to use sheltering strategies and to give students the chance to try out their L2 in nonthreatening environments and to keep stress at a minimum. ELLs will have a chance to go through the stages of acculturation without it becoming a debilitating process.

ELLs' emotional well-being can be enhanced if we offer them a positive, accepting school environment. Although prejudices and racial boundaries cannot be eliminated completely, schools and programs must strive to make the environment a better one, not only for ELLs but for *all* students. Multicultural awareness programs and activities need to be ongoing to sensitize school personnel, students, community members to the needs and feelings of others.

Thus, we all endorse a pluralistic perspective that celebrates diversity characteristics of students for supporting their adaptation process to the American school culture and the acquisition of its English language.

Myth: *"When Learning ESL, the L1 and L2 Should Be Kept Separate within Home and School Environments"*

Dr. Gonzalez: Based on my own experience as a multilingual person, I know that bilingualism is rarely completely balanced due to different levels of language competence in different content areas and topics. That is why it is completely normal for bilinguals to use code switching (i.e., use of two languages within the same sentence) and code mixing (i.e., use of two languages between sentences) when communicating with another bilingual person. Code switching and code mixing are normal sociolinguistic rules learned by young children in their natural and daily social and home context. These are legitimate cultural ways of communication for many language-minority communities in the United States such as the Hispanic groups. That is why it is so important for teachers to learn the traditional and contemporary lifestyles, and cultural and linguistic characteristics, of language-minority communities.

Dr. Yawkey: This is a most interesting misconception because it involves much misinformation about development of L1 and L2 in many areas. First, it assumes that the brain is a finitely constructed vessel and as such can only hold a certain amount of content, or simply "stuff." With the idea that there is only room enough in the brain for one language, we may think that by separating their uses exclusively in school (English) and for home (native language/s), the students are less language-confused resulting in less cognitive impairment. Of course, this myth has no basis in scientific research. And, even at a level of observed and lived reality, all of us know or can recall that countries such as Switzerland are multilingual, with the major languages of German, French, and Italian. And the Swiss are multilingual, not "multi-limited" in cognition or in languages. Equally so, for individuals in Holland, Germany, and France, for example, who within one to three hours can drive to *all* three different countries *all* speaking different native languages and *all* these folks being able to converse in these three different languages. Second, some educators may feel that in-depth exposure to speaking only English translates into greater English language fluency. But, exclusive or greater exposure to English does not produce or guarantee that the students learn it. In this situation, "more may not be better" because what is said may be far "over the heads" of the students.

At another level, one of my colleagues explains support for this misconception by stating that "focusing only on English" in Berlitz schools proves that English can be mastered by focusing and using it exclusively. He fails to carefully examine the facts that conversational English based on rote memory is far different than academic English required in classrooms. English of subject-matter classrooms is based on subject matter, context, and spontaneous language generation rather than memory of language isolated phrases and sentences.

Dr. Minaya-Rowe: Dr. Gonzalez and Dr. Yawkey have addressed this myth in a very convincing way. I would like to point out the research evidence indicating that in classes where there L1 and L2 are used, ELLs acquire English language skills equivalent to those acquired by children who have been in English-only programs (Ovando, Collier, & Combs, 2003). The L1 support is crucial for ELLs to learn all what they need to learn in school in addition to learning English. Instructional programs need to give ELLs the support of their L1. Using ELLs' L1 in the classroom enables them to avoid falling behind in schoolwork, and it also provides a mutually reinforcing bond between the home and the school. In fact, the home language acts as a bridge for children, enabling them to participate more effectively in school activities while they are learning English.

Two-way bilingual programs have been shown to benefit from extended intensive exposure to minority (ELLs) and majority (English-speaking) languages and students learn language and academics using both languages. The research clearly shows that two-way programs are not detrimental to learning content material in that language, as long as the home language continues to develop and is supported (Lindholm-Leary, 2001).

Thus, the three of us bring personal and research-based experiences to support the use of L1 and L2 in an interactive, dynamic, and flexible manner.

Myth: *"Facility of Young Children for Acquiring a L2"*

Dr. Gonzalez: There is a commonly held misconception by laypeople that young children can acquire a L2 with no effort, in a fast manner through immersion in the "sink or swim" approach. In fact, research-based information provides support for the opposite position, that adults have a greater facility for acquiring a L2 in all domains, with children doing better only in pronunciation. Children are NOT better language learners than adults because at a young age they are still developing the conceptual abilities necessary for language learning and content knowledge development. That is, children are developing in a parallel manner the cognitive and metacognitive and metalinguistic abilities necessary for L1 and L2 acquisition, such as literacy ability, conceptual learning, and topic knowledge.

In contrast, adults already have completed their conceptual and content knowledge development up to a level that allows using cognitive, metacognitive, and metalinguistic skills as a tool for learning a L2. That is, adults can transfer literacy skills from their L1 to their L2, as well as memory strategies, learning strategies for content knowledge and for language development. This phenomenon is well explained by inter-language theory and a process approach for L2 learning. Another construct explaining this phenomenon is the foundational hypothesis stated by Krashen, in which he made a distinction between acquisition of a L1 in an informal setting via exposure to social meaning, such as the home natural environment, and learning a language within a formal setting, such as school via the exposure to language forms (within a traditional linguistic approach to second-language learning).

Moreover, even young children can have a nonnative accent when acquiring a L2 at a young age. In fact, children can have an accent if their L1 is more developed than the L2, resulting in young children transferring phonological characteristics of L1 to their L2. For instance, I have witnessed this case for my own 8-year-old child, whose L1 is English now regardless of some degree of use of Spanish at home, because of exposure to schooling in regular English classrooms since age 2. He has an advanced social and academic competence in English and an intermediate competence in social Spanish, and he talks in Spanish with an English accent, adding sounds to vowels and not being able to pronounce consonants and consonant clusters that are unique to the Spanish language. This is a dynamic phenomenon, because he used to have a native-like Spanish accent before age 2-and-a-half, when Spanish used to be his L1 due to exposure to a Spanish-dominant family environment.

Dr. Yawkey: As Dr. Gonzalez has very aptly pointed out, younger children do not have greater facility for acquiring L2. This particular myth has convinced many well-intentioned language specialists that the younger child can learn English "more easily and more quickly" than the older ones. Therefore, English-only or English language immersion should be the mode of schooling when ELLs come to kindergarten or Grade 1. The "more easily and quickly" phrase favoring younger over older children is simply a myth. Some people believe this myth from other perspectives. Some point to support this myth states that children's minds or brains are more malleable or flexible and therefore learn English faster than older children or adults. However, research results show that older children are far more efficient, much faster, and more effective than young children in learning English. The older children have greater generalizing abilities between native and English languages and use more learner strategies than the younger children. In fact, the younger child compared to the older child may experience greater difficulty because she does not yet have access to learned strategies and/or memory techniques for grammatical rules or has just acquired so far a lesser amount of vocabulary. The language learning tasks that are easier and more efficiently learned for older children and adults compared to younger children include grammar, vocabulary, syntax, and literacy. Older children and adults have already established some competencies in these four language areas in their L1 and this learning can transfer to the English language. However, acquiring and using native-like pronunciation may favor younger children compared to their older counterparts and adults. Here, practice effects of spontaneity and constant, "un-embarrased" usages of verbal exterior and interior/self speech become helpful factors with younger compared to older children and adults. Of course, in these comparisons, many other affective and social factors weigh heavy on assisting development of English language competencies. These include factors such as: motivation, social contexts in which L2 is used, and the students' attitudes toward the English language.

Dr. Minaya-Rowe: I would like to reiterate Drs. Gonzalez's and Yawkey's responses to dispel this myth. The younger-is-better hypothesis does not have strong empirical support in school contexts. Older children are better L2 learners than are younger ones (Dulay, Burt, & Krashen, 1982). Only pronunciation is one aspect of L2 learning where the younger-is-better hypothesis may have validity. A number of studies have found that the younger one begins to learn a L2, the more native-like the accent one develops in that language (Dulay et al., 1982). This may be because pronunciation involves motor patterns that have been fossilized in the L1 and are difficult to alter after a certain age (i.e., sensitive period) because of the nature of the neurophysiologic mechanisms involved. It may also be that we need to develop effective strategies to teach pronunciation and intonation in a L2. Younger children do not necessarily have an advantage over older children and, because of their cognitive and experiential limitations when compared to older children, are actually at a disadvantage in how quickly they learn a L2.

Thus, all of us jointly support the importance of cognitive, affective, and social factors in L2 learning, resulting in older children and adults becoming better L2 learners due to a bigger repertoire of learning strategies. However, younger children enjoy greater neuropsychological malleability due to sensitive periods for acquiring new sounds, resulting in higher performance in language pronunciation patterns in L2 in comparison to older children, adolescents, and adults.

Myth: *"L2 Learning Is Parallel to L1 Learning: Search for Panaceas and Simplistic Theories and Practices"*

Dr. Gonzalez: Teachers keep searching for the "general theory of L1 and L2 learning" that can explain how to teach and assess ESL students. In reality, L2 learning is a complex and multidimensional process that can only be explained by multiple factors represented in different theories. That is, no one theory can explain this phenomenon, but different theoretical perspectives can explain only some aspects of the L2 learning process. Another problem that we educators face is that research conducted under different theoretical perspectives produces contradictory findings and explanations of the L2 learning process. This is due to different theories endorsing different philosophies, data collection methodologies, and interpretations of data.

Researchers are also subjective in how they select theories and methodologies for their studies, and how they explain their results based on some hypotheses, principles, and philosophies. Researchers are also subjective in the selected methodologies, such as the collection of data through specific instruments, the focus on specific variables and levels of analysis (such as language as grammatical structure, social context, cognitive or cultural processes involved in language use, etc.). That is why I believe it is so important for teachers to do "soul searching" and develop their own personal theories, beliefs, and hypotheses for explaining the L2 learning process that should be based on their own personal and professional experiences while interacting with ESL students. There are many ways of implementing best educational practices, depending on the teaching styles and personalities of individual teachers. Different ESL learners also require adaptation of the curriculum and teaching methodologies, requiring in teachers problem-solving skills and critical-thinking abilities. Educators need to take risks to change their educational practices and make informed decisions (know why applications of theory do work under what contexts, and for whom—specific individual differences of learners) about instructional strategies that optimize learning in their ESL students.

Educators need to analyze similarities and differences across theories in relation to themes or core constructs or concepts, principles, findings, and educational implications. For instance, some themes that could be used include: (1) universal versus individual differences and culture-specific characteristics, (2) emphasis on internal or external factors affecting development and learning, (3) active or passive role of students in learning processes, (4) study of learning and development as a process or as a product, (5) relation to real-life social experiences such as home and school environments (i.e., level of stimulation at home and school such as learning opportunities and available mentors, community and neighborhood characteristics; and socioeconomic status including degree of acculturation and level of education of parents, number of siblings, etc.), and (6) educational applications to the classroom.

Due to this complexity and multidimensionality of factors affecting L2 learning, educators need to assume an *eclectic teaching approach* that results from their personal selection of approaches that fit beliefs endorsed and personality characteristics. We referred to this eclectic teaching approach in Chapter 3 as a pluralistic view of L2 learning and teaching. As Spolsky (1989) stated,

> There are many ways to learn languages and many ways to teach them, that some ways work with some students in some circumstances and fail with others. That is why good language teachers are and always have been eclectic: they are open to new proposals, and flexible to the needs of their students and the changing goals of their course. (p. 15)

Dr. Yawkey: This myth is quite challenging to intellectualize and even more difficult to operationalize in the classroom. As to whether or not there are parallels between acquisition of L1 and L2 is still a very much researchable and debatable issue and question. Many teachers would not say or admit to the belief that L1 and L2 are learned in the same manner and at the same rate. However, if we examine practices used in our ESL and regular mainstream classes we see this myth that learning L2 in the same way as L1 is very much alive and well. In many instances, this myth forms a cornerstone of many classroom practices. An immediate example comes to mind from recent ESL observations in ESL classrooms—one at the middle school and the other at the university. The ESL students in both settings were following what is believed to be similar processes of L1 acquisition applied to L2 learning. I am speaking about the division or bifurcation within the language literacy learning processes where listening and speaking processes are taught first to ELLs. Then, reading and writing follow listening and speaking when mastery or criterion levels are met. Dr. Gonzalez's comments made previously were that L2 and L1 are very complex processes that are explained by multiple factors. Dr. Gonzalez, here, is making very important distinctions.

In other words, L2 learning is not so simple as a contrast between or a sequential ordering of processes within L1 matched against L2(s). In reality, it may be the nature of the language being learned coupled with other factors such as social class; deductive or analytical versus inductive talk that distinguishes mainstream and culturally diverse populations; sources of language learning as in peers versus adults; and so forth. Additional research definitely needs to explore these associated and affiliated factors within L1 and L2 acquisition.

In a previous discussion, Dr. Gonzalez notes that "no one theory can explain . . . [L2 learning] . . . but different theoretical perspectives can explain only some aspects of the L2 learning process." In Chapter 3, we saw some outstanding examples of differential theories and their diverse explanations in describing L2 learning processes. And, yes, these explanations can be contradictory. Yet, rather than throw the "theories out with the baby's bath water," I would challenge us to examine these theories closely. See which theoretical principles we believe in and use in classroom applications and which have produced sound results for us above levels of intuition. These principles become sound pivotal, foundational points upon which we can hang personal teaching experiences and beliefs. This perspective has benefits because we provide documentation and justification to the L2 learning processes and procedures we use in the classroom. As we move further into No Child Left Behind legislation, these foundational, pivotal principles can easily be turned into observational statements that can be used in assessment and in re-teaching.

A few words on conflicting and even contradictory outcomes between various theories are in order. In her seminal text, Spada (1990) noted that outcomes of L2 theories differ because of several factors such as differences of curricular organizations and programs. In addition, I would suspect that differences in the types and kinds of instructional, pedagogical strategies used by teachers in facilitating L2 acquisition would play a role. These differences alone could easily account for variations in results and in the power of these theories to predict outcomes in L2 acquisition and learning.

Dr. Minaya-Rowe: I agree with Dr. Gonzalez and Dr. Yawkey that this myth addresses the easy way to solve the challenges of educating ELLs. They both conclude that no one theory can explain L2 development. For at least three decades, researchers have tried to compare L1 and L2 development and have contended that indeed there are predictable stages of development and that there are similarities and differences. Others point out that there are sufficient numbers of similarities between L1 and L2 development to support a common theory. In my opinion, some important findings from the research point to the classroom as an appropriate environment for L2 learning, the pivotal role of social interaction in L2 development, and both input and output are important in the L2 acquisition process to receive comprehensible input and for opportunities to practice the L2.

We have explained in Chapter 4 that Vygotsky's Zone of Proximal Development and Krashen's *i + 1* are similar concepts, both offering insights into the cognitive processes involved in language development. Contrary to Piaget, who proposed one level of cognitive development, Vygotsky and Krashen implied two levels: an actual level and a potential level. While Vygotsky stressed the *importance* of social interaction, Krashen stressed the *nature* of the input.

Methods of L2 instruction, like models of cars, have varied over the decades. However, meaningful interaction about content of interest in the L2 is now in the driver's seat. Educators can help ELLs learn their L2 by believing that the student can understand more than he or she can say and lead him or her to communicate. What students learn when they acquire a L2 is not separate parts (e.g., words, sounds, sentences) but a system of social practices with conventions and systematicity.

All in all, we recommend the use of an eclectic collection of philosophical, theoretical, and educational applications that have been demonstrated to work as pedagogies in the L2 classroom. This pluralistic or eclectic approach can work provided that the ESL teachers build a nurturing social environment that stimulates cognitive, linguistic, and socioemotional development and progress in academic achievement among ESL students.

THIRD MYTH: NEED TO LINK ASSESSMENT TO INSTRUCTION FOR UNDERSTANDING DIVERSITY AS SEPARATE FROM LEARNING PROBLEMS

Myth: *"Fix the Difficult-to-Teach ESL Students in Special Education Settings"*

Dr. Gonzalez: I strongly believe that educators need to stop supporting the easy side of the "blaming the victim" approach, and instead endorse "the benefit of the doubt" approach to understand that most ESL economically disadvantaged students may experience learning difficulties because of social factors negatively impacting their potential for learning. That is, the latter approach expects educators to use different cultural and linguistic experiences brought to the classroom by ESL students as assets or strengths for learning and developing their cognitive, linguistic, social, and emotional developmental potential.

Dr. Yawkey: This myth can be rephrased to read something like what I have heard in university classroom settings as I teach graduate-level in-service ESL teachers. The rephrasing goes something like the following: "ESL students have learning disabilities, not language learning problems." In other words, "our ESL kids speak English just fine except that they are flunking academic subjects and don't understand these subject content language concepts." This returns to the commonly understood idea already discussed that social language differs from academic language. Diagnosing, evaluating ESL students on the bases of social language and placing them in special education based on this diagnosis and evaluation represents a "misdiagnosis." Metaphorically speaking, diagnosing an ESL student on his social language abilities in the playground and generalizing that he is "learning disabled" in academic-oriented classroom courses confounds perceived English social language fluency levels with perceived English academic language fluency levels. Generalizing from the playground to the classroom we intuitively think that this student should have the ability to perform just as well in academic classroom settings. This is not the situation. Unfortunately, this type of language bridging between social and academic language achievement goes on continually. As teachers, we must understand that ESL students need time and much help to develop their academic English language content.

And, we must share our thoughts about this "blaming the victim approach."

Dr. Minaya-Rowe: I strongly agree with Dr. Gonzalez' message to cease the "blaming the victim" approach; I would like to add that unfortunately ELLs continue to be misplaced in special education, not because of disabilities but because of English-language limitations. Legislation specific to bilingual special education does not exist. ELLs with disabilities are protected by both bilingual and special education legislation. Educators need to exercise caution and exhaust the resources available to them before making a referral for special education assessment.

Thus, our message is quite simple, but powerful. ESL learners need developmental time to unfold their learning potential to master English as a L2 and as a tool for learning academic content areas. Unless ESL educators provide genuine learning opportunities within a high-quality educational programs we cannot continue "blaming the victim" as a suspect of learning disabilities. The latter is a most important consideration, especially when ESL learners come from economically disadvantaged and language-minority backgrounds.

Myth: *"Exposing LEP Students to a Monolingual Regular English Curriculum Helps Them Learn English Faster"*

Dr. Gonzalez: On the contrary, I strongly oppose English-only immersion because it makes non-English-speaking children engage in a developmental regression to their infant and toddler years of nonverbal development. Non-English-speaking preschoolers or kindergartners would have to start over again by learning their first words and engaging in telegraphic speech and babbling conversation as they naturally acquired their L1 during their infancy and early toddler years. Using their L1 to learn content at up to developmental level and chronological age levels will help young ESL children to learn English faster, while keeping their academic achievement up to standards appropriate for their grade. Taking away the L1 of the child to replace it with English within an ESL or bilingual transitional program only creates semilingual or alingual children who do not have proficiency or dominance in either their L1 or L2.

Not having any language as an abstract tool for thinking and learning creates external teaching or instructional problems, which affect negatively their academic achievement and development. As mentioned in the discussion of the previous myth, the ultimate effect is the national endemic presence of a high school dropout rate and overrepresentation of ESL children in special education under the most common misdiagnosed labels of "learning disabled," or "language disordered," or "mentally retarded." Misdiagnosis results from confounding low-quality and inadequate instructional programs (educational and social external factors) with genuine internal biological or neurologically based dysfunctional syndromes. In reality these "learning difficulties" are created by inappropriate external stimulation received in curriculums that represent a language and culture that non-English-speaking children find meaningless.

I believe that the ideal instructional program is a two-way bilingual or developmental approach, in which both languages are used as methods of teaching and as tools for stimulating holistic development across linguistic, cognitive, social and emotional, and academic content domains. Even within this ideal instructional environment, development of academic language proficiency in English as a L2-learning tool will take about 5 to 8 developmental years. Development takes maturational time, and development cannot be rushed, as data-based socioconstructivistic and developmental studies since the early 1960s until the present show consistently.

Dr. Yawkey: As I teach ESL graduate-level in-service courses to teachers and administrators, I have experienced firsthand the popularity of this belief among both school and community colleagues. However powerful, it is still a myth and misconception based on rather much misinformation about our ESL learning and learning of students in general. The rationale for this approach is relatively simple if we move beyond the political terms used by many to describe this procedure. The terms I refer to include: *immersion* and *sink or swim* or *English-only*—all of which produce instant debate and arouse discussion "temperatures."

Basically, the thought here is to have ELLs join classes at Pre-K to Grade 12, that are all instructed in English. The reasoning here is simple. It is thought that ELL students put into English environments receive benefits of hearing and listening to English and exposing the ELLs to as much English-based learning as possible increases their English language acquisition. So, "more English is better" because the ELLs learn English quicker because there is more time spent on tasks using English. This reasoning is used as well in schools that have a revolving door theme for their bilingual and/or ESL programs. The revolving door notion is placing "newcomer" ELLs into native or English language support programs. Then within 90 days the ELLs are exited to mainstream English-only classrooms. The movement from ESL/bilingual programs is based largely on ELLs attainment of BICS (i.e., social, not academic, language usage). In other words, the ELLs have acquired the L2 if they can show it by speaking it with some degrees of English language fluency. This "dolby" sound environment of "total classroom English" creates artifacts of increased English exposure but not concomitant increases in English language acquisition and mastery. Besides, I have experienced firsthand these rapid-fire, revolving door programs specializing in transforming native languages into social English language usage. And, in visiting and watching the ELLs in these English classrooms, the ELLs, for the most part, pick seats near one another and, with self-selected seating, cluster in the back of the classroom. If the concern was continuing English language development, the recommended seating could be in "seating in the center or middle" of the classroom so that non-ELLs and ELLs would be able to peer-to-peer communicate and the ELLs might get added benefits of modeling English language usage.

Without special considerations built into the school curriculum tapering English-only classrooms to the individual ELL student's levels of English language acquisition and using grouping variations, simply admitting ELL students to English language classrooms for English exposure and awareness does not necessarily speed up English language acquisition. Much rests on the teachers and administrators to provide varieties of English and native language programs such as sheltered English, pull-ins, pullout programs and other varieties. In addition, we teachers need to use much more scaffolding strategies to amply key points in conceptual language mastery and bridge native-to-English-language understandings.

Dr. Minaya-Rowe: This myth is common in people who feel that the best solution to educating ELLs is to place them in the same classroom as native-English speakers and to follow the regular curriculum. They stress that ELLs do not need specific instruction to attend to their L2 learning needs and that all instruction should be in English. Obviously ELLs have more exposure to English but they do not necessarily have more comprehensible input. It is language comprehension, not just "heard" language that makes L2 learning happen. Thus, ELLs are only provided with noise with detrimental results: (1) ELLs fall behind subject matter curriculum, and (2) ELLs will not learn the L2.

The conditions for ELLs in the regular mainstream classroom may not be optimal. ELLs are usually aware that they cannot interact in the L2 as can native-speaking peers. This can inhibit them, especially in initial stages of seeking and obtaining contacts with other students and the teacher(s). Another important consideration is that ELLs, as any L2 learner, need a preproduction period in which they begin to comprehend but often say very little. In their early attempts to speak, they are bound to make many grammatical errors. It takes a very sensitive and well-trained mainstream teacher to accept these developmental errors, to allow very short sentences, and to address them in a manner that does not affect the ELL's motivation to continue learning the L2.

Thus, contrary to popular belief, "the sink or swim approach" of immersion into English regular classrooms for ESL students negatively impacts their academic language development in English, and ultimately their development and academic achievement across areas. Immersion in regular English classrooms with no other pedagogical support creates "disabling classrooms" for ESL students, resulting in further delays in English language learning and development, and ultimately increasing dropout rates and special education misplacements.

Myth: *"Mainstream Academic English Is the Only Acceptable Standard"*

Dr. Gonzalez: Educators need to dispel the myth of a topic-centered academic language as the only acceptable normative style in school. ESL students bring to school the real-life language they have learned in their minority homes and social communities, which probably use more topic association but is also perfectly appropriate for expressing abstract academic concepts. For instance, when I have studied ESL Hispanic children from low SES backgrounds, I have found that their concept formation is expressed through vocabulary commonly used in real life, which also conveys categories and abstract use of concepts and language. That is, an ESL child may not be able to identify elephants as mammals that live in the Sahara desert and have a specific diet; as the typical response of a middle-class mainstream child would be because she or he has been schooled and raised in a mainstream family. However, an ESL child can demonstrate abstract knowledge by engaging in analogical reasoning, as she can compare how the parts of an elephant relate to objects from different category domains (e.g., the elephant's ears are like giant leaves that are moved by the wind; they are also like a rug because they are flat; and also like a tortilla because besides being flat they are also rounded). The ESL child can also demonstrate flexibility of thinking, creativity, awareness of real-world knowledge, and ability to elaborate based on networks of prior knowledge, and the use of assimilation as a learning strategy. Based on this example, an educator has the choice of focusing on the negative or weak aspects of the ESL child development, such as lack of academic vocabulary according to age level; or on the positive aspects of learning, such as the ESL child's strength for concept formation processes at or above age level when using real-life social L1.

Unfortunately, many schools choose to have a single pedagogical register and purpose for educating all children, in an equal manner, with no respect for individual differences and needs, such as children who came for diverse language and cultural backgrounds. In such schools the "standard" language is only English, representing a middle-class mainstream school culture, and the curricula is preplanned and prepackaged, in which minority languages and dialects of English have no value. The ideal school setting for ESL students needs to value children's genuine way of using language (whether minority or mainstream). In this ideal educational settings, ESL children are allowed to talk and express their different cultural identities, interests, and experiences with language, which do not "fit" the homogeneous curriculum of the mainstream school culture. For instance, child-centered, literature-based, real-life communication situations can be used by educators with ESL students in order to talk, and write and read about real events and objects in culturally and linguistically familiar environments. The use of play, interaction within culturally appropriate settings, and cooperation of teachers and parents as facilitators of learning is key for the academic success of young ESL children.

Dr. Yawkey: This and other myths and misconceptions can be argued from many different perspectives. Here, English language as the only supported medium of expression in schools, government departments, businesses, and so forth needs examination. Federal and state laws do require that schools, businesses, and so forth provide equal but not "special" treatment to non-English speakers. Said differently, discrimination based on whether or not we speak English is prohibited under U.S. law—both constitutional and civil. However, we in the United States and most of the technologically advanced countries worldwide realize that speaking English is one of the primary means and languages of communication between people within and across nations of the world. We also can't deny federal-or state-funded services to nonnative speakers of English because they speak with accents; this and other actions become discrimination. All English speakers, limited-English speakers and non-English speakers in the United States are indeed protected under "constitutional due processes." The big problem here is one of compliance with these federal and state constitutional and civil laws. In my opinion, it is our responsibility as enlightened educators working in ESL fields to do more work so that there is greater compliance with these constitutional and civil laws. In this and related areas, we still have much work to do.

Dr. Minaya-Rowe: The U.S. Constitution specifies no official language and proponents of the English Only Movement have proposed that English should be the official language because a "common language benefits our nation and all its people" (U.S. English, 1990). The English Only Movement rhetoric of national unity cannot convince supporters of quality education for ELLs as the movement attempts to terminate bilingual education services designed to ease the adjustment of ELLs to American society. Current legislation (e.g., Proposition 227 in California; Proposition 203 in Arizona; Connecticut's PA 99–211) mandate a one-size-fits-all approach for ELLs known as "structured English immersion," a program not to exceed one year despite the lack of scientific evidence for its effectiveness. They push ELLs into mainstream classes at the beginning or at earlier stages of their L2 development. So the issue is teacher quality. Even with emphasis on hiring and retaining bilingual teachers, the rank of teachers continues to fill with white, female, middle-class, monolingual teachers who have had limited interracial and intercultural experiences and lack adequate ESL training. In general, preservice teacher preparation programs have not offered sufficient opportunities for learning to teach ELLs. Therefore, much of this learning takes place on the job.

Thus, professional development opportunities for ESL and all teachers need to expose them to federal policy and research-applied information supporting the value of using L1 and culture to educate ESL learners. In addition, cultural ways of using language for social and academic interactions need to be validated in the ESL classrooms, for both L1 and L2 as language becomes a major tool for thinking and learning in culturally appropriate manners.

FOURTH MYTH: ROLE OF TEACHERS AS CULTURAL MEDIATORS AND COMMITTED ADVOCATES FOR ESL STUDENTS AND THEIR FAMILIES

Dr. Gonzalez: I have always advocated for the role of teachers as cultural mediators, resource people, and collaborators with parents and school personnel for developing mentorship relationships with ESL students and their families. I perceive that the role of teachers as cultural mediators is to help ESL students and their families adapt to the school and community cultural environment. In addition, committed teachers hold the double role of acting as "social workers" in order to advocate as partners with parents for the best interest of ESL students, by helping parents in three important ways: (1) understand federal and state educational policy that applies to their children, (2) learn about community resources for meeting the health needs of their families, and (3) refer students and parents to the appropriate community agencies or school personnel who can assist them further in their individual needs (e.g., application to the free lunch school programs, medical and dental care, etc.).

My experience with Hispanic parents is that in some situations school personnel had to help them in finding appropriate housing (e.g., moving from an unsafe neighborhood that had created anxiety and stress in their children as they witnessed robbery, assault, and other signs of violence), clothing for cold weather (sometimes a new experience as snow is not common in Latin American subtropical and tropical regions), preparing and taking the driver's license exams, filling out papers to register their children in school, learning how to use bank accounts, learning how to buy a car and apply for a loan, learning how to read bus route maps, and so on. In general, educators and school personnel become cultural mediators for helping their students and their families to adapt to their daily-life new routines and school and cultural realities, which demand the development of new social knowledge and skills (e.g., learning a new language) for which they are ill-prepared (e.g., their literacy levels may not be up-to-level to the reading skills necessary to take a driver's license exam even in their first language—L1).

In addition, I believe that intervention strategies used by educators and parent–teacher liaisons, such as parent educators, need to take into consideration the minority families' values and cultural patterns present in educational goals and children's caretaking practices. Understanding the particular idiosyncratic characteristics of the community and family in which the child lives is necessary because minority groups vary widely between different cultures (e.g., Hispanics, Asian American, Native American) but also within ethnic groups. For instance, some factors affecting ethnic diversity are that: (1) Puerto Ricans have unique characteristics different than Mexican Americans, and other Central American and South American groups; (2) socioeconomic status makes a difference also between and within minority groups; and (3) number of generation also makes a difference for level of acculturation such as degree of proficiency of the minority and the English language.

Moreover, for educators to become committed advocates of ESL students and their families, they need to learn empathically about the ethnic background of students and to develop a habit of sociocultural observation for understanding idiosyncratic cultural patterns and avoiding stereotypes and overgeneralizations. By attending community events, such as festivals or local restaurants, educators can understand firsthand their students' experiences as they occur in the genuine cultural and linguistic environments. The challenge of educators is to discover and link the personal and school lives of their ESL students together with their experiences at school. In sum, I believe that by becoming true mediators between home and school experiences, educators become mentors who can offer meaningful interfaces of the bicultural identities of their ESL students between their home and school daily-life experiences.

Dr. Yawkey: We now examine the roles of cultural mediators and ESL advocacy for culturally and linguistically diverse (CLD) populations, whether they are our students and families or others in our neighborhoods and communities. The ideas of cultural and linguistic mediators and CLD advocacies is refreshing and something that many of us do currently and have done in the past. Any of us who raised and lived in the 1950s through the 1980s and in large urban cities such as Pittsburgh or Philadelphia, Pennsylvania, or Trenton and The Amboys, New Jersey, and so forth, these concepts for many of us are hardly new or novel. Next-door neighbors and peer group members speaking different languages with different religions and different cultural customs were really rewarding times and were tremendous growth experiences. We all in a sense were mediators and advocates for each other since we all belonged to various CLD populations. We had to follow the civil calendar in the United States for work, for school, and for all responsibilities such as banking and shopping. However, from boyhood to adulthood and growing up in a large urban city, myself and my peers were surrounded by 14 different cultures and different native languages. With Greeks, Russians, Ukranians, Polish who were Christians and Jews, with Chinese from China and others from French Indochina and several Hispanic families migrating from Puerto Rico, we lived our cultures and native languages, daily, weekly, monthly, and yearly. What rich environments these were for developing cultural and linguistic mediators and CLD advocacies.

So, in very early life, we came to realize that some of our friends for family and cultural reasons followed different family celebrations based on different calendars. With friends following the Gregorian and the Julian and two different lunar calendars, it was great times for developing cultural and linguistic awareness and even learning different native languages and participating in different religious and community celebrations. In my opinion, we now as ESL specialists need to regain our original, show our learned, or redevelop new senses of cultural and linguistic appreciations including committed advocacy. As cultural and **linguistic mediators** and committed advocates, support and demonstrate helping CLD families and their students in various ways in schools and communities. So, in a sense, we become "cultural and linguistic brokers" and bridges from CLD populations to greater understandings of their roles and responsibilities and to appreciate the many support services available for them.

In playing roles of CLD mediators and committed advocates, in my opinion we, as ESL teachers and administrators, must first examine our own cultural underpinnings. In understanding the countries' of origin of our own parents, grandparents, and other relatives, it is not difficult to get a cultural sense; that is, a CLD awareness. Different religions, different social customs and native languages all *make us unique, yet all make us one . . . Americans.* As we come to grips with our own previous and/or present cultural and linguistic foundations, we can better come to know CLD populations and develop mutual understandings. First, examine our own stereotypes; this self-examination and self-awareness usually begins by thinking and/or talking about the CLD stereotypes we have and those we know. By trying to under-standing the origins of our stereotypes and realizing some of the purposes they may serve, we are in better positions to take on roles of CLD mediators and committed advocates (Couchenour & Chrisman, 2000).

Next, we need to learn about distinctive characteristics of CLD families and their impacts of their children's school support roles and educational achievement. For example, Kim (2002) reports differences among Korean American families on forms of parental involvement. Some Korean American families show very high levels of home-based parental involvement with their children in content subjects and in additional educational endeavors. Kim reported that other Korean American demonstrated much lower levels of home-based parental involvement and higher levels of school-based parent involvement. For example, knowing these variations within this particular CLD group and across other CLD groups arm us in developing our cultural mediator and advocacy roles. By gaining and using information of our CLD populations for advocacy and cultural mediators, we can build bridges between our CLD populations, our schools, and communities. In addition, and by using these roles as mediators and advocates, we ourselves demon-strate positive living and learning strategies and model cultural pluralism.

Dr. Minaya-Rowe: I concur with Dr. Gonzalez and Dr. Yawkey that teachers have a role to play for ELLs and their parents. I would like to reiterate that an important concern of schools and the school systems they represent is the aca-demic and language achievement of ELLs and want parents to be involved in schools. Educators feel that parents and the communities they represent have a role in their children's education because parents can not only improve and maintain student achievement, but they can also participate as a group to challenge the claims that schools are failing because of lack of parent partici-pation (Bermúdez & Márquez, 1996). Language-minority parents may not be familiar with the school's expectations in parent involvement outside of their homes.

We have known for a while that parent-involvement practices are more important in the child's academic success than are race, level of education, and socioeconomic status. Schools and teachers need to clarify the role of parents in schools and what parents' expectations of their role should be. The spec-trum of parental support can be described from simple parental support of school policies with home reinforcement of school skills, to parents as advo-cates and change agents at the decision-making level.

Parents that participate in the school know how to help their children succeed. At the same time, school administrators and teachers are responsible for the form, frequency, and likely results of the information sent to the parents, particularly parents of ELLs who are new to the language, the culture, and the educational system. For example, schools are responsible to make sure that: (1) the information can be read and understood by all parents; (2) parents check frequently with their children for messages from the school; (3) parents work with the school staff to revise or improve school policies and ways of communication; and, (3) parents work with the school administration and teachers if their children's attendance, grades, conduct, and course work are not satisfactory.

Teachers and school–community liaisons need to include all parents in communications from the school (e.g., parent–teacher conferences using the language parents feel more comfortable with or using translators), phone conversations with parents about their children, parent involvement, frequent and genuine communications about their children's program or progress. Finally, parents who are involved consider as very good teachers the ones who have high interpersonal skills. Teachers rate parents higher in helpfulness when they follow through with learning activities at home regardless of parent education, race, or socioeconomic status (Bermudez & Marquez, 1996).

OUR THREE VOICES BECOME ONE: AN EPILOGUE

In sum, throughout the discussion of educational myths negatively impacting ESL students, we all have endorsed a pluralistic view of education and schooling that includes different languages and cultural backgrounds as part of America's educational values and beliefs, processes, and products. As Dr. Yawkey stated so well here, "Different religions, different social customs and native languages all *make us unique, yet all make us one . . . Americans.*" In this book we emphasize the conceptual difference between integration (leading to multiple languages and cultural identities) and assimilation (leading to enforcing mainstream culture and language only). We strongly stand behind an integrational approach to the linguistic and cultural adaptation of ESL students and their families, in which they can maintain their linguistic and cultural diversity by becoming bilingual, bicognitive, and bicultural.

As portrayed in this book since Chapter 1, and throughout its 9 chapters, ESL students are *not* a new phenomenon in the U.S. public school system. ESL students started to be part of America's schools since the middle 1800s, with a peak during the Ellis Island years since the late 1800s until the early to middle 1900s. Foreign-born and second-generation ESL students and their families from a southern and eastern European background, coming through Ellis Island, comprised millions of low-achieving students in U.S. public schools from the late 1800s until the early 1900s. We have forgotten about this historical fact of our nation of immigrants: U.S. public education has a precedent of trying to accomodate ESL students' low-achieving groups since the 1800s. It is a myth that these Ellis Island ESL students sailed through the U.S. educational system using a "sink or swim approach." In this book, we hope to make our readers aware of the fact that schooling of ESL students *may take generations*, and that the value of schooling lies in educators serving as social agents to facil-itate their linguistic and cultural adaptation process to access and inte-grate into middle-class America. Many ESL students of the Ellis Island era did "sink" and became dropouts or underachievers (see Chapter 1 for historical data). It took two or three generations of U.S.-born children of eastern and southern European groups to develop cultural and linguistic adaptation to mainstream America. The most important factor that helped increase the immigrant students' academic achieve-ment was the presence of teachers and school administrators from their minority background.

Today, about one-third of the U.S. current population (100 million out of the 270 million) are descendents of at least one ESL individual who came to the United States through the Ellis Island gateway. Most of these descendents of Ellis Island immigrants have forgotten their ESL roots, and are now considered to represent mainstream groups, another myth far from reality. Yet, in subtle characteristics we can still recog-nize their eastern or southern European backgrounds, such as their last names (many times anglicized or mispronounced), their few kept family traditions such as holiday celebrations and food, their religion, and other protected cultural and linguistic processes and products. Thus, we are hoping to awaken among teachers from a so-considered "mainstream" background, their ability to *make a personal connection to their family ESL ancestry*, and to become aware of the important role of ESL immigrants in their own family history, and their role in U.S. sociohistorical reality in the past, pres-ent, and future—and by doing so, to develop rapport, commitment, and advocacy to nurture, mentor, and mediate the cultural and linguistic adaptation process among the increasing number of ESL students that populate today's U.S. public school classrooms and buildings.

By gaining cultural awareness, educators can develop positive attitudes and intrinsic motivation for supporting their ESL students' learning, development, and academic achievement. Such high-quality educational support requires taking a holis-tic perspective to the instruction and assessment of ESL students. In this book we have endorsed a holistic vision for both ESL students' educational and teachers' profes-sional development. Teachers need to educate the whole child, encompassing not only academics but, most important, social and affective development and general mental and physical health and safety. Furthermore, throughout this book we have endorsed the position that the professional development of teachers needs to infuse in them a holistic vision of education that aims to develop cognitive and ethical and moral abili-ties for ESL students. Throughout this book we examined myths commonly held by pre-service and in-service teachers about the effect that having an ESL back-ground can have on Pre-K through 12th Grade students' learning, development, and academic achievement. Table 9.2 presents a summary of the 10 myths and the pos-sible solutions offered throughout our extensive discussion and dialogue presented in this chapter.

TABLE 9.2   The Ten Myths and Solutions Discussed by the Authors

MYTH	SOLUTION
1. Having a L1 other than English puts students at-risk of underachievement	Understanding and differentiating between external and internal factors affecting development and learning in ESL students
2. Stimulating learning in ESL students requires only providing a cognitive-academic experience and immersion into mainstream English-only classrooms	Understanding similarities and differences between monolingual students' learning and developmental needs.
3. Concentrate on academics, no need for nurturing the "whole" learner, including social, emotional/affective development	Some ESL children might have to deal with culture and language shock. While focusing on academics, the emotional and affective factors such as individual differences, temperament and personality characteristics, attitudes, values, and beliefs are important as well.
4. When learning ESL, the L1 and L2 should be kept separate within home and school environments	Code mixing and code switching are normal for a bilingual or multilingual person. There is no research support that a person's brain can only deal with one language at a time. Exclusive or greater exposure to English does not produce or guarantee that the students learn it.
5. Young children have greater facility for acquiring a L2	Research results show adult L2 learners can transfer literacy skills from their L1 to their L2. They can also use memory strategies, learning strategies from content knowledge and for language development. For younger learners, "unembarrassed" usages of language exterior and interior/self speech become helpful factors. To help adult or older learners, motivation and social context factors are to be considered in developing English language competencies. For younger L2 learners, literacy skills and other language strategies are helpful in their L2 language development.
6. L2 learning is parallel to L1 learning	L2 learning is not so simple as a contrast between or a sequential ordering of processes within L1 matched against L2. The processes influenced by many factors such as social class, deductive or analytical versus inductive talk that distinguishes mainstream and culturally diverse and so forth. Different L2 learners require different adaptations of curriculum and teaching methodologies.

7. Fix the difficult-to-teach ESL students in special education settings	ESL students need time and help to develop their academic English language content.
8. Exposing LEP students to a monolingual regular English curriculum helps them learn English faster	When L2 learners use their L1 to learn content up to developmental and chronological age levels, they can learn English faster and keep their academic achievement up to appropriate grade level.
9. Mainstream academic English is the only acceptable standard	Using language in cultural ways for social and academic interactions needs to be validated in the classrooms for both L1 and L2 because language becomes a major tool for thinking and learning in culturally appropriate manners.
10. Teachers are teaching languages and other subjects only	Teachers should play the role of cultural mediators and committed advocates for ESL students and their families.

SUMMARY

Our most forceful message throughout the chapters of this book, captured in our two main themes, is that teachers need to rethink and rediscover the learning potentials of ESL and *all* students, and forcefully endorse and demonstrate through their classroom practice that *high-quality teaching can make a difference.* The ESL theoretical and philosophical approaches, pedagogy, and instructional and assessment strategies proposed in this book represent best educational practices that committed teachers can use for developing L1 and L2 academic skills in ESL students. Best educational practices need to include and value the cultural, linguistic, and socioeconomic backgrounds of ESL students, in relation to content areas and methodologies used. We also endorse linking assessment to instruction through making teachers active participants in classroom-based authentic assessments. We fully support the possibility for teachers to become advocates of ESL students by contributing to and collecting assessment evidence that documents classroom performance across long periods of time. This set of recommended educational practices all have as a core message to stimulate teachers to become *committed* **advocates** for helping ESL students in their cultural adaptation process to achieve at higher developmental levels.

By examining the most commonly held myths in this final chapter, we give closure to this message and the two themes by *infusing cultural awareness* among ESL and *all* teachers. We hope that we have been able to inspire teachers to develop *moral responsibility* and to become *committed advocates* for ESL students. We hope that we have been successful in stimulating readers to engage in self-reflection about the philosophical orientation that they use the most in their practice (based on an "Ericksonian" concept of searching for a professional "identity").

In closing, this book has presented as a central message two themes across chapters, and this concluding chapter discusses these two themes in relation to myths commonly held among educators in order to reiterate this message and infuse cultural awareness among all educators. By making a connection between the *past, present, and future of U.S. education's history*, educators can help solve our challenge of closing the academic achievement gap between today's ESL students and their mainstream counterparts. In the pluralistic school environment that we have envisioned in this book, ESL and all teachers and parents collaborate as partners for increasing ESL students' achievement and developmental levels though high-quality education and parental school involvement that transforms research-based knowledge into educational practice in the classrooms.

Best wishes and successes,
V. G., T. D. Y., & L. M. R.

REVIEW QUESTIONS

1. What is a "wait-and-see" approach? How can ESL students benefit from it? What should ESL teachers do to identify ESL students' potential?

2. Does stimulating learning in ESL students only require providing a cognitive-academic experience and immersion into mainstream English-only classroom? Explain.

3. Why is it important to also stimulate the social, and emotional/affective development of ESL students while teaching subject areas?

4. Do ESL teachers and families need to separate L1 and L2 learning environment for ESL students? Explain.

5. What does research say about the widespread idea that young children acquire a L2 faster and better than older children or adults?

6. What can educators do to avoid misdiagnosing ESL students as having some disability or handicapping condition (i.e., learning disabled or language disordered, speech handicapped, or mentally retarded)

7. Do ESL students learn faster in a monolingual regular English classroom? Explain.

8. What is the meaning of the concept of ESL teachers as cultural mediators? Explain.

9. How can ESL teachers become advocates for ESL students and families? Give examples.

10. List at least ten important concepts that you learned from this book. Why are these ten concepts most important to you and all ESL teachers?

CRITICAL THINKING QUESTIONS

1. Study carefully the information presented in Table 9.1. Reflect about some possible myths that you may also believe in. Discuss how the theories and concepts, and their educational applications discussed throughout the book can help you to change your views about how ESL students learn and develop.

2. Study carefully the information presented in Table 9.2. Select two myths and discuss how the possible solutions offered by the authors can help ESL and all teachers to dispel their misconceptions and develop new conceptual knowledge. Think about possible scenarios in which this newly developed knowledge can help ESL teachers to meet the educational needs of ESL students and their families.

ACTIVITIES

1. Study carefully the information presented in Table 9.1. Interview a colleague about his or her opinions about how ESL students learn L1 and L2, how they develop and learn, how to increase their academic achievement, and what is the effect of internal and external factors on learning in ESL students. Analyze your colleague's views and identify any possible myths held. Are your colleague's views based on research-based information or commonly held myths? How can you help your colleague change his or her misconceptions and develop new knowledge?

2. Study carefully the information presented in Table 9.2. Select the myths that you actually have heard colleagues use, and think about professional development activities that can help your colleagues modify these misconceptions. How can you most effectively persuade your colleagues to change their perceptions, attitudes, cultural values, and beliefs about ESL students' learning and development?

GLOSSARY

advocates   Teachers act as "social workers" in order to help ESL students and their families to understand the federal and state educational policy that applies to their children, to learn about the community resources for meeting the health needs of the ESL students' families, and to refer ESL students and their families to the appropriate community agencies or school personnel who can assist with their individual needs.

cultural mediators   Teachers help ESL students and their families to adapt to the school and community cultural environments.

myths   Commonly held misconceptions, which are not based on objective information or factual evidence or research studies. Myths are acquired unconsciously or unvoluntarily as beliefs and values present in the cultural environment in which teachers live. Myths can be implicitly held as part of the school culture that surrounds teacher training programs and its faculty and administrators. Myths also can be present in school systems as part of curriculum objectives and standards and administration.

REFERENCES

Bermudez, A. B., & Marquez, J. A. (1996). An examination of a four-way collaborative to increase parental involvement in the schools. *Journal of Educational Issues of Language Minority Students, 6*, 33–43.

Brown, H. D. (2001). *Teaching by principles: An interactive approach to language pedagogy*. White Plains, NY: Addison Wesley Longman.

Calderón, M. E., & Minaya-Rowe, L. (2003). *Designing and implementing two-way bilingual programs: A step-by step guide for administrators,* *teachers and parents*. Thousand Oaks, CA: Corwin.

Chamot, A. U., and O'Malley, J. M. (1994). *The CALLA handbook: Implementing the cognitive Academic Language Learning Approach*. Reading, MA: Addison-Wesley.

Couchenour, D., & Chrisman, K. (2000). *Families, schools, and communities*. New York: Delmar Thomson Learning.

Dulay, H., Burt, M., & Krashen, S. (1982). *Language two*. New York: Oxford University Press.

Gonzalez, V. (2001). The role of socioeconomic and sociocultural factors in language-minority children's development: An ecological research view. *Bilingual Research Journal, 25*(1, 2), 1–30.

Heath, S. B. (1983). *Ways with words: Language, life and work in communities and classrooms.* New York: Cambridge.

Kim, Y. Y. (2002). *Communication and cross-cultural adaptation.* Clevedon, England: Multilingual Matters.

Lindholm-Leary, K. J. (2001). *Dual language education.* Clevedon, England: Multilingual Matters.

Ovando, C. J., Collier, V. P., & Combs, M. C. (2003). *Bilingual and ESL classrooms: Teaching in multicultural contexts* (3rd ed.). Boston: McGraw Hill.

Rogoff, B. (1990). *Apprenticeship in thinking: Cognitive development in social context.* New York: Oxford.

Rong, X. L., & Preissle, J. (1998). *Educating immigrant students: What we need to know to meet the challenges.* Thousand Oaks, CA: Corwin Press.

Spada, N. (1990). *Second language teacher education.* Cambridge: Cambridge University Press.

Spolsky, B. (1989). Formulating a theory of second language learning. *Studies in Second Language Acquisition, 7,* 269–288.

Teachers of English to Speakers of Other Languages (TESOL). (1997). ESL Standards for pre-K–12 students. Alexandria, VA: Author.

Thomas, W. P., & Collier, V. P. (2003). The multiple benefits of dual language. *Educational Leadership, 61*(2), 61–64.

U.S. English. (1990, May). The door to opportunity. *Roll Call.*

INDEX

Page numbers in **boldface** indicate figures and tables.